KENNEDY, JOHNSON AND NATO

Kennedy, Johnson and NATO is an incisive reassessment of Anglo-American defence relations, which form a crucial part of international security.

Andrew Priest closely examines this key relationship by focusing on the so-called Nassau agreement of December 1962. He clearly places Nassau in its context and shows how multi-level collaboration continued between the US and UK in NATO despite growing tensions over American involvement in Southeast Asia and Britain's global role. First, he shows how agreements made between Presidents and Prime Ministers shape alliances by encouraging interaction between politicians, government officials and military personnel at various levels of formality. Second, by focusing on the NATO area, he assesses US–UK attitudes to European and North Atlantic defence.

Traditionally, studies of US–UK relations at this time have tended to concentrate on developing difficulties between Presidents and Prime Ministers (particularly Harold Wilson and Lyndon B. Johnson) over global issues. This study demonstrates the 'dynamics of alliance' through a nuanced approach at high-political, official and 'working' levels, across different administrations in the US and UK. Although more recently some authors have successfully integrated such a 'multi-layered' approach particularly to studies of nuclear affairs, they have tended to treat the 1962 Nassau agreement as something of a dénouement.

This book will be essential reading for students of US foreign policy, British foreign policy, Anglo-American relations, European–American relations and the history of NATO.

Andrew Priest is Lecturer in International Politics, University of Wales, Aberystwyth. He obtained his PhD in 2003 at the Department of American and Canadian Studies, University of Birmingham.

CONTEMPORARY SECURITY STUDIES

GLOBALISATION, CONFLICT
AND THE SECURITY STATE
National security in a
'New' strategic era
Robert G. Patman (ed.)

THE POLITICAL ROAD TO
WAR WITH IRAQ
Bush, 9/11 and the drive to
overthrow Saddam
Nick Ritchie and Paul Rogers

BOSNIAN SECURITY AFTER
DAYTON
New perspectives
Michael A. Innes (ed.)

KENNEDY, JOHNSON
AND NATO
Britain, America and the
dynamics of alliance,
1962–68
Andrew Priest

KENNEDY, JOHNSON AND NATO

Britain, America and the dynamics of alliance, 1962–68

Andrew Priest

Routledge
Taylor & Francis Group

LONDON AND NEW YORK

First published 2006
by Routledge
2 Park Square, Milton Park, Abingdon, Oxon OX14 4RN

Simultaneously published in the USA and Canada
by Routledge
711 Third Avenue, New York, NY 10017

*Routledge is an imprint of the Taylor & Francis Group,
an informa business*

Transferred to Digital Printing 2009

First issued in paperback 2012

© 2006 Andrew Priest

Typeset in Times New Roman by
Newgen Imaging Systems (P) Ltd, Chennai, India

British Library Cataloguing in Publication Data
A catalogue record for this book is available
from the British Library

Library of Congress Cataloging in Publication Data
A catalog record for this book has been requested

ISBN13: 978–0–415–38534–3 hardback
ISBN13: 978-0-415-64949-0 paperback

FOR MUM AND DAD

CONTENTS

ACKNOWLEDGEMENTS

Some of the material in Chapters 3 and 5 of this book appeared in 'In American Hands: Britain, the United States and the Polaris Nuclear Project, 1962–1968', *Contemporary British History*, vol. 19, no. 3 (September 2005), pp. 353–76, while parts of the research for Chapter 6 are developed in 'From "Hardware" to "Software": The End of the MLF-ANF Debate and Rise of the NATO Nuclear Planning Group' in A. Wenger, C. Nuenlist and A. Locher (eds), *Transforming NATO in the Cold War: Challenges Beyond Deterrence in the 1960s* (Routledge, forthcoming, 2006). I'm thankful to Taylor and Francis for permission to reproduce this material here. Many people have helped in many ways with the writing of this book, and it is a great pleasure to say 'thank you' to them here.

First, the University of Birmingham's School of Historical Studies and Graduate Travel Fund provided me with funding to undertake this project. A generous grant from the British Academy then allowed it to be completed.

My colleagues, many of whom I count as friends, have helped me enormously with advice and practical help, and I thank them all. My greatest debt is to Scott Lucas who supervised my thesis and has shaped my work immeasurably with his testing questions and comments. I'm particularly grateful to Martin Alexander for his advice and assistance and I would also like to thank Jonathan Colman, Stuart Croft, Saki Dockrill, Gerry Hughes, Peter Jackson, Andrew Johnstone, Alistair Morey, Martyn Powell, Alistair Shepherd, James Vaughan and Carl Watts for helping in numerous ways.

Several people deserve special mention. Francesca has provided me with inspiration and support, and I owe her a great deal. Karen has encouraged me throughout, despite having her own book to finish, and I cannot tell her how much our time together and her enthusiasm for medieval monasteries mean to me. Finally, this book is dedicated to my parents, Shirley and Michael, with love and thanks for everything they have done for me.

ABBREVIATIONS

ABM	anti-ballistic missile
ANF	Atlantic Nuclear Force
BAOR	British Army of the Rhine
BDS	British Defence Staff
BJSM	British Joint Services Mission
CA	Churchill Archives Centre
CMND	Command Paper
CNO	Chief of Naval Operations (US)
DCNS	Deputy Chief of the Naval Staff (UK)
DOD	Department of Defense (US)
EDC	European Defence Community
EEC	European Economic Community
FRG	Federal Republic of Germany
FRUS	Foreign Relations of the United States
HMG	Her Majesty's Government
ICBM	intercontinental ballistic missile
JCS	Joint Chiefs of Staff (US)
JFK	John F. Kennedy Library
LBJ	Lyndon B. Johnson Library
MLF	Multilateral force
MMD	mixed-manning demonstration
MOD	Ministry of Defence (UK)
MRBM	medium range ballistic missile
NAC	North Atlantic Council
NATO	North Atlantic Treaty Organization
NHC	Naval Historical Center
NPG	Nuclear Planning Group
NPT	Non-proliferation treaty
NSAM	National Security Action Memorandum
NSC	National Security Council (US)
NSF	National Security File
OAB	Operational Archives Branch

POF	President's Office File
PRO	Public Record Office
RAF	Royal Air Force
RG	Record Group
RSF	Regional Security File
SACEUR	Strategic Allied Commander, Europe
SACLANT	Strategic Allied Commander, Atlantic
SHAPE	Supreme Headquarters Allied Powers, Europe
SNFL	Standing Naval Force Atlantic
UK	United Kingdom
US	United States
USAF	United States Air Force
USDD	United States Declassified Documents Series
WHCF	White House Central File

INTRODUCTION

On 11 January 1968, British Foreign Secretary George Brown met his American counterpart, Secretary of State Dean Rusk, in Washington DC. Brown, who was exhausted at the end of a whirlwind round-the-world trip he had commenced one week before, had bad news. He told Rusk of the British government's decision to advance its withdrawal from global defence commitments as quickly as possible. This meant terminating its presence in Singapore, Malaya and the Persian Gulf by 1971 at the latest, bringing forward previous plans by between two and five years. Now the entire British defensive effort would be directed towards the North Atlantic area, Brown said. Rusk was dismayed at the decision and subjected Brown to a lengthy and devastating verbal onslaught. He wanted the British to reconsider. Another US official persisted: 'Be British, George, be British – how can you betray us?'[1]

Just five years before, in December 1962, members of the previous United Kingdom (UK) government had emerged triumphant from talks with their American counterparts at Nassau in the Bahamas. During the meeting Prime Minister Harold Macmillan received assurances from President John F. Kennedy that the United States (US) would provide its Polaris missile delivery system for British nuclear submarines operating in the North Atlantic and integrated within the North Atlantic Treaty Organization (NATO), thus prolonging the UK deterrent for at least the next twenty years. This agreement brought to an end some days of tension in relations between the two governments following the US cancellation of Skybolt, an air-launched missile previously promised to the British. Now with an adequate replacement for Skybolt in place, the Anglo-American defence connection appeared to have been secured and British global commitments reconfirmed.

This book examines the years between the Nassau agreement and British withdrawal from the 'east of Suez' area in order to better understand the dynamics of Anglo-American relations as British foreign policy became increasingly focused on the NATO area. It does this in order to engage with three related areas of scholarship: first, historiographical debates about Anglo-American relations during the 1960s; second, generalizations that can be made about the nature of Anglo-American cooperation and alliance, especially in the cold war; and third, the growing literature on US foreign policy during the 1960s (and especially between 1963 and 1969) looking 'beyond Vietnam'.

On the first theme, the mid and later part of the decade witnessed a series of tensions between London and Washington over such issues as the unilateral declaration of independence in Rhodesia and the American conflict in Vietnam. Furthermore, the White House was deeply disturbed to witness British devaluation of sterling in 1967, which it had done so much to prevent for years before. The UK east of Suez withdrawal, therefore, merely compounded an already delicate diplomatic situation.

Historians have therefore attempted to explain how US–UK relations moved from a position of apparent mutual understanding in the early 1960s to one of mistrust and tension at the end of the decade. Many have seen the premiership of Harold Macmillan in the UK between 1957 and 1963 as a period of unparalleled peacetime Anglo-American cooperation in which he reinvigorated the US–UK relationship after the difficulties of the mid-1950s and especially the Suez crisis of 1956. Much of Macmillan's success appeared to have been predicated on his strong personal bond with successive presidents. David Dimbleby and David Reynolds suggest, for example, that 'Macmillan's close friendships, first with Eisenhower and then with Kennedy...restored a relationship that had nearly been destroyed over Suez' and Macmillan's biographer Alistair Horne talks of 'the intimacy and warmth that characterized the Macmillan–Kennedy *entente*'.[2] While many acknowledge the tensions and strains inherent in the relationship, the vast majority see the strong bond between president and prime minister as crucial in facilitating a positive working partnership during this period.[3] In contrast, scholars have then tended to see the period that followed Macmillan's resignation and Kennedy's death, both in late 1963, much less favourably. Far fewer scholars have examined the period between 1964 and 1970 but those who have tend to interpret it as a fallow period in US–UK relations when personal relations between leaders were less important as tensions between London and Washington at the highest level grew. D.C. Watt even goes so far as to say that Anglo-American relations in these years 'were conspicuous by their absence'.[4]

In recent years new studies of the period have produced a more nuanced picture. The question of a lack of a personal rapport between the British prime minister, Harold Wilson, and the US president, Lyndon B. Johnson, the Vietnam War and British withdrawal from east of Suez continue to cast a long shadow with Sylvia Ellis suggesting that Britain and America had 'a *Not* So Special Relationship' at this time.[5] Yet Ellis, Jonathan Colman, John Dumbrell, Alan Dobson and others have written studies of the Johnson–Wilson years showing some of the strengths as well as the weaknesses of relations.[6] Dobson prefers to call the years between 1961 and 1967 'The Years of Transition' in Anglo-American relations, while Colman notes the difficulties of maintaining strong relations between the two governments and leaders when there was such an 'asymmetry of power' caused by structural weaknesses in the British economy.[7] Saki Dockrill's recent study of the 'east of Suez' withdrawal has also highlighted some American understanding of British economic problems and defence reassessments.[8] Moreover, the notion of a flourishing 'special relationship' during the Kennedy–Macmillan years has received the revisionist treatment from such scholars as Nigel Ashton and Scott Lucas.[9] This book aims to build upon this literature to provide a more balanced study of US–UK relations in the Kennedy–Johnson years.

On the second area of engagement dealing with broader ideas about the Anglo-American relationship, the classic text is Richard Neustadt's *Alliance Politics* which examines the 1956 Suez crisis and 1962 disagreement over cancellation of the Skybolt missile. Neustadt's interpretation suggests that the nature of Anglo-American 'crisis' behaviour during the cold war was rooted in the close relationship between the two bureaucracies which led to 'muddled perceptions, stifled communications, disappointed expectations, [and] paranoid reactions'.[10] Neustadt claims that elements of the first three are evident in relations between all allies, but only the fourth, 'paranoid reactions', can be seen between the closest of allies. As important as Neustadt's theory is, Louise Richardson notes that it is limited by its attempt to compare two very different 'crises'.[11] Clearly crises between allies are very important in coming to an understanding of alliance behaviour; they are an extension of day-to-day contacts and often have long antecedents, and this book revisits aspects of the Skybolt episode and the Nassau conference in Chapter 2. Yet the contention of this study is that 'crises' need to be placed within the context of negotiation in order to understand the US–UK relationship.[12] Chapters 3 to 6 therefore examine the consequences of the Nassau agreement for US–UK relations within NATO, focusing in particular on the so-called Multilateral Nuclear Force.

This also suggests that the importance of 'sentiment' as a force in Anglo-American relations should be downplayed. Robert Keohane has identified four areas to explain the relationships between actors in the international system: 'indifference', 'instrumental interdependence', 'situational interdependence' and 'empathetic interdependence'. 'Indifference' suggests that states have nothing to do with each other. 'Instrumental interdependence' means that a state will be concerned with the welfare of another actor when the action the other actor takes could affect the first state. 'Situational interdependence' develops the notion that improving the welfare of another actor may improve one's own (here he uses the example of global economic interdependence), and finally 'empathetic interdependence' suggests that an actor may be interested in the welfare of others for its own sake and regardless of the effect it has upon themselves.[13]

In an influential article published in the mid-1960s, Raymond Dawson and Richard Rosencrance suggest that 'empathetic interdependence' or 'sentiment' is crucial in coming to an understanding of relations between Britain and the US after 1945, claiming that a theory based on national interests 'cannot explain the Anglo-American alliance'.[14] More recently, John Dumbrell has also discussed the importance of 'sentiment' in the 'special relationship'.[15] Yet Dawson and Rosencrance's claim simply does not stand up to close scrutiny. While sentiment may have some bearing in the way that the Anglo-American relationship developed at certain points during and after the Second World War, shared interests were more fundamental in the continuation of a strong Anglo-American bond during the cold war. This applies as much to the re-establishment of co-operation in nuclear weapons development at the end of the 1950s and its continuation throughout the 1960s as it does to other areas.[16] This book, therefore, does not dwell on the need to understand whether Kennedy and Macmillan, or Johnson and Wilson had good personal relations and instead stresses the importance of areas of mutual concern for their respective governments.

Therefore Keohane's ideas of 'instrumental interdependence' are far more useful in explaining the changing nature of US–UK relations. Broadly, Britain and America were drawn together after 1945 because of shared perceptions of a Soviet threat. In the mid to late 1960s, the utility of the relationship was tested primarily because of the disagreement over aims and objectives in Vietnam, the influence of domestic politics on foreign policy-making and global reassessments of foreign and defence policy in the light of economic exigencies and changing priorities and perceptions of threat.

Crucial to this was how the US–UK bilateral relationship functioned within a multilateral setting in relation to other major allies. Relations in NATO therefore provide a good framework for this, especially during the 1960s. In particular interactions with the other two key European allies, France and the Federal Republic of Germany (FRG), shed light on how US–UK bilateral relationship worked. The Nassau agreement explicitly raised the concept of multilateralism in order to encourage the participation of France and the FRG in a trans-Atlantic military project. That the specific proposal to which the US and UK implicitly committed themselves ultimately proved fruitless should not diminish present day views of its contemporary importance. While it failed in the long term, it had significant consequences for US–UK attitudes towards the alliance in the years that followed as West Germany became a more prominent NATO member and France withdrew from NATO's integrated military structure. This study therefore contends with some of Marc Trachtenberg's conclusions about the finality of the European settlement in 1963.[17]

Finally, this book examines US policy towards NATO and Europe during the 1960s and therefore seeks to produce a more balanced picture especially of the Johnson years. The Vietnam War has dominated the historiography of the Johnson presidency and most accounts fit Harlan Cleveland's observation of President Johnson's attitude towards foreign policy: 'I had a feeling that he thought that this was somehow grander, nobler, more honest, I don't know, but something special, and he was a little bit afraid of it'.[18] The idea that Johnson was a domestic policy president who disastrously lost his way in foreign policy has dominated perceptions of his presidency. Thomas Alan Schwartz's *Lyndon Johnson and Europe* has perhaps been the most important revisionist account of Johnson's dealings in foreign affairs but several other works have also made important contributions.[19] Schwartz has stated that the Johnson administration achieved much more in dealing with its European partners than has hitherto been acknowledged and this study agrees with that thesis.[20] During the 1960s, major reforms within NATO made it a more viable and effective forum for discussion, dealing with the French challenge to its very being and maintaining an American commitment to the security of Europe despite the war in Vietnam. Chapters 7 and 8 examine these issues in some detail, in the context of increasing British emphasis on the NATO area as they withdrew from their global commitments.

This book argues that the 1960s saw a complex process of re-negotiation of US and UK regional roles and global strategy. The development of NATO-related policy between the two countries thus permits an alternative assessment of the Anglo-American defence 'alliance'.

1

ANGLO-AMERICAN DEFENCE RELATIONS IN NATO

During the cold war the relationship between the United States and the United Kingdom was central to NATO. For the most part, shared political and military ideologies shaped the North Atlantic Alliance from its inception. Although there were serious disagreements and some divergence of aims and methods, developing mutual Anglo-American suspicion towards the government of the Soviet Union from the late 1940s gave rise to a post-war military coalition between Britain and America that helped to create and drive the alliance, as well as operate as a bilateral link within it.

Recent scholarship has suggested that the important role of Britain and the US in the formation of NATO should not be over-estimated.[1] Such scholarship emphasizes the multi-polar nature of the conflict and the need to see both the British and American contributions within the context of other allies and these allies' impact on strategy and policy formation. This is undoubtedly correct, but it should not ignore the huge contribution of Britain and the United States. The influence of these two allies was a result of America's domination of the nascent Western sphere and the re-establishment of its close relationship with Britain during the early cold war. Britain's influence occurred because of its continued role as a power with global interests and in spite of its weak economic position in the aftermath of Second World War. Indeed, Ritchie Ovendale suggests that the British, and particularly post-War Labour Foreign Secretary Ernest Bevin, were responsible for 'educating the Americans' to the Soviet threat in the years after 1945 and were thus crucial in the formation of the alliance that would stand against them. Ovendale argues that President Harry Truman was unprepared for the Soviet threat to Europe and was making plans to reduce long-term American commitments between 1945 and 1949, when NATO was formed.[2]

Whatever the strengths of Ovendale's argument, it is clear that the developing cold war strengthened existing bonds between Britain and America, as well as create new ones. David Reynolds has called these institutional links that were formed and nurtured in the early years of the cold war *specialités*.[3] These were areas of related co-operation that are often seen to be unique to the Anglo-American alliance and fall into four broad categories. The first and perhaps most difficult to encapsulate is diplomatic consultation; a complex and sometimes informal structure of institutional ties that allowed discussion to take place between the two bureaucracies at many different levels. Second is military co-operation, particularly between naval and air forces. Third, the collection and analysis of intelligence, most scholars agree, was a key development in cold war Anglo-American relations and is one that remains unique and often hard to discern because of its secretive nature. But it is clear that a mutually beneficial relationship emerged with the US establishing important intelligence centres within the UK and in such places as Cyprus and Hong Kong, while the British undoubtedly benefited from a harmonious relationship between the bureaucracies of the US Federal Bureau of Investigation and Central Intelligence Agency, and the British internal security service MI5 and its external counterpart MI6. Of an even more controversial nature but one that is, like intelligence, seen to be unique to the Anglo-American relationship is the development of co-operation in nuclear affairs.

In the immediate aftermath of Second World War American unilateralism and fears about nuclear proliferation resulted in the so-called McMahon Act of 1946. This act precluded nuclear co-operation with other countries, including the UK. This was a serious blow to British ambitions of sharing in the American atomic project as they had done during Second World War and caused strain in the relationship with their US allies. In the short term it resulted in the British deciding to try to produce its own weapon from early 1947. Yet it also led to a series of British attempts to develop bilateral links with the Americans in order to gain information on atomic matters.[4] In this endeavour they achieved some success, particularly in promoting joint efforts in uranium processing and purification.[5] From mid-1948, the British government agreed to a build-up of American conventional forces in the UK in response to the Soviet blockade of Berlin. Even by this stage the American government had gained permission to use British bases for atomic bombing missions.[6]

This British desire to remain in the nuclear field provided them with benefits as NATO strategy evolved into the 1950s and gave them a significant role in the evolution of American strategic thought.[7] Atomic weapons came to play an increasingly central role in the strategic doctrine of NATO as American global commitments became greater. In an Anglo-American context this nuclear dominance provided opportunities for further co-operation, often to the exclusion of other nations.[8] Although tensions existed over both conventional and nuclear strategy, the clearly established (though often informal) channels of co-operation meant that these tensions could generally be resolved at a working level: generals, admirals, officers, diplomats and politicians consulted and co-ordinated with their counterparts on a regular basis to establish joint positions and formulate policy. These institutional relationships within the US and UK military and political establishments undoubtedly oiled the machinery of co-operation.

Yet the period of Atlanticism in Anglo-American relations should also clearly be set in the context of the growing tensions between Britain's regional and global roles. While the US government was eager to maintain worldwide British defensive commitments (as it continued to be throughout the decade that followed), it also became increasingly aware of the limitations this placed on the British. At the very least, the perception among American policy-makers was that the British were simply not the global power they once had been. D.C. Watt has even argued that this perception was arguably more important than reality and it contributed to further diminution of British power because the Americans so often chose not to honour their relationship with the UK.[9]

Anglo-American relations also had a huge impact on relations with the other NATO allies. With the exception of the disastrous Suez expedition in 1956 and its effect on relations between Britain and America, Anglo-American relations generally remained strong throughout the 1950s. Indeed, Suez encouraged the British to strive for reconciliation and reaffirmation of the relationship during the premiership of Harold Macmillan in the UK. This impacted on both countries' relationships with other key allies within the alliance. As other major powers, and in particular France and the FRG, gained in economic strength and diplomatic power, the United States increasingly had to balance the continued prominence of Anglo-American understandings with the needs of the alliance. The bilateral relationship between Britain and the United States in the 1950s was therefore constantly informed by multilateralism. This set the stage for the pre-occupations of NATO policy-makers during the Kennedy and Johnson administrations.

Eisenhower, the new look and NATO

When Dwight D. Eisenhower became president of the United States in January 1953 he was determined to gain the initiative in the cold war with the Soviets, which he believed had been lost during the presidency of his predecessor, Harry S. Truman.[10] This involved a large-scale effort to thwart communism in many areas of the world, whether this took the form of a military, political, cultural or economic threat. Europe remained central to this struggle as the Eisenhower administration continued to believe that the greatest global military threat to Western, and therefore American, security came from the Soviet designs on Western Europe.

NATO was well established by the time Eisenhower assumed the presidency. Formed in 1949, the alliance had developed a political as well as military apparatus, taken in new members (Greece and Turkey in 1952) and now faced further extension through the potential inclusion of the FRG. The latter proved to be the most pressing concern in the first years of Eisenhower's administration with the struggle to ratify the European Defence Community (EDC) in order to include the Federal Republic in the defence of Western Europe. For Eisenhower and his secretary of state, John Foster Dulles, Britain was the key partner in their attempts to persuade France and others to agree to the treaty.[11] Eisenhower and Dulles urged ratification while simultaneously pressing for European powers to sustain or even increase their defence levels in Europe as the Americans contemplated troop redeployments of their own.[12]

For the British, maintaining or increasing forces dedicated to the defence of Europe was an unrealistic and even an unwarranted goal. Economic troubles, continued emphasis on global over regional policy and (a perception at least of) a reduction in East–West tensions following the death of Soviet dictator Joseph Stalin in March 1953 suggested that the Americans were following a misguided European strategy. The British Chiefs of Staff consistently told their political masters that the chances of all-out war in Europe were unlikely, resulting in British unwillingness to meet the force goals that the Americans were setting. Yet it was clear that this lack of adherence to US demands was likely to lead to strain in the Anglo-American relationship, thus leaving the British with a dilemma.[13]

Therefore in 1952 they took the initiative, producing a paper on defence and global strategy that had a huge influence on American NATO policy in the years that followed. What became known as the Global Strategy Paper was developed in parallel to the explosion of the first British atomic device. In the paper the politicians and military officials chose to emphasize nuclear deterrence at the expense of a conventional build-up for the very reason that they believed all-out war with the Soviets to be unlikely and the new weapon at their disposal offered a different set of strategic options. Deterrence therefore became the central pillar of British defence in Europe and this had a profound influence on American and therefore NATO strategy as a whole.[14] The British pressed their concerns about American pre-occupations in NATO defence, while simultaneously recognizing that this would also help them in their quest to revive the Anglo-American nuclear relationship. Eventually, Dulles responded.[15]

These British ideas struck a chord in Washington because Dulles and Eisenhower were also concerned about the cost of containing the Soviet Union by conventional means and wanted to avoid fighting expensive and unpopular wars, as the US had recently done in Korea. The two men therefore sought to cut military spending and US conventional forces by building stockpiles of atomic and nuclear weapons. The US now possessed enough nuclear firepower to make this plan a reality by posing a credible enough threat to the Soviet Union. In November 1953, Eisenhower approved National Security Council Paper (NSC) 162/2 ordering the Joint Chiefs of Staff (JCS) to base their military planning on consideration of the use of nuclear weapons, or, as the president explained to congressional leaders the following year, 'to blow the hell out of them in a hurry if they start anything'.[16] This became known as the massive retaliation doctrine and five months later Dulles announced that the administration would 'depend primarily upon a great capacity to retaliate, instantly, by means and places of our choosing'.[17]

The so-called *New Look* policy must be seen in context, however. First, massive retaliation meant consideration of the use of nuclear weapons rather than allowing them to be used as a matter of course.[18] Second, one of the major components in NSC62/2 was the need for the United States to maintain alliances and in particular NATO.[19] In effect, Eisenhower recognized that the US could not support all its emerging global commitments alone and the assistance of strong Western European nations was essential.[20] Third, although American adoption of the

'New Look' reflected the influence of the British Global Strategy Paper, the two were not identical. Generally, the British welcome the centrality of nuclear weapons in the US strategy, but there were some significant differences in specific areas and they certainly did not view all of the American strategic changes as entirely favourable.[21]

Yet with the continued US push for a conventional build-up of European conventional forces in the form of the EDC and its overhaul of NATO policy to take in the 'New Look', the US appeared to be pursuing almost contradictory policies.[22] Moreover, the prospect of nuclear annihilation stirred fears in Europe and led to considerable misapprehension at American intensions. French refusal to ratify the EDC in 1954 and the subsequent failure of the treaty shocked the US administration and it was left to the British and in particular Foreign Secretary Anthony Eden to help resolve the remaining question of the West German contribution to Western defence by proposing that it be allowed to enter NATO. This solution was rapidly agreed to by the other NATO members and put an end to a painful period in transatlantic relations.[23]

For the British, their centrality in NATO affairs by the middle of the 1950s through their initiatives towards West Germany and nuclear deterrence disguised the reality of a weakened position. In fact, the nuclear initiative had come about because, in the words of Anthony Eden's private secretary, 'we cannot spend more on defence, cannot reach our goals, better abandon them and make do with what we have'.[24] The 'New Look' was therefore less of a strategic innovation than a political necessity. Moreover, the failure of the EDC and American reappraisal of its European policies in 1954 and 1955 placed pressure on the UK to maintain a long-term conventional commitment to Western Europe.[25] NATO policy was thus intimately connected to the British global role, to which both the British themselves and increasingly the Americans with their own new-found global commitments attached such importance. These two elements converged to drive a period of Anglo-American cooperation that gained momentum in the later part of the decade.

The 1957 defence review and Anglo-American rapprochement

When Duncan Sandys became UK defence minister in 1957, he saw that the British defence burden was unsustainably high. It now accounted for 10 per cent of gross national product, and 7 per cent of the working population. National Service also represented a considerable drain on the nation's resources. Sandys, along with the new prime minister Harold Macmillan, recognized this lack of sustainability and attempted to rectify this with the 1957 Defence White Paper.[26] This document set out British doctrine for the next four years and reflected many of the concerns of previous reviews, privileging nuclear deterrence and committing the government to ending national conscription.[27]

Although NATO was of considerable concern to Sandys and the Ministry of Defence (MOD), the legacy of empire now meant that British attitudes towards the alliance were increasingly tempered by their perpetual concern with defence of the Middle and Far East. As before, the British strategic debate within NATO remained entangled with the ramifications of internal defence wrangling over policy east of the Suez Canal, but in 1957 this was particularly acute as a result of the Suez crisis the previous year. This episode had seen the British and French invade the Sinai Peninsula to try and regain control of the Suez Canal from Colonel Gamal Abdel Nasser, the Egyptian leader. Suez had exposed both the political impotence of the UK in the face of US political pressure and military inflexibility in launching a campaign outside of Europe.[28]

The difficulties of maintaining a British world-role were combined with the continued belief in the efficacy of nuclear weapons. During his tenure as minister of supply from 1951 Sandys had followed the line of the British Chiefs of Staff in developing the 1952 Global Strategy Paper, eager to find ways to save money on conventional forces and in particular the surface navy. One place to do this was the carrier force. In global terms, Sandys reasoned, carriers were a huge invest-ment, reducing funds to the overstretched British aircraft industry and seemingly duplicating the land-based strategic bomber programme.[29] Sandys also attacked the strategy of broken-backed warfare that had been enshrined in the 1954 Defence White Paper and would have involved NATO navies going into combat following a short nuclear exchange on continental Europe by the Superpowers.[30] Although Sandys had some sympathy with the aims of broken-backed conflict, his main aim was to reduce the fleet to a minimum, including the carrier component. Attacking the broken-backed concept was therefore his way to achieve this.[31] This policy found favour at the highest levels, as evidenced by a missive from Eden's private secretary to the prime minister in July 1956: 'I cannot believe that the maintenance of NATO naval forces, with an associated Command Structure, to keep the Atlantic open in global war is essential to maintaining American involvement in Europe'.[32]

Sandys' aggressive tactics were somewhat ironic when the Suez episode had so recently exposed the weaknesses of a flexible military capability. Carriers had been crucial in the Suez operation as many British bases had proved to be unus-able, but the landings had also pointed the way to producing more effective amphibious warfare by using helicopters and improvised commando carriers. Suez had demonstrated that speedy intervention was required to deploy rapid mobile forces in any future conflict.[33] Yet this, once again, showed the priority in British military thinking of a global strategy at the expense of NATO. In the short term, the British admiralty made a successful case to save the carrier force with the argument that they were essential for mobile air power in limited conflicts.

Following Suez and the plans to abolish conscription, First Sea Lord Mountbatten took the idea of amphibious warfare to the Chiefs of Staff. They agreed that a carrier force could be a useful asset for mobile air power in limited conflicts. This in turn convinced Sandys, in spite of his long-running antipathy to the carrier force, to postpone his plans for cancellation. The force was saved at the expense of some other changes, including the cancellation of missile cruisers and the demise of battleships. But it was only a stopgap measure and the Admiralty counter-attack focused on securing hardware for worldwide operations at the expense of NATO. Once again the east of Suez area remained vital in British military planning.[34]

Suez had also threatened schism within the US–UK political relationship, when US economic and diplomatic pressure on the British in October and November 1956 forced their withdrawal from the Sinai Peninsula. This low-point in relations between the two powers highlighted the huge imbalance in their respective economic and military might. But instead of signalling the end of Anglo-American collaboration, it encouraged British policy-makers and military leaders to restore it. They evidently felt that they needed the United States in order to operate on the world stage and therefore sought to establish closer military and political links to ensure this happened.[35] The key figure in this policy of Anglo-American rapprochement was Harold Macmillan, who succeeded Eden as prime minister in January 1957 following the disastrous events of Suez and Eisenhower's re-election. Macmillan was determined to reinvigorate the Anglo-American relationship that had been damaged over the conflict in the Middle East by cultivating his personal relationship with the American president, a task that was undoubtedly made easier because Macmillan had known Eisenhower during Second World War in North Africa.[36]

For Macmillan, these interests were primarily to maintain Britain's global role and he therefore supported Sandys in his attacks on NATO conventional forces. Macmillan made no secret of the fact that maintenance of British worldwide commitments was his top priority and that he would reduce British commitments to NATO to a minimum. He therefore supported Sandys aims to reduce the British Army of the Rhine (BAOR), initially from 77,000 to 64,000 men with a view to reduce it further to approximately 43,000 by 1962. By 1958, they had largely succeeded, agreeing a deal with West Germany that the BAOR would comprise 45,000 troops by 1961.[37]

Macmillan's dual track policies of Anglo-American rapprochement and the reduction in conventional forces were made possible by advances in the nuclear field, where the UK now strove to produce a hydrogen bomb. Some in the UK felt that a credible nuclear capability was a *sine qua non* for Anglo-American revival, although this was just one in panoply of British government aims driving the policy forward. From the start of the hydrogen bomb project in 1954, Winston Churchill, prime minister at the time, had viewed its development very much in terms of Britain's influence on the world stage. Moreover, as Sandys' designs on the Royal Navy illustrated, one of the most attractive features from the perspective of military planners and policy-makers was the savings that it could facilitate in conventional defence, thus making the east of Suez policy easier to realize.[38]

Anglo-American nuclear collaboration

The developing 'special relationship' between Britain and the United States from 1957 was important for a number of reasons. Primarily it brought the two countries closer together and fulfilled combined strategic and political needs. For the British, it allowed them to gain the means to deliver nuclear weapons effectively and for the US it provided an additional reliable ally with the means to threaten the Soviet Union and tied the British more firmly than ever into the defence structure of NATO, while drawing them away from giving overt nuclear assistance to the French and therefore fostering a true European nuclear deterrent.[39] And yet the independence of the British nuclear deterrent was a growing source of controversy within the alliance.

From 1955 and especially in the years that followed Suez, a series of decisions by the British and Americans rejuvenated the unique relationship in nuclear affairs that had been curtailed in 1946. The determination of successive Conservative governments to maintain the British nuclear deterrent brought them closer to their American allies and the ease with which the nuclear relationship at many different levels could be facilitated even before any formal agreements had been made is striking. While this may have been a direct consequence of improved personal relationships at the highest level, it was helped by mutual co-operation at many levels below. Attitudes towards Anglo-American nuclear co-operation were already becoming more favourable on both sides of the Atlantic with rapid progress on the British deterrent and American production of increasingly sophisticated delivery systems. The evolution of Polaris, a solid propellant ballistic missile for use in submarines, in the United States from 1955 soon aroused interest in its potential for the UK for example. Technological and strategic advances in the US had combined with political pressure from a committee set up by Eisenhower that undertook a review of future weapons policy to drive the Polaris scheme forward.[40] Soon after the first amendments to the McMahon Act were passed, some members of the US Congress began to note that the Polaris system could have advantages to the UK.[41]

As Eisenhower and Macmillan's personal relationship blossomed, the US administration's attitude towards the British deterrent also began to change. In May 1957, the first UK hydrogen bomb was exploded. In Washington this signalled one of many steps towards a rapprochement with the UK in nuclear weapons collaboration. Another took place in October that year when the Soviets launched the Sputnik satellite into orbit around the earth. Sputnik caused great fear in the US as it seemed likely that the Soviets could now produce an intercontinental ballistic missile (ICBM) capable of hitting the United States from Soviet territory. Development of credible nuclear delivery systems therefore became a priority for the US, as did co-operation with reliable allies.[42]

The events of 1957 led directly to revision of the McMahon Act the following year. In 1954, the McMahon Act had been partially amended to allow details of civil nuclear technologies and some information on weaponry to be made available to the UK. Subsequently, from the start of his tenure as prime minister, Macmillan had been remarkably successful in his efforts to build on this amendment.[43] He quickly reached an agreement on supply of nuclear information to other countries and in October 1957, announced the 'Declaration of Common Purpose' between the US and UK with President Eisenhower.[44] For the British it turned out to be more of a grand rhetorical statement that made little difference at working level.[45] But it paved the way for further amendment of the McMahon Act in June 1958 and the *Agreement for Co-operation on the Uses of Atomic Energy for Mutual Defence Purposes*, which allowed the British to receive nuclear secrets as authorized by the president.[46] Macmillan even agreed to have US Thor missiles on UK territory under a dual key arrangement giving either leader a veto.[47] Following the 1958 McMahon Act amendments, Britain was also able to procure a marine nuclear propulsion plant from the US for its first nuclear powered submarine HMS *Dreadnought*.[48]

By this time, close co-operation between British and American military counterparts had facilitated a tentative exchange of information on the Polaris missile. At the end of 1957, in personal correspondence with Mountbatten, US Chief of Naval Operations (CNO) Admiral Arleigh Burke enthusiastically endorsed the nascent US Polaris project. Recently, there had been a great effort to accelerate Polaris, Burke told Mountbatten, and the US Navy hoped to have a usable weapon in late 1959 or early 1960. Polaris was more sophisticated than other weapons being developed at the time because by placing the missiles on submarines, which could not be tracked, they were rendered almost totally invulnerable. A submerged vessel would also give a more stable platform for launch.[49] 'We are not behind schedule in any component', Burke proudly told Mountbatten, 'and are as much as four years ahead of schedule on some of our more fortunate components'. Finally, Burke reported that he expected some of Mountbatten's technical personnel to make the trip to the US soon in order to view the Polaris undertaking first-hand.[50] In response to Burke's candidness, Mountbatten soon declared to colleagues that now the US Polaris project was out in the open, he was 'encouraging everyone to introduce this topic into their general conversation'.[51]

Despite this sentiment, it seems that the Royal Navy did not make a concerted effort to impress the viability of Polaris upon the cabinet.[52] Its reasons for this were institutional, strategic and economic. As the first lord of the admiralty, Selkirk, explained to his predecessor, Lord Hailsham, in January 1958, although he wanted to 'percolate slowly but gradually into the minds of our colleagues the future possibilities of submarines equipped with the...Polaris', he stressed: 'I repeat I do not want to go too fast on this because it would divert attention away from other current problems. Moreover the development is necessarily some little way off and at the outset its cost would frighten the Chancellor.'[53] Selkirk still recommended that Hailsham introduce the concept to his counterparts in the cabinet at a convenient time. While Selkirk's assertion that completion of Polaris was 'some little way off' was undoubtedly true, it was likely to be developed at least as quickly as other US missiles. This would suggest that the Admiralty thought its role would be to agitate for Polaris, once it had been proven, for introduction further down the line, perhaps as a replacement for Blue Streak, the missile the British were then developing as their deterrent.[54] This was confirmed by the Deputy Chief of the Naval Staff (DCNS) in February, who suggested the Admiralty should go 'all out' to persuade the powers that be to opt for Polaris after 1965.[55]

Simultaneously, the Admiralty recognized the limits of its actions on politicians, who would have to make the final decisions about which service would maintain Britain's nuclear deterrent in the long term. Any political lobbying would imply 'a major revision of the national policy for the deployment of the deterrent' that they simply did not have the strength to muster.[56] Although revision of the McMahon Act would allow the UK to receive most of the necessary technical information from the US, changing to a sea-based deterrent was likely to upset the military balance in the UK.[57] The Royal Navy's reticence therefore reflected broader institutional thinking and tensions between nuclear and conventional defence that had been ongoing for a number of years with the Royal Air Force (RAF) endorsing a stronger nuclear approach, with the navy retaining a belief in the need for conventional forces.[58]

More than political or strategic factors, it was the cost that primarily hampered any immediate British ambitions for a seaborne nuclear deterrent. The Admiralty now estimated that the total cost of building one Polaris submarine would be £24 million, £6.4 million of which would be in US dollars. This omitted £5.75 million ($16 million) for the missiles themselves and an unknown amount for the warheads. The attraction of Polaris as a weapons system was therefore offset by the concern that it would detract from other areas.[59] The Navy simply did not want to pay for a strategic deterrent when its own conventional forces were under threat and therefore awaited government moves towards Polaris before it made any move itself. If the political powers then made it clear that they wanted to negotiate with the Americans for the weapon, the Royal Navy would put in for the appropriate funds.[60]

Finally, British concerns extended to the potential relationship with American counterparts and US–UK political relations as a whole. Strong Anglo-American co-operation was already paying dividends for the British now they had so much information with which to make a bid for Polaris, but the nature of any future agreement between the UK and US governments remained completely unknown. At this early stage (while the UK was still developing an ostensibly independent deterrent in Blue Streak), buying a missile direct from the US would undoubtedly prove to be controversial, as the Admiralty recognized:

> This... implies that we virtually forego any possibility of having a wholly British deterrent. This may well be the fatal weakness in the case for Polaris, since it is hardly conceivable that any British Government will commit itself on a long-term basis to being dependent on American agreement to use the deterrent... It follows logically from the foregoing that serious consideration should be given to the possibility of developing our own Polaris missiles, perhaps under the umbrella of interdependence.[61]

Still unwilling to move too quickly, the Admiralty therefore recommended they wait for two years, 'by which time we would know, more certainly, how the

Americans were progressing in their development of the 1500 mile Polaris, and whether there was any possibility of obtaining this weapon from them without unacceptable conditions'.[62]

It seemed impossible to make any progress on obtaining Polaris in the short term, so the British concluded that while work on Blue Streak continued they should not press for a sea-borne deterrent and could perhaps consider working with the French, Germans or Italians to produce a solid fuel weapon.[63] In particular, the need for closer co-operation within NATO would suggest that working with the French on the Blue Streak delivery vehicle was an option that should be explored with the Americans.[64] And if Polaris was ever made available to the UK, the missile would have to be developed in Britain 'to avoid the political disadvantage of not having the deterrent completely under UK control'. Achieving this independence was the main advantage of developing Blue Streak.[65]

Meanwhile, the flow of data on Polaris continued apace. In April 1958, for example, members of the British Joint Services Mission (BJSM) in Washington were made privy to more information about the US Polaris project when they attended a Navy League Symposium in the city. This visit went so well that members of the delegation suggested they should not advertise the fact that they had 'managed to get in so very well "on the ground floor" '.[66] Simultaneously, Burke wrote to Mountbatten once again to recommend the Royal Navy joining at some stage, while detailing costs and strategic considerations of developing such a deterrent.[67] The following month Burke went further and suggested that a UK liaison officer could be appointed on the Polaris programme to keep the British better informed.[68] Mountbatten happily took this opportunity, endorsing the scheme to the MOD in London. This low-level interaction on Polaris contrasted sharply with co-operation between the American and British air forces on Thor, where RAF officers were not allowed to attend firings. [69]

Beyond this, little more was done and by early 1959, although Burke was becoming more insistent in his support of Polaris, urging Mountbatten in one of his letters to 'Put our deterrent to sea, [w]here real estate is free'.[70] Burke had to acknowledge, however, that it was outside the remit of the US Navy to convert this support into political action from the US government.[71] Burke had little more good fortune in persuading the British defence minister of the veracity of Polaris. In Washington the previous October, the new minister of defence, Harold Watkinson, had requested a private audience with Burke with a view to possible Polaris production in Europe, but came away with the impression that the missile was not what the British required because at that time a range exceeding 1700 miles could not be guaranteed. Watkinson's reaction was so negative, it seemed to representatives at BJSM, 'that [the] Minister is by no means sold on Polaris, nor on solid propellants in the long term, in spite of the CNO's salesmanship'.[72]

Watkinson's suspicions of Polaris were re-confirmed over the next few months. Watkinson knew that the British purchasing missiles from the United States while making the submarines and warheads themselves would put the UK deterrent at the mercy of American whim. Moreover, the building of submarines would not begin until 1965 and the first submarine launched in 1969, more than a decade away. Finally, he saw that the Royal Navy was still by no means convinced about taking over the deterrent from the RAF. Watkinson may have been warned off further at the beginning of the following year when it was estimated that the total cost of Polaris would be some £800 million for nine submarines and 125 weapons.[73] Finally, despite the mounting cost of Blue Steak, Polaris was still unproved and the government appeared unlikely to curtail Blue Streak's development until it had a viable alternative.[74]

Macmillan's nuclear policy was now one that increasingly relied on the US, what he termed a policy of 'interdependence'. This strategy was the prime minister's acknowledgement that despite possession of the hydrogen bomb, the only way for Britain to continue as world power was to harness United States know-how, particularly its nuclear capability.[75] Interdependence was a contentious policy. The stark differences in relative US–UK defensive capabilities, in addition to the relatively primitive UK nuclear capability, made the notion of interdependence appear closer to dependence upon the US, and therefore hard to justify. The US nuclear arsenal was self-sufficient, whereas the very reason that Macmillan had wanted the McMahon Act amended was to make use of American nuclear materials, particularly tritium. And while Eisenhower had entered into the partnership because of the Sputnik launch and in order to give the US more strategic flexibility, the nuclear forces under his control could still act independently, but Britain's nuclear forces could only be effective when tied into American ones. Even the development of the UK's supposedly 'independent' deterrent Blue Streak missile from 1953 utilized technological information supplied by the US, as well as American financial support.[76] Dependence was in fact the order of the day for Britain and from 1958 it continued to grow.[77]

None of these factors had altered substantially by the time of the crisis over Blue Streak and the decision to scrap it in the spring of 1960.[78] Yet Skybolt, another unproved weapon, was quickly adopted in its place.[79] The primary reason for this was the need to find a quick alternative. Skybolt promised to prolong the life of British V-bomber force, from which it would be fired, into the next decade and so would not require the building of new delivery systems (such as submarines). It thereby gave the RAF greater strategic flexibility and range at an affordable price.[80] Skybolt would also not unbalance the delicate relationship between the Royal Navy and RAF. The latter was the designated carrier of the British nuclear deterrent and to alter this in favour of the navy would undoubtedly have meant major changes in the strategic balance between the two forces. This would have been politically difficult at a time when the UK was becoming dependent on another country to supply the deterrent.

It was therefore the political rather than strategic considerations that dominated the decisions made on Skybolt, a concern for the US Navy. Despite his awareness of this delicate political situation, Burke was worried over the agreement. When he learnt the details of the offer, namely that the British would purchase Skybolt for the period from 1965 to 1970, the CNO wrote to the new First Sea Lord,

Admiral Charles E. Lambe, to explain that 'the Polaris system is here and now and Skybolt is very much in its R & D stage...I would expect there to be considerable misgivings among our people, mostly scientists, as to whether or not it would be advisable ever to produce it [Skybolt]'.[81] In reply, Lambe's deputy W.T. Couchman (covering for Lambe, who was seriously ill) concluded that Skybolt was merely 'a relatively cheap blood transfusion to keep [the] V-bomber force alive' and the plan was still to purchase Polaris for the later 1960s.[82]

The MOD retained an interest in Polaris and requested a study on the timing of alternative programmes that envisaged the British receiving Polaris in the late 1960s. Simultaneously, the Admiralty now estimated that as early as 1965, subject to American agreement, it would be possible for the UK to purchase a four Polaris submarine force at a capital cost of under £200 million and annual running costs in the region of £9 million, yet the government continued to place too much emphasis on Skybolt.[83] The political nature of inter-service rivalry also played a part in the Skybolt decision. Tory determination to maintain the V-bomber force was combined with substantial pressure from air forces on both sides of the Atlantic.[84] In Couchman's opinion, Watkinson had been 'advised by interested parties in very optimistic terms, about Skybolt's state and prospects'.[85]

Yet the commitment made between Eisenhower and Macmillan at Camp David on Skybolt in March 1960 was ambiguous and as the talks over British adoption of Skybolt developed, an important strand emerged. The US State Department in particular was unwilling to sanction a purely bilateral agreement over a replacement for Blue Streak and instead required commitment to a proposed NATO medium range ballistic missile (MRBM) strategic nuclear force. Following the talks, additional phrases were also used by the US that Skybolt would be produced 'subject only to United States priorities' and this offer was 'dependent on the successful and timely completion of its development programme'. In June, another clause stating 'either party might terminate its interest at any time' after 'prior consultation with the other' was also inserted.[86] A further complication was the delicate linkage between Skybolt and British agreement to offer the US a Polaris submarine base at Holy Loch in Scotland with the British and Americans both using the potential of a deal over the base to consolidate their respective bargaining positions on Skybolt.[87]

The rise of multilateralism

The MRBM force concept raised during the Camp David negotiations soon became the most important and controversial strand of Anglo-American discussions. Plans for this force drew directly upon the American development of the Polaris missile, representing the increasing centrality of a sea-based nuclear strategy to the future of the Atlantic alliance and a shift away from plans within NATO to dedicate MRBMs to continental Europe. In 1957, as part of a broader review of NATO policy, the Strategic Allied Commander, Europe (SACEUR, NATO's highest ranking military officer) General Lauris Norstad had requested a force of MRBMs to be placed under his command, intended both to plug a supposed gap in alliance defence and to modernize its weaponry.[88] Norstad envisaged a land-based force in addition to the stockpile concept already being developed by the Eisenhower administration. As Polaris was to be a crucial weapon in the American arsenal, with mobility on land as well as at sea, planners at Supreme Headquarters Allied Powers, Europe (SHAPE) posited the notion of a mobile, land-based Polaris system, camouflaged in trucks and railroad cars, and able to fire at reasonably short notice. If deployed in Europe, Polaris would also have been able to reach far into Soviet territory.[89]

Unfortunately for Norstad, his presentation of this plan to NATO, along with development of a tentative suggestion for Polaris missiles to be built in Europe for the use of the alliance, elicited a negative response from key figures in the State Department. They concluded that, as the French were beginning to demand national access to nuclear weapons, the Germans would soon follow. Ability to produce these weapons and then use them on continental Europe could, they surmised, result in development of weapons that could then be fired by a country acting unilaterally. It was as a result of this that Eisenhower's Secretary of State, Christian Herter, (who had succeeded Dulles) commissioned former State Department official and Harvard Professor, Robert R. Bowie, to study the defence needs of the alliance.[90]

As Bowie's inquiry was ongoing the word 'Polaris' was entering the British vocabulary at the highest political levels, but the British government was aware that any deal was likely to involve committing the deterrent to NATO in some form. Even before the Camp David meeting, the British had been trying to avoid the prospect of making a commitment to a NATO force and had succeeded in gaining the stationing of Thor missiles on UK territory on a purely bilateral basis. But they were soon coming under renewed pressure to submit to a joint force.[91] During the first months of 1960, the Foreign Office had explored the possibility of a Polaris deal in the future, but the fear of an MRBM force predominated. 'We should, in all circumstances, wish to be satisfied that there would be no conditions attached' the embassy in Washington was informed. As part of this enquiry, the embassy was to ask 'Whether it will be possible, at a later stage, to make [the] Polaris missile system, and perhaps the submarines themselves, available to us... and what the prospects are for developing a more effective version of this missile'. Developing the British nuclear deterrent with the US was therefore the preferred option, but this also left the problem of how to deal with France. Although the Foreign Office preferred that NATO nuclear weapons remain under US control, it questioned whether Western Europe should be more closely associated with the British–US nuclear partnership.[92] As the British position on Skybolt looked more secure, the offer of the Holy Loch base was linked with a desire for Polaris submarines in some form (whether bought or leased). Macmillan therefore not only saw the importance of the agreement for Anglo-American relations, but he also wanted to emphasize the value of the base agreement to the whole alliance.[93] The sticking point continued to be connection of Polaris to an MRBM force.[94]

During a meeting at Downing Street in June 1960, the subject of acquiring Polaris had even been discussed, but generous terms were required of the US. In the prime minister's opinion, the missiles had to be delivered without strings, with one or two submarines and an option for the British to build their own in the future. These would all have to be under 'sole ultimate control of the United Kingdom government, whatever practical arrangements have to be made as regards their operational control'.[95] This line of thinking may have been stimulated by reports that US Secretary of Defense, Thomas Gates, had suggested a 'lend-lease' agreement on two or three Polaris submarines, with the UK buying Polaris missiles and assigning them to Strategic Allied Commander, Atlantic (SACLANT) as part of the MRBM force. But British Ambassador in Washington, Sir Harold Caccia, reported from Washington, 'On MRBMs we have had much discussion but no decisions.'[96]

Talk about Polaris contemporaneously with the Camp David agreement supports Ian Clark's thesis that Macmillan's choice was not simply picking Skybolt over Polaris in 1960, but that Skybolt was intended for the 1965–1970 period with Polaris to follow.[97] The notion of Skybolt in the short-term and Polaris in the medium to long-term dominated the politico-military mindset from this point onwards. Prior to a Macmillan meeting with Norstad in July, for example, Philip de Zulueta, the prime minister's private secretary, suggested keeping their options open by making clear their desire both to make use of Skybolt 'if it works' and getting into 'the Polaris business as an insurance for the remoter future'.[98]

British political interest in Polaris was always tempered by fear of Norstad's MRBM force being part of any potential Polaris deal, particularly as American interest in the scheme grew. De Zulueta warned the prime minister of the dangers of subscribing to such a force, both for British nuclear independence and the entire French position in the alliance. Simultaneously, he foresaw the negative effects of opposing the plan outright when the Americans supported it and might attempt to tie it into the Skybolt/Holy Loch deal.[99] De Zulueta therefore recommended that independent UK control of Polaris arising out of a future deal with the United States could be 'disguised by some NATO cloak'. If they opposed the Norstad plan too vehemently, he surmised, the Americans could decide to keep the missiles only on American soil or do an independent deal with Germany (presumably to station land-based missiles on their soil or enter a seaborne MRBM scheme).[100]

Therefore, the Admiralty's decision not to press the Polaris deterrent on the government in the early stages of its development was understandable. Before the Blue Streak missile was cancelled, the Admiralty knew that the government could not afford to gamble upon Polaris when it was unknown first whether it would either be made available and, if it was, on what terms this offer would be made. And even though Macmillan and Watkinson made some tentative moves towards

Polaris in the summer of 1960, it appeared impossible to broker a deal without raising the spectre of the MRBM NATO force.[101]

With the rise of the MRBM and the Anglo-American rapprochement, British possession of a nuclear deterrent and American assistance for it had profound implications for other NATO allies, particularly as the UK emphasized the 'independence' of its deterrent from NATO and the SACEUR, implying that it was intended for national use. Moreover, the perpetual dominance of nuclear weapons in the psychology of the London and Washington defence establishments during the Eisenhower presidency inevitably diverted attention from conventional commitments within the alliance. While the British were still concerned about the levels of defence expenditure, defence spending had in fact been steadily decreasing since the end of the Korean War and debates about the EDC, when France and Britain were spending the same percentage of their gross domestic product as the United States. But by the end of the decade the debate in NATO about the role of nuclear weapons and their efficacy in maintaining great power status while reducing conventional commitments was becoming ever more intense.[102]

The question was increasingly fraught as France sought its own nuclear status, raising fears that West Germany would do the same. Traumatized by its defeat in Indo-China at Dien Bien Phu in 1954 (and American refusal to provide outright military support), the continued struggle in Algeria and its part in the Suez crisis, France had pressed forward with the development of its *force de frappe*, an independent nuclear force.[103] With the return of General Charles de Gaulle to the French presidency following the fall of the Fourth Republic in May 1958 the French nuclear programme was accelerated, throwing the country's position in NATO into doubt. De Gaulle was eager to redefine the role of the alliance and France's position within it and in September 1958 he produced proposals to advance these changes. The so-called *September Memorandum* greatly disturbed Anglo-American allies and culminated in the withdrawal of the French fleet from NATO the following year.[104]

The development of a French nuclear capability proceeded as the diplomatic gap between France and the US widened. Eisenhower's attempts to mollify de Gaulle had failed and while the US conceded the sale of enriched uranium to the French in 1959 and further assistance the following year, other information, including details of nuclear reactor technology for submarines, was withheld. It was clear to the French, therefore, that the amendments to the McMahon Act had been made with great bias towards the UK to the exclusion of France, which initially hoped it might be included. And despite conciliatory measures taken by Eisenhower towards de Gaulle on tripartite talks during 1959, relations were becoming frosty and would grow worse. In February 1960, the French exploded their first atomic bomb in the Sahara Desert.[105]

Meanwhile, France's relations with West Germany were growing warmer, as they had been doing since de Gaulle's return to power. The German Chancellor, Konrad Adenauer, shared some of de Gaulle's suspicion of the United States and moved towards something of a rapprochement with the general at the end of the decade. Germany had undergone deep introspection in the early years of decade over remilitarization and NATO membership, while France was eager to keep its grip on world power status, but the two leaders found much in common during the final years of the decade.[106] And despite some suspicion in the Federal Republic over de Gaulle's tactics in the alliance and determination to lead in Europe, relations remained strong.[107]

The German question increasingly dominated American policy and strategy towards Europe. In particular, growing American fears that Germans would at some point in the future demand national access to nuclear weapons began to be voiced in Washington. American retreat from tripartite co-operation with the French and British allowed renewed promotion of the MRBM force, fearful that the French might one day share their knowledge with the Germans. Bowie's study led to an adaptation of the original Norstad proposals and formed the basis of what would eventually become known as the NATO Multilateral Force (MLF). First, Bowie recommended building up the conventional forces of the alliance. Second, he advocated constructing a collective submarine force under the direct control of NATO, with the submarines being given prior authorization to fire if a direct attack on Europe occurred. Furthermore, Bowie proposed the development of a multilateral force of submarines in the longer term, if it was desired by the European nations of NATO. In this force, he concluded, crews comprising at least three NATO nations would man each submarine and therefore a system of control would have to be devised. During the final weeks of his administration, the force idea gained momentum and discussions took place at the highest level.[108] President Eisenhower tentatively embraced Bowie's report and Herter took it to the NATO council in December 1960, just one month before the president left office.[109]

2

SKYBOLT, POLARIS AND NASSAU

Eisenhower's successor offered the promise of a new era. John F. Kennedy was young, dynamic and articulate and when he took office in January 1961 he sought to translate these personal qualities into policies. Just as Eisenhower had believed that his predecessor's administration had run out of ideas, so Kennedy wanted to reinvigorate US policy-making during his presidency. He brought in many young, dynamic individuals, people who reflected his style of thinking and his way of working.

Kennedy introduced a raft of new policy initiatives to deal with different areas of the world. He attempted to build better relations with Latin America, the so-called Alliance for Progress, and with Africa at a time when it was emerging from the colonial era. He also faced challenges in Southeast Asia. But it was in relation to Western Europe that he faced his greatest test. Europe was the key to American success in its foreign policy, it continued to be the focal point of east–west confrontation and Kennedy wanted a united Europe and an effective NATO. He therefore sought better policies for dealing with European allies and to revise the doctrine of massive retaliation.

And yet it is arguable how much these policies really differed from those of his predecessor. Broadly, he continued to operate within clear cold war parameters. His call in his inaugural address, for example, to defend any friend and oppose any foe was classic cold war rhetoric. Thus, one can argue, the substance of American policy largely remained the same. In relation to NATO, although Kennedy sought new and potentially important changes during his first months in office, there was a significant degree of continuity from his predecessor. Kennedy's idea about moving away from the doctrine of massive nuclear retaliation to a more flexible response was not especially novel and there is some evidence that the Eisenhower administration desired this during its final months. Moreover, Kennedy's approach seems to have remained something of a long-term policy objective designed to cajole European allies to increase conventional force quotas, another perennial theme of US NATO policy, rather than an achievable aspiration during Kennedy's term of office. In this respect, the notion of sharp change in the direction of US NATO policy in the 1960s can be questioned.[1] Kennedy also continued to explore the possibility of creating the collective NATO nuclear force when there had been no pressure from the outgoing Eisenhower administration for him to do this.[2]

Kennedy's relationship with Britain also fits this paradigm of continuity. Although Macmillan was instrumental in developing an even stronger personal bond with Kennedy than he had with Eisenhower,[3] and this led to a number of foreign policy triumphs, there were significant disagreements and even crises from 1961 and 1963.[4] Once again, US–UK relations must be seen in the broader context of Britain's negotiation of its global role. The nature of both British and American politics at the time meant that a number of competing agencies and power bases within the US sought a reassessment of the Anglo-American relationship that brought Britain down to a level with other comparable European powers, notably France and West Germany. The most obvious way to do this was in reducing the burgeoning nuclear relationship with Britain.

Kennedy faced pressures from within his administration and the North Atlantic Alliance over the issue of the British deterrent. Many believed that a British 'independent' nuclear force was outdated and they should be discouraged from pursuing this. Yet the Kennedy administration maintained the deterrent in the form of Skybolt, despite spiralling costs and questionable reliability until late 1962. When the US Secretary of Defense felt he had no choice but to cancel it, calls within the administration to end the British nuclear weapons capability were renewed. The British therefore faced the termination of their nuclear project a mere five years after the Anglo-American partnership had been renewed.

In response, Harold Macmillan apparently pulled off a brilliant coup at his meeting with President Kennedy at Nassau in the Bahamas in December 1962. Ostensibly meeting to discuss a whole range of issues, the Skybolt topic dominated their conversations and the prime minister used his personal influence with the president to persuade him to renew the American nuclear commitment. Although it covered a number of subjects, the communiqué issued at the end of the conference included a separate 'Statement on Nuclear Defense Systems', which confirmed that the US had agreed to provide the UK with Polaris missiles, minus nuclear warheads, in place of Skybolt. The communiqué stated that this decision had been 'considered in the widest context both of the future defense of the Atlantic Alliance and of the safety of the whole free world'.[5]

The cancellation of Skybolt caused what many have seen to be a diplomatic 'crisis' between London and Washington that has been the subject of much academic inquiry.[6] Scholars have seen it as a microcosm of breakdown and reconciliation within the Anglo-American alliance to be compared with Suez in 1956 and demonstrating inherent problems in the Anglo-American alliance. Part of the fascination is how such an episode could occur when Anglo-American relations under the Kennedy–Macmillan partnership were good and a culture of nuclear collaboration had developed since 1957. Yet it is increasingly clear that structural and strategic limitations placed on each service in both the US and UK came into play as the relative merits of each delivery system became known and these hampered decision-making at the highest level. Furthermore, although significant tensions and misunderstandings developed between Washington and London in late 1962, these also have to be seen in context. Competing agencies within the US government certainly favoured termination of the UK nuclear programme and saw the cancellation of Skybolt as a way to achieve this. But the consensus of opinion within the administration moved relatively quickly towards an under-standing of the British need for a replacement in the days before the Nassau conference. This puts the Nassau agreement into perspective, suggesting that Macmillan's bravura performance to the American delegation in the Bahamas was not as decisive in securing Polaris as might first be suggested, and its primary importance was in the finer points of detail, particularly how the Polaris system would be assigned to NATO, rather than whether or not the British would receive the system. This assignment was, perhaps deliberately, left vague.[7]

In short, reconciliation between the British and American governments at Nassau has been overstated. Although it was not 'a kind of charade' as Marc Trachtenberg suggests,[8] both sides were consolidating their bargaining positions before the negotiations began. While the US government demonstrated a good deal of insensitivity to the British plight in the way it handled the situation, the British had knowledge of the likelihood of cancellation that they did not fully utilize.[9] In addition to the intra-governmental problems in Britain, this demon-strated the inherent limitations in the informal structures of a US–UK military alliance. But, more importantly, when the crisis arose it lasted only a matter of days, if not hours, as the American announcement that Skybolt development would be curtailed was followed swiftly by implementation of plans to give the British Polaris. Thus, the entire episode should be seen as part of the Anglo-American negotiation in nuclear affairs that had been ongoing since 1946.[10]

It also brought the British policy of 'interdependence' into sharp relief. While the Americans had given the British a nuclear deterrent, the extent of its inde-pendence was questionable. Moreover, with the rise of the MLF, the question of whether the US would relinquish a degree of nuclear control also came to promi-nence. This vexed policy-makers on both sides of the Atlantic for the duration of the Kennedy administration and beyond. Kennedy's ambivalence towards the MLF was derived in part from his desire not to relinquish control over nuclear weapons. Thus Kennedy's decision to provide the British with Polaris kept them firmly tied to the US while, for presentation, he persuaded Macmillan to agree to provide the deterrent for the defence of NATO. It seems the British were well aware of the implications of 'interdependence' for them and attempted to find other areas of the Anglo-American relationship where they could take the lead role because the nuclear relationship with the US appeared to be too much like dependence.[11]

Finally, the Nassau agreement also had profound alliance-wide implications. Britain's nuclear deterrent was in itself of great significance to other NATO powers, but with a concession by Macmillan on the collective NATO nuclear force other players were brought in. France was offered Polaris on the same or similar terms as the British while American policy-makers sought a way to bring Germany into nuclear and conventional aspects of the alliance. In order to succeed, the participation of the other major NATO powers, most notably West Germany and Britain, was required to make the force viable. Therefore Nassau brought together strands of US policy and informed debates that would go on in NATO for a number of years.

NATO policy and the nuclear force

In his first months in office Kennedy was primarily concerned with conducting a more thorough review of NATO strategy than the former president had done, a task delegated to the former secretary of state, Dean Acheson. On 24 March 1961, Acheson produced 'A Review of North Atlantic Problems for the Future', which eventually became National Security Action Memorandum (NSAM) 40, a wide-ranging paper encompassing political, military and economic influences on the alliance. In dealing with military strength of the alliance it emphasized both the need to build-up of conventional European defences along with centralized American nuclear control. It would be the responsibility of the president to 'direct use of nuclear weapons if European NATO forces have been subjected to an unmistakable nuclear attack or are about to be overwhelmed by non-nuclear forces'. Under this presidential control, however, the paper recommended that the US should commit perhaps five Polaris submarines to NATO for the duration of the alliance, with a view to providing more seaborne missiles in the near future.[12] A significant amount of the paper was also concerned with how the US should approach British and French nuclear forces. The directive urged that the US should not assist the French in seeking to attain a nuclear weapons capability, except as part of a joint NATO nuclear force. Simultaneously, it argued for the UK to commit its strategic forces to NATO, while recognizing the difficulty of gaining British acceptance on this without the US committing Strategic Air Command forces in the UK in the same manner. Finally, the directive opined:

> Over the long run, it would be desirable if the British decided to phase out of the nuclear deterrent business. If the development of Skybolt is not warranted for US purposes alone, the US should not prolong the life of the [British] V-bomber force by this or other means.[13]

With the Acheson review ongoing the British were led to believe that plans for a collective NATO missile force in Europe had been shelved. Sir Harold Caccia informed the Foreign Office that the British were being told ahead of anyone else of developments in US strategic thinking and at this stage the US was planning to commit five Polaris submarines on the same terms as the Americans committed their Sixth Fleet, with a long-term plan to introduce an MRBM force if others wanted to propose such a plan. It would, Caccia stated, 'take no such initiative themselves'. This contradicted rumours from earlier in the month 'that the State Department, at least, were far from abandoning the idea [of a NATO MRBM force]'.[14]

Less than two months later, Kennedy himself confirmed that rumours of the death of the collective force had been greatly exaggerated. In May, Kennedy told the North Atlantic Council (NAC) meeting at Ottawa that the five Polaris submarines would be committed to NATO and, although remaining under US command, they would be:

> subject to any agreed guidelines on their control and use and respon-
> siveness to the needs of all members...Beyond this we look to the
> possibility of eventually establishing a NATO seaborne force which
> would be truly multilateral in ownership and control, if this should be
> desired and found feasible by the allies, once NATO's non-nuclear goals
> have been achieved.[15]

Kennedy may have made this announcement at this time for a number of reasons, including the need for a new initiative in the wake of the recent Bay of Pigs disaster in Cuba and deteriorating relations with the Soviet Union, especially over the status of Berlin. He was certainly attracted to the idea because it advocated the new doctrine of flexible response contained in the Acheson report, which would encourage the European nations of NATO to augment their conventional forces, but required little action on his part. The two qualifications Kennedy made on allied acceptance of the force and on NATO reaching its conventional force goals reinforced his view that this was a long-term initiative. As Kennedy did not believe Europeans would fill their conventional force quotas, he paid little further attention to the matter of a joint force and little progress was made during the first year of his presidency.[16] Even the commitment of the five Polaris submarines was not of immediate concern and with the production of Polaris still ongoing, the Pentagon was unwilling to sanction the assignment of so many vessels before 1964 at the earliest.[17]

But JFK had already done enough to convince a group of State Department officials of his enthusiasm for a NATO nuclear force. Indeed, Kennedy's inclusion of a multilateral option in his Ottawa speech had been under the suggestion of these 'Europeanists', sometimes called 'theologians'. They included George Ball, Under Secretary of State for Economic Affairs and then, from November 1961, Under Secretary of State; Henry Owen, a member of the Policy Planning Staff; Walt Whitman Rostow, chairman of the Policy Planning Council; Henry Rowan, Deputy Assistant Secretary of Defense for International Security Affairs; and William R. Tyler, Assistant Secretary of State for European Affairs. Some of these had already collaborated on the recent Acheson report and the Bowie paper for the previous administration. They advocated European strength and unity as the best way to ensure its secure future. They saw opportunities in this force to achieve such goals, and believed a military case could be made by tying it as closely as possible to Norstad's MRBM plan.[18] Specifically, these collective force advocates saw a sea-based force as superior to a land-based one because it was less likely to elicit demands for nationally controlled missiles from the countries involved (specifically Germany). Such demands were bound to cause tensions both within the alliance and between the US and Soviet Union. In military terms, a sea-based strategy reduced vulnerability in comparison with missiles stationed on the European mainland, both from attack by the Soviet Union and seizure by the nations in whose territory they were based.[19]

The 'theologians' quickly began to dominate areas of debate on NATO and Europe within the US administration.[20] This had significant implications for the British whom the Americans knew were strongly opposed to the MRBM force, particularly any land-based version.[21] Although Kennedy's plans for the MLF did not advance significantly, by December 1961 when Macmillan met with the president in Bermuda, the State Department was pressing for an emphasis on the multilateral solution to the MRBM problem at the expense of the British independent deterrent. In particular it stressed that the president should not make further commitments to the UK nuclear deterrent while discussions about MRBMs were ongoing in NATO. And in regard to the MLF, 'We should stress the need to respond constructively to European, and particularly German, concerns regarding control of nuclear weapons since these concerns, if disregarded, will add to pressures for national nuclear programs.'[22] In light of the NSC of 21 April 1961 concerning the long-term US desire to phase out the British deterrent and questions of future policy, 'we should not extend military nuclear co-operation with the British beyond present levels'.[23] In contrast to these specific State Department aims, the Pentagon urged the president to take up broader defensive matters with Macmillan, such as the need to bolster conventional NATO defence, reintroduce conscription and augment the BAOR, as well as maintain global commitments.[24]

The 'theologians' ' approach was not well received by NATO authorities. Norstad still perceived the land-based MRBM problem to be acute and his request for such weapons had sparked interest from others in the alliance. In January 1962, the Strategic Allied Commander, Atlantic had expressed his concern 'about the use of Polaris submarines as European MRBMs' and pointed out 'that the type of MRBMs he understands are needed in Europe and Polaris submarines are not the same thing at all'.[25] Yet his concern, along with Nortad's, for a land-based element was being pushed aside in favour of the seaborne component and the president was advised that land-based missiles would simply be too provocative:

> Governments would demand a special national role in the peacetime deployment and control of any missiles on their territory, and the possibility of national seizure of such missiles in wartime would frustrate the whole point and purpose of a multilateral force. Serious European and Soviet concerns would be generated by the prospect of deployment of MRBMs on German territory. The evident presence of MRBMs with the warhead aboard travelling about European roads might stimulate neutralist and anti-nuclear sentiment and demonstrations in some countries. If an accident, possibly induced by sabotage, involving even the threat of nuclear contamination occurred on land, the political damage to

NATO would be serious. For all these reasons, the US position – since it was first made public in the President's Ottawa speech – has been that a multilateral MRBM force should be seaborne.[26]

Norstad's antipathy towards a sea-based force carried little weight. Appointed by the Eisenhower administration, he was clearly coming to the end of his term and later that same month it was announced that he would leave the post of SACEUR at the end of the year.[27]

The president's decision to opt for a collective force proposal hid his concerns.[28] In March 1962, Kennedy met with his advisers to review the progress that had been made since the Ottawa declaration, almost one year before, in dissuading the French from pursuing their national nuclear programme, particularly whether US attempts to guide them away from this position was not making them more determined to combine their resources with the Germans.[29] He was worried that in offering the joint MRBM proposal to the French and Germans, other nations might be excluded. He then expressed further concern that 'we were pouring our money into the ocean in this proposition in order to satisfy a political need whose use was dubious'. Specifically, Kennedy questioned whether the Europeans would sign up to a force in which the US retained its veto. In response, Bowie maintained that the political need was enough and while Kennedy's Secretary of Defence, Robert S. McNamara, played down the military requirement for MRBMs and highlighted the continued desire for a conventional build-up in Europe that might be compromised by the force, he grudgingly conceded that the political aspect was important.[30]

Kennedy's concern also extended to the finer points of detail. In April, studies conducted by State officials Henry Owen and Henry Rowan on the force proposal became NSAM 147 and therefore part of official US government policy. Although recent emphasis on the US nuclear submarine capability might have suggested submarines as the obvious choice for this force, Kennedy and the US JCS objected to the suggestion that the United States might share control of NATO-assigned Polaris submarines. So while the final draft appears with this paragraph on control still intact, the memorandum was issued with the instruction that it 'should not be volunteered by the US'. And in a discussion between the president and secretaries of state and defense, a decision had been made not to agree the paragraph. The paragraph stated that

'the US should consider some form of multilateral NATO control . . . over the Polaris submarines committed to NATO, if this is strongly desired by our allies', although it stressed that this would not be allowed to compromise operational effectiveness of the force and continued that 'Any multilateral control over these Polaris submarines would lapse when they were replaced by a multilateral MRBM force.'[31]

The Kennedy administration knew that the US retained overall nuclear superiority over the USSR and would continue to do so in most fields. Although the Soviets had 'made technological advances at rates at least equal to those achieved by the US in several areas which are of prime significance to the Soviet national defense posture' the US maintained six more nuclear submarines with a further sixty-one planned for the future. Soviet submarines also possessed only three or six short-range three-megaton cruise missiles each.[32] Immediate questions were therefore raised in the US about the military necessity of the force, despite the continued worry of a missile gap with the Soviets, particularly on MRBMs.

Despite such reservations, the force itself was clearly taking shape in US minds. The proposed force was now a 'modest sized (in the order of 200 missiles) fully multilateral NATO sea-based MRBM force'. It would involve 'adequate allied participation, so that it did not appear to be thinly disguised US–German operation', all of the costs 'should be equitably shared' and 'a sufficient degree of mixed manning' was required 'to ensure that one nationality does not appear to be predominant in the manning – and is not, in fact in control – of any vessel or of the missiles aboard any vessel'. The final section on control almost anticipated (albeit unknowingly) the future of the force:

> The US should indicate that it wishes to ascertain the views of its allies concerning the control formula...In connection with NATO considera-tion of the multilateral force [however] the United States should make it plain that transfer of nuclear warheads and procedures for using the force without United States concurrence would require amending exist-ing United States law and could well entail other obstacles depending on the character of the arrangement.[33]

Even in the early stages of the collective force idea the Kennedy Administration was clear about the difficulties of implementation. NATO Secretary General Dirk Stikker was pessimistic about the chances of British and French participation when he met US officials at the ministerial meeting in May. While at present the British were satisfied with the package of assurances, guide-lines and information, he suggested that the French were bound to give priority to their independent nuclear *force de frappe*. State Department official, Foy D. Kohler, agreed that there were problems, but said the MRBM force might have to proceed without the French and that the British might eventually come around.[34]

Washington was keen to stress that its enthusiasm for the prospective force rested on a European initiative, or in the Secretary of State, Dean Rusk's words, it did not want to produce a ' "US plan" for other countries to shoot at'.[35] In June 1962, Kennedy had met with officials from the British Embassy to explain cur-rent US thinking on the force. The president's advisors confirmed that they now envisaged a multilaterally owned, manned and controlled seaborne force with Polaris missiles, but it required European input. Foy Kohler pointed out to the British 'that the Americans intended to leave it to the Europeans to take the lead'. Foreign Secretary Lord Home disagreed. 'Although they [the US] profess to wish to leave the Europeans to make the running in this matter, [they] are in fact intent on promoting their own idea of a multilateral force', he reported to new British ambassador in Washington, Sir David Ormsby Gore.[36] Yet the president had not been convinced by the 'theologians'. As he told US NATO ambassador, Thomas Finletter, the military case had not been proved, the cost of undertaking the force was great, and he opposed a NATO MRBM force being a substitute for increasing alliance conventional force goals. As he concluded, 'my estimate in light of these factors is that the probability of final affirmative action on this MRBM force is low at present'.[37]

Renewed American pressure for the MLF from June caused considerable tension in the relationship with the British and other allies. The government in London saw that the French were opposed to an NATO MRBM force and American solutions would not impress General de Gaulle. Any support for the Americans would complicate relations with France and other allies. As Watkinson told the prime minister, 'Our policy of opposing the idea of a NATO MRBM force is quite clear, and I hope that we shall maintain it as it stands.'[38] The British objected to the clumsy presentation of the plan, particularly without consulting Norstad (when it appeared to undercut some of his ideas) or other allies, including West Germany.[39] They also saw little military value in the MRBM force and disagreed with the Americans about the political value such a force would have in providing cohesion within NATO. Ironically, this opposition brought them far closer to the position of the French than it did to the Americans.[40]

The British nuclear deterrent and Skybolt

With the rise of the MLF and the long-term US strategy of phasing out national nuclear deterrents the British nuclear project looked increasingly precarious in the early 1960s. This was compounded by significant technical problems on Skybolt. In the final six months of the Eisenhower administration, the president's Scientific Advisory Board had recommended that serious consideration be given to curtailing its development and Thomas Gates had made a move to cancel and remove it from his last defence budget in the final weeks of the Eisenhower administration.[41] As reports of this filtered down to British defence officials in Washington during December 1960, Watkinson even went so far as to warn Macmillan that production of Skybolt might be curtailed. With this in mind, the British sought assurances that the missile would still be produced. These assurances they duly received with the information that the planned date of deployment still stood at 1964.[42]

The British were also reassured when McNamara immediately increased the budget of Skybolt, thus apparently demonstrating his faith in the project. In the first year of the administration the British received reports that McNamara was willing to commit atleast another $50 million to it, prompting further agitation from Burke.[43] Despite some concern in the MOD, Skybolt appeared to have been saved, thus allaying UK fears throughout 1961. Then in November the MOD received a report that McNamara was willing to invest as much as it took to guarantee success, perhaps even an additional $100 million. In making this decision, staff in the ministry learnt, McNamara considered the amount of money already spent, the continued uncertainty of the strategic situation and the apparent competitiveness Skybolt still appeared to offer at this time. The Skybolt Director at Douglas Corporation (Skybolt's prime contractor) reinforced such optimism telling the UK chief scientific adviser, Sir Solly Zuckerman, that all was according to plan. McNamara confirmed this himself when he met Watkinson in December 1961, saying that the research and development costs were now likely to total to some $492 million. The US was still pushing ahead despite this huge cost, 'because its great importance to the bomber force of the United States as well as the United Kingdom, in the year 1966 to 1970 was recognized'.[44] But these American assurances were not without qualification and the British were aware that one possible outcome was cancellation even though the financial injection was welcome. McNamara went on to explain that there were 'considerable doubts as to whether the missile would prove sufficiently reliable, even if the required limits of accuracy could be achieved'.[45]

Yet it was also significant that on assuming office McNamara ordered the Polaris programme to be speeded up by some nine months over and above Gates' previous recommendation. The first five Polaris submarines were now required during the current financial year instead of the next (1962).[46] Kennedy's defence budget message to Congress in March then promised a total of twenty-nine Polaris submarines, an attestation to McNamara's great faith in Polaris according to the British Embassy.[47] Yet Watkinson remained convinced that Skybolt would succeed and there was no need to seek Polaris at this stage.[48] Even President Kennedy could not dissuade the British from continuing to rely on Skybolt. In January 1962, he informed the Secretary of State for Air, Julian Amery, directly that Skybolt might not work and Britain should not rely on it. Amery was greatly disturbed and Kennedy tried to reassure him. As David Nunnerley concludes, the importance of Skybolt to government policy meant that 'ministers discounted the more alarmist reports they were getting, preferring instead to put their faith blindly in the optimism of the contractors and the American Air Force'.[49] The underlying reasons for this continued to be the need for a rapid solution to the deterrent problem and continual fear of any other deal being tied to a NATO nuclear force.

Yet as McNamara was reassuring the British, he appeared to be taking an increasingly hostile view of national nuclear deterrents and the NATO force proposal. McNamara had initially toyed with the notion of a 'counterforce' strategy involving high-technology equipment pinpointing chosen targets for nuclear attack and therefore avoiding high levels of civilian casualties. Controversy and general antipathy towards this from the US military and European governments pushed it to the periphery as it gave way to new initiatives. Then in a secret speech to the NAC in Athens in May 1962, as well as a subsequent public (and widely reported) statement at the University of Michigan at Ann Arbor in June, McNamara advocated building up European conventional forces while condemning national nuclear programmes, implying instead that unified American central control was required.[50]

The US State Department and British and French governments reacted with dismay and even fury at McNamara's words. The State Department was disturbed that McNamara's statement appeared to undermine the call for a NATO MLF. Although McNamara's plan had similarities to the NATO force, as it also strove to limit national nuclear capabilities, the collective force plan downplayed American central command and foresaw a day when the US might relinquish its veto over it. And while McNamara claimed that he supported the MLF idea, its evolution would have diverted attention from the strengthening of conventional forces. Both the UK and France were angry that their national deterrents should apparently be singled out. The UK was particularly livid that the US secretary of defense should make such a brazen attack on its deterrent when the US government was developing a nuclear capability for the UK in the form of Skybolt. McNamara was quick to cover himself, claiming that his call had not been aimed at any government in particular. But the damage had been done.[51]

The McNamara speech effectively ended serious US considerations of substantially aiding the French with their nuclear programme. In the first months of his administration Kennedy had told Macmillan that aiding the French would be 'undesirable'.[52] Yet the president's attitude had changed, fearful of the economic wastage that the independent *force de frappe* entailed for the French and the impact it would have on NATO more broadly. Kennedy was also concerned with negative balance of payments with European countries exacerbating the increased defence expenditure brought about by the Berlin crisis, as well as continued plans to create a more flexible defensive posture in NATO. If technical help could be provided, he reasoned, perhaps some of these issues could be controlled. The British, on the other hand, were interested in the benefits tripartite nuclear co-operation between the US, France and Britain could bring them and they encouraged the Kennedy administration to consider such a course of action.[53]

Britain now had to balance its need for American help in defence with its growing interest in joining with the other six members of the European Economic Community (EEC). From July 1960, this became an official objective of British foreign policy and towards the end of 1961 negotiations for entry began.[54] Unfortunately for the UK, its application coincided with increasing strain between the two superpowers over the status of Berlin and de Gaulle's renewed attempts to steer the six EEC members in a direction ordained by him, specifically a *union d'etats*. Compounding this was the inevitable problem of the British nuclear deterrent being so closely connected to the US, while the French strove for independence. Members of the UK government agitated for closer co-operation with France on nuclear issues during the first months of the Kennedy Administration, with some encouragement from the president and officials.[55]

In the spring of 1962 the president authorized the Assistant Secretary of Defense for International Security Affairs, Paul Nitze to examine ways the French could be aided in their nuclear programme. This had widespread support among personnel in the Pentagon, Central Intelligence Agency and White House. Kennedy was also under considerable pressure to facilitate French capability from his Ambassador in Paris, James Gavin.[56] This culminated in a meeting between Nitze and director of armaments in the French defence ministry in Washington in March 1962.[57] But with the opposition of the State Department to consider, as well as his commitment to the joint NATO force, Kennedy withdrew support the following month. McNamara tipped the balance, arguing that assistance for the French in this area would give the green light to other potential nuclear powers to blackmail the US in order to gain its help. The president agreed with this prognosis, giving a press conference on 18 April reiterating that there had been no change in US nuclear policy towards France. He then instructed US officials not to discuss sharing with the French on nuclear matters. This decision was based in part on the damaging effect that aiding the French nuclear programme could have on West Germany.[58] It had the effect of placing the multilateral nuclear option in NATO at a higher point on the American agenda.[59]

Meanwhile, others within the US administration were putting pressure on the president to reduce nuclear assistance to the British in order to ease their entry to the EEC. National Security Advisor McGeorge Bundy told the president on 24 April 1962 'that our close cooperation with the British does not depend on British aloofness from Europe or on the existing preferential treatment of the British on nuclear matters':

> We want the British in Europe, and we do not really see much point in the separate British nuclear deterrent, beyond our existing Skybolt commitment; we would much rather have British efforts go into conventional weapons and have the British join with the rest of NATO in accepting a single US-dominated nuclear force. The question of British membership in Europe is now urgent. The nuclear question is less pressing from our point of view, simply because the time does not look right for a solution. Certainly there is nothing for us in any possible British notion that the UK might pay its entrance fee to the Common Market by providing nuclear assistance to the French. In such a case the British would be appeasing the French with our secrets, and no good would come of it. I strongly agree with Jean Monnet [Head of the Action Committee for the United States of Europe] that the Common Market and the nuclear problem should be dealt with one after the other and not both at once. Our discussion of the MRBM problem should fill the gap in NATO while the Common Market and the UK are working out their basic arrangements...So I think the answer is that the President of the United States has every right to sustain the special relationship with the UK as long as the fundamental basis of that relationship is cooperative common effort, and not special preference. After all, we would like a special relationship with the French too, if only it could involve some real cooperation.[60]

Bundy's hopes were understandable. US policy statements suggested that in the long term (and crucially once the EEC negotiations were out of the way) US efforts should be directed at ending the British nuclear deterrent, or at least placing it within a NATO context. This would jeopardize any 'special (nuclear) relationship' the US felt it had with the UK.

Bundy's views were echoed by the State Department, which also took up the mantle of the April 1961 NATO Policy Directive. Although there was no overriding clamour to end what it saw as the preferential relationship with the UK in the nuclear affairs, State officials felt that it should certainly not be exacerbated in the future at the expense of Britain and the EEC. As part of long-term policy, the NATO nuclear force therefore continued its ascent in the State Department and the Secretary of State, Dean Rusk, came under increasing pressure from his subordinates to ensure any future British nuclear role was placed firmly in this context.[61] He was told in May 'the heart of the matter is that we should avoid any actions to increase the degree of our special nuclear relationship with the UK. We should make it clear that we are not prepared to extend that relation, notably in regard to the creation of a UK Polaris missile force'. A longer-range recommendation here was for the British to assign their V-bombers to NATO and for any American nuclear aid to be given to the European Community, rather than the British or French on a national basis, or even NATO.[62]

Contrary to these hopes, Macmillan saw British nuclear co-operation with France as a possible *quid pro quo* for British EEC entry. In April and May, Macmillan began tentative talks with successive French Ambassadors. He then met de Gaulle in June at Champs. It is unclear whether Macmillan actually made the nuclear co-operation for European entry offer, as the official record makes no mention of it, but it seems clear that some form of co-operation was discussed.[63] Significantly, Macmillan's ideas were not aired either in public or in discussions with Washington. As the US was becoming increasingly vocal in opposing the idea of national deterrents he had reassured Rusk in April that no such *quid pro quo* would be offered to de Gaulle, although he conceded that a European nuclear force with some British component was a possibility after UK entry to the EEC was assured. The following month, he was also dissembling in responses to questions over the issue in the House of Commons and even had to guard against opposition from his own ministers, particularly in the Foreign Office, who continued to see the US as the natural nuclear ally for the UK.[64]

Despite Macmillan's assurances to Washington, the US government, and State Department in particular, remained concerned that British assistance to the French would upset relations between all three countries. On the eve of Macmillan's visit in April, a paper written by leading 'theologians' claimed that Macmillan might try to persuade the president that Franco-British nuclear co-operation would improve France's relations with NATO to secure French participation in a NATO force, rather than the real motive, which was to gain British entry to the EEC.[65] While State was not especially concerned with the British making certain information available from the period before the 1958 amendments to the McMahon Act, any provision of material beyond this presented 'enormous difficulties' because of legal, technical and administrative difficulties it would create. A paper prepared for the president in May concluded: 'The simple answer to the question regarding UK–French nuclear cooperation without the United States is...that it is difficult to see how it could be made to work to the satisfaction of any of the three countries.'[66]

To the British, US policy was increasingly contradictory. They were concerned that the Americans desire for a MLF alongside a broader discussion of NATO nuclear affairs would upset already tense relations with the French at a time when the EEC negotiations were entering a crucial period. With continued French opposition to a NATO nuclear force, Macmillan was against entering discussions with allies about nuclear matters for fear of complicating Britain's EEC negotiations.[67] He explained to the foreign secretary that if they could not persuade the Americans to 'keep quiet about the Common Market, I would hope that we could at least impress on Rusk the importance of leaving the nuclear question, and indeed the re-organisation of NATO, over until our negotiations with the six have come to a head'. To Macmillan the British and French nuclear deterrents were established and the Americans could do nothing about them, while French refusal to place troops returning from Algeria under SACEUR's control meant there was little point in McNamara and Rusk making speeches and launching plans. 'If the Americans have a "grand design" for Europe, they are much more likely to achieve it if they can talk less now', he concluded.[68] Moreover, the introduction of McNamara's proposals at Athens and Ann Arbor did not sit easily with the MLF proposals. They did not agree with the American assertion that the German nuclear question needed to be dealt with quickly and did not want to initiate a discussion about control of any future force.[69]

Meanwhile, British plans for nuclear co-operation with the French continued. In June, Watkinson met his opposite number in Paris, Pierre Messmer, to discuss possible collaboration on missile firing nuclear powered submarines. Then a drastic Cabinet re-shuffle by Macmillan the following month brought Peter Thorneycroft to the top job in the MOD. Following his attempts to work with the French on Blue Streak during his tenure as aviation minister, Thorneycroft was even more favourably disposed than Watkinson to the European option, particularly the opportunity afforded by a French company's request on behalf of the navy to receive information on the *Dreadnought* propulsion system. With the support of the Admiralty and Julian Amery, Thorneycroft warned the prime minister not to support the Foreign Office view that they should, in Home's words, 'let go the submarine sale'.[70]

It is hard to gauge what Thorneycroft told the US as regards the British situation with France. The British record of a meeting in September between British officials and Walt Rostow shows that Thorneycroft explored the possibility of both a European nuclear force without an American veto and British nuclear help to the French at crucial points in the forthcoming EEC negotiations. In the American version, Rostow was much clearer in his support of any European force's total integration so as not to allow withdrawal of any units for use as a national deterrent. Thorneycroft also urged Rostow that 'no discussion on nuclear matters be launched currently which would interfere with the delicate Anglo-French negotiations over the EEC'.[71]

Whatever the details of policy, it was clear that tensions were developing between the United States and United Kingdom over American plans for a seaborne MLF and ideas about aiding the French. In September, London expressed fears that US determination to press on with the multilateral scheme might prejudice its own initiatives on nuclear collaboration with the French and at the same time raise general policy discussions within the alliance.[72] The following month, on 15 October, the British agreed to allow a company to seek a contract with the French for sale of the propulsion unit to the French navy. Simultaneously, Washington agreed in principle to sell a nuclear powered 'hunter-killer' submarine to the French government. This caused deep concern in Downing Street, although it did not know that the Pentagon was proposing going even further. On 25 October, Nitze resurrected ideas about sharing nuclear and ballistic missile technology with the French, including information on nuclear submarines and perhaps even selling the 10,000 kilograms of weapons grade Uranium-235.[73] All such plans were to be shelved however, first as the crisis over Soviet weapons in Cuba became apparent and second because Skybolt was becoming a mater of great concern – so much so that it could no longer be deferred.

The cancellation of Skybolt

By mid-1962, doubts in British minds over Skybolt were reinforced from lower levels. In August, Zuckerman, who received regular reports from the United States Air Force (USAF) and Pentagon on its progress, concluded that his personal assessments of Skybolt's progress were generally 'somewhat less rosy than the information sent to us'. And the embassy in Washington warned that there was 'an element of doubt in some DOD [Department of Defense] circles that [the] MOD is not 100 per cent in favour of Skybolt. This is particularly serious as McNamara is now being invited to approve allocation of funds.'[74]

While equivocal, McNamara still tried to keep the British up-to-date with developments, although this was complicated by his relationship with Peter Thorneycroft. Thorneycroft's style was very different to McNamara's and the Americans knew he was less well disposed to the US than his predecessor Watkinson had been.[75] McNamara now estimated that the cost of Skybolt would rise to $2.5 billion over three fiscal years and might not prove viable even then.[76] Although McNamara made no firm decision, he warned Thorneycroft of the situation in September when the new defence minister was in Washington. Yet McNamara's concerns were not sufficiently heeded by Thorneycroft, who, according to Donette Murray, 'returned home dismissive of McNamara's pessimistic account of Skybolt's problems and happy that all was progressing as expected'. Furthermore, the acute global situation during the Cuban missile crisis, the following month, helped to divert Anglo-American attention from the impending doom of Skybolt.[77]

This pattern of missed opportunities continued for the next two months. It may have been caused by US obfuscation in its statements, yet Washington always kept the British in mind. Pentagon officials even argued later that the very fact the US prolonged the life of Skybolt for as long as it did indicated sensitivity to the British position.[78] Yet now it was becoming increasingly difficult to contemplate prolonging it any further because of huge technical difficulties. On 31 October, the USAF liaison officer warned the MOD that McNamara had threatened to cancel the missile unless the first guided launch was successful.[79] The same day the British Desk in the State Department prepared a paper for William Tyler on the likely political fallout from cancellation.[80] Noting the implications for the Conservative Party and the UK nuclear deterrent, the paper emphasized the importance of the US–UK relationship, particularly as the US relied on so much British military 'real estate', and how cancellation might be seen as ' "double-crossing" our oldest and closest ally . . . it would be a serious blow to our whole alliance system'. State suggested close consultation to avoid awkwardness and embarrassment, possibly in the form of a letter from president to prime minister.[81]

The British now sought clarification. Reacting to some positive British reports on Skybolt, Thorneycroft wrote to McNamara to tell him this was 'welcome news indeed'. Yet he was clearly worried, concluding that 'the Skybolt programme . . . is, as you know, a central feature both of our defence policy and of our collaboration with you'. This letter may have been an attempt to smoke McNamara out.[82] In this regard Thorneycroft was reasonably successful; McNamara's reply was much less optimistic, stating that he had 'long had reservations as to the success of this most complex and expensive system'. The next set of tests would decide the course of action to be taken, he said, and promised to keep the minister informed.[83] Despite this, the MOD decided that it would be 'premature' to involve the prime minister and president at this stage.[84] This decision was based on the belief that clearer indications of cancellation would be forthcoming, a sentiment reinforced by the British Defence Staff (BDS) in Washington:

> During various conversations today we found that the gravity of this matter from a UK point of view was still not fully appreciated. However there is little doubt that all concerned realise they are dealing with dynamite and as a result we gather that no decision to cancel is likely to be made without prior and full consultation with the UK.[85]

This explains something of the British mindset. The very nature of the Anglo-American alliance reinforced the British belief that it would be wholly unreasonable of the US Administration to cancel Skybolt, which they were after all producing for the British as well as their own air force, without prior consultation. Complacence in London to the plight of Skybolt was reinforced by unsound information emanating from across the Atlantic. On 13 November, USAF staff in Washington informed Ministry of Air staff in London that the USAF had passed their arguments for the retention of Skybolt to the Pentagon and these were 'sound'.[86]

Simultaneously, however, Thorneycroft was moving towards a more realistic assessment of Skybolt's state and the need for an alternative. In early November, the US secretary of defense once again talked about imminent cancellation in a telephone conversation with Thorneycroft and Ormsby Gore and offered to come to London to discuss alternatives.[87] Arthur Hockaday, Thorneycroft's private secretary, signalled that he was 'especially depressed by McNamara having gone so far as to mention alternatives' and that they should not take the bait, instead encouraging Ormsby Gore 'to fight the battle...on the wider political issue'. In contrast, Thorneycroft himself reacted calmly. Cutting through such arguments he emphasized his personal concern for the deterrent gap if Skybolt was cancelled and that 'He would settle for four Polaris submarines here and now without strings, and that we should be put in a position to build our own by 1970.'[88]

What developed in Thorneycroft's mind between then and the early days of December was a future Polaris force for the 1970s with the US government loaning the British use of two or three Polaris submarines for the interim period.[89] He articulated this to the prime minister as news of the cancellation was starting to filter through on 7 December. Thorneycroft now required the Kennedy Administration to re-affirm its commitment to an independent British nuclear deterrent and 'to undertake to give us options to acquire what we need for this purpose'. He continued:

> What this will be requires careful working out with them, but it will include the purchase by us of a number of Polaris missiles with control and navigational equipment; the loan of two or three complete Polaris carrying submarines for a period of years until our own submarines are ready; and technical help in assisting us to create, maintain and operate the force.[90]

This ignored the crucial fact that any Polaris deal was likely to be tied to some kind of joint MRBM force. It would be difficult for the US to be seen to be giving the British a nuclear delivery system without strings, as it would be perceived as reneging on earlier commitments made to other NATO partners and incur the ire of the French. And as the British Chiefs of Staff recognized at the time, the Americans would argue that simply assigning British and American (perhaps with some French) forces to NATO would not satisfy the Germans in the long term.[91]

The prime minister, who remained wedded to the Skybolt option, also undercut Thorneycroft's ideas. Macmillan made the decision to pursue Skybolt because of the domestic impact its cancellation would have had, particularly when anti-American sentiment in Britain had been roused by Dean Acheson's speech claiming that Britain had 'lost an Empire and has not yet found a role'.[92] Macmillan's intervention so late in the day meant that he lacked an understanding of the finer points of the case. As a result, he wanted to call the Americans' bluff, recommending that they should tell Washington they were planning to finish Skybolt on their own. In the prime minster's opinion, 'it might just stop the Americans cancelling the project. It would certainly be very embarrassing for the Administration to abandon a weapon which their own Service Chiefs favour and then see us go on with it'.[93] While Macmillan's solution ignored the egregious technical difficulties the USAF was experiencing with Skybolt, it was more demonstrative of the prime minister's attitude towards Britain's relations with the US at a crucial time in the EEC negotiations. This proposed political arm-twisting could in fact achieve little if the US announced that the missile would indeed be cancelled and it was highly unlikely to induce them to rethink their decision. Moreover, it ignored the strategic reality that if the US cancelled Skybolt it would be discredited as a deterrent. Once again though, overriding political necessity took precedence over such strategic considerations.

By the end of November, the Americans had effectively decided to terminate the Skybolt programme.[94] As this fact became clear within the US administration, the ambassador in London stressed that because cancellation would have so many ramifications for the British they should be given the maximum of time possible to make decisions, prepare plans and present them to Parliament and the public. 'Abandonment now could have the most fundamental consequences to defense policies of the UK, its relationship with ourselves and other allies, and its participation in evolving common defense efforts,' the American ambassador in London, David Bruce, stated. He concluded that McNamara's coming to London to meet with Thorneycroft would be 'highly desirable'.[95] Another State Department paper declared that cancellation of Skybolt would be 'extremely unfortunate from a political point of view'. Citing the likely British reaction that the US was trying to reduce their world power status, the paper suggested that it would leave 'deep scars'. Only two alternatives were available: to help the British with Skybolt or to provide them with one or two Polaris submarines 'initially ... under at least a superficial multilateral umbrella'.[96]

Yet if McNamara thought that Thorneycroft and the rest of the British government had been given ample time to consider the implications of the Skybolt cancellation and would be roused by the hints he had given to Ormsby Gore and Thorneycroft he was much mistaken.[97] Indeed, before the crisis broke, both parties were trying to play down Skybolt as an issue.[98] On 29 November, as the British prepared for Macmillan's talks with de Gaulle at Rambouillet and then Kennedy at Nassau the following month, Skybolt was still only the second of twelve main discussion points on the agenda for Nassau.[99] In the US, it came under a sub-heading within 'nuclear matters', which was itself under the fourth point (headed 'Atlantic Community') of a five-point agenda.[100] Similarly, although McNamara had warned Bruce in November of Skybolt's almost certain fate, Bruce made no call to action. 'Perhaps if [the Skybolt] matter [is] decided it would be wise to have President discuss it at Nassau with Prime Minister', Bruce commented blithely at the beginning of December and as late as 14 December, the American Embassy in London felt it necessary to warn the State Department explicitly that Skybolt had become a major issue in Whitehall.[101]

Even the British were not as rash and uncompromising as has been thought previously. Despite notions that the British tried to play up the crisis in order to consolidate their bargaining position with the Americans, the prime minister, possibly fearful that such attention would jeopardize Britain's EEC application, sought to play down the nuclear aspects of the Nassau conference, while Ormsby Gore agreed with Rusk that Skybolt should not be placed as a specific item on the agenda 'as we wanted to reduce speculation about the future of Skybolt to a minimum'.[102] On 9 December, with unconfirmed rumours of Skybolt's' demise swirling round Whitehall, Macmillan was still urging 'a cagey line' and suggesting that they could play Skybolt along for a year 'to avoid political difficulties at home'.[103] Two days later, in the midst of the crisis, de Zulueta wrote to Ormsby Gore to inform him that Macmillan felt that the issue of Skybolt would inevitably be the most urgent one on the agenda in Nassau. 'I do not know if you will think it wise to mention this to the President; of course, we shall not wish to play Skybolt up in the publicity but no doubt the press will do this for us.'[104]

De Zulueta was right, as by then it was no longer possible to keep a lid on news of Skybolt's demise. McNamara volunteered to deliver the blow, with Secretary of State Dean Rusk, who probably did not want to get his hands dirty with the Byzantine State Department politics concerning Britain and nuclear weapons, delegating what should have been his task to a man who was not known for his political finesse.[105] When he spoke to reporters in London shortly after his arrival, McNamara emphasized that one of the main issues he would discuss with Thorneycroft was Skybolt, the cost of which was spiralling while several tests had failed. This statement alone upset members of the British government and sent the press into a furore.[106]

By the time Thorneycroft and McNamara met on 11 December, it was clear that the Skybolt issue was now an acute concern to both sides. When McNamara confirmed that the US would not continue with the programme, Thorneycroft made an impassioned speech in which he reiterated the importance of the British nuclear deterrent to US–UK defence relations. Continuing, he rejected McNamara's offers of the British continuing Skybolt, accepting the Hound Dog system as a replacement or creating a NATO MLF.[107] What is certain is that both were constrained by the briefs they had been given by their respective leaders and could therefore probably come to no concrete decisions, but the record now shows that discussion of Polaris as a replacement for Skybolt took up a considerable portion of their meeting. Previous accounts have tended to play down the importance of the Polaris discussion. According to Richard Neustadt, for example, 'Thorneycroft was waiting for an offer of Polaris; McNamara was expecting him to ask for it.' While Neustadt concedes that McNamara mentioned Polaris, it was within the context of an MRBM force and was therefore not especially significant when this was probably within his brief. Donette Murray states that this offer only exacerbated the situation, because it had always been one of the key barriers to British acceptance of Polaris.[108] During this discussion, Thorneycroft claimed that Polaris had been mentioned before and that Admiralty studies had indicated a UK Polaris 'hybrid' programme might have its first operational submarine by 1969 if it had help from the US on missiles, navigations and communications components. McNamara stressed the legal, political, technical and financial issues that that would be raised by such an agreement and suggested that the UK could think about building this fleet in conjunction with others. Thorneycroft was clear however. Although he was 'the keenest of multilateralists... he had to maintain Britain's independent role – he had no choice'. Cancellation of Skybolt would be 'desperate', but he concluded, cancellation without an adequate alternative would be 'quite impossible'.[109] Of more significance, however, were meetings between Thorneycroft and McNamara at the meeting of the NAC in Paris between 13 and 15 December. Just prior to his leaving Washington McNamara had discussed with the president and Rusk the possibility of offering Polaris, perhaps to be developed in conjunction with a MLF. While Rusk objected, the president broadly agreed with McNamara's ideas.[110] Thus, McNamara and Thorneycroft discussed Polaris as an alternative to Skybolt, although McNamara could make no official offer at this stage.[111] This suggests that both sides were slowly beginning to establish a position from which they could negotiate at Nassau. Simultaneously their perceptions of the likely outcome of the talks were beginning to converge.

Macmillan's position had also changed. With Skybolt now totally discredited he sought viable alternatives and it was soon very obvious that the only choice was Polaris. Yet he needed to keep up the pressure on the Americans in order to extract concessions from them and the best way to do that was to keep up the appearance that the Americans had let him down over Skybolt. He contacted Ormsby Gore about this, but made it clear that this was not to be discussed with the Americans. He also sought to move the nuclear issue to the top of the agenda because the outcome of the Nassau discussions would affect the entire British defence posture, an implicit threat to the US.[112]

In fact, Washington had already been acting to avert a crisis in the days before the Thorneycroft–McNamara meeting. From 10 December, tentative plans were afoot to offer the British Polaris missiles and, in the following days, this became the focus of American policy.[113] Kennedy asked his Special Assistant for Science and Technology, Jerome B. Wiesner, in tandem with the DOD to consider alternatives that could be offered to the British. While Wiesner responded with a number of options, only two appeared to him to be viable. British continuation of Skybolt, either with or without US help was possible, but likely to increase both production costs and delay the time when the missile could go into service. Supplying a slightly modified Hound Dog missile for British V-bombers was also valid, although, as he recognized, the British had no interest in it. Another possibility was direct cost sale of land-based Polaris or Minuteman missiles for hardened sites in the UK. The advantages here would be that they could be deployed quickly (in 1964) and would probably not make the UK any more vulnerable to a pre-emptive strike than having Skybolt bases on their soil. The final two options were, however, the most practicable. The first was a 'Polaris-type submarine force', which Wiesner thought, 'by far the most satisfactory force since it would be highly invulnerable and would remove attack targets from the UK itself'. The sale of complete submarines built in the US would almost certainly be too expensive, therefore:

> A much better approach would be to sell Polaris missiles, excluding warheads, at a cost of about $1 million each to the UK and to provide technical assistance to the UK in the production of its own submarine and nuclear reactors. This approach does have the disadvantage that it would delay the operational availability of the first Polaris-type submarine to about 1969. I understand that the UK has shown definite interest in this approach.

In addition, Wiesner's ultimate recommendation was the most ambitious, comprising a mixed force of V-bombers with Hound Dogs, land-based Polaris or Minutemen and Polaris submarines. Although this final recommendation would be the most expensive, Wiesner estimated that it would still almost certainly be cheaper than Skybolt.[114]

While McNamara was away at the December NATO ministerial meeting, his deputy, Roswell Gilpatric, drafted a parallel memo to Wiesner's suggesting three possible military (rather than political) possibilities in the light of Skybolt's imminent demise. The first was its continuation in order to subsidize British production, the second withdrawal of US help with the British deterrent and the third to provide technical information and components for some kind of alternative. According to Gilpatric, the first solution 'would only put off the day of reckoning', the second (even if it was combined with a US statement of support for a British independent deterrent) was 'too drastic to consider seriously at the present time' and so it was the third that became recommended DOD policy. Polaris was the prime candidate for this substitution, as Gilpatric explained:

> The British are well along in the development of a nuclear powered submarine. They would neither need nor request US assistance for the submarine-unique part of the system. It becomes analogous to the Vulcan Mark II bomber that would have carried Skybolt. They would require our agreement to sell Polaris A-3 missiles ex warhead, and to sell (or perhaps only to describe) equipment uniquely required to operate and launch the missiles. These parallel the Skybolt arrangements.[115]

The under secretary's recommendation was to swap Skybolt for Polaris, rather than make additional demands of the British. Pentagon advice was therefore much more pro-British than State Department, and by implication anti-French, although there were still limits on this help. Gilpatric did not recommend, for example, plugging any gap in the UK nuclear arsenal that would occur before Polaris came into existence. But the die had been cast.

The State Department view was evolving in a considerably different direction under the influence of the 'theologians'. They wanted to ensure the British were clear that the Americans would not give them a nationally owned and manned replacement for the cancelled weapon.[116] In a summary of their collective position on the eve of Nassau, they stated that neither Britain nor Europe would benefit from a hasty decision on a replacement for Polaris and it recommended a considered approach. Ideally, the State Department desired the prime minister to accept Skybolt, while it conceded that this was not a likely scenario. The central dilemma therefore became one of timing. Although the present acute political crisis over Skybolt apparently threatened the Macmillan government, State feared the situation could be made worse by an unwise decision taken as the EEC negotiations continued. Thus the question of an alternative was 'most likely to be sensibly answered if the answer is returned *after* the present sensitive and distraught period of EEC negotiations'. In order to do this, the US and UK could make a joint declaration that they had decided to curtail development of Skybolt and were examining alternatives.[117]

Consideration of possible European reactions was even more crucial to State Department thinking and once more it saw opportunities to demonstrate a reduction of the British nuclear role. In order to placate European governments, 'the UK might announce that it was ordering several Polaris MRBM submarines from the US, and was prepared to have other European countries join with it in their financing, manning and control'. Alternatively, the UK and US could jointly announce the creation of a pilot force. Again it conceded that neither of these two alternatives was likely to be acceptable to the British.[118] Yet in the view of the State Department, public opinion in the UK appeared to be retreating from support of a nuclear policy because of its costs and impact on alliance nations thus offering opportunities for State Department policy. 'This important and promising possibility of a UK phase-out from national deterrent would be greatly weakened if we now allowed the UK – in a moment of great difficulty – to strike out in near panic in a direction whose implications neither the UK nor we have had an opportunity fully to consider', it concluded.[119]

On 16 December, the president made a decision and largely overruled the State Department. In a meeting with his key advisers (except Rusk, who also did not go to the Bahamas) Kennedy explored the possibility of giving Macmillan the system he wanted. Although George Ball raised objections, the president took a pro-British position arguing, 'that the cancellation of Skybolt implied some obligation to provide a substitute, on our part'. Going on the advice of Bruce (who was also not at this meeting) that this was primarily a political problem that would be raised when the UK Parliament met again in January, the president attempted to 'meet the prime minister's needs for this hour and he thought only the prime minister could decide this question'. The meeting finally approved a general proposal concluding that 'we would offer components of Polaris missiles to the British', although, 'it would be a condition of this offer that the British would commit their eventual Polaris force to a multilateral or multinational force in NATO'. In addition, the UK would have to agree to build up their conventional forces.[120]

In other words, despite the general impression of a lack of preparedness given on both sides at Nassau, the US already had the essentials of the Polaris offer three days before the conference even began. And despite Kennedy's attempt to sweeten the Skybolt pill with a 50–50 Anglo-American development plan that he offered to Ormsby Gore on the presidential aeroplane from Paris the day after the meeting with his advisors, he was ready to relent and give the British Polaris.[121]

The State Department was now less than satisfied with what they saw as a change of policy that affected the whole of NATO and began to turn their attention to presentation of any Polaris deal.[122] As Kennedy prepared to leave for the Bahamas, Tyler and Rostow wrote to warn Rusk of how the Polaris sale should be handled. To divert European attention away from the bilateral aspect of the potential agreement, they argued of the need to 'limit the damage' as regards the UK and EEC following the 'gloomy' meeting between de Gaulle and Macmillan at Rambouillet to discuss British entry to the Common Market earlier in the month. It was up to the US to stress to other European nations that they should proceed 'by exploiting the condition that we have imposed on the UK', in other words the joint NATO force. In this way, the State Department perceived the Polaris sale as a 'transitional arrangement', whereby UK submarines would eventually be merged into the larger NATO force. Finally, Rostow and Tyler lobbied against extending the agreement to France, as this would undermine the argument that Polaris was just a follow-on from Skybolt, which could be seen by the USSR and European nations to presage a Polaris sale to West Germany.[123] Rostow's fears were underlined when he wrote to Kennedy independently the same day. 'I have rarely seen so dangerous a gap between a high level decision and the judgement of junior subordinates, in both Defense and State, and on both sides of the ocean' he said, somewhat cryptically, before proceeding to outline his opposition to the likely resolution. Again, Rostow's main fear was the apparently irreconcilable nature of the Polaris sale with the Brussels negotiations, particularly as he surmised that British public opinion was now calming down after the Skybolt furore, and so it seemed that Polaris might be unnecessary. But his main concern was directed towards allies of the US in NATO, most notably France and Germany, and their perception of any agreement.[124]

The point of greatest clarity to emerge from these State Department explorations was that the Skybolt issue had largely been resolved. A Polaris offer was now the most likely outcome. Indeed, this was beginning to be reflected on the other side of Atlantic in the MOD where it seemed to have become a prerequisite for any deal in the Bahamas (although Macmillan apparently remained cautious).[125] 'I must tell you as strongly as I may' Sir Robert Scott, permanent secretary of the

MOD, told Thorneycroft, 'that in my opinion the future of the British deterrent lies under the water' He continued: 'We need American support, of course, but I feel that some support will be forthcoming on the demise of Skybolt.'[126]

The Nassau conference

Details of the discussions that took place in Nassau over the two days of 19 and 20 December 1962 have already been well documented.[127] It remains an incredibly complex summit, however, conceived in the aftermath of the Skybolt controversy and subject to many competing interests. Tensions between the two sides were undoubtedly compounded by Macmillan's precarious domestic position that had forced the cabinet re-shuffle in July and the recently resolved Cuban missile crisis. Yet some of the participants have also said how positive the atmosphere was.[128] Yet the Polaris deal was brokered fairly swiftly, partly because of the pressing time constraints on both parties, not only because of Macmillan's need to announce a decision quickly following the declaration of Skybolt's imminent demise but also because of US action behind the scenes in the preceding days.

While Kennedy had decided on a course of action that included supplying Polaris to the British, he did not offer it straight away. Instead, he established his negotiating position by proposing the new Skybolt deal he had offered Ormsby Gore on the Nassau-bound presidential aeroplane and had mentioned to the prime minister in an informal talk the previous evening. Kennedy suggested that it could be produced purely for the British, but with the US continuing to put in 50 per cent of production costs. Macmillan reacted as Ormsby Gore had apparently predicted he would, with reservation, if not outright hostility.[129]

By this point, Macmillan had already given a lengthy and eloquent presentation on the history and importance of Anglo-American nuclear co-operation. In particular, he stressed that he and Eisenhower had discussed the possibility of the British gaining Polaris at their Camp David meeting in 1960. When the president explained that the great difference between Skybolt and Polaris was in their respective political ramifications for Britain's relations with Europe, Macmillan disagreed. He had made it clear to de Gaulle at Rambouillet that if Skybolt was indeed to be scrapped he would require the Americans to provide a viable alternative, meaning Polaris, or Britain would have to produce its own, he said. Now, he claimed, he could see little point in giving de Gaulle Polaris on the same terms, or indeed widening the deal to include Germany. Macmillan:

> Did not believe...that a switch from the lame horse, Skybolt, to what was now the favourite, Polaris, would upset France and Germany because they accepted the different backgrounds of their national history. If, however, it would help the Prime Minister would consider making some arrangement which might in practice be little more than a gesture but which would have a moral effect.[130]

46

Although discussion of Skybolt as an option persisted throughout this first meeting, and McNamara gave Macmillan a summary of its technical possibilities and difficulties, discussion was already moving away from it. The complicating factor was the MLF, which Kennedy began to press in conjunction with any offer on Polaris. This was unsatisfactory to Macmillan, who remained highly suspicious of the force and was unconvinced that it would satisfy German nuclear aspirations. Yet by the beginning of the afternoon meeting on the first day, it seemed clear to Macmillan 'that the situation now was that the US had agreed to sell Polaris missiles to the UK, which would construct the actual submarines and the warheads'.[131]

The president had now forsaken the State Department line expressed in the previous days, with the one crucial concession that Polaris could not be seen to be totally independent and assignment to a NATO force was required. This proved to be the most intractable element of the negotiation, as it dealt with the political presentation of an extremely volatile area of alliance policy. Macmillan wanted Polaris on the same terms as the Skybolt agreement, without strings. An early US draft agreement, on the other hand, said that the submarines would be 'assigned to NATO'. Yet once again the president came towards the British position, recognizing 'that it was in the UK interest to define "assigned" as loosely as possible so as to satisfy British opinion with regard to an independent role', a definition that would be interpreted differently in Europe. Macmillan naturally wanted something blander, his government having opposed such assignment since at least 1960.[132]

With presidential concession on assignment, members of the State Department saw the chance to gain political credence for the NATO nuclear force in Europe. Their inability to prevent the sale of Polaris missiles had been something of a defeat and the symbolic move towards a NATO force was now the only face-saving option left open. From the beginning, George Ball (the highest-ranking State Department official present) argued that discussion 'should be done in a multilateral context' and that the US envisaged a force with mixed-manning and no right of withdrawal.[133] The following day, absent State Department officials Robert Schaetzel and Rusk cabled their comments to the Bahamas stressing that 'The ultimate objective of the agreement will be the development of a multilateral force.'[134]

For Macmillan, the combination of defining assignment on Polaris alongside the NATO force caused great difficulties and he had to tread warily in order to keep all his ministers and advisors on side.[135] Few in his Cabinet saw much merit in the multilateral scheme and when he cabled the Foreign Office in London at the end of the negotiations that, 'I have discussed this with Alec Home, Peter Thorneycroft and Duncan Sandys [now minister of aviation] and the four of us feel that this draft statement gives us what we want', this hid some considerable dissatisfaction between them.[136] At the end of the first days' discussion, for example, Thorneycroft minuted Macmillan to object to the latest American draft:

> Under these proposals we would not in fact have (nor could we ever claim to have) an independent nuclear deterrent... I am strongly against any attempt to find a formula which glosses over the very deep and wide chasm between us.

Thorneycroft believed that while Macmillan was bound to proclaim that the independence or what he would term 'interdependence', of the British nuclear deterrent had been secured, this arrangement tied Polaris too firmly to NATO. Thorneycroft even went so far as to suggest winding up the talks as soon as possible, with a statement that the US had withdrawn Skybolt and although 'possible alternatives have been discussed...it has not been possible to reach a decision'.[137]

Macmillan also remained unsatisfied with the terms of the American offer. He wanted at least the appearance of more independence for the British deterrent and was determined to get this agreement. With the American desire to see the British deterrent tied to NATO, the prime minister emphasized British commitments in the non-NATO area (the example he chose was over the defence of Kuwait). His position was clear: the British would have to have the option of using their deterrent when they wished or face the possibility of reassessing their global defensive posture. And, adopting some of Thorneycroft's language, even the prime minister seemed to be threatening a walkout of the conference if acceptable terms could not be agreed.[138] His tactics worked and the next American draft made a looser connection between Polaris and the NATO force, a satisfactory arrangement.

As the agreement was being finalized on 21 December Macmillan contacted the cabinet to explain the deal, only to receive a reply expressing its members' concerns. Despite expressing appreciation of his efforts, they suggested changes to the details of Polaris' assignment along with a report that they were 'worried and not sure that the political repercussions of the action proposed have been sufficiently considered'.[139] The chief whip wondered whether Polaris was worth the cost when it would not be operational before 1968: 'Would it not be possible to pause and study at leisure possible alternatives even if these are more costly.' What the cabinet objected to primarily was the provision of a supposedly independent deterrent: 'They are troubled by the price...that we are having to pay and the commitment to a multilateral policy and they feel this is only acceptable if our independent control of our Polaris force is clearly and unambiguously expressed.'[140] The prime minister faced further dissent from two influential officials in the MOD, Solly Zuckerman and Robert Scott, who complained of 'the very serious risks of the proposed arrangement' for the British Polaris force.

> The claim that it is 'independent' can be made, but only with difficulty...
> In fact, we shall be spending vast sums of money in order to make a contribution to a multilateral force the object of which is political rather than military.[141]

Yet with the Americans able to claim that they had made two fair offers, one concerning Skybolt and one on Polaris, either walking away or pressing for a better deal were both highly problematic courses to follow and Macmillan pressed his cabinet to accept as quickly as possible.[142]

Key members of the State Department also remained unsatisfied although for a very different reason. Concern here rested with the perennial problem of presentation to other alliance members. Back in Washington, as the conference in the Bahamas drew to a close, Rostow expressed his concern to Ball regarding the draft statement that he had been sent. He pointed out that the multilateral and conventional aspects of the agreement had to be stressed, and on the latter suggested the wording could be 'tightened or strengthened'. In playing down the nuclear aspects, Rostow took the established State line that had been articulated to Kennedy as he left for the conference. Ball replied that it was 'the best we can do' and expressed some satisfaction with the outcome, possibly believing that non-nuclear aspects could be sufficiently expressed. 'It was a long hassle. I can tell you that we here feel pretty good about the thing and the boss does too. Please don't under estimate', Ball said.[143] But Rostow was not satisfied and reiterated his fears to Rusk later that day, again focusing on how the pact would be presented to other NATO powers:

> Reuter's despatches (on the basis of UK briefings) are already portraying the arrangement as simply an extension of the UK national deterrent into the 1970's, with no hint of an eventual multilateral force. This kind of picture could do us and the UK (in EEC negotiations) the most serious damage on the continent, particularly Germany; it is important to set the record straight.[144]

Yet the Americans did try to deal with their other two main European allies as the conference was concluding. The French were the main concern and the president despatched a message to de Gaulle informing him of the outcome of the conference. In explaining the Polaris settlement he had come to with the British, he told the French president that he would consider 'a similar agreement with you, should you so desire'.[145] Yet the Americans also had to ensure not only that the West Germans were not alienated by the agreement but that they reacted positively to its multilateral aspects. As the conference broke up this became the key component, with the Dean Rusk emphasizing that they would keep in constant contact and that the German situation was at the forefront of their thinking.[146]

Following the conclusion of the conference, Ball and McNamara spoke to the press to explain the deal that had been struck. They tied the deal to broader NATO issues, including the Kennedy administration's attempts to prevent nuclear proliferation, the need to build up a conventional alliance capability and the desire to maintain the cohesion of the Western alliance.[147] Yet most of the questions dealt with the specifics of the bilateral deal with the British and the offer that Kennedy then made to the French. In answering these questions, both men sought to stress the unique opportunities the Nassau agreement apparently heralded, particularly the assignment of Polaris submarines to NATO.[148] In order to deflect criticism, briefing officers were instructed to reiterate the collective force aspect of the agreement, that Nassau had been 'the most important and constructive of their discussions' and the Nassau meeting would become a 'landmark'.[149]

The State Department wanted to salvage the multilateral aspects from the Nassau accord. With the bilateral aspects dominating the discourse on the subject, the need to focus on the broader implications for the alliance were clear and the theologians were developing ideas about the expanding the role of NATO responsibilities, especially in terms of political consultation and out-of-area roles. In the aftermath of Nassau, Rostow told William Tyler that the US should undertake serious and systematic efforts to develop an alliance policy in outside areas. Factors such as growing global interdependence, the likelihood of a Chinese nuclear capability and rapid decolonization made this imperative, he suggested. Nassau also argued for greater emphasis on nuclear consultation. The Cuban missile crisis had recently highlighted the need for crisis consultation and without some kind of attention, 'the Nassau decisions have within them the potentiality of perpetuating and, for some time at least, crystallizing distinctions in nuclear status between Great Britain, France and Germany'.[150]

3

THE POLARIS PROJECT AND NATO

In the immediate aftermath of Nassau, Dean Rusk wrote to various American missions in Europe. He told them he was concerned that NATO members had formed the impression that the Kennedy–Macmillan meeting in the Bahamas had led to far-reaching decisions being made without consultation of other allies. He wanted to stress that the issue of Skybolt had been essentially a bilateral matter. It would therefore not have been possible to consult NATO members in the NAC meeting held just before summit at Nassau because the decision to cancel Skybolt had not been finalized then. Moreover, he said, the president and prime minister only decided at Nassau that the decisions they were making could offer opportunities for the alliance as a whole.[1]

As Rusk's message shows, the US faced problems in presenting the Nassau agreement to other members of NATO. As the leading power it had to avoid giving the impression that it was purely bilateral. In particular, State Department concern centred on the need to make the UK deterrent an integral element of NATO, hence the inclusion of language about a multinational and multilateral force. Immediately after Nassau, Walt Rostow expressed concern about achieving this but stressed that the British must take part, even if this was through 'token participation'.[2] Yet the Americans recognized that London would try to emphasize the independence of Polaris.[3] The British wanted to concentrate on the bilateral aspects of Nassau in order for them to get Polaris into service as quickly as possible and avoid the broader alliance-wide questions that Nassau raised.[4]

Yet in addition to the US promise of Polaris missiles for UK submarines and support facilities, in paragraph six of the agreement both sides had agreed to allow some of their existing forces, including US strategic forces and those from UK Bomber Command, to become part of a NATO nuclear force and targeted according to NATO plans. The paragraph stated:

> The Prime Minister suggested and the President agreed, that for the immediate future a start could be made by subscribing to NATO some part of the forces already in existence. This could include allocations from United States Strategic Forces, from United Kingdom Bomber

Command, and from tactical nuclear forces now held in Europe. Such forces would be assigned as part of a NATO nuclear force and targeted in accordance with NATO plans.

Paragraph seven said that the US, UK and other allies would participate in an MLF. Macmillan and Kennedy then affirmed their commitment to a multilateral NATO nuclear force to be examined with other European allies, although there was no further explanation of what this would comprise. To complicate matters further, the UK Polaris capability was apparently to be a part of this force, although there was some contradiction over whether this would be fully integrated or just loosely assigned.[5]

In some respects the British were successful in maintaining the American focus on the bilateral aspects of the agreement rather than the broader alliance aims. From early 1963, close Anglo-American co-operation allowed the British to develop the Polaris deterrent rapidly. Although the US Polaris project remained the top priority throughout,[6] the British were extremely successful in garnering working level American support for their own venture. In order to achieve this, members of the UK Polaris team successfully nurtured existing working level channels as well as creating numerous new ones. Although this relationship highlighted many of the power imbalances in the US–UK relationship, it also allowed the British Polaris project to be advanced at a significantly reduced cost.[7]

Yet in American minds there were three distinct strands to the Nassau agreement, of which the bilateral Polaris project was only one. Following the Nassau agreement, a post-Nassau steering group was set up in Washington.[8] It made clear that the Nassau pact comprised three parts: the bilateral US–UK Polaris agreement, the assignment of British, Americans and perhaps other countries' units to NATO and the creation of the MLF. Although the Americans gave immediate priority to the British Polaris project, they did not want to downgrade the other two. In particular, they felt that national units could be assigned to NATO relatively quickly under the terms of paragraph six of the communiqué and pressed forward with this.

This produced a tension in the first year after the Nassau agreement as the Americans attempted to persuade the British to see a commitment to NATO as an integral element of the deal they had made. This had implications for Britain's regional and global roles. For Britain, a key concern remained how they could satisfy alliance needs with minimum forces in the North Atlantic area.[9] Therefore one of the key elements of the Nassau agreement was that it allowed them to play up their non-NATO commitments, the primary area of concern for the Conservative government, despite promises to augment the BAOR in 1962 and 1963.[10] The British were therefore largely successful in promoting their concerns. Moreover, as the end of the Kennedy administration approached, the importance of committing British forces to NATO in the short term decreased as the NATO MLF gained momentum.

Crucially, the UK, US, and indeed European governments, remained confused on the multilateral aspects of Nassau. It appeared from the text itself that the

British Polaris force had been committed to NATO in a multilateral context and yet the UK government remained unwilling to make such a commitment. From Macmillan's perspective, British public opinion would not countenance tying the British deterrent into such a force. Yet in the months following the Nassau meeting, the NATO MLF became a central feature of the North Atlantic agenda. So while the Polaris project proceeded apace, the question of how the UK deterrent and other forces would be assigned within the alliance took on far more political significance.

These debates took place within the context of continuing American pressure for a change in strategy and build-up of conventional forces but Kennedy continued to face challenges in pursuing this policy. First, the European nations of NATO, and in particular France, were chary of the increase in conventional force commitments that the change in strategy suggested.[11] Moreover, Secretary General Dirk Stikker, who did not want to press for a revision of NATO strategy at this stage, accused the US of following its own agenda. This new US policy, according to Stikker, was an attempt to make strategy fit certain types of weapon that the US was now developing.[12]

Post-Nassau implementation

Almost as soon as the Nassau meeting was over, preparations for the British to participate fully in the US Polaris project began. It was imperative to organize quickly because of the nature of the Polaris agreement: whereas other Anglo-American bilateral agreements, including Skybolt, had been the result of detailed technical negotiations, the Polaris project began with only a vague political statement. In an attempt to flesh out the Nassau communiqué, McNamara immediately informed the MOD that he hoped to see a British delegation in Washington in early January. The US Navy 'was all set on technical level' by the beginning of January, he reported.[13] It was now time for the UK to respond. The MOD found this a daunting task, but a military and scientific delegation was hastily assembled.[14]

Before being dispatched, the Foreign Office emphasized that members of the delegation would explore the technical aspects of the system rather than political implications of the Nassau agreement.[15] The MOD noted that the, 'purpose of their mission is entirely technical and, although their discussions with the Pentagon may touch on implications of multilateralism, they are not expected to have any contact with the State Department or to hold discussions on the political aspects of the Nassau agreement'. As Home pointed out to Macmillan, however, it was impossible to separate questions of equipment from the political framework within which it would be used. Yet what the government wished to avoid were wide-ranging discussions especially with the advent of the multilateral questions on NATO's agenda.[16]

In line with the prime minister's political aims, the first technical consideration was 'to ensure the independent control and operation of the British Polaris fleet'. It was particularly crucial at this stage because of the vague wording of the

Nassau communiqué. The MOD wanted control to be extended to all fields, including communications, services and maintenance.[17] This raised immediate concerns in the State Department in Washington at a time when its members were trying to emphasize the alliance-wide aspects of the agreement. The American Embassy in Paris, for example, had noted with some alarm that the British Ambassador Sir Pierson Dixon, who met de Gaulle at the beginning of January, told the French president that the British would be glad to discuss aspects of the Polaris agreement with him. To the chagrin of the Americans, Dixon stressed that the Polaris force would be 'British manned, British armed and British built' stressing 'very heavily the independent deterrent capability that Britain would have under the arrangement'.[18] It also stood in stark contrast to the presentation of the Nassau agreement to NATO allies, when the British representative claimed that the arrangements for Polaris 'had to serve [the] long-term interests of [the] Alliance'.[19]

The 'independent' clause of the Nassau communiqué therefore presented a conundrum for some US policy-makers. Paul Nitze cautioned that 'we cannot...allow ourselves to be dragged into nuclear war by independent action of a NATO ally. For this purpose, we have to insist upon advance notice of any use of nuclear forces.'[20] McNamara had no such qualms. He argued 'we should tie the UK Polaris force so closely to ourselves that their capability of independent action would be minimized'. One way to do this, he said, was to connect the UK force to US support forces, therefore allowing the US militarily to dictate the way that the Polaris force operated. By doing this 'If their force was withdrawn, it would have either no capability or a lesser one because of the lack of support'.[21]

On 9 January, the delegation met with US Secretary of the Navy, Fred Korth, and others to talk in general terms about the formulation of a Polaris agreement. This discussion was primarily concerned with the type and number of missiles each submarine would carry, where the UK crews would be trained, how much the US would be involved in this process and how reliant the UK would be upon American shipbuilders and producers of equipment.[22] Two key factors were already apparent by this stage. First, despite any misgivings in Washington about the supply of nuclear delivery systems to Britain, the Pentagon staff was forthcoming with the offer of both equipment and training to the UK. The second related factor was British willingness to rely on the US. It seemed obvious to the British contingent that in order for the British Polaris to succeed, this was inevitable. The initial report of the fact-finding mission to the United States concluded that 'because of the small number of Polaris submarines in mind for the Royal Navy, it would be grossly uneconomical to design and build our own system complete, the Americans already having in service at sea a proved system'.[23] The British did not disguise their interest in making use of American shipbuilders and suppliers to test and fit equipment for the British programme.[24] Even before the team had been put together, First Lord of the Admiralty Carrington told Thorneycroft 'we must buy in the USA every item of sub-installed Polaris weapon system that they will sell to us'.[25] And at the meeting with Korth, the team established that the two courses for the Royal Navy as regards training were either tutoring British personnel in the US, who would then return to the UK to train others, or relying on the US Navy to conduct all the training. Either way, the US would be intimately involved.

On its return to the UK, the Polaris fact-finding team reported to the MOD that its mission had been almost entirely successful: 'US Polaris visit went off very well from our point of view . . . and had useful practical results as well as demonstrating momentum of the project.'[26] The State Department concurred that Zuckerman and party had had 'useful conversations' and were glad to respond to the British request of a small party of US naval officers headed by Nitze to go to the UK.[27] 'We can now see how this "acte de presence" would help HMG [Her Majesty's Government] in demonstrating progress toward an agreement about Polaris' they concluded. Once again, the talks would be primarily technical, although the Americans were also wary that this would allow the British to downplay the multilateral aspects.[28]

The British request for an American team was an effort to allay public and political fears that the Americans might, in Thorneycroft's words, 'do another Skybolt' and cancel Polaris without consultation.[29] A visible official US presence was considered essential when members of the press were harbouring concerns over the US commitment to the Nassau agreement.[30] The prime minister had even voiced such fears, asking Thorneycroft, in the week after Nassau, how long it would take the UK to build its own Polaris system from their own designs if the government was 'driven into a corner . . . either as a bluff or as a reality'.[31]

The series of meetings between the British and American teams in London also generally went well, and the Americans were keen to press ahead with the official Polaris agreement regardless of discussions within NATO. Yet differences were already apparent over the commitment of British forces, particularly V-bombers, to NATO. The British favoured a loose connection of their entire force, while the Americans wanted a small, more closely assigned force so as to make 'sizeable impact on NATO now'. The British tried to play up the fact that they wanted to assign large numbers of forces because the alliance 'should be seen to have a nuclear punch which was both long-range and powerful'. There was also discussion of the role of tactical battlefield weapons, which the Americans did not want to be included in any NATO nuclear force.[32]

Furthermore, the subject of research and development costs was 'one unexpected development' raised during the course of the various discussions.[33] It derived from McNamara's desire to amend the errors of the Skybolt era, where British participation in a wholly American venture was not a partnership but what he termed a 'charitable contract'.[34] He also wanted the Nassau agreement to be seen as a 'full and beneficial exchange' to the benefit of all NATO allies.[35] Peter Thorneycroft was disenchanted with this move and determined not to allow the British to agree to an open-ended commitment over Polaris costs, especially as the A-3 version of the missile that the British had chosen was still in its developmental stages.[36] Kennedy and Macmillan eventually finalized details of the development costs, which it was decided should be 5 per cent of costs incurred after 1 January 1963, although this had, in fact, cautiously been agreed to by Zuckerman and Pentagon official John McNaughton during Zuckerman's Washington trip.[37] McNamara also attempted to shift the balance following this compromise by requesting a further $36 million for overhead costs likely to be incurred by the US in providing Polaris. He intended this to be for the use of facilities in factories, offices and storehouses. The British delegation was eventually able to negotiate a revised figure of $17.5 million.[38]

Contrary to any notion that McNamara might have been displaying displeasure at the Nassau developments, he was in fact approaching them in a characteristically pragmatic manner. Recognizing the inherently open-ended nature of the US Nassau commitment, McNamara felt 'our objective should be to assist Britain and France to acquire, at the least possible cost, the nuclear force which each is determined to develop anyway'. Shortly after the Nassau meeting, in a lengthy, lucid and sometimes vehement attack on previous alliance policy, McNamara claimed to colleagues that withholding technical knowledge merely compelled the two European nations to spend precious resources that could be put to better military use. And he was 'unwilling to joint [sic] with the UK in an uneconomic enterprise' as 'inefficiencies in their nuclear program...will affect their costs and ours in other areas of defense'. Yet the research and development stipulation over Polaris existed because of the need to develop and understand cost-sharing in NATO 'which is now not there'. 'NATO has depended on the US more than both they and we realize. In essence, we have assisted their [European allies'] economic growth by bearing the major share of the defence costs of the Alliance', he stated.[39]

Tensions remained as to exactly how Polaris would be assigned and what sort of contribution it would make to NATO. The British wanted to emphasize their Polaris deterrent and the difference it could make to NATO, while the US wanted closer adherence to the MLF.[40] The US also wanted to stress its commitment of three Polaris submarines to NATO and therefore press the British to make a similar commitment.[41] But members of the Kennedy administration recognized that they would have to ' "Put on steel helmets" and live with Macmillan's overemphasis of national aspect'.[42]

Allied reactions to Nassau

In the short term, the key issue on Nassau was the European reaction to the deal and members of the State Department continued to urge caution in the presentation. They were pursuing two methods that appeared to contradict one another in order to achieve this. First to quell any accusations that Polaris represented a new-found nuclear 'special relationship' between the US and UK they argued that it was merely a continuation of the Skybolt arrangement. Second, they stressed that signing the Polaris agreement would tie the UK Polaris capability into the MLF and could therefore even be considered as a transitional arrangement whereby the British deterrent would be surrendered to the force in the long run. But the

Skybolt deal had offered no multilateral dimension to the alliance and this made the Polaris as straight swap for Skybolt line harder to argue with conviction. Moreover, Rusk recognized that the British would push the independent aspect of the nuclear force, rather than the multilateral, for domestic political reasons. But most in State remained hopeful and by the beginning of January their prevailing view was that the British would come over to the multilateral option with the course of time, the present position merely being a stalling tactic.[43]

Washington could make no such claims about the French. By the beginning of January, the British Embassy in Paris was reporting that de Gaulle was unhappy.[44] This view was confirmed in the New Year when Charles Bohlen, US ambassador in Paris, met de Gaulle. The general told Bohlen that he saw very little advantage to France in the Nassau offer. Britain had maintained a reasonably steady nuclear relationship with the US that the French had not had; UK technology had also advanced differently from France and so they would be able to make use of submarine-launched missiles as it had submarine and warhead technology that the French simply did not. De Gaulle also said that he had 'a very poor opinion of the possibilities of a multilateral force'. Bohlen concluded that de Gaulle had not seen enough benefits to his country in the Nassau accord to make it worthwhile signing up to the multilateral aspect.[45] The government in London also recognized that the chances of de Gaulle accepting the Polaris offer were slim. In addition to the fact that France did not have the technical capability to accept the offer, de Gaulle would have found it very difficult to have accepted an offer made by the 'Anglo-Saxons' into which he had no input.[46] Furthermore, with the pact's adherence to multilateralism it was difficult to see de Gaulle doing anything other than rejecting.[47]

As expected, on 14 January de Gaulle gave a press conference in which he rejected the American offer of Polaris and the MLF. Even more importantly he vetoed the British application to join the EEC claiming that they were not yet ready to join the Common Market and that their inclusion would fundamentally change the nature of the EEC.[48] He implied that the Nassau meeting had had a significant impact on his decision to use his veto, insisting to Adenauer, for example, that Macmillan had 'deceived' him because he had told him nothing about his plans for Nassau when they had met at Rambouillet.[49] He suggested that this was either a sign of the British prime minister's duplicity if he had known he was going to ask Kennedy for Polaris or subservience to Washington if he had not.[50]

Yet it seems highly unlikely that the Nassau agreement had any material effect on de Gaulle's decision to veto. As the US recognized, although the presentation was more stark than it had been in past, de Gaulle's move against Britain (and thus by implication America) did not represent a radical departure.[51] He had almost certainly made the decision before Nassau, and perhaps as soon as three days after the end of the Rambouillet meeting.[52] At the most, the American Embassy in Paris suggested, the Nassau agreement had simply 'crystallized' de Gaulle's decision to end the Brussels negotiations.[53] In response, Rusk was firm that de Gaulle's behaviour did not warrant a new undertaking with the French or an attempt to 'sweeten [the] Nassau offer without any concomitant change in French policy, since at this juncture such change seems highly unlikely'. Instead, pressing ahead with the UK agreement on Polaris and the NATO MLF with other NATO allies was crucial.[54]

In Bonn, there was confusion as to exactly what Nassau offered them as well as some anger at the way the offer had been made.[55] This caution reflected a split in government attitudes. Konrad Adenauer was frustrated that the Americans had done a deal with British and the offer to the Germans seemed to be an afterthought. In a meeting with Stikker, Adenauer dismissed the idea that Germany was at the forefront of American and NATO thinking, saying 'this was once [the] case but no longer'. He was suspicious of the Nassau agreement and clearly thought that the UK had extracted many concessions from the US, although the German foreign minister, Gerhard Schroeder, was more positive saying that Nassau was a 'step in the right direction' and the multilateral aspects should be emphasized.[56]

Surveying the scene, Macmillan tried to make the best of the situation. He had written to Kennedy days later to express his gratitude to the president for the 'strenuous' but 'rewarding' talks in Bahamas and was optimistic that the Nassau pact represented a balance between interdependence and independence.[57] On 19 January he and Kennedy exchanged pleasantries on the telephone. Now when the conversation came round to Nassau almost a month before, the prime minister still told Kennedy that he had 'loved' the meeting and Kennedy concurred that it was all 'very good, very good'. Negative domestic reaction to the agreement had clearly shaken the prime minister, however:

> Both you and I thought we'd done a fine job; when we got home we were told we'd made an absolute mess-up of it. But I thought therefore of broadcasting. But then I thought, No, I'll leave it alone. It's all quietening down. I think when we get the Debate in about a fortnight, I can put the whole thing in a proper perspective and I think we shall get it right.[58]

Macmillan's apparent satisfaction with the Nassau agreement hid his disappointment with the reactions of many in Britain and the rest of Europe in the first weeks of 1963.[59] Much of the British press had claimed that the NATO commitment compromised British independence and the offer to the French ended any notion of a 'special relationship' with the US.[60] And as he admitted to Kennedy in their telephone conversation, de Gaulle's move against Britain had left the EEC in 'a very bad situation'. He continued: 'I think this man has gone crazy – absolutely crazy'.[61] Yet dismay at de Gaulle's wrecking tactics in Britain served to deflect attention from the Nassau agreement and its impact on relations with the US. Macmillan had noted immediately after the veto, 'By a curious paradox de Gaulle's attitude is cementing that very Anglo-Saxon Alliance which he professes to dislike'.[62] And David Bruce was now able to report that the bitterness over Skybolt's cancellation and the associated wave of anti-Americanism had been erased by de Gaulle's veto, rising unemployment and the recent death of popular Labour leader, Hugh Gaitskell. Most British people, he reported, were now satisfied with the Polaris offer.[63]

Co-operation and negotiation on Polaris

In mid-February, political talks began in Washington on moving towards a formal agreement and how the forces would be assigned under paragraph six. This brought them into conflict with the Americans in NATO.[64] The Americans wanted reaffirmation of the Nassau declaration in the Polaris sales agreement, while the British resisted for fear of reigniting some of the controversy Nassau had aroused. The two sides also disagreed as to the extent of the NATO commitment they would make. The British wanted to assign all their V-bombers, while the Americans wanted a much smaller commitment but one that was tied closely to NATO with the others free to be used outside the NATO area. All points clearly related back to the MLF, with the British pressing towards a rapid commitment of nationally manned forces 'to provide immediate political impact'. Although broad agreement was reached, it was clear that the British had a different inter-pretation of their commitments under paragraph six from the Americans and their obligations towards the MLF and the assignment of tactical nuclear forces.[65] Although Kennedy seemed more in line with British thinking than many within his administration, the Americans maintained that it was unwise at this time to raise broad questions of political control on these forces and they therefore wanted their assignment to be as loose as possible.[66]

Kennedy clearly wanted some action in order to demonstrate progress and pressed for implementation of paragraph six. William Tyler had met Denis Greenhill of the British Embassy in Washington to discuss the matter in the mid-dle of February and Kennedy held an informal meeting to follow up on the issues it had raised on 9 March. No notes of the meeting were taken, although Bundy issued a memorandum for McNamara and Rusk. A few days later the president reiterated his desire for speedy implementation of paragraph six of the Nassau accord to his colleagues 'in the event our proposal for a MLF was not acceptable to the Europeans'.[67] He also wrote to Macmillan to say that the US should 'join full steam with you in making these forces and their new command a reality not later than the Ottawa meeting in May'.[68]

As a result, rumours in London began to circulate that the US was more committed to assigning forces to NATO on this basis and was moving away from MLF, which George Ball was quick to quash.[69] The emerging confusion between assignment of multinational and multilateral forces was clearly causing tension in NATO, a development Macmillan was happy to ignore now the British had Polaris: 'The more I think of it, the more constructive I believe our Nassau dec-laration was. In whatever form our plans emerge, the spirit in which they were launched has undoubtedly been more and more understood as the weeks have passed,' he wrote to Kennedy in the middle of the month.[70] Yet the MOD and Chiefs of Staff remained solely interested in the assignment of Polaris to NATO and increasing pressure within the alliance over land-based MRBMs and MLF only made this position more secure.[71] This upset many in the US, including the president, especially over Mountbatten's vocal opposition to MLF.[72]

Progress on Polaris had also been rapid and the Polaris agreement was signed in April 1963.[73] This was a high-point for US–UK relations. Yet with the MLF question now high on the NATO agenda, the British remained concerned that with the bilateral issue of Polaris so intimately entwined with the multilateral one in the Nassau statement, failure of the MLF (or in worst case scenario the break up of NATO) might prejudice supply of Polaris missiles to the UK.[74] Even after the agreement had been signed, the MLF hung over the Polaris project and a fear developed that, as one report put it, 'our planning might be overtaken by the events of multilateralism'.[75] With talks on the MLF gaining momentum, however, the British had to be circumspect about an approach and sought assurances from Washington on this matter while playing down their opposition to multilateralism.[76] Assurances were duly received. Yet this was not enough and Macmillan claimed that in order to quell any public and parliamentary unease about the independence of the deterrent, he needed to make these American assurances public. But the State Department in particular was concerned that this might give the impression that its support for the MLF was beginning to wane. Although they relented, this was primarily because they wanted no confusion that could lead to another Skybolt situation and they asked Macmillan to reiterate support for the MLF.[77]

By this time, a pattern of close co-operation between the British and American Polaris teams had already been established. Increasingly this was the responsibility of civil servants and particularly military officials, rather than ministers. David Bruce remembered that although there were still some exchanges between McNamara and the MOD, the project was typified by links established at a lower level. There was not, he noted, any cause for further intervention from people like himself at policy level.[78] During this trans-Atlantic exchange, the opportunity for members of the British Polaris team was unprecedented. As part of a close-knit Anglo-American partnership, they were privy to information and techniques not divulged to any other nation. There was a full imparting of information on the part of the Americans from early 1963 and 'the [British] negotiating team met with the greatest goodwill from the Americans, and especially from the US Navy, which augur[ed] well for the future of the Polaris venture'.[79] Much of the work was conducted by the British and American liaison officers and within a joint steering task group, which met for the first time in June.[80]

In correspondence with Macmillan in May, Kennedy appeared to be broadly satisfied with the way Nassau had developed since the previous December. The Polaris agreement was, he said, 'clear and good' and the nuclear force assignment 'well on its way'. Yet he recognized the problems over MLF, the third and most difficult strand.[81] Clearly, the British still viewed the commitments made at

Nassau in different terms to the Americans and it was the assignment of forces, both multinational and multilateral, which were the cause of the most significant concerns. While the Americans saw the British contribution to the MLF as an entirely separate entity from the Polaris commitment, the British believed that the MLF included the mixed-manned component in conjunction with the assignment of US and UK forces.[82]

Yet any lingering fears about the veracity of the American Polaris promise had proved to be unfounded. With occasional exceptions, the US–UK team were able to establish close and profitable working relationships with each other. US concerns about the impact of the British Polaris project on its own work existed, but this did not prevent the staff from providing considerable technical support from January 1963. The co-operation of the liaison officers and guiding influence of the task group were both crucial to this process. By the end of 1963, Deputy Under Secretary of State at the Foreign Office, Lord Hood, was able to report that US co-operation had been 'excellent' and there was considerable hope that they could keep to the timetable.[83]

Yet the decision to assign British forces and Polaris, when it was completed, to NATO raised a series of contentious issues during the post-Nassau months. The tentative commitment was primarily political and made little difference in military terms.[84] But it was significant in framing reactions to the development of the British deterrent. Many in the UK reacted negatively to the assignment and the prevailing British position was that the assignment of British forces had to be kept as loose as possible. This contradicted American interpretations of a small, tightly controlled NATO force.

With a lack of agreement over exactly what commitment each side was willing to make, the multinational element of Nassau was downgraded as 1963 progressed. It was clear that France would not participate and the British would not make the kind of commitment that Stikker, Norstad or even the Americans would accept. The German 'problem', especially after fears raised by a Franco-German treaty signed shortly afterwards, was becoming more pronounced and momentum on MLF growing.[85] The MLF therefore became the primary focus of American NATO policy. Growing German interest and French refusal to participate both facilitated an improvement in its fortunes. The 'theologians' also continued to exercise considerable influence and reiterated their concerns about the need for European unity in the wake of de Gaulle's veto and the dangers of West Germany being left adrift within the alliance.

4

THE MLF AFTER NASSAU

While paragraph six of the Nassau Statement made reference to US strategic forces and elements of British bomber command being assigned to NATO, paragraph seven went further. It stated: 'the President and Prime Minister agreed that the purpose of their two governments with respect to the provision of the Polaris missiles must be the development of a multilateral NATO nuclear force in the closest consultation with other NATO allies'. Paragraph eight, however, went on to describe the provision of Polaris missiles to the UK and claimed that these British forces would be 'targeted in the same way as the forces described in paragraph 6'.[1]

There was therefore some confusion as to what the provisions in paragraphs six, seven and eight meant. The Americans came to believe that the British had signed up to a 'NATO force' comprising, first, a commitment of British and American national forces (as under paragraph six) and, second, a multilateral nuclear force to be created, manned and controlled by Britain, America and any other NATO nations that wished to join. The British either failed or refused to understand this at Nassau and in the weeks that followed its conclusion. They claimed that their commitment of V-bombers and then afterwards Polaris to NATO absolved them of any responsibility in the MLF.

The aspects dealing with the NATO multilateral nuclear force therefore proved to be far more problematic to implement than Polaris did and produced more tension between London and Washington. For one, Polaris was a bilateral arrangement. In contrast, the NATO force envisaged many alliance nations participating and as a result suffered huge complications. Moreover, while the Americans attempted to clarify their position and approach in early 1963, the contradictory language used at Nassau ensured that more questions were raised than answered in the weeks that followed.[2] The crucial questions for most in Europe were, who would control this force and how would decisions over its assignment and targeting be taken? These had not been addressed in the Nassau pact, ensuring months of detailed, and sometimes fruitless, talks among NATO nations.

In the UK, both the Tory Government and Labour Opposition were reticent to become involved in MLF for a number of reasons. The Tories could see little military justification for an MRBM force in Europe as long as the American nuclear guarantee remained. The UK was also now promised Polaris and saw no merit in expending further resources on what it saw as a less effective force. In political terms, the MLF appeared to be a military solution to a lack of political unity in NATO and potential West German calls to share in nuclear weapons technology seemed to be a long way off. Labour opposed the force for some of the same reasons and because of their stated opposition to the Nassau agreement itself. Ongoing opposition from the Chiefs of the Defence Staff was on the grounds that the force was militarily suspect, as it was soon clear that the force would be based upon surface rather than submarine vessels, and that mixed-manning was not practical on a grand scale. Despite some support in the Foreign Office, heavy-weights such as Mountbatten and Solly Zuckerman both opposed the MLF plan and placing large numbers of MRBMs in Europe.[3]

Such testing considerations could not prevent the MLF proposal from gaining political credibility during 1963. Although de Gaulle had rejected the scheme when he also prevented the British entering the EEC, the MLF received support in other areas of Europe. Initial reservations in West Germany soon gave way to general acceptance and even some enthusiasm. The German government saw MLF as a way to retain the American nuclear guarantee while gaining an increased stake in the nuclear affairs of the alliance. Smaller European powers also wanted to increase their participation in NATO and some saw MLF as a relatively inexpensive way to do so.

Yet even West German support for MLF was qualified in the period immediately following Nassau.[4] America's relations with Germany were in a period of flux at the time; the differences in style between the new dynamic leader of the United States and Konrad Adenauer, elder statesman of the Federal Republic, were obvious.[5] This heralded a distinct cooling in relations between the two nations, something the bilateral Nassau agreement did little to rectify.[6] Indeed, a Franco-German treaty of friendship and co-operation signed in January 1963, less than a month after Nassau, smacked of an almost mathematical response to the exclusion tactics of Britain and America at the conference the previous month. The United States remained fearful throughout 1963 that it heralded possible nuclear co-operation between the two countries.

However, the Germans never made an open choice between France and the United States. Simultaneous to the signing of the treaty with the French, Adenauer told Kennedy of his interest in the MLF and his intention to co-operate on the nuclear sharing programme with the US.[7] Yet opinion within the Federal Republic remained divided. Beyond MLF, the Franco-German treaty amounted to little and in practice on other issues, such as the test ban treaty and the Kennedy round of trade negotiations, Germany took the American side. Moreover, the Kennedy and Adenauer eras came to an end almost simultaneously and this, along with the pragmatism of new German Defence Minister Kai-Uwe von Hassel in his dealings with McNamara, led to an easier working relationship between the US and Germany. As far as MLF was concerned, once de Gaulle had refused to participate, the way was left open for MLF-advocates to push the German cause with renewed vigour.[8]

Primarily, these advocates were the same 'theologians' who had dominated the issue for the first two years of the Kennedy administration. Their enthusiasm and determination kept MLF at the forefront of US NATO policy during 1963. Led by George Ball, they maintained pressure on Kennedy from the time of Nassau right up until his assassination in November. These men regarded MLF as a politically unifying force in NATO; they feared future German interest in obtaining nuclear weapons and saw MLF as way to stymie this while drawing the Germans into the NATO fold. And with the French absent by mid-January 1963, Ball and his cohorts were free to press the MLF case on other NATO partners far harder than the president intended, in the hope that Europeans would embrace it, if not with a similar fervour, then at least with a degree of enthusiasm befitting such a grandiose project.[9]

Kennedy allowed them to do this without much enthusiasm or belief in the chances of success. He recognized the great difficulty of gaining acceptance within NATO for a political idea, but one that was also supposed to have a military purpose and yet had little ground roots military or political support. The issue of an American veto also troubled him as he was aware of the huge contention that would be caused by any hint of a German 'finger on the nuclear trigger', while also recognizing that the Germans would not be willing to pay large sums of money for participation in a force that gave them little in return. Without the French, by January 1963 the force had already lost some of its credibility and without the British, Kennedy feared that any deal might be perceived as a German-American one at the expense of other allies and the Soviet Union. Yet following his declaration of support for a multilateral concept at Nassau, the president found it difficult to back away. He therefore made a British agreement to participate in the MLF (whatever that meant in the long term) a priority.[10]

MLF after Nassau

When the British and American delegations had produced their communiqué at Nassau in December 1962, prospects for the MLF within NATO were far from good. A State Department message to American embassies produced during the Nassau conference had recognized that, in line with the British tentative approach, European support for the force was at best qualified. Primarily, the European concern was cost. Responding to Norstad's complaint about the state of NATO defences as well as the tentative US initiative, the United Kingdom delegation to NATO suggested that the alliance would have to be content with the shortfall in its military capacity or simply reconcile strategy with the resources available. The Italian delegation concurred, stating its low gross national product would mean that its contribution to the prospective force would be limited. Some of the smaller countries expressed more enthusiasm for the seaborne nuclear force, Belgium's delegation stating that it was 'quite interested' in examining the proposition.[11] The responses improved in the days and weeks after Nassau, with Greece, Canada and the Netherlands expressing greater interest in the proposals.[12]

Yet it was the Federal Republic that remained the top priority for the US and the MLF proposal had been created very much with the Germans in mind. Washington felt that Germany was likely to become disaffected with its place in NATO if it was not offered something more substantial than token membership of the alliance, which in the long term meant an access to nuclear weapons. But German possession of nuclear weapons was hugely contentious and likely to be a disastrous public relations exercise if it ever happened.[13] Moreover, the German government had not requested nuclear weapons, nor was there any evidence that it would do so in the near future. This provoked concern in some quarters of the US government that offering them a taste of nuclear power in MLF would whet their appetite and create a desire where none had existed before.[14]

Yet Washington did not want the MLF to be seen as a US-FRG project and strongly desired another large European power to join in order to give the MLF more credibility. The focus in Washington was therefore on getting the British to accept that they had committed themselves to the MLF.[15] For the British, the cost of gaining Polaris was that they were also now committed to examine the MLF. In the weeks after Nassau, the intimate connection between the two became more pronounced and it was impossible for them to back away. The British working group on implementing the Nassau accords initially seemed to believe that the Americans would accept assignment of units under paragraph six and seemed incensed when it became clear that 'American officials speak of the multilateral aspects of Nassau as if they were something other than the NATO nuclear force to which we intend to assign certain nuclear forces, and then express fear that we are not going to support these aspects sufficiently'.[16] Peter Thorneycroft soon recognized that they would 'not make much progress over Polaris unless we can at the same time open discussions on that part of the Nassau Agreement to which the Americans attach so much importance, namely the subscription of some of our existing nuclear forces to NATO and plans for the formation of a multilateral force'.[17] Some initial reports on the British reaction were quite positive. Finletter met with Robert Scott days after de Gaulle's veto and Scott himself raised the issue of MLF, saying 'that Britain intended to support vigorously and immediately the effort of the US and other allies to create a multilateral force in accordance with Paragraph 7'. Yet Finletter acknowledged that Scott's definition of 'multilateral' may have been different from Washington's and he may have meant something more closely akin to a multinational commitment.[18]

Many of the main tenets of the MLF had been put in place by the US Nassau steering group by the end of January. Building on the Owen-Rowan paper of the previous year, the steering group decided that participation would be open to all NATO members and at least three were needed to participate. Initially the force would comprise some 200 weapons and these should be an integral element of NATO's strategic arsenal.[19] Much remained unclear, however, and subsequent discussions on MLF revolved around a number of key topics. First, the allies needed to decide the type of vessel to be used. Would it be a surface ship or a submarine? Second, 'sharing' had to be clearly defined. How would the costs and responsibilities be split between participating nations? How would command and control operate, and could the force operate without a US veto? Kennedy himself also wanted to know about the prospects for greater alliance cohesion brought about by the force.[20]

The issue of control was the most important and complex one, and the one on which the viability of MLF rested. With military, and more specifically nuclear power increasingly being used as the benchmark of world power status, the MLF was a tantalizing offer to many NATO countries. Yet with this offer came both responsibilities and costs. West Germany, for example, was expected to pay a substantial sum of money in accordance with its population and relative power within Europe towards the force. In return, the West German government would expect at least some say in targeting and deployment of the new force. Yet Kennedy remained reticent to shift the locus of power from the United States towards Europe. And German interest in the force was also troubling because the prospect of nuclear weapons being in German hands was unsettling, not just for the Soviets but also other NATO allies.[21] It was also difficult to see the president relinquishing his control over firing decisions to SACEUR. McNamara in particular remained concerned that such a move would increase the risk of accidental firing, which remained a possibility even with US control intact. McNamara's view was in complete opposition to the prevailing State Department opinion, as he maintained that such an issue could not be fudged when the Germans and Italians would want to know whether a US veto would continue to be in place before they would commit themselves.[22] After lengthy discussions, surface vessels were adopted as the preferred vessels for the force.[23]

The Merchant mission

Regardless of these problems, Kennedy needed a European commitment on the force for it to retain its credibility. He therefore made a decision to send a special envoy on MLF, Livingston Merchant, to Europe to open the forum for allied discussion.[24] With German support for the force growing and the need to make MLF more than an American-German bilateral undertaking clear, bringing the British on board became an imperative part of his campaign. McGeorge Bundy told his colleagues this at an NSC meeting in February: 'if the British support a surface force, the Europeans would be more favourable toward it'.[25]

Even at this stage, Kennedy's awareness of European perceptions following the Nassau conference and his incipient pessimism about the chances of success for MLF were both clear. Before dialogue on MLF was officially underway, Kennedy noted opposition to the scheme:

> He said it was his impression that the British were not for it; the French were clearly against it; and the Italians did not have a deep-seated interest in it. The Germans reportedly were interested, but once they realized how little they were getting for their money, they might look at it differently.[26]

He also wondered whether the appeal of the MLF might fade as the Europeans realized the US was unlikely to surrender its veto. In February he told George Ball that he did not want Washington to be too close to MLF because 'Livy is probably not going to be very successful and we don't want it to look like it is an American initiative and an American failure'.[27]

As Merchant left for Europe, the White House wanted to stress not only the importance of his mission but also that the US was not trying to foist solutions onto the Europeans. It also wanted to emphasize the alliance-wide aspects of the mission over the intricate details of the MLF.[28] Yet when Merchant and Finletter made speeches promoting the MLF to their NATO allies in Paris, reactions were mixed. While Germany, Italy, Belgium and the Netherlands appeared eager to know more, Greece, Turkey, Canada and Britain expressed only 'qualified interest'. European press reports were also highly critical. The British representative to NATO, Evelyn Shuckburgh, said that the MLF was of 'terrific' importance to NATO as its failure might lead to the failure of the alliance. '[The] UK therefore would give all possible support to US efforts on MLF and UK expected to participate to degree indicated'. Yet as he went on to claim that the Nassau talks had not dealt with MLF, this clearly meant assignment of certain British forces to NATO under paragraph six.[29] In contrast, the Germans reacted much more positively to Merchant's presentations. Von Hassel told Merchant that the Germans viewed the MLF as a 'real force to strengthen NATO and bring all allies closer together'.[30]

London and Washington both remained well-informed of each other's respective positions. In March, with Merchant's arrival in London imminent, Macmillan expressed to David Bruce his scepticism of the importance of MLF either to the FRG or NATO. The main difference between Britain and the US was on how to deal with the question of FRG equality in the nuclear field, the prime minister said. He believed that German concern was political rather than military and might be satisfied with a place on a NATO 'executive committee'. Moreover, MLF was going to be expensive and he believed that this would drive other small countries away.[31] By now, rumours in London were already suggesting that Kennedy was not pressing the Merchant mission more stridently because the president was losing faith in the MLF. On the same day, in an observation of great prescience, British government adviser, Alistair Buchan suggested to Home:

My own impressions from recent talks in Washington...is that McNamara and the wiser heads in the State Department realize that there is a high probability that the kind of approach to NATO consultation and control embodied in the multilateral seaborne force and the Merchant mission may well fail or run into the sands, and that they will quickly have to consider a more political approach to the improvement of the NATO machinery itself and to a stronger reflection of European interests and capabilities within it.[32]

Yet Macmillan remained polite and positive in accommodating Kennedy's request for Merchant to get a fair hearing. He told the president that he was 'very interested to hear how Merchant gets on', and expressed the hope that he could meet up with Merchant to discuss the proposals. The prime minister continued that he was 'very anxious to give what help we can in forwarding this plan'.[33]

Merchant's party had two days of talks with the British in London on 12 and 13 March. The British gave a decidedly cool reception to the group and initial reactions were guarded.[34] Although Macmillan made a point of welcoming the party personally, along with other members of his cabinet, Bruce commented that he had 'no detailed knowledge' of MLF and seemed surprised that the fleet was to comprise surface vessels. Merchant reiterated that for the MLF to be a real success it would require the UK inside from the start and they should make a contribution to match their power and influence.[35] Lord Home went on to say that while the British 'had no quarrel in principle with the concept of the MLF...We ourselves would find it difficult to make a huge contribution to the force'.[36] The British military delegation was prepared with more detailed questions and expressed concern over various aspects of the force including the technical specification of the vessels, the military value of the force and the question of the US veto.[37]

During a second day of meetings, Bruce reported that, the British were 'more forthcoming' but that there was clearly much work still to be done to convince them to participate.[38] Home had modified his position slightly. He reassured Merchant that he would explain to the NAC the complementary nature of paragraphs six and eight of the Nassau agreement, in other words a multilateral arrangement in conjunction with assignment of V-bombers and Polaris by Britain and America. Moreover, he would, he assured Merchant, also 'tell them that the United States proposal for a multilateral force had the full backing of Her Majesty's Government'.[39]

With Merchant's trip to Europe producing mixed results, Kennedy retained his ambivalent attitude towards the MLF. In a meeting in March, the president reiterated that: 'In his own view our present proposal on the MLF, in which we continued to require unanimity on the political decision, as we should, and in which we offered merchant ships instead of submarines, did not represent anything very attractive to the Europeans.'[40] Yet in correspondence with other NATO leaders he maintained his interest and increased the pressure on dissenters to join. Just three days later, as Merchant was completing his series of meetings in London, he wrote to Macmillan again extolling the virtues of MLF. This time he stressed the progress Merchant had already made in Bonn and proclaimed the 'special value' British participation would have.[41]

The 'theologians' were also using Merchant's mission as a springboard for progress on MLF. On the same day as Kennedy wrote to Macmillan, Rusk sent a telegram to Ambassador Bruce in London emphasizing the need for the UK to become a full member of the new force. The secretary told Bruce that 'Not only would the political impact of the Multilateral Force be enhanced, but [the] course of European Atlantic development might be given a new lift if [the] Macmillan Government could be persuaded to take [a] more enthusiastic position on MLF'.

Somewhat playing on the French veto of British entry to the EEC, Rusk's note displayed the State Department's tendency to cajole other nations over this issue when it stated that 'if the Macmillan Government cannot be brought to see these larger issues of UK's relations to the continent, the natural evolution of events may conspire to damage British basic interests and position in the world.'[42] Although Rusk's signature appeared on the telegram, its drafting was the work of George Ball and Deputy Assistant Secretary for Atlantic Affairs Robert Schaetzel, both of whom were taking over and directing this policy to an increasing degree. Simultaneously other 'theologians' were also pressuring Rusk.[43] This State Department pressure had given the proposal considerable momentum by the end of March: in a memorandum to the prime minister, the new Cabinet Secretary Burke Trend reported gloomily that he feared swift progress was being made on the MLF discussions because Merchant's mission 'seems to have been unexpectedly successful so far'.[44]

When Merchant reported to Washington it was clear that the British political position was now such that although they were unwilling to dismiss him out of hand, they could give him nothing more than vague assurances of support. Merchant said that the British were decidedly less enthusiastic than the Germans about MLF. He could only take solace in the fact that this German enthusiasm could be used to enhance the US diplomatic position:

> I think the British will find great difficulty in staying out of a nuclear venture like MLF lest it become a new US-FRG 'special relationship'. These two countries, with the US would certainly be an adequate starting nucleus and sufficient to avoid the charge we were working on a bilateral nuclear deal with Germany. If Britain did decide to join, Italy in my judgement could not stay out.

He had, he admitted however, encountered considerable difficulties when discussing the matter with the British, although he reported that later in their discussions the British were talking about what sort of a contribution they could make.[45]

By the end of the spring and the completion of the Merchant mission, Kennedy's own position was still one of detachment and he remained fully informed of all views. In late March, the presidential confidant Arthur Schlesinger wrote to the president about the British situation, urging caution at least in part because US support of such an ambitious plan did not sit easily with previous statements urging a conventional build-up (as in Athens and Ann Arbor). Mixed-manning was, he claimed, 'universally derided' and in the three months since MLF had officially been a part of US political doctrine, British government support was 'tepid', the press were 'baffled' and Labour and the Liberals 'hostile'.[46] Two days later, Schlesinger reiterated his fears saying that there was no obvious desire for nuclear weapons in Germany and the British remained worried that rather than satisfying them this initiative would whet their appetites.[47]

Bringing the British in

Kennedy now required a new initiative to persuade the British. With reports of Adenauer's interest in the surface force growing, Kennedy needed more support from other NATO powers and particularly Britain.[48] Several times during a meeting with advisers at the beginning of May, he stressed that the British should be more fully informed of the US position. He also reiterated the idea that:

> On the diplomatic side...getting UK participation in the MLF was the most urgent item of business. This was particularly important to avoid giving the impression of a US/German arrangement. Moreover, the British might be reminded that the MLF was an integral part of the Nassau commitment.

He repeated this as 'the first order of business' at the end of the meeting.[49]

A week later, Kennedy resorted to personal diplomacy by requesting Macmillan's help in persuading the cabinet. On 9 May, David Bruce had written to Rusk to inform him that Foreign Office opinion was now becoming more sympathetic to MLF in response to Adenauer's growing interest and his acceptance of surface ships for the force.[50] The 'key problem' was now Macmillan 'who, in their [high Foreign Office] view, [was the] only [one] President can move'.[51] '[M]y main purpose', Kennedy wrote to the prime minister the following day, 'is to ask if you and your colleagues can now make a definitive commitment to participate in the multilateral force'. This would, he assured Macmillan, 'put an end to what is otherwise the very real possibility of a Franco/German co-operation in nuclear weapons systems in the narrow Gaullist spirit'. The president concluded with a rhetorical flourish, saying 'I do want you to know once again that while I see the costs as well as the opportunities, for us both, I am convinced that the moment for a determined advance together is here.'[52] He reiterated this view to his close friend David Ormsby Gore in Washington, saying that although the British might be able to offset some of the costs, he did not believe 'that a cheap ticket can be arranged without deeply weakening political effect of British participation'.[53]

Four discussions on MLF then took place in the British cabinet between 9 and 19 May, all dominated by negative reports about MLF. During the third meeting, it was even suggested: 'it might become necessary to inform the United States Government that, if they persisted in promoting the multilateral seaborne force, we could not contribute to it'. The objections centred on the force's limited military value, the need for diversion of resources from other commitments and the standard objections towards the FRG gaining access to nuclear weapons.

> Alternatively, we could maintain that our assignment to NATO of our V-bombers (and ultimately our Polaris submarines) represented a sufficient discharge of the obligation, which we had assumed during the Nassau discussions to contribute to the new NATO force; that our

resources, if deployed to the best advantage, did not permit us to make any further contribution; but that we were well disposed in principle to the concept of the multilateral force and would be prepared to consider assisting its creation by providing: – (i) free of charge, the use of facilities existing for the benefit of our own Polaris submarines (ii) against payment, additional logistic facilities and services and, possibly later, nuclear warheads.[54]

Although a high degree of indecision still existed by the time of the final meeting, it seemed that the cabinet was moving towards participation in talks, without a firm commitment to take part in the force itself.[55]

This cabinet position represented the middle ground between a hostile MOD and a more genial Foreign Office. Following the cabinet discussions, Thorneycroft and Home each produced separate memoranda arguing their respective cases on MLF. Home's memorandum was cautious, recognizing the importance of the issue to the US and the need to examine the concept of mixed-manning more closely. Thorneycroft, however, suggested that the worst outcome from a US perspective would be the British joining a drafting group before ducking out at the last minute. His concluding remarks included the warning that Britain should take the 'utmost care before we proceed with proposals for which the military case is non-existent and the political case both doubtful and controversial'.[56]

At the NATO meeting in Ottawa at the end of May, the British and American delegations met to discuss the MLF with the British retaining their public, sceptical position. Members of the negotiating teams included Rusk and Tyler on the American side and Thorneycroft and Home on the British. The British tactic in this meeting was to suggest that not only was the MLF militarily unwarranted, it was also not viable. The US delegation countered this with assurances that their Joint Chiefs had concluded just the opposite. But shortly afterwards Dean Rusk summed up the British attitude as being that the 'military would be terribly critical and, what's more, it will cost loads of money'.[57] Whether or not Rusk's pithy summary was correct, Ormsby Gore almost precisely restated the same sentiment when he spoke with the president the next day. With the military objections so significant, both agreed that the forthcoming visit of US Admiral Claude V. Ricketts to London in order to discuss technical matters was crucial.[58]

Ricketts was a keen supporter of the multilateral project and was dispatched to European capitals in June to develop military aspects of the project upon which Merchant's more politically-oriented mission had not. His prospects for success in persuading those in London were poor, as previous US–UK navy liaison and examination of the issues had already prejudiced MOD thinking on the topic. The previous month, Mountbatten had told the Thorneycroft 'that the recent technical discussions Navy-to-Navy have produced nothing to change their mind that the Americans have underestimated the vulnerability of a surface ship force'.[59]

Despite this, the prime minister seems to have remained relatively sympathetic. As one of the chief architects of the Nassau agreement he had a responsibility to uphold the decisions made there and had, at least in his relationship with the president, to appear eager to discuss the possibilities of MLF in the months afterwards. His domestic position meant an inability to adopt the multilateral clause swiftly, but his lack of diplomatic bargaining power and close relationship with the president rendered outright opposition to MLF impossible. Macmillan therefore had to accept Kennedy's requests to examine the force in a serious manner, despite the opposition in political and military circles, while protesting to Washington that little could be achieved in the short term. In expectation of Ricketts' arrival, Macmillan urged Thorneycroft to tell the Chiefs of Staff that 'they must take him [Ricketts] seriously'. He continued:

> A good deal of harm has been done in American minds by the way the British staffs have given the impression that they have closed their minds in advance. After all, the Americans have done an immense amount of work and study and I hope our staffs will discuss the practical and defence aspects on a very objective basis... I think this is really vital if I am to convince the President that we are giving the American plans the careful thought which all the work they have put into them deserve.[60]

In the event, Ricketts' visit in June did little to change the British government's disposition towards the force, particularly on the question of its vulnerability. In his meeting with Thorneycroft and leading military figures, numerous points of contention were not answered to their satisfaction and the meeting did not go the admiral's way.[61] In short, Ricketts' trip had little or no effect in converting the London sceptics. Following the meeting, Lord Hailsham, now minister of technology, argued that the political value of MLF was limited 'unless we suppose that the French, Germans and Italians are too lacking in intelligence to understand the military weakness of the case'. Echoing this view, Thorneycroft informed the prime minister:

> I think Admiral Ricketts felt that every opportunity had been given him to present not only the technical arguments but the wider defence considerations relating to the proposed force. I feel bound to say that on the latter he was remarkably unconvincing... In the light of these discussion it does not seem possible to support the case for these proposals on military grounds, and it is certainly difficult in such circumstances to say what political value attaches to them.[62]

While perhaps not entirely content with the Tory government's position, Kennedy was realistic about its chances of implementing the multilateral dimension of Nassau in the short term and over the summer he allowed the issue to slip. Little progress had been made and the diplomatic and military missions to Europe had highlighted more entrenched opposition than perhaps even the president had expected. He had recently accepted an invitation to meet with Macmillan at

Birch Grove, his country home in Sussex, at the end of June.[63] As he prepared for the meeting he was told that although Macmillan did not look as vulnerable as he had the previous year, he was still weak. He also had what one American report described as an 'obsession' with brokering a nuclear test ban treaty and would therefore not have risked provoking the Soviets by pushing for rapid agreement over MLF when it could be construed as proliferation by another name.[64] Macmillan simply could not implement the full Nassau decisions because 'his ability to do so has now been weakened'.[65]

Others within his government were also once again tentatively pursuing nuclear co-operation with the French. Despite American opposition and the subsequent French veto on British EEC membership, Thorneycroft, who retained his scepticism of the American connection, saw possibilities in this course and from June 1963, the idea took hold. It was discussed at the highest level in the Foreign Office, and in July Thorneycroft met with Pierre Messmer to discuss the potential joint development of delivery systems. Intriguingly, the idea of a trade for British EEC membership remained. This time, however, Macmillan was more cautious.[66]

The final months of the Kennedy administration

Although Kennedy maintained a degree of pressure, he was moving away from any speedy decision on MLF by the middle of the year. British intransigence was certainly a major factor, although German enthusiasm was certainly not universal and oftentimes muted.[67] The German press was generally disparaging of the proposed force.[68] And even Adenauer, who had accepted the concept in January 1963 and the surface vessel compromise later in the year, began to change his mind as the year progressed.[69] Yet Kennedy could not afford to cancel the proposal, having been associated with it for so long and after it had built up expectations in both Washington and abroad.[70] After Bundy, now the most influential voice in Kennedy's inner circle on the topic, sent what was to prove in the long run a vital memorandum on 15 June 1963 calling for some radical rethinking on MLF and as what enthusiasm Kennedy had had for the project faded further, he began to send out subtle signals to indicate his changing attitude.[71]

Following the Ricketts visit and Bundy memorandum the president became less rigid and more open to suggestion over the proposal. While he told the British that he still wanted some sort of commitment as set out at Nassau that would allow talks to be initiated, he was unwilling to press too hard. Instead, he now began to see MLF as an entity to be modified or manipulated to suit the needs of the moment. With the development of plans to limit nuclear proliferation and attempts to work towards a nuclear test-ban treaty, the MLF proposals were coming under increasing scrutiny from the Warsaw Pact. Kennedy did not want to compromise a deal with the Soviets that was a short-term reality for a long-term plan that might even destabilize relations. As the record of their meeting at Birch Grove records, 'the President indicated his feeling that if in fact a test ban agreement came in sight, it would be desirable and possible to modify our plan for the multilateral force'.[72] He reiterated his concerns about the MLF to Rusk in July when he acknowledged the lack of enthusiasm in Europe and warned him against giving the impression that the US was trying to 'sell' the MLF. But he also reiterated his desire for British participation in any talks that were to be held.[73]

With the perennial questions of organization, control and support becoming increasingly complex and European support for the force divided, the president introduced two new initiatives. The first built upon ideas discussed at the end of the Eisenhower administration.[74] This was to create a 'test' case for the MLF in order to demonstrate the viability of one aspect of it, so-called 'mixed manning'.[75] It would involve officers and ratings of the different participating nations living and working together on board the same vessel. This was to be an integral part of the MLF, representing shared ownership and unity and the 'theologians' interpreted this move 'as a full hunting license for the zealots'.[76]

Kennedy's position seemed to be subtly shifting back towards support for the force, although, once again, this was difficult to discern, and his reasoning remains unclear. It may in part have been because the British seemed in a slightly better situation. Although the Conservative government remained in a precarious position, agreement on the partial test ban treaty in July and August seemed to have reinvigorated Macmillan.[77] He was, Ormsby Gore reported, in 'such a state of euphoria...that Alec [Home] doubts whether he now has any intention of resigning'.[78] In private, Kennedy was now much more bullish. On 30 August Bundy told colleagues that the president believed the US should begin consultations with Congress as 'we are now in the correct posture on MLF. Last spring we were too far out ahead of our allies trying to "sell" the concept.' Somewhat contradicting the evidence he said that the Germans were now on board and although the British would not come in as long as Macmillan was pinning election hopes on the results of Nassau, 'After the election a change may be possible'.[79]

In the UK, the Foreign Office position was now also becoming even more favourable. On 11 September, the initial US report into the viability of a mixed-manned demonstration ship was produced and it encouraged other NATO nations to participate in this exercise by stressing that it would not commit countries to take part in the MLF.[80] The next day, Home issued a lengthy memorandum detailing his thoughts following discussions with Dean Rusk in Moscow. Rusk had reproached the foreign secretary for the British government's change in attitude from the time of the Nassau agreement, while Home had deduced that the Germans and Americans were now committed to MLF. Indeed, Home's assertion that 'The Germans regard it as politically essential to escape from their present position of inferiority to the other major powers' had echoes of State Department rhetoric. Although he urged caution, the foreign secretary suggested 'we are now faced...with a situation in which it is more than likely that the multilateral force will come into being whatever attitude we adopt to it' and he therefore argued for some kind of UK participation in such a force because it would be difficult for the government to justify staying outside. Echoing fears expressed after Nassau, he suggested, they 'could not exclude the possibility that a hostile attitude on our part to the MLF might prejudice the supply of Polaris missiles to us under the Nassau Agreement'. Finally, when tentatively proposing alternatives to MLF, he surmised that in order 'To meet the political requirements, any such proposals would have to accept the principle of mixed-manning.' To this end, 'If possible there should be a pilot project, to test the effectiveness of mixed-manning in practice and the participants should agree not to go further unless the pilot project proved effective.'[81]

Yet Kennedy's initiative in proposing the so-called mixed-manning demonstration (MMD) could also have been brought about by his continued dissatisfaction with the MLF proposal and realism that the British and others were unlikely to accept it as it stood. He knew that the British on the whole remained sceptical even though reports of Home's conciliatory position were transmitted back to Washington by the American Embassy and then by Ormsby Gore himself.[82] Yet in face-to-face meetings with the foreign secretary the following month the president expounded the advantages of Britain joining in with a single mixed-manned ship in relation to MLF because it involved no real commitment at all. He told Home that 'there was no hurry' regarding MLF and in connection to the MMD, and his comment that 'the ship could sail around for as much as a year and a quarter or a year and a half and the Germans would be satisfied' was based on the political difficulties encountered. By the time the MMD was completed, he said, the situation would be known. He reiterated this later the same month, when the president recommended joining a mixed-manned demonstration as it 'would help to give the impression of momentum, would in fact be a time consuming exercise and he hoped that we would see the advantage to us joining for this very reason'.[83]

Kennedy's second initiative to convene multilateral discussions in Paris also on a non-committal basis once again showed that he saw no immediate solutions to British participation. And once again the British were reluctant to join. Yet with Kennedy's apparent renewed interest in the force, the 'theologian' cabal were pressing for progress to be made through extensive congressional consultations.[84] Moreover, Kennedy's reassurances that agreement to participate in formal talks would not entail a commitment to participate in the MLF had to be taken seriously. And so on 27 September the British announced that they would enter detailed discussions. Although their statement acknowledged the importance of the MLF proposal and the reaffirmation of this by Kennedy and Macmillan at Birch Grove, the tone was tentative:

> the United Kingdom Government do not feel that they could in good faith enter into these discussions on terms of reference which imply...[a] degree of commitment in principle to participation in a mixed-manned force of surface ships, especially since they have publicly *questioned* the value of a force of this kind in relation to the expenditure of resources which it would entail and this issue is now under examination in the

context of the NATO strategic review. *Therefore, if they are to take part in the discussions it must be on the clear understanding that it does not commit them to participate in such a force.*[85]

So while overall the attitude of the British government was negative, its promise to at least talk was an admission that the MLF might come into existence and, as the British newspaper the *Economist* saw the dilemma, the British government had already 'missed too many international buses' in the past by not talking.[86]

On 11 October 1963, the first meeting of the MLF steering group met at Port Dauphine, Paris and immediately approved a military sub-group, which would meet in Washington on 18 October to begin examining the proposal for an MMD.[87] With the establishment of groups on both sides of the Atlantic, the British reiterated that 'if they [the UK] are to take part in the discussions it must be on the clear understanding that it does not commit them to participate in such a force'.[88] This view reflected that taken by other European governments chary of commitment to talks being taken as commitment to MLF in Washington. The Dutch government told the British that it 'had decided to participate in the study group discussions on the same basis of no commitment as we have'.[89]

As before, the reactions to Kennedy's initiatives in London were split along Foreign Office-MOD lines, bringing the two departments into conflict with each other. The Foreign Office reacted most favourably, especially welcoming the proposal for the demonstration ship, while emphasizing that the pilot project would have to prove effective before further action could be taken.[90] The MOD disagreed with this assessment. Although 'one of the greatest charms (from our point of view) of the Multilateral Force Working Group is that it consumes time and sheds the cold light of reason if not scepticism on a superficially attractive idea' it was not so supportive of the MMD concept for practical reasons.[91] During the talks on the proposed demonstration in Washington, the deputy permanent secretary of the MOD, Frank Mottershead, suggested that British 'should not encourage this experiment'. He continued:

> The practicability of mixed-manning a single surface ship has not been seriously questioned, and exaggerated significance would be attached to the 'success' of a single experiment, which would add to the momentum of the concept. Moreover to provide suitable personal for one crew would be comparatively easy; to provide 25 crews would be another matter. Even if other countries wished to make the experiment HMG would not wish to participate by providing RN personnel.

This was rejected, however, as being 'not really acceptable to the Foreign Office'.[92]

Washington remained up-to-date on these internal debates. The American Embassy in London, summarizing British policy towards France, explained:

> The Foreign Office is sympathetic to the idea of the MLF providing a means by which the UK can work closely with the US, Germany, Italy

and other European countries to strengthen the cohesiveness of the Atlantic alliance and counteract French attempts to develop an exclusively continental system. But Parliament is not enthusiastic and the Defense Ministry dislikes the proposal.[93]

It concluded that British indecision on MLF had undoubtedly disappointed the Germans and had the effect of reducing British influence in Atlantic affairs.

Yet it was difficult to see what sort of commitment the British could make before the election due sometime over the following year. In spite of the surge Macmillan had received as a result of the test ban treaty signing in August, little had been achieved. In some respects his government was in an even worse state than it had been at the end of the previous year, apparently on the verge of being torn apart. It was widely recognized in Washington that the figure of 'SuperMac' had long since disappeared, indeed the prime minster's position looked increasingly untenable as the scandal over Secretary of State for War John Profumo's sexual indiscretions continued to produce more revelations and the prospect of an election drew ever closer.[94] For the British then, participation in the MMD became more attractive for the very reason that each would take a considerable time to complete. In October, the British Embassy argued that two main political points regarding the talks and proposals should be considered.[95]

In contrast, the State Department's MLF protagonists intended to use progress on the demonstration as a springboard for the full-scale MLF. They refused to see MMD as a time-wasting tactic and instead thought that MLF talks could produce an international agreement before the end of that year; six months before the MMD was scheduled to start. At the beginning of October, John Barnes from the Foreign Office met Howard Furnas from the State Department, who had been appointed head of the MLF Negotiating Team. When Barnes raised the difficulty of reconciling the idea of 'finishing [MLF talks] before Christmas' with the fact that the MMD would take at least a year to show results, he received the reply 'that the demonstration was not intended to be judged by the countries concerned before they made up their minds on the force. It was merely intended to give a head start to mixed-manned force if it was decided to set one up.'[96]

During the final weeks of the Kennedy administration, therefore, the MLF appeared to be regaining some momentum. The military sub-group met for the first time in Washington on 17 October to consider the demonstration proposal.[97] Before the end of the month, it had produced a report concluding that the MMD was feasible. The sub-group's conclusions, however, indicated the inherently limited nature of the proposed demonstration. Most significantly, the sub-group recognized that the MMD 'should be of some benefit to the Multilateral Force', although it did 'not cover all aspects of mixed-manning as envisaged for the MLF' as it presented 'only a portion of the whole problem'.[98]

The MOD was quick to seize on the shortcomings of the proposed demonstration and saw few benefits that they could draw from it. They pointed out that time would be wasted whether they joined or not. The Admiralty also worried about having to find the officers and ratings needed to participate when British forces were already so overstretched.[99] Yet with Foreign Office encouragement, UK government policy was now moving towards more substantive participation in the MMD. The Foreign Office maintained its position against a token contribution because full-scale MMD participation would improve relations with both the US and West Germany. It claimed that the project possessed 'political importance'. By November Home was the new prime minister, following Macmillan's resignation on the grounds of ill-health the previous month, and his private secretary Oliver Wright informed Arthur Hockaday of the MOD that 'President Kennedy evidently attaches great importance to the demonstration' and therefore it was important to maintain influence from within.[100]

Kennedy even appeared to be making bold moves within his own government to prepare for the MLF to come into existence. Since the previous month, George Ball had been encouraging congressional consultation on 'a *very quiet* basis'[101] Kennedy had resisted this pressure, perhaps for fear of arousing even more opposition to the proposal. Yet in his final days he gave Ball and the others permission to follow this course and begin briefing congressmen. As John Steinbruner suggests, this provided the 'theologians' with a wider mandate and thus was bound 'to provide an additional test of the President's position'. Official approval from the White House for this move came on the eve of President Kennedy's trip to Texas in November.[102] Two days later, the president was gunned down by an assassin's bullet in Dallas.

What Kennedy would have done had he lived remains unclear. Thomas Finletter later claimed that Kennedy's actions in support of talks in Paris and action on the MMD from the autumn of 1963 indicated that he wanted to take a stronger lead on MLF policy, although Finletter conceded that 'this is my impression. I can't document it. I can't prove it, but the evidence is strong to this effect.'[103] Based on the evidence available it is clear that Kennedy adopted myriad attitudes towards the MLF during his presidency and especially following the Nassau agreement. On the whole he expressed almost continued scepticism in private while supporting the MLF as a solution to the 'German question' in public. So while he attempted to persuade and cajole Macmillan through his personal relationship with him and offer Adenauer assurances that Washington was set on the MLF, he would often simultaneously state his pessimism about the chances of success for the force with his key advisers. McGeorge Bundy, who was increasingly the most important voice for the president on this topic, arguably captures the essence of Kennedy's attitude on the question of MLF when he says the president 'probably would have given different answers on different days'.[104]

Despite his apparent activity in the autumn and in particular his move towards congressional consultations in November, it is likely Kennedy had concluded that he could play the long game and wait for the results of discussions and the test ship. It was clear that the talks in Paris were going to be slow in coming to any significant decisions; and Kennedy told Home quite explicitly at the beginning of October that the demonstration ship would take some time, perhaps up to a year and a half, to produce results. William Tyler reports that after saying this, the president laughed and said: 'Of course Bill Tyler will still be around then, but some of us may not be.'[105] Although in a quite different, unexpected and tragic way, Kennedy was extremely prescient. His untimely death bequeathed the consequences of these MLF debates to his successor.

5

WASHINGTON AND THE
LABOUR PARTY

Harold Macmillan resigned barely more than a month before Kennedy's death. His successor, Foreign Secretary Lord Home, who renounced his title to become Alec Douglas Home, presided over a forlorn Conservative government in what was to be its final year in office. The British people seemed to want a change, especially as the Conservatives had been in power for more than twelve years by the time Home took office. The new prime minister with his aristocratic background and lack of dynamism seemed unlikely to reverse the fortunes of his party.

Waiting to succeed the Conservatives was the Labour Party under the leadership of Harold Wilson. Wilson, a young and much more vibrant presence, promised 'a new Britain' forged in the 'white heat of technology'. After being out of power for so long, Labour wanted to come to office with a radical agenda for Britain that would take it into a new era. With the dissolution of the empire and growing importance of the EEC in British foreign policy, it seemed the time was ripe for a new dynamic force in British politics. However, despite hefty leads in opinion polls during 1963, it was far from certain that the Labour Party would be able to muster the collective will to forge a sizeable majority in Parliament. Internal splits and tensions did not augur well for the party.

Moreover, with Kennedy dead and Macmillan out of power, the prospects for close Anglo-American relations as the highest level looked poor. Home and President Lyndon Johnson developed little rapport and the Americans regarded the Labour Party and Harold Wilson, whom they considered to be the prime minister in waiting, with some suspicion.[1] Washington considered Labour to be more anti-American than the Conservatives and less dedicated to the principles of NATO. This view was compounded by Labour opposition to the Nassau treaty and its promise to 'renegotiate' the agreement if it came to power.

And yet during 1963 and 1964, Wilson was relatively successful in alleviating many of Washington's fears. He did this by reining in the more radical Labour elements, uniting the party behind him and steering clear of controversial issues such as disarmament that had caused schism during the late 1950s and early 1960s. The left wing of his party was broadly satisfied with criticism of Tory claims that Polaris was independent and the right was content with equivocation over whether he would scrap the deterrent. It was an effective compromise in an effort to achieve power.[2] In this way Wilson maintained consensus at a time of deep popular disaffection with the Tories. And despite some bellicose rhetoric during the election campaign, Wilson assured Washington that there would be few breaks from Tory policy on foreign and NATO policy; Labour's obligations to NATO and British global commitments remained strong.

The Labour Party, nuclear weapons and NATO

Internal Labour Party debates about the British nuclear deterrent reflected a split between those who espoused a 'socialist' foreign policy and those who believed that the national interest should dominate decision-making on international affairs. Those on the socialist wing disagreed with placing the national interest at the forefront of policy-making because it did not sit easily with Labour claims to represent the workers and oppressed around the world. They saw the reduction of tensions between East and West as the primary role of governments in the modern international system. In contrast, 'Atlanticists' believed that it was impossible to deal with the complexities of the international system in such a manner and however much they wished to adhere to socialist principles, the competitive reality of international affairs meant that national interests had to come first.[3]

Both these camps also had to contend with the fact that Britain's dire economic situation and the deterioration in its international position had resulted in reliance on the United States. This meant that the post-war Labour government under Clement Attlee had adopted a more 'Atlanticist' approach to foreign affairs, especially in support of the Marshall Plan and the creation of NATO itself, than many on the left-wing were willing to countenance. Left wing stalwarts such as Aneurin Bevan had resigned from the government in protest at a military build-up in the early 1950s that they felt was unjustified.[4] Yet many also accepted that the Soviet Union had become a repressive and authoritarian regime that was willing to snuff out democracy within its sphere of influence, and therefore those who supported a pro-Soviet stance began to lose influence.[5]

Throughout the 1950s, therefore, the Labour Party (now in opposition) had maintained a relatively positive view of the American guarantee to Europe through NATO. Certainly those at the vanguard of the party were not willing to countenance anything that would undermine the treaty, particularly as it also cemented relations with another key ally, West Germany, and despite some opposition to Adenauer's policies towards East Germany.[6] Despite some continued pacifist and anti-American views from those on the left of the party, and elsewhere, the vast majority of the parliamentary and grass-roots Labour Party continued to support strong relations with the US through NATO.[7]

Yet the American nuclear guarantee raised issues among many on both the left and right wing of the party. It was a Labour government that in 1947 had made the secret decision to pursue the manufacture of atomic weapons after being cut out of the American nuclear programme. While controversial in itself, the development of the hydrogen bomb, Soviet advances in delivery systems and the increasing need for reliance on the US raised the issue once again at the end of the 1950s, sparking a heated debate that threatened to split the party along social-ist/Atlanticist lines. Some opposed nuclear weapons outright, especially on moral grounds, but the vast majority supported some form of nuclear capability whether it was in order to enhance Britain's global status, nurture links with the US or to demonstrate a degree of independence from Washington.[8]

Labour Party infighting on the subject of the nuclear deterrent reached its zenith in 1960. Changing attitudes towards the nuclear deterrent were exacerbated by the Conservative Party's decision to adopt Skybolt in 1960, showing the degree to which Britain now relied upon the US for its missile delivery systems. Labour leader Hugh Gaitskell then lost a vote at the party conference in 1960 when a res-olution supporting unilateral disarmament was adopted. Ultimately, the vote was only just carried and it was reversed the following year, but this episode demon-strated just how divided the party was on this issue.[9] Peter Jones suggests that the reversal of the unilateral disarmament resolution in 1961 may have been because nuclear weapons were becoming less important as an issue for the Labour Party by the early 1960s, particularly as many were re-thinking attitudes towards British foreign policy in the light of Macmillan's move towards the EEC.[10] The move away from unilateralism also represented Gaitskell's increasingly strong position that augured well for Labour's electoral chances.[11]

The Labour Party did not welcome the Nassau agreement. Even as it was being completed, the American Embassy in London reported that it was 'doubtful' as to whether Labour would accept Polaris without significant controversy within the party and a considerable amount of external pressure to do so. It also seemed unlikely that it would be willing to merge the deterrent in some form of NATO or European context as the Americans wished.[12] On Christmas Eve 1962, shadow cabinet member George Brown gave an interview in which he said that it was 'nonsense' for the Conservatives to claim that Britain now had an independent nuclear deterrent, although he was evasive about whether Labour would repudiate the agreement.[13] In the debates that followed, however, Labour opposition became far clearer.[14]

Harold Wilson as Labour leader

In January 1963 Hugh Gaitskell died suddenly of a rare disease. In Andrew Thorpe's words, this 'threw the party into something of a panic'.[15] Gaitskell had been gaining ground on the Tories and the expectation both in Britain and abroad was that a Labour victory was the most likely outcome of the forthcoming con-test. Now with its charismatic and popular leader gone and a general election imminent, the chances of victory seemed to be slipping away again.

Moreover, Washington viewed the contest for a new leader with some suspicion. The US considered that if the successful candidate did not unite the party behind him, this might seriously undercut Labour's chances of beating the Conservatives.[16] The two leading candidates, Harold Wilson and George Brown, both had their faults. While Wilson was considered to be the most likely candidate to win, current deputy leader George Brown was perceived to be far friendlier to US interests although his bouts of heavy drinking were seen to be a hindrance. Washington noted that in the debates on the Nassau agreement, Wilson had taken a highly critical line. He had played upon reports that the Macmillan government was trying to do a deal with the Germans to give them a nuclear capability in return for entry to the EEC. He described any potential Western European collective nuclear deterrent as 'narrow, nationalistic, intransigent, revanchiste' and claimed that endowing Germany with nuclear weapons would end any hope of resolving east–west tensions.[17]

The momentum was with Wilson and in mid-February he was elected to replace Gaitskell. The same month, Albert Irving of the American Embassy sent a memorandum dubbing Wilson the 'Next British Prime Minister'. In a thorough and lengthy character sketch, Irving summarized Wilson's personality thus:

> We see Wilson as the hard-driving, left-of-center socialist intellectual with strong egocentric drives and intense ambition from the age of ten; as the single-minded careerist with on occasion not much scruple, weaving and bobbing like a cork on the political waters; as the essentially friendless and withdrawn lone-wolfer pursuing his goals of personal advancement with relentless concentration and a minimum of compromising commitment; and we see him as the nearly unmatchable parliamentary performer (the present House of Commons being what it is) who can hold attention with wit, and style, and telling punch in debate.[18]

Irving recognized that despite his tendency to side with the left of the party, in recent times, this had begun to change and in the international arena, and especially in the US, he wanted to be seen 'as the moderate democratic socialist leader of an empirical, middle-of-the-road Labor Party'.[19] Irving noted that he had reaffirmed his support for NATO, but stressed the need to build up non-nuclear components, improve consultation and provide more effective controls over nuclear weapons. He also noted Wilson's opposition to Britain's deterrent or a shared Western European weapons system, although 'It is unclear what a Labor Government would do under his leadership with the Polaris weapons if Polaris formed... part of the British or a NATO-shared arsenal'.[20]

With his position as leader secure, however, Wilson did little to clarify his views on the Nassau agreement, particularly the multilateral aspects. Although by the end of February, the British Embassy reported on the 'now familiar Labor opposition to [the] UK independent deterrent to establishment [of] European deterrent', Wilson was not opposed to arrangements for more safety catches on the nuclear trigger, although he was clearly concerned that a German finger would be provocative to the Soviet Union and therefore should be avoided. Yet, Wilson was not willing to state outright that Germany should be excluded from any MLF arrangement, and on Polaris he would not be drawn on whether

Labour's stance meant an absolute rejection of the Nassau agreement. By this stage he was using the term 'renegotiation' to explain what Labour would do in relation to Nassau if it won the election. He claimed that the Americans were as dissatisfied with the Nassau agreement as Labour was and spoke to American concerns about the need for conventional forces, particularly the BAOR, which the Labour government would be able to augment with its savings in nuclear defence. He repeatedly stated sympathy for the broad thrust of the Kennedy administration's foreign policy aims.[21] In turn, Washington seemed increasingly satisfied with the broad implications of Wilson's pro-NATO stance.[22]

Labour's views were further fleshed out by a meeting between Labour foreign affairs spokesman Patrick Gordon Walker and Livingston Merchant at the end of March. In an account of the meeting by the American minister in London, which also provided a whimsical character profile of Gordon Walker who was likened to an academic, politely listening to opposing views. Gordon Walker wanted the Americans to feel at ease with the new leader of the Labour Party. He told Merchant:

> I suppose everybody is wondering about our Harold. You won't find him too difficult. He is a man very hard to pin down. I doubt that he has any strong convictions about anything. He doesn't feel passionately about things the way Hugh Gaitskill [sic] did. Hugh believed that a party leader should always lead. Harold is much more of a compromiser. In some ways he is like Attlee and your Harry Truman. He likes to listen to all views on any subject and then arrive at a policy which will satisfy most people.

So although Wilson was extremely Intelligent, Gordon Walker said, 'he always operates short-range – and by short range I mean that he keeps his eyes on the period three months to six months ahead'. Gordon Walker concluded this character sketch with the observations that 'You won't find Harold too hard to deal with if we come to power...Our Harold is behaving very well lately...He is being very cautious these days. You will find him alright on NATO and broad policy lines; after you get to know him, you will not find him too difficult.' With some understatement, the minister reported that 'Gordon Walker's auditors were somewhat startled to hear a possible foreign secretary thus describe a possible prime minister.'[23]

On the issue of nuclear affairs Gordon Walker was very specific; the Labour government would take the British out of the nuclear field as soon as it could by letting the V-bomber force run down and not replacing it with Polaris. He played up the need for American defence saying that there was no doubt the Americans would come to the aid of the Europeans and therefore there was no need for the British to have the deterrent as well. Britain could therefore concentrate on building up other defence forces. He conceded that Labour did not have all the figures on which to make a final and definitive judgement, but reiterated the British view that the MLF was not needed because the German desire for nuclear weapons had been overstated. Naturally, Merchant countered with the standard American arguments in favour of MLF and Gordon Walker claimed: 'He was not completely convinced, but he was much more impressed than he expected to be.'[24]

By now, the American Embassy was reporting that Wilson seemed 'confident and poised' in his new position as Labour leader. He was also looking forward to a visit to Washington later that month.[25] Bruce put it in even starker terms saying that the Labour leaders were 'a limely [sic] lot, exuding confidence, contemptuous of the present government, convinced of their ability, if elected, to revive the British economy, and perform other near miracles'. Bruce thought that Wilson would take a generally pro-American line and warned his superiors against attempting to impose American views on their partners when Labour was so opposed to the MLF.[26] Schlesinger reported to JFK on the significant progress that the Labour opposition was now making. The Macmillan government, he said, 'reeks of decay; and the press and opposition, sensing a rout, are moving in for the kill'. Although Schlesinger recognized there were problems with Wilson and that his principles and abilities could be questioned, he was certainly trying his best to show his pro-American sensibilities and deny that there were any fundamental differences between Washington and the Labour Party, except perhaps on trade with the communist bloc and the MLF.[27]

When Wilson arrived in the US he met Walt Rostow and told him that Labour's priority on taking power would be a review of British defence, which he believed 'will prove to be a mess'. In this regard the two primary areas under review in addition to general defence matters were the 'renegotiation' of Nassau and NATO policy. On the MLF, Wilson expressed his concern in terms of the effect it would have on Britain's global role: 'The maintenance of a world position for Britain on a conventional basis is, in his view, more important than moving expensively or pretentiously forward in the nuclear field', Rostow reported. Wilson conceded that his mind was not closed on MLF and somewhat optimistically Rostow concluded from this that Wilson would 'jump with both feet into the MLF' because it would give the British a say in alliance nuclear control *vis-à-vis* the Germans and save money on his budget.[28] Arthur Schlesinger concurred with this generally positive impression of Wilson: 'I can report that he has made a favourable impression here. [Presidential adviser] Averell Harriman...tells me he is a changed man from the pompous and conceited person whom Averell knew 15 years ago as head of the Board of Trade', he told the president. Schlesinger also reported that Wilson now even seemed to be a little 'cagier' about attacking MLF.[29] Yet when Wilson met Rusk the same day, Wilson reiterated his fears about the MLF giving the Germans a finger on the nuclear trigger and provoking the Soviets.[30]

Labour and the MLF

With Labour's attitude towards NATO evolving in a generally positive direction during the first months of 1963, Washington remained concerned about its continued opposition to the MLF. Foreign affairs spokesman Patrick Gordon Walker remained particularly vocal. Gordon Walker had made his and Labour's views on the MLF known when Merchant visited London in March 1963. He said that the MLF could only be one of two things: either a 'sham' because the Americans would in fact keep their finger on the trigger, which in the end would not satisfy the Germans, or it would be a European deterrent with many fingers on the trigger, which would make it 'feeble and incredible'. He said he could not see a Labour government that gave up its nuclear deterrent in order to put the savings into conventional forces agreeing to put more money into a collective deterrent 'of which it would gravely doubt the value'.[31]

Labour's problem, however, was that events seemed to be overtaking them and there was a distinct possibility that a deal on MLF might be struck before the election. Speaking at the end of March 1963 to the Foreign Press Association, Gordon Walker articulated the emerging view that while a Labour government would find it hard to renege on a MLF agreement if one had already been made by the time it came into office, it could not support the MLF in its present form and opposed giving Germany nuclear weapons in the foreseeable future. He said, he felt that Labour's relinquishing the deterrent if it came into office would enhance Labour's ability to augment British conventional forces and bring a balance between forces and political control.[32]

Gordon Walker's scepticism was further enhanced by meetings with the president and McNamara at the end of May. He told McNamara that there could be no equality in NATO until the Germans were on the same level as the British and the French, and therefore Labour intended to move out of the deterrent business and let the US have the nuclear monopoly in return for an 'intimate voice' on nuclear control. He also asked that the Americans make no irreversible decisions on MLF while Labour was trying to push through this policy. In turning conventional Labour Party wisdom on its head, a *lack of* nuclear weapons would give Labour bargaining power.[33] McNamara's responses convinced Gordon Walker that the Pentagon was far less convinced by MLF than the 'mad keen' State Department, and even the president had to admit that there were problems.[34] Gordon Walker was much more positive when he met Merchant again, telling him that he accepted the 'political justification for the MLF and its military effectiveness' and that although the best solution following Labour's renunciation of Nassau and ending the British nuclear programme would be to gain assurances from the Germans that they would never seek nuclear weapons, if this was unsuccessful then the Labour government 'would throw itself wholeheartedly into the MLF'.[35]

The rest of the year passed with Wilson continuing to consolidate his position as leader while sniping at the MLF concept.[36] As Kennedy prepared for his European trip in June he was told that Wilson had succeeded in uniting the Labour Party behind him 'at least temporarily'. In contrast, the Tories and Macmillan were looking very vulnerable.[37] When Macmillan did resign, however, Labour seemed to be slightly taken aback. George Brown came to Washington in the days that followed and Bundy reported that although Brown was still 'bouncy', he was somewhat less confident than when Macmillan was in office and there was a sense that Labour was still 'yet to have the measure' of Home. Brown was still very much opposed to MLF, Bundy reported, and there was clearly some annoyance in Washington because Labour appeared to have teamed up with the Italian Socialists to oppose it.[38] Wilson continued to claim that the MLF was built on the fundamentally flawed supposition that the FRG wanted nuclear weapons and claimed he had received word that if Willy Brandt became Chancellor he would denounce such aspirations.[39] The shadow defence spokesman, Denis Healey, like Patrick Gordon Walker earlier in the year, was willing to concede openly that if other courses remained blocked and the MLF came into existence then the Labour government would join rather than remain outside.[40]

Labour and the Johnson administration

By the end of 1963, the nuclear question was far less volatile for Labour than it had been just a few years before. This allowed the leadership to develop its position in more detail and with less public attention than before. It soon became clear to interested parties in Washington that it was adopting a much more favourable position towards the deterrent. In February 1964, Gordon Walker visited the US once again and spoke with Rostow, telling him that the Labour Party was now trying to keep its options open. At present, it was still planning to end the deterrent, converting Polaris submarines to conventionally armed 'hunter killers', although it might retain them as part of the British national deterrent if this was deemed necessary (that is, the programme had advanced beyond the economic point of no return). Moreover, Labour had not dismissed assigning Polaris to what he called a 'European Force'. He expressed his continued opposition to MLF, however.[41] A brief glimmer of hope for MLF advocates in Washington was that if Labour did win office and decided to scrap Polaris then the MLF might look like a better bet to other partners, although the difficulty of persuading the British to join would still remain.[42]

Gordon Walker was very much in line with his party leader, who was also developing his public position so as not to foreclose any policy options. Wilson followed Gordon Walker to Washington in March and while he stressed both the importance of conventional forces to the future defence posture of the UK and claimed that Polaris would 'not add anything significant to Western deterrent striking strength', he gave himself an escape clause. At a press conference in Washington in March he stated:

> We believe there is a need for a very much expanded conventional naval ship-building programme in Britain and we would hope to convert them [Polaris submarines] from their present design to nuclear powered tracker submarines. If they got, in a sense, past the point of no return here, we would obviously be prepared to offer them for the Western deterrent within NATO on whatever basis NATO is going to be organised.[43]

The day before this, however, Wilson had met the president and told him in categorical terms that a Labour government would end Britain's nuclear deterrent. In stressing his support for NATO and the Atlantic community in general, Wilson informed the president that scrapping Polaris would save £300 million 'which could used to put back the British fleet on the high seas' and increase conventional forces in the alliance. He reiterated the idea the following day to McNamara, when somewhat prophetically he said that if a country as small as Britain tried to have 'a little of everything' it would wind up with 'a lot of nothing'.[44]

Perhaps Wilson took this position because he could use it to bargain with Washington. The Labour leader was fully aware of both the prestige of Polaris and the diplomatic muscle towards the United States that it gave him. Reference to conventional force posture pushed the right buttons in the Pentagon, while demonstrating Wilson's solidarity with Healey's position on NATO strategic reform. Moreover, the threat to cancel Polaris was likely to induce some concern in the US capital and might make them think about ways in which they could lessen its effect. To this end, Wilson may have expected Johnson and McNamara to dissuade him from making such a move. More likely he wanted to extract concessions on MLF, his threat on Polaris a move to cajole the president into reducing his support for the NATO force.[45] Following his visit, Gordon Walker further articulated Labour's ideas in an article in *Foreign Affairs* in which he reiterated the notion that ending the deterrent was intended to be part of Labour's effort to mediate a more sophisticated policy which would give it a greater role in American nuclear planning.[46]

Throughout the 1964 general election campaign, therefore, 'renegotiation' of the Nassau treaty and Polaris agreement remained one of the Labour Party's main aims. Labour saw many faults in the agreement made between Kennedy and Macmillan in 1962, as the party manifesto articulated:

> The Nassau agreement to buy Polaris know-how and Polaris missiles from the USA will add nothing to the deterrent strength of the Western Alliance, and it will mean utter dependence on the US for their supply. Nor is it true that all this costly defence expenditure will produce an 'independent British deterrent'. It will not be independent and it will not be British and it will not deter... We are not prepared any longer to waste the country's resources on endless duplication of strategic nuclear weapons. We shall propose the re-negotiation of the Nassau agreement. Our stress will be on the strengthening of our conventional regular forces so that we can contribute our share to NATO defence and also fulfil our peace-keeping commitments to the Commonwealth and the United Nations.[47]

In order to limit the possible effects of cancellation, Denis Healey stated publicly that if Polaris was cancelled, the submarines could have their mid-sections removed and be used instead as nuclear powered, conventionally armed 'hunter killers'.[48] Yet commentators in the UK were already speculating that if Labour came to power it was likely to retain Polaris, particularly if it was difficult to have the submarines converted, within the context of some kind of NATO force.[49]

As the election approached, Labour's chances of an outright, crushing electoral victory seemed increasingly remote. Despite Wilson's success in uniting his party the Tories' strategy of waiting as long as possible in the hope that the improving economy would bring people back to vote for them seemed to be paying dividends. In June Labour's lead in the polls had been some 20 points, by September it was just three. In the event, Wilson's election in October 1964 was a very narrow victory. The election gave Labour 317 seats and the Conservatives 304, leaving Labour with a working majority of just five.[50] Despite this result, it was seen to hold great significance in Washington, perhaps 'a turning point in Atlantic affairs', as Dean Rusk told the president just over a week later.[51]

The decision to retain Polaris

Following Labour's victory, the US moved quickly to soften the blow of any Polaris cancellation. Days into the new administration, Ormsby Gore (now Lord Harlech) spoke to McNamara, who reported that there would be 'no ill-feeling' on the part of the US if the UK decided to cancel the Polaris programme. Somewhat paradoxically, however, McNamara told him that there were 'mixed feelings' within the US administration about Britain deciding to drop out of 'the future deterrent business'.[52] McNamara may have been trying to balance the conflicting views between the executive, Defense and State Departments, but it seems more likely that it was an appeal to the UK to maintain at least some of their present commitments around the world, which he perceived could be achieved more effectively and at a lower cost to the British taxpayer by remaining in the nuclear game. He may even already have decided that Wilson's position had been a bluff.

On the other hand, Labour's pre-election pledge appealed to the State Department 'theologians' who were still smarting at the results of Nassau and keen to end Britain's nuclear role. George Ball told Bundy that 'What Wilson and Denis [Healey] have told Ball in the past is their thought was to phase out with V bombers, get out of the Polaris deal and help us run [Strategic Air Command at] Omaha'.[53] The State Department was cheered by reports that 'the Royal Navy has plans which will permit turning the Polaris submarines into "hunter killer" [sic] submarines, if Labor so decides, any time before mid-1965', although this would depend on the US making the cancellation costs as low as possible.[54]

A number of factors now influenced the new Labour government's thinking on Polaris. The first was cost. Days after the narrow victory, Healey asked the Chief Polaris Executive whether Polaris submarines currently being developed could be converted to hunter killers. This was possible, he reported, although such a conversion would result in cancellation of some £40 million of equipment, depending on American willingness to divert the parts to other purposes at minimal costs. He recommended completing four of the boats, while converting the fifth to a hunter killer thus reducing the capital cost of the programme by £15 million. If, however, all five were converted to hunter killers, he reported, the cost would be reduced by some £200 million over ten years. But as Healey recognized, hunter killers had a different strategic role to Polaris and so conversion into hunter killers did not solve all of the problems.[55]

Healey also had to consider the strategic credibility of any Polaris force. He was concerned about the ability of the navy to maintain a credible force in the 1970s if that force was kept at a minimum, meaning three submarines. To remain credible, it would be necessary for at least one submarine to be available to patrol at any one time and with three this was difficult to guarantee. In contrast with five, two could be constantly deployed.[56]

Moreover, the relationship with the US at different levels was a factor in his thinking. Good navy-to-navy relations were essential, as the Chief of the British Naval Staff explained to him. His thoughts on this are revealing for their honesty and, although they lead back to retention of the deterrent in the hands of the navy, a degree of reticence clearly remained:

> As regards the technical benefits these are of course useful. We have a very close liaison with the USN on the Polaris Programme and we are learning a lot about the Polaris system itself. However, it is perhaps fair to point out that we have for many years maintained an excellent liaison with the Americans on a wide range of other naval matters of mutual interest and benefit; there is no reason to suppose that this would not continue even if the Polaris Programme were renegotiated or cancelled. Nevertheless on a Navy-to-Navy net such a change might well have long-term effects in that we would, in US eyes, be seen to be dropping-out of a major naval role.[57]

Such factors were important, but Wilson's decision to retain four Polaris submarines also turned on political and economic, as well as strategic considerations. Wilson claims in his memoirs that when he spoke with Gordon Walker and Healey before the conference began it was 'clear that production of the [Polaris] submarines was well past the point of no return', and the decision was made to continue with the project on this basis.[58] Healey's recollections are somewhat different and worth quoting at length:

> The navy told me that, though the hulls for two Polaris submarines were already laid down and long-lead items had been ordered for two more, it would still be possible to convert them into hunter-killer submarines at no additional cost. Moreover most of the senior admirals were reluctant to take on the Polaris force within their existing budget at the expense of other ships, and were uncertain whether they could find the additional

skilled personnel to operate and service Polaris. When I gave Wilson and Gordon Walker this unexpected news they asked me not to let other members of the Cabinet know; Wilson wanted to justify continuing the Polaris programme on the grounds that it was 'past the point of no return'. I did not demur.[59]

This 'past the point of no return' argument became the one that was used to justify the decision to the public. Contracts were up and running, and apparently conversion to hunter killers could no longer be contemplated.[60]

Labour's decision to retain the Polaris capability therefore rested primarily on its strategic value in comparison to economic cost. A submarine launched deterrent gave the UK a degree of flexibility that a similarly priced conventional capability simply could not. The expected cost of Polaris was estimated to be some £150 million less than had been spent on the V-bomber force. Healey argues that the small running cost amounted to just 2 per cent of the annual defence budget and retention was justified because Polaris fitted neatly into the revision of NATO strategy at the time.[61] Beyond the alliance, there was a possibility that it could have been deployed in a global role, a concern of Harold Macmillan at Nassau. China had exploded its first atomic bomb the day Labour was elected and it was feasible that Labour could re-deploy in the Far East if it had been able to renegotiate Nassau without cancellation.[62]

Beyond the intangible addition to Britain's worldwide prestige that came with a nuclear capability and the need to compete and co-operate with France in the nuclear field, the diplomatic potential of Polaris also influenced Wilson's decision.[63] As the MLF negotiations seemed to be gaining in momentum when Labour took office, staving off a quick decision on the force would be more likely if the British retained nuclear weapons. With the retention of Polaris, Wilson was able to promote his own alternative to the MLF, a force comprising various elements including the British Polaris force and a mixed-manned component. The decision to retain Polaris was therefore also made with the MLF in mind.[64] By Christmas, it was 'abundantly clear' to Denis Healey that the Polaris programme would be continued in some form, and, in Harold Wilson's words, the 'general feeling' at Chequers was in favour of three submarines with one mothballed.[65]

The White House was genuinely pleased with the new developments.[66] Mountbatten confirmed Labour's position and perhaps to assuage US fears that this would militate against the UK conventional defence role and therefore justify retention of Polaris as a cost-saving measure he reassured the State Department that the Royal Navy would still get a second new carrier.[67] At the beginning of the following month, during an uneasy meeting between Ball and Wilson, the new prime minister told Ball how he had been forced to accept that 'merely to hand over the British Polaris submarines on a non-returnable basis would be political suicide'.[68]

Home and the Tories were quick to pick-up on the apparent u-turn in Labour Policy. During a characteristically raucous parliamentary debate on defence issues in December, the Conservative leader accused Wilson of surrendering Britain's independent nuclear deterrent. Unlike the Conservative policy, Home argued, Labour's proposals made Britain dependent on the United States and other NATO nations even after 1968 when the Polaris fleet was due to be completed. Wilson rebutted this assessment saying that whatever the assignment of the submarines, even after this date the UK would remain dependent on the US for specialized materials in order to run it, as well as, in the case of emergency, intimate discussions with them over when to fire it.[69]

Labour's position on the British nuclear deterrent appeared to have shifted considerably from the time Wilson became leader and the narrow election victory of October 1964. Even as the election approached, Patrick Gordon Walker wrote that Britain could simply not afford a 'full nuclear armoury' and dismissed the notion of an independent nuclear deterrent as 'far fetched'.[70] Yet, as Chris Wrigley has noted, it is very difficult to disentangle the style and substance of Labour Party foreign and defence policy during this period.[71] By the time the Labour manifesto was published with the promise of a 'renegotiation' of the Nassau agreement, Wilson had already modified his position to a considerable degree and once in power, the factors in favour of retention were clear. Polaris was a credible deterrent that could be delivered quickly and within cost. This would make it easier for Britain to fulfil more of its global obligations in the short term at least. Washington was also broadly in favour of retention and with the promise of a commitment to NATO in some form, it demonstrated Labour Party adherence to the alliance as well as possible relief from American calls for conventional troop increases. The 'past the point of no return' argument adopted by the Wilson government was then something of a smokescreen to disguise the economic and strategic benefits that Polaris was calculated to bring. Furthermore, by reducing the number of boats from five to four and emphasizing the commitment to NATO, Wilson could demonstrate an ostensible 'renegotiation' of Nassau.

Wilson's decision was undoubtedly made easier because the two major issues that had dominated in late 1962 and early 1963, namely the British application to the EEC and the Nassau agreement, had become far less important to the British electorate. With de Gaulle still in power and the Polaris project ongoing, there was little prospect of Britain joining the six in the near future.[72] But the decision to keep Polaris was also made with the prospect of an imminent 'nuclear sharing' agreement between the US and West Germany very much in mind. This issue continued to dominate the NATO agenda and would prove to be one of the most challenging issues for Wilson during his first months in office.

6

THE END OF THE MLF AND
NUCLEAR SHARING

President Kennedy's death in November 1963 had marked the start of a period of stagnation in plans for the MLF. Lyndon B. Johnson assumed the presidency with relatively little knowledge of the NATO nuclear force project. To him, the MLF was a public commitment that Kennedy had made almost a year before and one that should be honoured – he seemed unaware of the Kennedy retreat from MLF during the summer of 1963, a view from which the State Department did nothing to dissuade him.[1] Indeed, only days after Kennedy's death, Dean Rusk asked George Ball for a paper (presumably intended for the new president) on the 'MLF business setting forth the key points of what it is'.[2] Although the president then reaffirmed US support for MLF (in line with Kennedy's apparent position), he appears to have spent a little more time on the subject in his first few months in office.[3]

Meanwhile, at operational level, work on MLF continued. Johnson approved congressional consultations in December 1963.[4] Then from June 1964, the destroyer USS *Biddle* began to operate with an international crew in a demonstration of mixed-manning designed for those countries that might participate to gain experience. The British had signed up for the demonstration on the basis that it entailed no further commitment and sent officers and ratings to participate. West Germany, Italy, Greece, Turkey and the Netherlands had also sent personnel to take part until the demonstration finished in December 1965.[5] The US Navy also made considerable progress in planning for the MLF. In December 1964 McNamara included a Polaris A-3 force as a component of the surface-to-surface missile capability with a view to an agreement being signed by July 1965 and the force coming into existence by mid-1971.[6]

In the UK, both main political parties continued to oppose the force. And yet there was no crisis during 1964 or 1965 over the nuclear sharing issue, despite Labour's electoral victory and the prominence of MLF on the international agenda. This can be explained by the advent of the Labour Government's Atlantic Nuclear Force (ANF) proposal in late 1964. The ANF was intended to comprise British and US submarines, V-bombers, some mixed-manned components (to which the British appeared unwilling and unlikely to contribute) and perhaps French participation in some form. The Polaris submarine component was particularly important to Labour as it would fulfil their promise to internationalize the force as part of their Nassau 'renegotiation'. It was, in many ways, a more realistic approach to nuclear sharing than MLF, as it was far less ambitious. As a result, ANF garnered a good deal more military and political support in the UK than the MLF ever did.

ANF was not designed purely to scupper MLF, as Harold Wilson apparently claimed to the cabinet.[7] As Susanna Schrafstetter and Stephen Twigge have recently contended, far from being a device to destroy nuclear sharing in the Atlantic Alliance, the ANF proposal served a number of key functions for the Labour government and may have solved some problems within the Atlantic community. They argue that it would have resolved the non-proliferation treaty (NPT), at the time still blocked by the Soviets because of the MLF proposal, while appeasing Labour left-wingers who advocated ending the British deterrent. Thirdly, it would have fulfilled some of the terms of the Nassau agreement as well as being welcomed by the Johnson Administration, which was favourable to Europeans taking a lead in Atlantic affairs.[8]

Ultimately, Johnson's tentative withdrawal of support from MLF in late 1964 resulted in the slow decline of nuclear sharing. His decision to slow MLF was the result of a meeting with Harold Wilson when it became clear that the new British prime minister would accept nothing less than a change in policy direction. It was followed the next year by the rise of a nuclear consultation committee in NATO that offered non-nuclear members some political participation in nuclear matters as an alternative to nuclear sharing. Even so, some members of the Johnson administration continued to view ANF as an opportunity to strike a deal on a hardware sharing agreement.

The MLF and the Home government

The tumultuous events of the Kennedy assassination in November 1963 led to a period of reassessment in American–European relations. Europeans remained unsure of exactly how the new president would handle NATO issues, while Washington was keen to assert leadership during a time of potential drift. Immediately following Kennedy's assassination President Johnson met the new British Prime Minister Alec Douglas Home and told him 'He was looking forward to the same cordial and intimate relationship with the UK as President Kennedy had. The prime minister echoed these sentiments with great emphasis.' The two men then discussed President de Gaulle and whether there was any indication of him softening his attitude towards NATO. Finally they both agreed that the US 'continued to attach great importance to the German question'. Therefore, although the MLF was not discussed explicitly, Johnson's emphasis on continuity with his deceased predecessor implied no retreat from it.[9] This was reiterated in the traditional exchange of letters of agreement between the president and prime minister about consultation on the use of nuclear weapons on British soil.[10]

As the US administration saw it, the Kennedy assassination had ushered in an 'atmosphere not of crisis but of uncertainty', compounded by new leaders recently taking office in West Germany, Italy and Great Britain. It therefore felt it was necessary to stress the importance of Europe to the US and continuity between the Kennedy and Johnson administrations.[11] A National Security draft paper written just over a week after Kennedy's death urged strong leadership at the start of the Johnson administration, a reaffirmation of the American commitment to Europe and encouragement of a European build-up of its own conventional forces.[12] Another written some six months later noted, 'While the military strength of the Alliance has remained substantial, its political morale has clearly deteriorated'.[13]

In the first months of the Johnson administration, the MLF was pushed down the agenda as problems over Berlin continued and French truculence within the alliance grew. In preparation for the December NATO ministerial meeting, the State Department position was that, 'No aspect of this subject [nuclear sharing] is ripe for action at this time'. And in relation specifically to MLF,

> We should refer realistically to the status of the preliminary discussions on the Multilateral Force now in progress in Paris and Washington, making clear our continuing support and, in bilateral discussions, our willingness to proceed toward establishment of the Force whenever the Germans and Italians are prepared to do so.

This implied that the US would consider leaving the British behind, but that it was not prepared to force the issues while other pressing subjects awaited discussion.[14]

The NATO ministerial meeting later the same month in Paris therefore concentrated on shoring up morale in NATO and avoiding further controversy. Yet the American government could not ignore the MLF issue and Robert McNamara duly pledged support for the force. In a sop to critics, however, McNamara acknowledged the need to improve 'US general purpose forces notably in ground force readiness, tactical air and mobility' in parallel with nuclear sharing.[15] Dean Rusk concluded that this approach 'had gone very well' and 'he had the feeling that differences within the Alliance were less grave than the public assumed and had been narrowed down'.[16]

The British, however, remained uncertain of American policy towards the MLF. 'There is...[some] thought that the death of President Kennedy makes the American commitment to the MLF plan less certain', reported Evelyn Shuckburgh in December. Continued confusion in Europe about the state of NATO, unstable political situations in some countries and several upcoming elections compounded this, he suggested.[17]

Moreover, the United States uncharacteristically seemed to be wavering in its commitment to provide Polaris at this time. At the beginning of 1964, President Johnson proposed a 'nuclear freeze' whereby 'It would be possible to maintain and replace missiles on a one-for-one basis and keep confidence in the missiles by some number of firings. [But] there would be no testing of new models.' The British government was eager to safeguard its national deterrent and Bundy reassured the prime minister personally that even if the US decided outdated V-bombers should be scrapped under the terms of any reductions, Polaris would be protected. 'The rationale would be different', Bundy told Home. 'The US would agree to a freeze on terms which would allow it to honor its agreement at Nassau and with regard to MLF.' Bundy's assurances were predicated on US assessments that any nuclear freeze would not be accepted by the Soviets in the short-term and McNamara assured Foreign Secretary Richard A. Butler that 'the British [Polaris] program would be provided for under the agreement'.[18]

Home was in an even more difficult position as regards MLF. In September 1963, just a month before Macmillan's resignation, Home (as foreign secretary) had written a memorandum detailing various courses of action the government could take. In conclusion he recommended that, although there were risks with every option available, the British should desist from outright opposition to MLF.

> In my view, we cannot take an entirely negative attitude to the multilateral force. We cannot prevent it coming into existence. Unless we take part from the start we may be unable to influence the shape which it assumes. If it comes into being as a going concern we may later want to join and have to accept the terms on which membership is offered. We do not want to repeat the history of our relations with the Common Market.[19]

He also reasoned that any hint of rejecting MLF while accepting Polaris would leave the British open to accusations of ignoring integral elements of a crucial Anglo-American agreement, Nassau. In addition to noting that hostility to the MLF might still prejudice the supply of Polaris missiles, he noted that the US might become increasingly reluctant to continue bilateral nuclear consultation in the longer term.[20]

This attitude may have influenced British acquiescence to American pressure over the issues of the talks in Paris and the demonstration ship. British agreement to participate in the MMD, which was announced on 10 January 1964, was a considerable coup for American MLF protagonists and the State Department officially approved the demonstration a few days later.[21] As they had done at the start of the Paris talks, however, the British maintained that that their participation in MMD was on the clear understanding that it entailed no further commitment to the MLF as a whole. In the House of Commons Denis Healey attacked his opposite number for the government's policy both over MLF and for agreeing to examine the demonstration ship proposals put forward by the United States. Thorneycroft retorted that they would examine proposals if they were put before them, 'but that would not commit us to the enormous expense of going in for this multilateral force any more than would the discussions upon which we are now engaged'.[22] The prime minister also made this clear to the cabinet.[23]

Home's approach to the MLF problem as foreign secretary made him chary of further reports on the decline in the fortunes of MLF now he was prime minister. Such reports began to circulate near the end of 1963 and by the start of the following year the British Embassy in Washington announced a US 'retreat' on MLF on what they termed 'scientific grounds'. 'I doubt it', the prime minister responded. 'Anyhow the German and Italian attitude is hardening – but the

Americans may be more inclined to play it long or find a variant'.[24] When he returned to the US later that month his suspicions were confirmed as he was told that although the Johnson administration 'appreciate[d] British participation in MLF talks and demonstration ship' it would proceed with the force without Britain if necessary.[25]

In response, the British attempted to slow progress on the MLF in two ways. First, they made it clear to Washington that no decision on MLF could be made before the election. Simultaneously, Peter Thorneycroft began to develop a tentative plan to include British Canberras, the projected TSR-2 aircraft and V-bombers along with American and West German equipment under SACEUR's command in one force. He presented the proposal to the NATO ministerial meeting in December 1963.[26] Butler stressed that this was not intended as an alternative to MLF.[27] The proposal gained credibility in the US State Department, which believed that the Tories might have been trying to widen support for MLF, particularly in the Royal Navy. Alternatively it suggested it might have been an attempt to reduce the costs of entering MLF by selling the TSR-2 to other NATO nations within the force.[28] MLF was still a priority for the State Department and the UK election was likely to hold up its progress anyway. It therefore welcomed a new initiative to propel the proposal forward. There was also some hope that a return to power by the Conservatives would mean progress on MLF.[29]

The president also became more active on the MLF at this time. It seems that he understood very few of the finer points in the MLF debate, but was persuaded that appropriate action could be taken to bring the force into being. In March 1964 Harold Wilson told the Italian Foreign Minister Giuseppe Saragut that the new US president's attitude towards MLF differed significantly from that of his predecessor. Johnson was cool towards the whole project, Wilson said. Saragut then related this to Thomas Finletter. When Finletter confronted Wilson with this accusation himself Wilson apparently replied, 'Yes, that's right, that's what we think. We think President Johnson is "indecisive" about the support he intends to give to the Alliance in general and to this nuclear sharing idea.' Finletter assured Wilson that this was not the information he had, but that he would take this query back to Washington.[30]

Meanwhile in Washington Dean Rusk wrote to Johnson advising him of action that should be taken towards Congress on MLF 'if we are to hold open the option of presenting it for action in early 1965', following US and British elections.[31] Rusk also observed that the British could reach no decision on MLF before their elections, but that a Conservative government would probably join. Moreover, he surmised, 'There seems to be a reasonable possibility that a Labour government would eventually do so, especially if the creation of the MLF ... were assured anyway. It is unlikely however, that a Labour government would reach an affirmative judgement quickly.'[32] Other advisers were not as optimistic, however. Bundy told the president that although there was a consensus supporting it in the US, McNamara, the JCS and William C. Foster, Director of the Arms Control and Disarmament Agency, had 'serious reservations'.[33]

Of more immediate importance to the president was his discussion with Finletter that took place the same day. Significantly, this meeting was also attended by George Ball, but not McNamara or Bundy.[34] Johnson was aware that there would be no congressional action in the current sessions and that British and Italian participation continued to be the main problem in making progress.[35] Finletter told Johnson that Wilson's comments to Saragut 'had complicated the problems for the Italians' and Saragut had asked Finletter 'to give a specific endorsement to the project so there would be no misunderstanding the American position'. According to Finletter, Johnson replied that he was 'tired of this nonsense. And we are going to go ahead with MLF; it is to the interest of all concerned; and there's going to be no indecision about the United States on this.'[36] The president (perhaps in reaction to Rusk's memorandum from two days previously) instructed George Ball to apprise Congress of the situation and Finletter to make the president's position clear to allies in NATO. He warned Finletter, however, that he needed to be protected, as he had not yet spoken to Congress himself.[37]

Johnson was therefore forced to make a statement on MLF because of Wilson's truculence, although his newfound interest may also have derived from the State Department's assertion that sceptical British politicians could be converted. Rusk had suggested, for example, that Home had come to acknowledge that the MLF was the only feasible solution to the nuclear problems of NATO following a discussion with Gerhard Schroeder in August 1962. Schroeder had convinced Home that MLF would bind the Americans to Europe, tie the hands of future German governments and keep the Federal Republic away from the French. The same logic could therefore be applied to the Labour Party. An attachment to this correspondence noted that Labour was trying to persuade the Italian socialists that a better approach to the nuclear problem would be 'in *improved consultation on use of nuclear power*', it acknowledged that Home had originally taken up this position, concluding 'perhaps Wilson will also travel the road to Damascus when he bumps up against the reality of German attitudes'. It went further on the British national deterrent, optimistically suggesting that 'Even [a] Labour government might have trouble doing this unless it could get, in return, something which British electorate would consider just as good. MLF could thus offer long-term alternative to [the] UK national program as well.'[38]

The Home government remained unwilling to commit before the General Election as the prime minister was wary that any rapid American movement on the force could have the effect of damaging existing British support at a time of political uncertainty. But maintaining good relations with Washington remained paramount. Although he suggested that he might talk to the president over the issue, the Foreign Office responded first.[39] At the end of April, Sir Pierson Dixon told the Foreign Office that General de Gaulle had said the MLF was 'going to fail' and if he was right it might contribute to the disintegration of NATO. Conversely, Dixon said, if it did succeed, de Gaulle was likely to leave the alliance anyway. In a sharp rebuff the following month, Dixon was told that he was 'on dangerous ground' in citing this latter argument when it could be used by opponents of MLF. Moreover, France was unlikely to leave NATO and, even if it did, this would not be the end because the connection between the United States and Europe was much stronger than one link.[40]

Yet pressure from Bonn on Washington and the forthcoming meeting between president and chancellor now gave a new momentum to MLF. Joint State-Defense talks concluded at the start of May that British participation was not a *sine qua non* for the MLF.[41] This message was relayed to London from Bonn on 11 June, signalling that a MLF charter was likely to be signed before the end of the year.[42] It was confirmed the next day when the president met the new West German chancellor, Ludwig Erhard. Erhard was favourably disposed to MLF and eager to press forward. The US now proposed a timetable calling for signature of a MLF charter by November or December.[43] Washington's only concession to the British was over the exact timing. In the days following the declaration, Bundy told Lord Harlech that while Washington and Bonn would go ahead, they would wait until the end of January if it was necessary to get other countries on board. The following month Washington informed Finletter that this position did not represent an American attitude of 'inflexibility and unrelenting pressure upon our allies to meet [a] fixed timetable regardless [of] political circumstances in states concerned and regardless [of] whether governments stand or fall'.[44] Simultaneously, Richard Neustadt, who had been brought back into the administration to prepare a report on Labour's likely attitude to MLF, recommended restraint before the British and American elections, followed by gentle pressure on Wilson with a view to a possible visit to Washington perhaps as early as late January. Washington needed to deal with Wilson's concerns over broader defence issues, the American veto, consultation and east-west relations, Neustadt argued.[45] But, he concluded, the US must

> leave him no possible excuse we can foresee for failing to proceed toward MLF in company with us and with the Germans...I surmise that if we get over this hurdle in good style, the stage will be well set not only for effective Anglo-American relations but for increasingly productive Anglo-German ones'.[46]

In Britain, the MOD remained concerned that the UK might be bounced by bilateral US–German pressure into making a commitment on MLF before it was ready to do so. In May, Thorneycroft had written to the prime minister claiming that if the Tories continued to show a proclivity for joining MLF then it might affect their chances of being re-elected. Thorneycroft also argued that any decision should be taken in light of allies' responses and Soviet sensibilities. 'I think there is some danger', Thorneycroft concluded to Home, 'of our drifting into a commitment, the precise nature of which we have not understood'.[47] The Johnson-Erhard declaration only exacerbated Thorneycroft's concerns and re-emphasized a growing split with the Foreign Office. At the end of June he wrote a personal letter to Home reiterating his deep concern on MLF and the need for the Conservatives to present a viable alternative. Again the Foreign Office took a more sympathetic line, with Butler suggesting that the UK needed to enter MLF in order to preserve a degree of control over it.[48] The next month Thorneycroft wrote to the prime minister again. This time he claimed to have obtained information that the US was planning to lift its MLF veto at some point in the future.[49]

By this time the eighteen month MMD had begun on the USS *Biddle*, bringing forth a new round of pressure from the 'theologians'.[50] At a special ceremony in Norfolk, Virginia, the USS *Biddle* was re-commissioned the USS *Claude V. Ricketts*, after the vice-chief of Naval Operations, a key supporter of MLF in the military, who had recently died.[51] Both Paul Nitze and Dean Rusk visited the ship and used it to promote the MLF. Rusk claimed that the MLF would improve prospects for non-proliferation and the participants in this new force could have an enhanced position in future disarmament talks.[52] This pressure and the inauguration of the *Ricketts* in turn brought forth renewed attacks from the Soviets.[53]

Further pressure against MLF was being exerted on the West German government both from France and from within the Federal Republic itself. Although French anti-MLF sentiment was arguably behind this, Erhard was also aware that German Gaullists could keep pressure on him and prevent passage of any imminent MLF treaty. The Chancellor thus required strong US executive action and its absence was frustrating. By the beginning of the autumn, the chancellor urged Johnson to make his commitment to the MLF cause even more pronounced through immediate dissemination of a preliminary MLF charter in order to get the treaty signed 'as early as the end of November or the beginning of December'. Whether he believed this was possible is hard to fathom, but his convincing victory in the September election had undoubtedly emboldened him. Erhard was also motivated in part by the possibility of the General Assembly of the United Nations adopting a resolution calling on those participating in MLF negotiations to desist and push instead for an NPT.[54]

Possible UN pressure was, however, secondary in Johnson's mind to the potential intransigence of Congress. From his perspective this was where the MLF was likely to fall. The president was intimate with the machinations of Congress, remained in touch with a vast array of senators and congressmen and knew that agreeing a MLF charter timetable with the Atlantic partners would be meaningless if its passage through the US legislature could not be secured. In short, Johnson doubted he had the votes. When it was claimed, for example, that influential Democratic senator from Arkansas and chairman of the Senate Foreign Relations Committee J. William Fulbright was in favour of MLF, the president was able to counter this as he had spoken to Fulbright some ten minutes earlier.[55] Furthermore, several politically influential people had began to agitate against the MLF in public.[56] Bundy candidly confirmed to the president in November that 'A curious collection of liberals, Joint Committee atom-guarders, and neo-isolationalists would probably beat the MLF today if there were a totally free, silent, secret vote in the Senate.' Bundy suggested that they might have to strike a bargain in order to get it through.[57] It seems that this congressional opinion stultified Johnson and in the weeks and months after the declaration with Erhard, the president once more reverted to inaction on MLF (probably because of his continued concern with domestic legislation). When Finletter met George Ball late in 1964 in Paris and discussed MLF, Ball apparently complained 'You know I can't do anything with the president. I'm sorry, I just can't.' Finletter believed this inaction was fatal.[58]

The Wilson government and the ANF

Ten days before the British General Election in October 1964 Wilhelm Grewe, German Ambassador to NATO, arrived in Washington. This hurried visit, for which the Johnson administration was largely unprepared, resulted in a clumsy attempt by the Erhard government to force the MLF issue. Grewe proposed a bilateral German–American MLF deal that was intended to stymie German Gaullist attacks on NATO. This was an embarrassment to Johnson, especially as the content of Erhard's proposal was quickly made public and the Americans had to reject it outright.[59] In private, Grewe told George Ball that while the British had forced delays on some issues, 'he thought the MLF was not too far from the defense doctrine of the Labor Party in the UK'.[60]

Immediately following Labour's election victory, David Bruce wrote to the secretary of state to take issue with an article in the *Sunday Telegraph* the previous week that the major stumbling block in Anglo-American relations would be the MLF, which the new prime minister wholeheartedly opposed. Bruce thought that Wilson was 'too clever by half to commit to such an egregious blunder'. But he was not prepared to countenance Wilson's diplomatic game-playing, arguing that Washington should not allow Wilson to use MLF as a bargaining chip, either towards the US or Soviets. Bruce believed Wilson might tell Moscow that he was going to sign-up to the American proposal, before dropping it in return for 'a spectacular Soviet offer on disarmament'. Moreover, Bruce saw danger in the intimate connection between the British nuclear deterrent and MLF for the US:

> A lesser danger is that in proposing to renounce Britain's independent nuclear deterrent, he [Wilson] will cherish expectations of receiving from us a greater quid pro quo than our own interests should permit. If, by what he calls 'renegotiation of the Nassau Pact', he could arrive at an understanding with the US that he could represent to his own people as establishing a special relationship with us on the control and use of nuclear military weapons, only short of an equal right to a finger on the trigger, he might well consider MLF accession a low price to pay. I think it would be both unwise and unnecessary for us to consider such an arrangement.[61]

Yet Bruce adopted a different position when he spoke to Ball a month later, saying it was time to be 'tough with British on MLF'.[62]

With the British election over the 'theologians' now used renewed German pressure to move towards a rapid agreement on MLF.[63] It was now almost one year since Kennedy's death and, apart from the April and June reaffirmations of American intent, little movement on the force had taken place. In response, the secretary of state's special assistant on MLF, Ronald Spiers, working to a timetable calling for the signing of a MLF agreement on 15 January 1965, argued that the US should seek assurance that the new British government would honour this. Accordingly, Spiers was willing to compromise on the size of the force (a reduction to 10–15 ships), include a US–UK agreement for a possible land-based element and increase US financial input with a concurrent UK reduction if Labour agreed to install its Polaris force as part of the deal.[64] The President also recognized that the change of government in the UK heralded important decisions with regard to the nuclear affairs of the alliance. These decisions related 'not only to the MLF proposals now under discussion in Paris, but to the interests and concerns of the new British government', he told Rusk and McNamara.[65] Yet the British remained confused over the President's intentions. On one hand, continuing discussions in NATO fuelled further fears that a bilateral American-German deal over MLF was imminent. It was also reported that both the Dutch and Italian governments had agreed to the MLF irrespective of the British decisions.[66] In a conversation with MOD officials, Roswell Gilpatric, who was shortly to head a presidential task force on nuclear proliferation, rejected this saying that Johnson was not firmly wedded to MLF. Stating that 'It would be untypical of the president to have taken up an entirely rigid position' Gilpatric suggested that fresh proposals might be welcome.[67]

An important element of Patrick Gordon Walker's visit to Washington immediately following the election was therefore to try and clarify Washington's position on alliance nuclear issues. It was also intended to pave the way for the president's discussion with the prime minister at the end of the year and tentatively introduce the new Labour plan for nuclear sharing. In discussions from 26 to 27 October, Gordon Walker sketched out their new proposals:

> What HMG [Her Majesty's Government] was thinking was, Gordon Walker said, a larger nuclear force consisting of British V-bombers, British Polaris submarines, if HMG decided to buy a certain number of them (three or four), an equivalent number of American Polaris submarines, and a mixed-manned element (MLF), which would play a less conspicuous role than originally planned. UK element would be committed unconditionally with no 'national interest' withdrawal clause. Whole force would be co-targeted with U.S. national nuclear deterrent. Britain would like veto in new force but considered American veto essential.[68]

'Although Britain would not be taking part in part in the mixed-manned surface element', Gordon Walker told Rusk, 'they would be contributing to the wider force and would have no nuclear forces in the Atlantic area other than those in the new force. They would thus be on the same footing as the Germans.' This became known as the ANF.[69]

Exactly where this proposal originated remains something of a mystery, although Wilson later claimed he had thought of it while in the bath. Regardless, this astute move by the British guaranteed them an extremely strong bargaining position in the weeks that followed. It gave the initiative to the new Labour government over the Johnson administration by building upon the Thorneycroft plan developed at the end of the previous year. It also purportedly fulfilled part of its pre-election promise to 're-negotiate' the Nassau treaty and demonstrated to the US the likelihood of Labour retaining Polaris, which would then be given to NATO for the life of the alliance. Finally, at the end of the meeting Gordon Walker suggested that the British put forth firm proposals but that this should occur in conjunction with the West German government, perhaps an attempt to prevent Bonn from moving too close to Washington on this issue.[70]

MLF supporters now had to respond. In conversation with his boss Dean Rusk on the following morning, Ball insisted that they make clear their position in support of MLF when they met Gordon Walker for lunch. At that meeting, Ball told Gordon Walker that even if V-bombers and then Polaris were assigned to NATO (as envisaged in the Nassau agreement) Britain 'would be having its cake and eating it if she refrained from taking part in the MLF'. McNamara was equally cautious when he explained, 'there might be a problem for the USA in the cost of contributing both to the MLF and assigning some Polaris [submarines] to the new force [ANF]'. As Gordon Walker pointed out, however, this appeared to be what was envisaged in the Nassau agreement and he argued whether it would really be that much of a burden for the US to contribute three Polaris submarines to the force. He then went further perhaps than he should have when Ball asked how the Germans could be made to feel they were on an equal footing with the British, by suggesting 'that one conceivable way would be for Britain to give up their nuclear weapons and for the Germans likewise to agree not to seek such weapons'.[71]

Although the US and UK governments had their differences, Gordon Walker's trip was largely successful. Despite his belief that the British had not fully evaluated the respective economic merits of MLF and ANF, Ball (who now felt that 'he had the assignment on the MLF as far as the department was concerned') expressed satisfaction, saying that the American delegation had had a 'good discussion' with the British. William Tyler agreed they should tell Bonn that the British were flexible on the matter but they would not accept the proposal as it was and Bundy concurred with this. But Ball suggested that 'if the UK agreed to put its Polaris into an Atlantic force subject to US permissive link safeguards, with transfer of ownership and flag to an Atlantic command, it would be hard for the Labor Government to justify it to the British people since it would cost far more than the participation in the MLF'.[72] From the British perspective, there was a small victory in the US postponing the date of signing an initial MLF agreement from 15 to 31 January 1965, as result of Gordon Walker's trip.[73]

Initial US reaction to the new British proposals was not unfavourable.[74] 'The British Labour Party has adopted a much more flexible and interested posture than it had taken in opposition', Bundy informed the president at the beginning of November. He continued:

Our response has been to show interest and to emphasize the importance of finding a system which meets the interests of the Germans. But we recognize and respect the British desire not to buy a whole new weapons system just two years after Nassau (to specialists in this subject, what is fascinating is the very close relation between Labour's [sic] current attitude and that of the Home Government – the only important differences are those of political imagery and on the whole those differences may make it a little easier for Labour than for the Conservatives to join in a new package deal).

Following his well-observed comments, Bundy called on the president to take strong action and suggested that a decision on the subject needed to be taken 'over the next 6 to 9 months'.[75]

There was even some movement towards a compromise on the question of mixed-manning. In private, the British acknowledged that mixed-manning was the only way 'non-nuclear countries can be enabled to take part in ownership and manning of nuclear weapons systems within the force, without transgressing the principles of non dissemination'. In this way, they continued to appreciate the retention of an American veto.[76] Moreover, the embassy in Washington reported that the State Department had ordered an examination of committing the same number of US Polaris submarines as the British to NATO under the terms of an ANF-type agreement. This examination even mooted mixed-manning the fire control elements on a purely Anglo-American basis because it would be the easiest way to gain the assent of Congress. This force would, however, only comprise a part of the ANF and surface vessels would still be a major element.[77]

In the United Kingdom, defence planning now took place with the creation of ANF very much in mind and discussion of retaining Polaris centred on its place within some kind of ANF.[78] Moreover, the MOD Defence Study Group saw the ANF proposal as a way to retain British interests outside of NATO and hoped to persuade the Americans that, in return for a substantial British contribution to ANF, the US government might buy a major British weapon. But it recognized the limited British bargaining position in this area suggesting, 'if we try to obtain too many concessions we may only arouse suspicion about motives for proposing an Atlantic Nuclear Force'.[79] Burke Trend told Harold Wilson 'the [ANF] project may have considerable attractions for the Germans in so far as it offers them the prospect of something approaching equality of status with ourselves within the Alliance'. But Trend also admitted that this would depend upon the extent to which the British government was willing to surrender its nuclear deterrent to NATO.[80]

Yet the Germans were largely unimpressed with the new proposal. After being told of Gordon Walker's visit by Johnson, Erhard reaffirmed his commitment on MLF to the president, although de Gaulle's truculence had convinced the Chancellor that no treaty could be signed before the following year.[81] In the days that followed, reports circulated that Bonn and Washington were still wedded to the original MLF.[82] Returning from meetings in Bonn and Berlin, Ball informed Rusk that the Germans were still 'eager' to have an agreement on MLF as soon as possible. He also reported that they found the British concept of a mixed-manned element merely constituting one part of the NATO force 'disturbing', although they had taken no firm position against it. Moreover, while von Hassel told Rusk and McNamara that the addition of Polaris to the force 'might be desirable', TSR-2, TFX and Pershings could not be included because they had a fundamentally different role.[83]

The Chequers weekend and December summit

In London shortly after Walker's trip to Washington Wilson decided that a series of meetings would be held at Chequers, the prime minister's weekend residence, to discuss Britain's east of Suez position, balance of payments problems and the ANF in preparation for Wilson's meeting with President Johnson in early December.[84] In the days before the Chequers meeting opposition to MLF undoubtedly drove the development of the ANF scheme. Zuckerman suggested to Healey that the ability of Britain to promote its interests within the MLF had been overstated and that participation 'will not halt a continuing erosion of our special relationship with the United States'.[85] Trend was, however, not optimistic that ANF would halt progress on MLF, merely that it would force the US to let the timetable slip for a few months.[86]

The ANF offered several advantages to the Wilson government, however. It could demonstrate that the 'supreme national interests' clause of the Nassau agreement was now no longer in effect (although it is doubtful whether Wilson would have acknowledged this publicly). Instead, the UK's Polaris submarines would be committed 'irrevocably' to the alliance. More subtly, however, the new proposal dealt with the control issue to the UK's advantage. With each member's right to veto any firing decision taken, Labour devised a solution to the problem of physical control within the force. In effect, although the UK could be constrained by other nations, it in turn could constrain and therefore remain independent. Moreover, as Saki Dockrill has recently argued, the ANF was ambitiously designed to be linked to 'the entire spectrum of US strategic forces' so that Britain could in effect have a role in running the US nuclear deterrent.[87] Simultaneously, the cabinet perceived ANF as an excellent bargaining chip with the United States that might allow force reductions in other areas of the North Atlantic so that the British could concentrate on their world role.[88] Finally, it was less likely to provoke Soviet reactions, as it did not advance nuclear sharing as one of its tenets and held open the door for the French to join.[89] Schrafstetter and Twigge state that, 'the ANF was a tight non-proliferation treaty disguised as an offer for nuclear sharing on the basis of equality'.[90]

Unfortunately Labour's presentation of ANF was compromised by continued attacks on MLF. When Lord Kennet, a minister with special interest in disarmament issues, delivered a speech to the NATO Parliamentarians Conference on 19 November promoting the ANF, he argued against the military case for MLF and played down the nuclear ambitions of FRG, which was a 'law abiding state'.[91] Two days later, the Wilson cabinet met at Chequers. It discussed the British global situation, the need to make defence cuts and nuclear sharing. Specifically, plans for the ANF were developed in some detail.[92] When Wilson returned from Chequers, he gave a speech in the Commons on 23 November heavily criticizing MLF.[93] This worried MLF advocates after Wilson's careful diplomacy of the previous weeks. Although David Bruce struck a conciliatory note arguing once again that 'it is a build up for bargaining position', George Ball took little heed of this, telling Wilson later of his concern about its divisive intent and concluding that the prime minister had used 'Gaullist language'.[94]

Ball's enthusiasm had not, it seems, been dented by an incipient pessimism on MLF developing in the White House. In contrast, McGeorge Bundy had begun to reconsider his position. Just two weeks after writing to the president to urge a decisive action, Bundy told Ball 'I am reaching the conclusion that the US should now arrange to let the MLF sink out of sight', and therefore 'we should ask the president for authority to work towards a future in which the MLF does not come into existence'. He cited seven reasons on which he based this view, of which the first was 'a deeply reluctant and essentially unpersuaded Great Britain'. Bundy also mentioned other important factors: a divided ruling party in West Germany, a weak Italian government, a setback in the struggle to limit nuclear proliferation, a protracted fight with Congress, a constitutional debate on NATO and a blow to Franco-German relations. In a telling caveat he indicated that from his own conversations with Johnson, 'I am sure that he does not feel the kind of personal presidential engagement in the MLF itself which would make it difficult for him to strike out on a new course if we can find one which seems better. I believe we can.'[95]

Although ostensibly working together, the internal struggle over MLF was now becoming a personal dual between George Ball in the State Department and McGeorge Bundy in the White House. Presidential action could still have been used at this stage, but Ball was on the defensive. Bundy's subsequent actions towards the president were now to be crucial in the campaign for nuclear sharing.[96] His growing influence with the president and negative attitude towards the MLF prepared the way for a change in the US position, although he was careful to support the German position in public.[97]

As the hour of the summit between Wilson and Johnson approached, Washington's primary fear was of a rift with London that might produce a re-run of the Skybolt episode. On 27 November Richard Neustadt and George Ball were in London to prepare for the summit and Neustadt told Patrick Gordon Walker that 'the noises coming out of London were similar to those which had preceded the Nassau talks, namely that we were in great political difficulties and that we were going to try and get the Americans to help us out of them'. Gordon Walker said that this was definitely not the case and promoted the ANF forcefully, arguing once more that an American agreement to put submarines into a NATO force was in fact contained in the Nassau agreement. He claimed the British were abandoning their withdrawal clause in this agreement in order to rely upon the American clauses and 'we would look ill upon it if they tried to get out of them'.[98] In a subsequent meeting with the prime minister, Ball remained determined to avoid a bilateral agreement in Washington that would give 'to the other NATO allies the impression of an Anglo-Saxon deal'. He conceded, however, that the line had been crossed at Nassau and now it would be difficult for the US to renege on its earlier position and criticize British retention of some form of nuclear capability.[99] Gordon Walker suggested to the prime minister that confusion with Washington over the British position appeared to have arisen over the words 'negotiate' and 'hard-bargaining', which officials in the US equated too closely with each other.[100] In Washington, Harlech downplayed comparisons with the Nassau summit: 'The situation is quite unlike Nassau...on this occasion all we need to do is...to try and discover the points on which we were and were not in agreement and how far apart we were, and perhaps try to bridge the differences.'[101]

US attempts to avoid any misunderstanding with the new Labour government were underlined following the first set of serious internal discussions about ANF in Washington. When Gordon Walker had met Neustadt on 27 November, Neustadt had produced a memorandum detailing discussion between Ball, Tyler, Bundy, Neustadt and McNaughton examining how ANF could be made to fit into the plan for MLF. Although it stressed that any arrangement would, by necessity, have to be non-discriminatory towards the Germans as well as substantially involve the British, it tentatively suggested offering the British help if they decided to cancel the Polaris programme and convert to hunter-killers (as Washington believed was still being mooted). Alternatively, if the UK agreed to join MLF they would ensure that the costs did not exceed their present nuclear commitments. Unfortunately, the assembled US officials also indicated their unwillingness to sanction placing US submarines in equal number to British, as 'It would create a special position for the Anglo-Saxons which would be psychologically bad.' Ball had also called on Gordon Walker to emphasize the necessity of the British joining, although the foreign secretary had surmised from talks with Bundy that the American position was more flexible than Ball seemed to imply.[102]

Little of Bundy's antipathy towards MLF was known to the British, although it was obvious that he was not pushing for the nuclear solution with the same fervour as Ball. On 29 November, Bundy met Lord Caradon, British representative at the UN, and Harlech, telling them 'that if mistakes had been made at Nassau in 1962 it was essential to do the right thing now'. Any arrangement Wilson and Johnson came to the following month should satisfy the Europeans and that the MLF should at least receive British blessing, he said.[103] In contrast, he maintained pressure on Harlech, telling him at the end of the month that 'nothing less than real (as opposed to token) participation in a mixed-manned surface force would satisfy the Germans and Italians'.[104] The Italians confirmed this to Rusk at the beginning of December when Giuseppe Saragut said that if the British joined, '95% of the political difficulties with the MLF would disappear'.[105] On 5 December, Ball sent a memorandum to the president urging that any US nuclear sharing solution had to fall within the framework of MLF. This, Ball argued, would mollify both Germany and Italy, thus proving 'that the United Kingdom has no special position'. He attacked ANF and dismissed the notion that Wilson could not provide enough military personnel for the MLF.[106] In a cover note Bundy expressed his support for this position, but also suggested that a fallback position could be adopted that would place the onus for the failure of MLF on the Europeans rather than the United States.[107]

At this late stage, the president was still unfamiliar with the finer points of the MLF/ANF debate, as became acutely clear in the days preceding the Wilson visit. It was left to Bundy and McNamara to explain that if Germany was 'cut adrift' (Bundy's words) it might turn towards France for nuclear assistance, and Bruce, Ball and Bundy collectively to summarize the British position. First they stated Wilson needed to demonstrate his handling of the Anglo-American relationship; second, he had to reduce the defence budget without scrapping Polaris; third, he wanted to portray the talks as a success in order to bolster his prestige and fourth, he had to balance donating the British deterrent to NATO alongside German non-acquisition of nuclear weapons. Bruce concluded by drawing the president's attention to the assurance Ball and Neustadt had given to the British that their participation was a *sine qua non* for successful talks with both the US and Germans on MLF. If this was also how the president presented it, the British would have to concede.[108]

Johnson was not convinced by these arguments and intervened to ensure that the tide began to turn against nuclear sharing. It was now only the third time he had found it necessary to confront the nuclear sharing issue in over a year as president and all three had been because of external pressure. His actions during December effectively signalled an about turn from those he had taken in April and June. He now felt uneasy about riding roughshod over British government opinion: 'Aren't you telling me to kick mother England out the door into the cold, while I bring the Kaiser into the sitting room? How will that look to Americans?' he asked rhetorically. In response to a point made by Dean Acheson that Anglo-American links were not as important as they had once been, the president said that other factors were more important in modern America, particularly opinion 'in the press or on the Hill'. Continuing, he demonstrated the success of Wilson's organized opposition to MLF since October:

> The President asked what he was to do if Wilson said 'No soap' on British participation on surface ships. He thought this was what Wilson would say, given Wilson's own recently expressed opposition. It's the

stand he would take in Wilson's place. 'What do we say then', he asked, 'where do we move from there?' He then asked, 'And if by chance Wilson should say "o.k.," can we get it across in Congress?'

Bundy's report that 'Kennedy had grown increasingly cool' towards MLF and deciding it was not going anywhere he 'had begun to back away in the summer of 1963' raised the president's interest. So too did Bundy's reference to the 10 June 1963 memorandum he had written for Kennedy recommending slowing the MLF process.[109]

Johnson received this with customary indignation. He was clearly disturbed at not being kept up to date with important developments on the MLF and being forced to make a decision with so little time before a foreign leader arrived for a meeting that Bundy had told him would be the most important Anglo-American encounter since December 1962.[110] This led to a broad attack by the president on foreign policy information and advice he was receiving and US dealings in world affairs more generally. He was 'new here' and said he needed better advice. Yet 'He was in the position of a Jack Rabbit in a hail storm, "hunkered up and taking it"'. Johnson apparently spent time 'needling his aides in turn' and it was left to Acheson to break the tension, saying 'Mr. President, you don't pay these men enough for this; even with pay raise.'[111]

At this stage Bundy still recommended that the president go all out and convince Wilson to submit. Yet while he prepared a paper with Neustadt on Wilson's likely objections to the force, he commented 'if he does not say "yes" then I think we should have a very careful look... and my own current view is that we might wish to take a wholly new attitude toward this enterprise'.[112] But he cautioned Johnson to handle the new prime minister with care. Wilson attached great importance to his meeting and was eager for a 'successful' outcome. If he did not get one it might damage him: 'you are strong and he is weak, and you have much longer experience of real power', Bundy suggested in a reference to Johnson's recent landslide in the presidential election and Wilson's tiny parliamentary majority. In the extreme, humiliation for Wilson might lead him to strike out in 'an emotionally anti-American way'. Bundy in fact thought this a highly unlikely scenario, but he also gave his estimate that the chances of getting Wilson to agree to British participation in the mixed-manned surface fleet were approximately four to one.[113]

The following day Johnson reported that he had read Bundy's June 1963 memorandum and as far as he could see no one was for MLF – not the British, French, Congress or even the Germans. Just because Acheson was for it, LBJ argued, was not enough because Wilson would simply not come on board. While Bundy suggested the possibility of reaching an agreement without MLF, Ball and McNamara argued that this would merely confirm what the sceptics had believed all along – 'that Washington didn't want it'. Johnson, conveniently forgetting the contents of his April and June declarations, retorted that he did not believe this was true because no full commitment had been given, but Finletter persisted, arguing that Johnson's prestige was at stake in Europe. The president responded that there was no point in trying to save your face because 'you'll lose your ass'. In April, Johnson had believed JFK had been in favour of MLF, but after reading Bundy's memorandum he saw that this was not the case. Kennedy was right, he concluded: 'If Europe isn't for it, then the hell with it'.[114] Although the meeting continued, the course of action had been set, or as the president said: 'if we're forcing the British and not satisfying the Germans, and only getting 30 votes in the Senate – then the hell with it'.[115]

These two discussions were revealing for a number of reasons. First, they pitted Johnson against his advisers. Ball and Finletter clearly took a strongly pro-MLF line as they had in the previous two years and from this point onwards, Ball was isolated in his position. Yet it was the actions of figures such as Bundy and McNamara, who both advocated some form of MLF agreement that were most revealing. Even Bundy argued at the end of the first day's discussion that unlike mid-1963 when Macmillan's government was mired in the Profumo scandal, 'Now there was a new British government and a much more promising situation.'[116] If it is true that, in Saki Dockrill's words, 'As Bundy saw it, the project did not possess a single attractive feature', then Bundy was playing 'devil's advocate', or at least trying to demonstrate a broad minded view to the president during these discussions.[117] His covering memorandum to the June 1963 memorandum was written 'partly because I feel that we have not given you a full and fair statement of the case against pressing hard now for the MLF'. While listing the usual objections presented, he concluded:

> *If* you go half steam ahead, there will probably be no MLF, but it will not be your fault alone. You will have kept the letter and spirit of the Kennedy readiness to move if the Europeans wanted it. There will be trouble with the Germans, but nothing unmanageable. There will be plenty of opportunities for debate, discussions and delay, and for gradual and ceremonial burial. Your wisdom, caution and good judgement will have the praise of liberals, of military men, of the British, of the French and of many Germans – and you will have freedom to make a different choice later if you wish.[118]

In the final hours before Johnson met Wilson, Bundy suggested that excessive pressure should not be placed on Wilson and the meeting merely 'a matter of exploration and discussion without decision'.[119]

McNamara also remained adamant throughout the meetings that MLF was a viable military solution for the alliance. When Johnson noted that Mountbatten claimed MLF had little military utility, the defense secretary disagreed, saying 'Mountbatten had frightened successive British Governments'. Even on the second day (6 December), McNamara argued that if the US dropped MLF, SACEUR would still push for an adequate MRBM arrangement and therefore the whole European MRBM argument would erupt again. In McNamara's eyes therefore, a sea-based MRBM force was preferable to a land-based one.[120]

In Johnson and Wilson's first meeting of their summit on 7 December, during which no record was kept, the president took a relatively hard line. He told Wilson, 'our folk were damned tired of being told that it was their business to solve all the world's problems and do so mainly alone'. Johnson pressed Wilson on MLF but agreed that it was important to keep the US finger on the nuclear trigger. Wilson rejected the MLF outright on technical as well as political grounds.[121] He then officially offered ANF as an alternative. US officials examined the proposals overnight and produced comments for discussion the following day. But further US disorganization ensued on 8 December as Wilson arrived for talks with Johnson at 11.30 am, only to find the president in a meeting with his officials finalizing their position on MLF and the British proposals. Denis Healey apparently called this 'Ball's last stand'.[122]

There was no definitive conclusion to the meeting then held between Johnson and Wilson. The detailed discussions between the British and American parties merely produced a series of points on the US comments and an understanding between Johnson and Wilson that ANF would be considered without formal commitment. It was becoming increasingly clear, in Philip Geyelin's words that 'MLF would lie in limbo, available for use in whatever new formula might emerge, but no longer the centerpiece of US nuclear policy for NATO.'[123] Yet, as Saki Dockrill has shown, Wilson and Johnson's first meeting of Wilson's premiership was not an unsuccessful affair, despite Wilson's relative inexperience as prime minister and wafer thin parliamentary majority making his political position uncertain. The British approach of working from their worldwide commitments towards European issues may have created 'a warm atmosphere throughout the Washington talks', but the careful preparation, awareness of mistakes at Nassau and luxury of producing only general consensus undoubtedly helped.[124] When discussing his plans to make a speech on NATO and nuclear issues, Wilson even apologized for his 'blooper' in late November, when he had attacked MLF in Parliament. He claimed that this had been made because of the need to carry his own party and the 'Gaullist' opposition of the Conservatives.[125]

Like the Nassau communiqué of December 1962, the joint statement issued by President Johnson and Harold Wilson on 8 December 1964 following their two days of discussion was open ended. The statement ranged over a number of topics, but in relation to NATO and the MLF:

> They recognized the importance of strengthening the unity of the Atlantic Alliance in its strategic nuclear defense. They discussed existing proposals for this purpose and an outline of some new proposals presented by the British Government. They agreed that the objective in this field is to cooperate in finding the arrangements which best meet the legitimate interests of all members of the alliance, while maintaining existing safeguards on the use of nuclear weapons, and preventing their further proliferation.[126]

Significantly no mention was made of MLF itself, although it had certainly not been removed from the NATO agenda at this point. It was, however, the beginning of the end for MLF, this meeting between prime minister and president marking the completion of one stage of nuclear sharing development plans and the beginning of another.

The fallout

Following the summit with Wilson, the president was left feeling dissatisfied. In the days afterwards, Johnson complained so much and questioned the value of having such meetings that Bundy had to reassure him.[127] Bundy also wrote to David Bruce in London in order to make the president's position clear, suggesting he warn Wilson off making any rash remarks in the House of Commons (the memory of the 23 November speech still in his mind). Moreover, Bruce was instructed to tell Wilson that Johnson would take a very different attitude towards the discussions if Wilson gave the impression that he had 'won a victory'.[128] Yet the US government had now accepted ANF as an alternative to MLF.[129]

Johnson's action in response to the talks with Wilson was to re-direct the course of the nuclear sharing issue. On 17 December 1964, the president produced NSAM 322 giving Rusk and McNamara 'guidelines for discussions on the nuclear defence of the Atlantic Alliance'. In short, Johnson informed the two secretaries that they were no longer to press any American proposals for nuclear sharing onto their European NATO allies:

> Unless I give specific instructions to the contrary, I do not wish any American official in any forum to press for a binding agreement at this time. I wish to maintain the positions established in our talks with Prime Minister Wilson – namely that the US is not seeking to force its views on any European nation, but wishes rather to find a way of responding effectively to the largest possible consensus among interested European allies.[130]

With this stroke he had sounded the death knell of plans for nuclear sharing and the MLF office was abolished.[131] Immediately following the Wilson visit, Frederick G. Dutton, a Democratic Congressman from California, wrote to McGeorge Bundy urging the president to sound out both Democratic and Republican opinion over the force, as there were many reservations in Congress. In a wry comment, Bundy noted to the president, 'I think you have anticipated him and probably you have as clear a sense if the current state of Congressional opinion as he does.'[132]

In Europe, many now had the impression that the MLF was no more. Even before 1964 was over a British official in Washington was quoted in the *New York Times* as saying that 'we are preparing to do nothing' over nuclear sharing. The New NATO secretary general, Manlio Brosio, appeared downcast with the current turn of events, but claimed that there would be new arrangements for nuclear forces within the alliance. French Foreign Minister, Maurice Couve de Murville, was not so sure and reacted with some glee to these developments, telling the British Ambassador that he believed MLF would now never come off 'since the differences between various protagonists will cause the whole project to collapse.'[133]

Yet President Johnson had not totally stopped progress on the MLF. Dean Rusk asserted afterwards that it did not take presidential action, 'it just required an understanding that we would not press the matter. We'd simply leave it on the table and let it die there.'[134] MLF did not die a quick death and the plan for nuclear sharing within the alliance remained for a considerable time after December 1964. Indeed, the momentum that had kept it going for the previous years could not just be turned off when it suited the president. Within the State Department, some were willing to keep the idea at the forefront of NATO politics, particularly now an alternative to MLF existed. Official support in Germany was also still reasonably strong and Wilson turned to the promotion of ANF in Europe and especially the FRG. He told the German foreign minister, Gerhard Schroeder, days after his return from the US that ANF had support in Washington and 'amounted to a credible deterrent with all participating countries equal in status'.[135] Wilson also mentioned a poll that showed growing support for such a force.[136]

The ongoing debate about the future of Polaris influenced the British government's ideas about the ANF. Labour conceived ANF as a receptacle for the Polaris deterrent with the submarines assigned to the force and only returned to British control in the event of the break-up of the NATO. Nuclear status assured greater control and diplomatic influence in the ANF if it ever came into existence and, as Healey told the prime minister in December, the decision to 'continue with a Polaris submarine Programme of some kind' was 'a corner-stone of our proposals or an Atlantic Nuclear Force'.[137] Furthermore, in January, Healey told Wilson that at least three submarines, and even better four, would help secure 'a significant American contribution of submarines and of eliminating or reducing the mixed manned surface component'.[138] Simultaneously, they conceived of a Polaris deployment in the Far East at some point in the future, which would be much more complex with only three submarines and much easier with five.[139] When Labour announced it would retain Polaris but cancel the fifth boat, it stressed the importance it attached to ANF in making this decision and that Britain could still make an 'effective contribution' to alliance defence.[140] The Foreign Office instructed its delegation to explain to NATO colleagues that 'this decision affects the terms of our offer to the proposed ANF'.[141]

In Washington, the prevailing view outside the State Department was that with the rise of the ANF and Johnson's refusal to press for a speedy solution, termination of plans for MLF was underway. Neustadt told Bundy at the beginning of January that he was glad the MLF had been laid to rest and he hoped 'we'll soon have heard the last of it'.[142] It was also significant that presidential adviser on disarmament John J. McCloy's memorandum to Gilpatric of the same day was written in the past tense:

> The MLF may have been clumsily presented and handled, but it was in an attempt to create a sense of collective security which would preclude return to national power balances...in my judgement, the concept of which it partook must now be abandoned in favour of a laissez-faire attitude such as we appear to be assuming.

Yet the MRBM and nuclear sharing issue remained and parenthetically McCloy urged that the British, Germans and Italians should still reach a rapid decision on laissez-faire arrangements, as drift could lead to deterioration in the alliance.[143] Bundy was keen to stress to the president, however, that 'his famous NSAM was a shift of tactics not of principle. He has not abandoned MLF. He regards it as a constructive proposal aimed at a real need.' Bundy wanted the president to make clear to both the British and the Germans that he had not abandoned the MLF or ANF.[144] And Gilpatric's committee on nuclear proliferation concluded that MLF policy should be carefully reviewed if any headway was to be made on an NPT, especially as it was clear that the MLF was 'a divisive factor' in NATO.[145]

Pressure still existed from within the State Department on combining elements of both MLF and ANF plans while progressing towards British surrender of their Polaris force, and these elements converged to drive the nuclear sharing policy from this point onwards. As Dean Rusk informed Gerhard Schroeder on 13 January:

> The British Government has now come up with an approach which we believe can, through negotiation, be accommodated to the principles we have been advocating in the MLF. In fact, in our view the ANF proposals can leave room for the MLF substantially as it was initially conceived. Moreover, a broader nuclear arrangement, such as the British propose, introduces a new and important dimension in creating the possibility of the United Kingdom's divesting itself of its independent nuclear deterrent.[146]

George Ball and the 'theologians' were more vocal. Ball pressed for a resolution of the nuclear issue in the short-term, bringing him into conflict with McGeorge Bundy once again.[147] Supporters within the military even suggested that the MLF proposal could be made more attractive to Europeans by dangling the carrot of the successor to Polaris in front of them. Although the weapon was in its early stages of development and would not be operational until 1970, it could feasibly be fitted to surface ships designed for Polaris A-3, just as in US Navy submarines designed for the same weapon.[148] In February, new British Foreign Secretary, Michael Stewart, met with Robert Schaetzel, Deputy Assistant Secretary of State for Atlantic Affairs, who said he believed the president required a decision on the nuclear sharing issue by the end of the year. He also informed Stewart that the president's recent inactivity on this issue was 'purely tactical'.[149]

Later the same month, Rusk proposed sending messages to European leaders, notably Wilson and Erhard, suggesting that they reach a decision to press forward with a MLF agreement as soon as possible. The president responded saying that neither Wilson nor Erhard was in any doubt about his position and there was also likely to be little movement before the German elections late in 1965. In response, Bundy 'wondered whether we should not ask ourselves a few hard questions about the whole MLF concept before we agree to any serious multilateral discussion in the spring and summer'. He was now, he said, reaching the conclusion that the MLF was never going to be the right step for all nations and perhaps they be should thinking about other alternatives 'which may be more modest but which are also more likely to happen'.[150]

By the time Patrick Gordon Walker (now out of government having lost his parliamentary seat) met William Tyler in March the president had decided not to pressure Wilson. Tyler reported that 'GW dismissed any prospects of reaching agreement' and claimed that not only had the Americans ended the MLF but the ANF as well because they had left it to the Europeans and 'This they were incapable of doing.'[151] Wilson now had to balance his support for ANF with continued opposition to anything that looked like MLF. In March the prime minister claimed that Erhard had told him he was not going to press the nuclear sharing matter this side of the German election and had agreed with Wilson that the MLF and ANF should both be 'a [sic] sort of sleeping beauty'.[152] Yet simultaneously he was also talking about the prospect of the ANF coming into being and the potential need to balance it with a Pacific nuclear force. This was quickly quashed as the US could always deploy more ships and submarines east of Suez and the prime minister felt it was unwise to end up 'being dragged at the American chariot wheels in an area where our policies sometimes differ', particular in regard to policy on China and Vietnam.[153] Once again in May, Healey assured Brosio that the MRBM solution could now be found through ANF, so that the SACEUR could have some of the most sophisticated weaponry in Western Europe at his command.[154] Even Mountbatten was willing to endorse ANF when he wrote an article for the *NATO letter*. He also discussed the British military effort in NATO at this time, noting that 85 per cent of the British fleet was earmarked for the North Atlantic area and even the east of Suez commitment could be recalled.[155]

The fortunes of the MLF suffered further during May as the activities of the MLF Working Group in Paris were slowed. Rusk told Brosio that this had occurred as an accommodation to the Federal Republic rather than to France or Russia, as the Germans did not want to push the nuclear sharing subject in the run-up to their elections. It was still in everyone's interest to keep some form of discussion going, however.[156] The previous month an intelligence paper had concluded that 'The outlook for agreement on such a force is not bright, partly because of British-German differences, but particularly because the Germans and others are anxious to avoid a confrontation with de Gaulle over the question.'[157]

By the time the demonstration ship *Ricketts* arrived in European ports during the spring and early summer of 1965, political and media interest in the nuclear sharing project was noticeably waning. The MMD had experienced some difficulties during its first weeks and months that had highlighted potential issues that would be raised by mixed-manning a whole fleet of ships.[158] By the spring of 1965 these problems had largely been overcome and the ship successfully completed a series of tests in the Mediterranean with the US Sixth Fleet.[159] Yet with the declining fortunes of MLF, European governments became reluctant to entertain the ship which led George Ball to issue a memorandum reinforcing the view that no country was to be pressured into receiving the vessel against its will. David Bruce concurred with Ball's instruction, suggesting that it was pointless 'to spend our diplomatic capital for so little purpose'.[160]

Government opinion in the UK remained cautious over the possibility of a port call from the mixed-manned ship.[161] In a note to his private secretary, Wilson wrote that he was, 'Not keen. They must know we entirely reserve our position [therefore] no celebrations.'[162] His reticence was related to the American Embassy in London.[163] Yet a low-key visit was agreed and Wilson stressed that no special attention should be given to the ship, although he commented that the press handling had been 'very sound'.[164] The low-key visit passed off with little incident. Press coverage was reasonably broad and largely favourable, and the captain told *The Times* that he 'had no doubt that what they set out to prove had been proved'.[165]

Yet the entire nuclear hardware sharing concept was now under attack from a different perspective. At the NATO ministerial meeting held from 31 May to 1 June in Paris, McNamara apparently 'out of the blue' and with no consultation of the State Department suggested a 'defence ministers select committee' to consult on nuclear issues. This was, McNamara said, with a view to improving allied communications, consultation and participation in conjunction with other measures. In the medium term this move substantially changed the political complexion of the nuclear sharing issue.[166] But initially McNamara and colleagues were eager to assert that it was in no way intended to cut across or replace the ANF/MLF discussions.[167] The Committee idea certainly did not faze Healey, who told McNamara 'In Paris it became clear that our ANF idea was [the] front runner.'[168] Continued British support for ANF was reiterated later that month as part of the British NATO Intermediate Review.[169]

The reaction of MLF advocates to the consultation committee was negative. There remained much confusion as to exactly what the new scheme promised and David Klein told Bundy that the State Department was trying to play down McNamara's idea, 'especially since the theologians see this as a possible poor man's MLF'.[170] Thomas Finletter's reaction was also telling. Finletter had been disaffected with US NATO policy since the Johnson–Wilson talks in December the previous year. Now he informed the NAC 'he proposed to recommend to Mr McNamara to drop the whole idea of arranging these consultations in NATO and to make such arrangements as he liked with individual Ministers of Defence'.[171]

By October McNamara was hinting to the British that the nuclear sharing venture, including ANF, might be nearing an end but that the Germans would be bought off only by adding 'some substance' to the committee.[172] Bundy, who recommended to George Ball what he called 'a fresh start on nuclear defense' the same month, now openly supported McNamara's position in Washington. Facing such opposition, Ball retaliated, arguing that a collective nuclear arrangement was the only way the German people would feel on a level with the British.[173] Others also refused to concede that the McNamara consultation proposal precluded the likelihood of nuclear sharing. Ronald Spiers argued as much when he claimed that the 'hardware solution' was still the best one for the nuclear problems of NATO.[174] Moreover, some of the 'theologians' tried to try extract political capital from the success of the *Ricketts* demonstration as it ended at the start of December.[175] As expected, the British did not react favourably to this and questioned the value of the demonstration.[176]

Yet even in the face of the McNamara proposal offering a chance to escape from a commitment on nuclear sharing Wilson clung to ANF. He explicitly told Harlan Cleveland, Finletter's successor as US NATO Ambassador, in mid-October that 'we still want ANF', although he rejected mixed-manning on board nuclear submarines or any other component of the force, implying that the units would be nationally manned with a mixed command structure. He also reiterated the UK veto requirement and the possible need to deploy east of Suez in an emergency.[177] By November the private Downing Street view was finally moving towards a straight decision between consultation, which might lead to an NPT, and nuclear hardware for Germany, where pro-MLF Erhard had been re-elected in September. Oliver Wright advised the prime minster that although the need for a decision between these two options might not appeal to Ball and the 'boys in blinkers at the State Department', it should appeal to McNamara and 'even more so to the President'.[178] Yet even at this late stage Healey still saw the consultative committee only as partial solution and looked to stimulate a discussion between himself, von Hassel and McNamara on 'wider nuclear issues'. Healey believed 'that the Germans for their part would welcome a firm commitment on the part of the United States Government to put into the ANF, or any form of collective force, the same number of Polaris submarines as the British are prepared to contribute'. Healey wanted to make clear, however, that any force would exclude mixed-manned components as McNamara had now informed Healey of his opposition to the concept.[179] Possibly in an effort to prevent the spread of rumours about the possible cancellation of Polaris,[180] Healey told NATO defence ministers of the newly formed nuclear consultation committee that that the whole of the Polaris fleet would be committed to a 'collective NATO force', regardless of whether the ANF came into existence.[181]

Throughout December, the official British position remained one of approval for ANF. When Wilson and Johnson met again, the prime minister reiterated his continued support for it and stressed his appreciation of Johnson's action the previous year in holding back from endorsement of MLF. This time Johnson was willing to accommodate the prime minister on the issue, stressing the difference in judgement between the German attitude and US–UK position. Moreover, discussion of nuclear sharing was of less importance than the previous year, taking place along with a cluster of other pressing issues such as the Rhodesian crisis, Vietnam and the impending British defence review. While Wilson expressed his preference for the nuclear consultative committee, he told officials that the ANF proposal was still on the table. LBJ assured him that he would not push MLF onto the prime minister as Wilson was still new to the job and the president 'did not want to foul up our relations being difficult on this'.[182] Even assignment of Polaris submarines to NATO with anything that even resembled shared ownership seemed to be 'tricky'. While it had appeared to be a possibility as recently as the previous month, Bundy reported, it was now much more doubtful.[183]

The president's refusal to press nuclear sharing onto the Europeans was confirmed in subsequent talks between the US and Germans, despite pressure from leading 'theologians'.[184] Gerhard Schroeder expressed his interest in the ANF proposal as a cornerstone of a MLF, recognizing the unacceptability of the original American proposal to other NATO members.[185] Yet, as Schroeder told the British Ambassador in Bonn, the ANF would have nothing to offer the Germans if it consisted of just US and UK submarines. In fact, the West German Government now designed a compromise solution that combined elements of ANF and the McNamara committee, comprising nationally manned US and UK submarines and multilateral control, but with some smaller NATO countries excluded from the latter.[186]

Perhaps even at this late stage presidential pressure could have been brought to bear on the UK and other European countries to force an agreement, but it seemed unlikely. When Wilson wrote to Johnson at the beginning of the New Year, he spoke only of the Nuclear Planning Working Group.[187] This led Bundy to comment that Wilson was 'moving away from the common nuclear force just as fast as he politely can'.[188] Although the president informed David Bruce that he still supported a US–UK–Germany agreement whereby the British and Americans might put in submarines and the West Germans just money, he explicitly rejected pushing the British to make a speedy decision and, as Bundy put it, 'make a hard issue of this question' in doing so. As Bundy saw it:

> My own impression is that the President is sympathetic to the German desire for a 'share', but strongly aware of the opposition which such an arrangement might produce among important groups here and abroad. He wants to go ahead with it if an agreement can be reached by the normal process of negotiation and discussion, but he is not willing to apply pressure at this stage.[189]

When David Bruce explained the president's position to Wilson, it must have seemed obvious that the Labour Government had successfully held its position. With nuclear sharing now moving into the background and the *Ricketts* demonstration completed, the presidential tactics of allowing matters to take their course were working very effectively. In February Sir Patrick Dean, the new British ambassador in Washington, suggested to the foreign secretary that '1965 was something of a year of drift'. Ignoring the nuclear planning committee proposal, Dean argued that in spite of slowing the progress on MLF/ANF, Johnson had offered no clear alternative or allowed one to emerge.[190]

This inaction from the president increasingly suited Wilson, who was now retreating from his position on ANF in favour of the consultative approach. Wilson told Bruce, he was still totally opposed to the Germans getting their hands on nuclear hardware and so a hardware solution was now out of the question and when the prime minister wrote to Johnson in February of 1966 he concentrated once again on the nuclear committee's utility as a 'forum for discussion of nuclear policy, strategy and planning'. But he insisted on telling the president that he had informed the Soviet government during his recent visit to Moscow that nuclear sharing was the best way to prevent German demands.[191] Moreover, the Labour Party's manifesto for the election in March included a reaffirmation of the ANF commitment.[192] But just two days before Labour was returned to power with an increased majority, Wilson told the president that he believed nuclear sharing was now no longer an option for the alliance.[193]

As late as April, Rusk wrote to the president voicing his continued support for nuclear sharing and arguing that the US should push ahead in order to strengthen the NATO military structure. While MLF advocates may have had a hand in the writing of this missive, the secretary of state told the president that the French withdrawal had brought the nuclear sharing issue to fore once more. Despite the rise of McNamara's consultative committee, or Nuclear Planning Group (NPG) as it became known, Rusk apparently saw the British 'playing games' with their independent deterrent and ANF. It was not, Rusk insisted, a direct competition between hardware and consultative solutions as the British appeared to believe.[194] And with de Gaulle's move to withdraw French forces from NATO's integrated military structure, thus provoking a political crisis within the alliance, there were calls to revive MLF in order to strengthen NATO and reassure West Germany.[195]

But with consultation now the preferred option Johnson issued an NSAM on 22 April that explicitly required examination of both consultative and hardware approaches. Yet it assumed that a 'NATO Nuclear Force' would be agreed upon after a consultative approach (and perhaps arising out of it) and ruled out either mixed-manning of submarines or the creation of a surface fleet capable of delivering nuclear weapons within any such force. This move was a typical Johnson tactic to counter accusations of inaction without forcing solutions on the Europeans and to encourage broader aims of alliance cohesion at a time when it was under attack from the French president.[196] At best MLF advocates could now look forward to a 'halfway house' with assignment of some units to a NATO force.[197]

Even Johnson's correspondence with the prime minister in May on the issue (following Wilson's return to power with an increased majority and a few days before Wilson met Erhard), despite its hectoring tone, was half-hearted, calling for Britain and the US to reassure the Germans in the wake of Nassau, the MLF and the ANF. Yet the president told Wilson 'I do not mean that I am wedded to any particular solution to this problem. We are doing staff work over a whole range of options. We should not foreclose any of them.'[198]

The US–UK position was now almost exactly in line. In May when Healey met Paul Nitze, the two agreed that in view of current French policy it was important not to mention MLF because it was likely to cause controversy between members of the alliance.[199] And in preparation for meetings the following month, the State Department stated candidly that the collective force option was 'Not now recommended'.[200]

The position of the Federal Republic was also changing. In July, the American Embassy in Bonn reported that despite nuclear hardware sharing remaining a long-term ideal for the West German Government, both Schroeder and von Hassel felt that they might be willing to give it up 'under certain circumstances', namely that the NPG evolved into an acceptable forum for nuclear planning and crisis management with good communications.[201] In Walt Rostow's words, the president simply did not want to 'wring the German necks' over this decision, but wanted to press ahead with the committee as events appeared to evolving in a healthy direction.[202] Rostow was also changing his view. By September he saw a nuclear non-proliferation agreement as a greater priority that any nuclear sharing agreement with the Europeans, arguing that the Soviets might accept American proposals for non-proliferation if Washington agreed that any future arrange-ments with Europeans, excluding those with the existing nuclear powers Britain and France, would exclude the US giving up its veto.[203] Furthermore, the fall of the Erhard government in September removed another key State Department ally on nuclear sharing. This was shortly followed by the US administration's sudden announcement in October 1966 that it had successfully agreed a treaty on non-proliferation with the Soviets.[204] The Johnson administration's equivocation on nuclear sharing has finally paid off. At the end of the year, Harold Wilson observed that the 'hardware solution' to the NATO nuclear problem looked as if it was finished.[205]

The MLF episode had been a debilitating experience for Washington and London. It had highlighted some of the differences in their respective approaches to alliance policy. But it had also demonstrated that the US government was far from certain that nuclear sharing was the correct solution for other NATO mem-bers. Ultimately, this allowed Wilson to exploit the situation to his advantage, first through the ANF, which then led directly to McNamara's suggestion of a consul-tative approach. It also resulted from the latitude both Kennedy and particularly Johnson had allowed their advisers. The 'theologians' in particular had been given a huge amount of room in which to press forward with their plans. But when Johnson intervened, he did so with considerable skill. Paul Hammond calls this the 'heroic presidency'.[206] The result was that the slow move away from MLF during 1965 and 1966 did relatively little damage to his prestige in NATO.[207]

With NPG work progressing by the end of 1966, the MLF and ANF were now unnecessary.[208] The State Department concluded that the Germans would probably maintain a public position calling for a hardware solution within the alliance but that the nuclear committee could satisfy them in the long term.[209] State admitted publicly on 12 December that although there was no notion of the NPG substituting MLF/ANF, there was no hardware solution in sight either.[210] When the NSC met the next day, McNamara expressed his relief that the situation now appeared to be resolved and that the NPG would 'end talk of the Multilateral Force'.[211]

7

ALLIES UNDER STRAIN

In an interview conducted shortly after the end of Johnson administration, Harlan Cleveland, who became the US permanent representative to NATO at the end of 1965, claimed that President Johnson was 'not very much interested [in NATO] because it wasn't producing very many problems and therefore it wasn't very interesting'. Moreover, Johnson's growing obsession with Vietnam resulted in his constant desire to explain to NATO why the US was acting in the way it was.[1]

If Cleveland is correct, Johnson's view of NATO was understandable. When he became president, the crises over the status of Berlin and nuclear weapons in Cuba were still both fresh in policy-makers' minds, maintaining a level of high tension between Moscow and Washington. Since then the alliance had stabilized. The onset of a thaw between NATO and the nations of the Warsaw Pact ushered in troop withdrawals and a reassessment of US commitments in Europe and the North Atlantic. Concurrently, rapid escalation of the American military presence in South Vietnam coincided with the end of the nuclear sharing issue. At the beginning of 1966 the US had almost 185,000 military personnel in South Vietnam, a figure that would rise above 385,000 by the end of the year.[2]

Yet this prognosis ignores some crucial factors. First, the failure of MLF had left many in the US and Europe uneasy about nuclear and military prospects for the alliance despite the existence of the NPG. The German question therefore still loomed large while alliance military planners continued to argue that shortfalls in MRBMs required urgent attention. As Johnson recognized in his numerous explanations of US Vietnam policy to alliance members, a tension had developed between the global and regional perspectives of alliance policy. Although NATO by its nature operated as a regional alliance, it had much broader implications. And as the US began to focus on Asia in its struggle for cold war supremacy the impact on the debate about NATO strategy was highly significant. By 1967, for example, half the US attack carriers, eight destroyers and one ammunition ship from North Atlantic waters had been reassigned to the Western Pacific. This increased in 1968.[3]

Escalation of the war in Vietnam also exacerbated already tense relations with the French and de Gaulle's resounding election victory in January 1966 afforded him the opportunity to renew his attack on NATO. With the treaty up for renewal in 1969 the Americans began making contingency plans for a French withdrawal. De Gaulle feared that the war in Southeast Asia might result in the US dragging the Europeans into a war with China while he also believed that the reduced threat from the Soviet Union rendered NATO increasingly outmoded. He therefore sought better links with Moscow and the nations of the east bloc.[4] Johnson dealt with de Gaulle's challenge fairly calmly, thus steadying the NATO ship. Most memorably he summed up his attitude to de Gaulle saying, 'when a man asks you to leave his house, you don't argue; you get your hat and go'.[5] Yet the French actions intensified debate about the purpose of NATO and reaffirmed that a nuclear hardware sharing agreement was not going to be reached.[6]

While the US spat with de Gaulle united the British and Americans, in other areas tensions developed. This was ironic when both wanted to maintain British global commitments and acknowledged the strain of, but need for, the British Army's presence in West Germany. Yet the British defence position was chronic. When Labour entered office in late 1964 defence spending was projected to grow over the next five years under Tory spending plans, despite a trade deficit, a weak pound sterling and a growing balance of payments problem.[7] If Labour was to maintain a worthwhile global defence presence it would need to address growing defence expenditure in the light of these adverse economic conditions, suggesting that defence cuts would have to be made. While one such cut could have been the Polaris deterrent, Labour reasoned that retention of it might allow cuts in other less politically sensitive areas of defence, particular in NATO, to ease the defence burden. During 1965, the financial situation had grown worse and reached crisis point with a balance of payments deficit and the distinct possibility of the devaluation of sterling. With its implications for the US dollar, this necessitated the Americans stepping in with a rescue package.[8] By the end of 1965 the US was extremely concerned about more defence cuts, which would have implications for the US and therefore had to be discussed at the 'highest level'.[9] During 1966 and 1967 therefore the British government progressively strove to trim the defence budget in order to bring it within acceptable and stable limits. A figure of £2000 million sterling was set and the MOD was asked to find savings of £400 million in the defence review. Yet this was not enough and more cuts were then required.[10]

The Vietnam War also caused major problems because it impacted on so many other areas of mutual concern. Wilson had to balance both his domestic constituencies while mollifying the US administration, but it quickly became clear that his refusal to send troops to support the American effort was a source of resentment to the Americans and LBJ in particular. Some in Washington even suggested that propping up the British economically should only be done in return for a British commitment in Vietnam. Thus the British bargaining position with the US was weak because of sterling and the need for assistance in dealing with the crisis in Rhodesia, and Wilson always had to acknowledge Labour support for US policy in Vietnam. This support was mostly no more than verbal but it also included British maintenance of their long-standing presence east of

Suez.[11] These tensions were then exacerbated by Wilson's mediation efforts in the war, especially during early 1967.[12]

Yet during 1966 and 1967, there were considerable achievements in NATO, and London and Washington found much common ground.[13] Much of this was due to strong levels of coordination at various levels of the defence and foreign policy establishments. Perhaps the most important relationship was between Healey and McNamara. Healey acknowledges the importance of this relationship, although he is also critical of McNamara's style.[14] Yet their personal and working relationship was strong, as epitomized by Healey's note to McNamara after a visit to Washington in February 1966: 'I was, as always, delighted to have the chance of a talk with yourself, and I found our half an hour together in the Pentagon on Friday afternoon particularly valuable.'[15]

Up to 1968, the US government's perennial aim towards both Britain and France was to prevent them becoming too inward looking as the process of de-colonisation took hold.[16] This reduced allied emphasis on NATO at a time when it was increasingly difficult for these countries to maintain a world role. In the UK, the worsening economic situation meant Britain's global position was increasingly precarious from 1964. Military spending was set to rise year on year, a key factor for Labour in its decision not only to cancel the fifth Polaris submarine but also the P-1154, HS-681 and TSR-2 aircraft. With these cancellations a ceiling of £2000 million was set for defence, while a promise to maintain east of Suez commitments was renewed. In order to achieve this, the government made deals with the US to purchase F-111 (formerly known as TFX), Phantom F-4 jets and Hercules transport planes. Labour was therefore willing to play down the importance of NATO both because of its desire to maintain a worldwide role and because of the pressure from the US to do so. In a speech shortly after becoming the prime minister, Harold Wilson had famously declared, 'We are a world power, and a world influence, or we are nothing at all.'[17] But this continued adherence to global commitments in the first years of power demonstrated that the new government could not match its aspirations to fiscal reality.[18]

The 1966 White Paper

When Labour had taken power in late 1964 the east of Suez question was still high on its agenda. No fundamental reassessment of the UK global role had yet taken place and major defence projects were still being planned with the Middle and Far East in mind.[19] The new carrier for the Royal Navy, for example, was designed for forward defence in distant territory and to relieve pressures on the current carrier force.[20] In struggling to maintain worldwide commitments, British NATO forces were permanently under pressure and Labour did little to redress this early on. As a result, throughout 1965 the Royal Navy had to remove escorts and other vessels from the Mediterranean for duties elsewhere.[21]

With ANF still on the agenda, NATO continued to be of vital importance to Anglo-American relations, but this pressure to prolong global commitments was taking it toll. In the first months of the Labour government, Burke Trend warned the prime minister:

> It is not easy to strike a fair balance between these conflicting consider-
> ations. But I should have thought that, at the present moment, when we
> are trying to reinforce the cohesion of the Alliance, particularly by our
> ANF project, we should be chary of any action which might seem to
> throw doubt onto our commitment to NATO.[22]

The MOD believed that the decision to retain Polaris and the ANF proposal had both demonstrated British commitment, and indeed its nuclear guarantee, to the alliance thus giving them a strong voice. As Healey argues, the cost of running Polaris was low and possessing the deterrent gave Britain a greater opportunity to participate in the strategy debate, as well as reinforcing the credibility of the American deterrent itself.[23]

Unfortunately for Healey while the UK financial situation was growing worse the desperate political and military situation in Vietnam resulted in increased US pressure for Britain to stand firm in its global position and maintain its land forces in Germany. Healey was realistic about Britain's ability to play these dual roles. In the middle of 1965 Healey informed McNamara that a major defence review was underway to ascertain how money could be saved and commitments cut or shared. The US secretary of defense was wary of such measures and urged restraint. McNamara did not see a naval intervention capability in NATO as a vital area for the UK to pursue and suggested that any cuts should be made in the navy, especially in the Atlantic. For his part, Healey was ready to curtail the United Kingdom's global 'intervention capability', which had proved to be so problematic in previous years.[24]

While Healey questioned the efficacy of globally committed naval forces, land forces in Europe concerned McNamara most. Naval forces were less politically sensitive than those on land, and McNamara foresaw congressional dissent brewing over the issue. Specifically, he was fearful that a cut in British forces based in Germany would provoke political reaction in the US, and a possible questioning of why US forces should be committed to Europe when Europeans were not concerned with their own defence.[25] The following month, McNamara reiterated this view. He told Chancellor of the Exchequer James Callaghan that it was possible for the British to reduce their defence expenditure from £2200 million to under £2000 million without reducing their political commitments around the world. Instead, the NATO area could be adjusted. To this end, the US could help by avoiding 'duplication' with the UK. McNamara warned Callaghan in no uncertain terms that cutting British commitments in either Germany or the area between Aden and Hong Kong would have what he called a 'deleterious effect on our own, on UK and on free-world interests'. In order to help the British, McNamara told Callaghan that other difficult decisions, like the cancellation of the RAF's tactical strike aircraft TSR-2, would have to be taken.[26] As the economic crisis deepened for the British, Washington's position remained that it was east of Suez and the BAOR that were sacrosanct.[27]

Therefore Washington was 'caught in a paradox' by demanding that the British persist in progressively more de-stabilizing tactics in order for the Americans to be able to continue with their own global role.[28] It required some cuts in the NATO area in order to continue UK deployments in the global sphere, but Labour knew the political difficulty of making such cuts without disturbing NATO authorities, allies and the electorate. This was without consideration of the economic factors making east of Suez and BAOR cutbacks more attractive. Participants at a State-Defense meeting in Washington in October 1965 concluded that US strategic interests would be adversely affected if the UK reduced its commitments either in NATO or the east of Suez area. But the situation looked bleak; a reorientation of present British commitments to NATO while attempting to economize would lead to a further degradation of forces and the US Joint Chiefs in particular concluded that the British nuclear deterrent should receive 'first consideration for reduction if economic constraints cause a reduction in British defense expenditures'.[29]

Yet with the Labour government now resolved to retain Polaris they began to consider deploying it in the east of Suez area. The Nassau agreement had tied Polaris to NATO except in emergencies and without its full contingent it was unlikely that they could have been put to use outside of this area before 1972. Yet, such a deployment had some advantages, primarily to relieve some of the strain of the global defence burden and thus providing a degree of nuclear parity between the British and Germans in NATO. At their meeting in December 1965 Wilson told Johnson that the British were considering this.[30] Wilson reported back to the cabinet that LBJ had expressed interest in the idea, but Rusk and McNamara were much more guarded.[31]

Walt Rostow also suggested that assignment of Polaris in Asia would be a mistake. As its primary purpose would be to cover vital Chinese Communist targets, Rostow suggested it would place a British veto over US China policy, when UK domestic opinion was unlikely to sanction an attack on China. Although the specific subject of re-deploying Polaris did not appear to arise the following week when US and UK ministers met, Rostow concluded that short-term financial assistance to keep the British east of Suez was all the US government could give at this time. In his opinion, Washington could not 'allow the British to exploit our short-term concerns in ways which would mortgage our long-term prospects for effective US, Asian and European action east of Suez'.[32]

Despite these signs of tension, Rusk told the British in January 1966 that 'he believed our positions were quite close together in this area [NATO]'. In turn, the UK delegation did all it could to reassure the Johnson Administration that it would continue to look beyond the North Atlantic. The British and American governments now faced both internal and external pressure to cut some European forces and felt that this might be necessary in the short term but were worried about the political implications of this for the alliance, particularly with the

126

French position as it was. The British therefore had to consider the European position as well as that of their American allies. Moreover, McNamara's concerns about German territory persisted, although he felt that it was the responsibility of West Germany to increase its forces because the US could no longer countenance the German 'paper army'. If it did not encourage such a build-up, he suggested, NATO might be undermined as Britain and the US made savings on foreign exchange costs and other countries (particularly Italy and the Netherlands) reacted with their own cuts.[33]

At the time of the 1966 British defence review, Washington resolved to maintain pressure on the British on their east of Suez role.[34] For the most part, the British reacted favourably to this and placed NATO on the back burner. The economic burden was becoming more significant, however, and more radical solutions were soon required. Healey informed Rusk and McNamara that the Royal Navy would take most of these cuts.[35] Although the quality of military hardware for the navy would be increased with new missile ships, nuclear-powered submarines and helicopters, most of the Royal Navy's activities would now be concentrated east of Suez. The cabinet had also decided to cancel the navy's new carrier CVA-01, intended to guarantee the east of Suez role into the late 1970s. The Royal Navy's three existing carriers *Victorious*, *Eagle* and *Ark Royal* were to be phased out by the mid-1970s. The immediate effect of this decision was the resignation of secretary of the navy, Christopher Mayhew, followed by the First Sea Lord, Sir Henry Luce, in protest.[36]

The decision not to build the new carrier had been made in part because of the previous Conservative government's agreement to purchase Phantom F-4 jets from the US. The Phantoms were intended originally to operate from existing carriers, but, crucially, they could also operate from ground bases after the carriers had been phased out.[37] The carrier cancellation was then given further justification by Labour's extension of its military commitments to US hardware. As part of the defence review Labour also agreed to buy F-111A jets from the US. In justifying this decision to the electorate, Labour argued that to keep one carrier stationed permanently in the Far East with the potential to despatch another within two weeks would cost in the region £1400 million over ten years. This was prohibitive. It had been considering the cancellation since coming into office and now argued that as F-111A could operate as effectively from land bases as opposed to carriers, it would be able to conduct a full role in the Far East thus obviating the need for carriers.[38]

Under the F-111A arrangement, which was signed on 21 February 1966, the UK ordered 50 aircraft worth some $700 to $750 million to the US for delivery between 1968 and 1970. Although this purchase was intended to save the UK money and thus allow them to keep a ceiling on defence spending, the deal presented a financial obstacle. The acute balance of payments situation continued to grow worse in the UK and such a major military purchase would only exacerbate it further. London and Washington therefore brokered a compromise. As part of the agreement, the US government resolved to examine the possibility of purchasing items of UK non-combatant naval equipment. This was not a new concept in the UK and had even been raised as a potential bargaining chip during the ANF/MLF negotiations.[39] It was also reasonably limited with the US Navy preparing for bids on eleven small ships, including minesweepers and salvage tugs, amounting only to some $60 million, which was 'consistent with the public interest of the nation'.[40]

If economic exigencies forced Healey to adapt his immediate position regarding Britain's regional role, he was still realistic about the long-term prospects for British defence. In describing the strengths of UK force structure for the 1970s, which would include airlift capability from the C-130s and now a crucial role for the F-111s, as well as the Polaris submarine capability, he acknowledged to McNamara and others the limitations of this force.

> Thus, he concluded that the British were not really giving up a relevant capability for the 1970s. (Mr Healey observed that in fact it is doubtful that the UK has the military capability today to deal effectively with an expanded conflict in Indonesia.) The ability to fight a limited war alone is the *big* option the British are renouncing, but Mr Healey argued that the British do not really have this capability militarily now and could not use it politically in the 1970s.[41]

As regards the French, Healey was eager to pre-empt the upcoming de Gaulle 'deinitiative' as he called it. He had recently learned of de Gaulle's decision to withdraw from NATO's integrated military structure and he clearly foresaw the need for Anglo-American alliance leadership and suggested bilateral contingency planning as a way to head off potential repercussions and presumably reinforce the link with the Pentagon. As expected, while not objecting to behind the scenes discussions, George Ball warned of creating the appearance of 'an Anglo-American cabal in NATO' and even McNamara said that the impression of collaborating against the French should be avoided.[42]

Washington still worried that the CVA-01 decision presaged further cuts outside NATO. 'Other British military bases and deployments (such as those in the Mediterranean) are clearly less vital to US interests, for the foreseeable future, than the BAOR, Malaysia–Singapore and Arabian Sea–Persian Gulf areas' was the joint State-Defense response. And while they were appreciative of UK maintenance of a robust commitment to NATO, they noted that the British position in Malta was of relatively low strategic importance because of the Sixth Fleet presence in the Mediterranean. It was only significant in political and symbolic terms to deter the Soviets and provide a route to Libya.[43]

But the F-111 deal was a source of great satisfaction in Washington. It put US bilateral military balance of payments with the UK in the black and provided 'solid evidence' that the UK had committed itself to a continuing east of Suez policy.[44] The US was in a strong position in Europe and so the UK promise to bolster its Asian commitment was welcome. President Johnson made reference to the deal in correspondence with prime minister in which he praised Wilson for the 'masterful way' he had tackled matching defence resources to the needs of Britain and the free world.[45] He spoke of the very important agreements (notably F-111) that had been brokered between McNamara and Healey. 'Our good work together in recent months,' Johnson said, 'shows how important it is to keep in touch with all these matters'. In a similar telegram at the beginning of March, the president told the prime minister, how much he appreciated Wilson's willingness to keep in contact; 'it is of great comfort to me and a good thing for our countries, the alliance and the world', he said.[46]

But further cuts in NATO continued from both sides. The US military budget for the financial year 1965–1966 contained no money for new destroyers, frigates or cruisers. Although McNamara continued to take an interest in NATO, the navy's role had been somewhat neglected since early in the Johnson administration because of McNamara's call for an increase in anti-submarine warfare capability as part of a move towards increasing flexibility in all areas.[47] By mid-1966, McNamara was asking the secretary of the navy to examine the possibility of removing an aircraft carrier from the Mediterranean.[48] British NATO cuts were also a cause for concern to European allies. In March, the Foreign Office sought to assure the German government that downgrading the UK naval presence in NATO was limited to escorts and smaller ships in the Mediterranean and was unlikely to affect SACLANT forces to any significant degree.[49]

De Gaulle's challenge

At the beginning of 1966, the Johnson administration appeared to be relatively sanguine on the issue of NATO. An intelligence report in February suggested that the organisation 'seems to have come through the past year relatively well, weathering but not surmounting two very critical issues: France's threat to withdraw in 1969, and the problem of nuclear sharing'. It noted that the other members of NATO had drawn together in the face of the French challenge and most had 'drawn a collective sigh of relief' that the multilateral nuclear issue had not been pressed.[50] Although the issue had not been solved and may cause problems in the future, the report concluded that the greatest challenge to NATO was the worsening war in Vietnam, which was 'casting an ever deeper shadow over the alliance'.[51]

As the consequences of the British defence review were being digested in Washington, however, de Gaulle renewed his attacks on NATO. While this was of obvious concern to the US and other NATO allies, it was seen within the boundaries of being an internal threat that did not seem likely to break up the alliance. It was also part of ongoing process that had been underway since de Gaulle's return to power. Although de Gaulle's withdrawal of French naval officers from alliance structures announced at the end of April 1964 had been damaging, it was his statements about the nature of the military relationship between the United States and Europe that caused most concern. The French action was 'profoundly disturbing', having long-term political significance at a time when other alliance members wanted to demonstrate their unity. It undermined a military system built up over some fifteen years, and Washington feared it could affect future planning and operations, particularly if the naval cuts presaged further changes in air and land commitments.[52] Moreover, with the US still advocating conventional build-up in the alliance, there was genuine fear that French withdrawals and British downgrading of forces would simply encourage other smaller powers to follow suit.[53] The US solution to the 'NATO–France problem' was to stress the alliance-wide nature of the threat and to reassert American commitment to the alliance. Washington wanted to resist the French attack by acceding to any French demands for NATO to leave France but refusing to bow to any French calls for a series of bilateral agreements rather than an integrated military structure. Washington also sought to encourage the return of France to the fold as quickly as possible while consulting with the other allies in order to maintain a sense of assurance and cohesion.[54]

By the beginning of March George Ball reported to the president that action by de Gaulle against NATO was now imminent.[55] The State Department reacted by giving instructions to their ambassadors stressing this was a transitory threat because de Gaulle would one day be out of power, that Washington was determined to resist it, but at the same time arguing that 'we should lean over backward to be polite and friendly to France, to President de Gaulle personally, and to all French government officials'.[56] Sure enough on 7 March 1966, Couve de Murville met Charles Bohlen to give him a letter from de Gaulle.[57] Despite his assurances of support for the alliance, de Gaulle's letter declared that French sovereignty could be 'impaired' by the presence of foreign military forces in France and French forces in the integrated military structure of NATO.[58]

The Americans were well prepared and remained guarded in their response. Presidential aide Francis Bator immediately urged a cautious line, arguing that the president should hear 'both sides of the argument in much greater detail'.[59] NSC staff member Robert Komer continued this theme: 'Do we want a full blown war with de Gaulle?' he asked. Although the Americans talked about strengthening NATO and facing up to de Gaulle, Komer questioned how easy this would in fact be. 'Indeed, the lessons of recent history all suggest that we stop, look and listen before flinging down the gauntlet to de Gaulle'. The French president was 'dead right' according to Komer that the lessening Soviet threat made it easier for him to make trouble and so it was wiser to wait and see 'while limiting the damage he can do'. As he pointed out, the real problem was not France, it was Germany.[60]

Harold Wilson attempted to turn de Gaulle's actions to his advantage. In the days after de Gaulle's missive, the British and Americans resolved to 'exchange ideas and notes' on the problem.[61] The prime minister then began to work on the president to stress the similarities in policy between their two countries at a time when de Gaulle was highlighting the differences between France and the US. Although de Gaulle's atavistic behaviour (his 'nineteenth century nationalism, his anti-American motivation and above all his bull in a china shop tactics' as Wilson put it) offered some opportunities for the alliance, Wilson was primarily concerned with the broader implications of these moves. Just because Europe appeared to be safe from imminent attack, the prime minister warned the president, this did not mean that the Soviet threat had abated.

> For example, he would say that the main centre of conflict has shifted to Asia, although he is unwilling to draw the natural conclusion that NATO cannot confine its attention to the Atlantic area alone and he remains determined not to become embroiled in the containment of communism in Southeast Asia. The General goes on from his premises to argue that since the dangers have lessened we should go over to what one might call peaceful attack and seek to promote a detente with the Soviet Union at the expense of the United States presence in Europe. Although we cannot be sure that the threat would remain dormant if NATO no longer existed to contain it, there is some attraction in both these propositions. We have armed, not merely to be able to resist attack if it should come, but so that we can parley with confidence. Where I disagree with him, and this is fundamental, is in his apparent belief that you can talk with the Russians from a position of weakness and disarray.

Wilson's tactic here was obviously to create the impression of Anglo-American alliance against French isolationist tactics when addressing the president. It was also significant that in order to do this he made reference to the situation in Southeast Asia as a reason for maintaining a strong alliance, suggesting that NATO, rather than any country acting unilaterally, could have a role to play there. Moreover, Wilson went on to argue that the problems communists were causing in the Third World was no reason not to take robust action in NATO 'to slim that vast military headquarters apparatus in Europe and possibly to streamline the actual level of our forces deployed on the continent, and above all to reach fairer arrangements about the foreign exchange costs which plagues us both'.[62]

The trilateral negotiations

By mid-1966, the British economic crisis forced both London and Washington into further action. Both were now aware that cuts needed to be made but with the escalation of the Vietnam War, the need for the allies to maintain their commitments in NATO and beyond was of the utmost importance. Although by May the American Embassy in London advocated the UK scaling back on some of its east of Suez operations, this was still within limits. It continued to place great importance on the British presence in Singapore, for example.[63] Relations were not helped by Labour's reaction to the bombing of Hanoi and Haiphong in May and June when Wilson and Healey publicly disassociated themselves from US actions.[64]

Furthermore, in July an economic crisis forced Wilson's hand. The economy had failed to improve and the situation became so severe that the possibility of devaluing sterling was discussed in cabinet. While this was rejected, Wilson and

131

his colleagues agreed on a set of unpalatable austerity measures in order to cut foreign exchange costs of overseas expenditure and foreign aid. These included a six-month freeze on wage and price increases, a new round of taxes and cuts in domestic and foreign spending, specifically another £100 million from the MOD's budget.[65] Many with the American administration understood the repercussions that the dire British situation could have for the American dollar and therefore its war in Vietnam.[66] Bator told the president there was now great concern about 'the UK problem... Wilson has clearly swallowed the necessary economic medicine. It is not certain that he can pull it off'. The Americans prioritized a good UK balance of payments situation and a strong position east of Suez and on the Rhine. Bator reported splits within the American administration. Secretary of the Treasury Henry Fowler believed that the economic health of the UK was paramount and excess pressure could and should not be placed on Wilson to maintain defensive commitment. McNamara on the other hand continued to believe that the east of Suez position should remain the top priority, while Ball put the BAOR higher but placed a premium on full participation in Europe.[67]

In order to do this, Ball pressed for a more radical remedy to the chronic British economic situation. Shortly before his resignation, Ball wrote to Johnson on the need of 'talking long-term' with Harold Wilson. He suggested possible UK actions that could facilitate entry to Europe. These included a decision by Wilson to give up the nuclear deterrent, a reduction of Britain's overseas role and the possibility of Britain forming an EDC. For its part, Ball argued, the US should refuse to continue to support sterling, only agreeing to co-operate if Britain pushed towards Europe. In this way, he suggested, the 'special relationship' could actually be improved.[68] But Ball was increasingly isolated within the administration. In June, Walt Rostow had insisted to the president that it be made 'bloody clear' to the British Embassy in Washington and the UK government that Wilson should support US efforts in Vietnam or Washington would 'find an excuse for the visit not to take place'.[69] Yet the visit did take place and was considered to be something of a success.[70]

For their part, the British did not fully understand the Johnson administration's concerns about NATO troop commitments. At the beginning of August, Patrick Dean reported Rusk as saying that the US was glad of assurances over the British east of Suez role and they continued to stress the importance of the BAOR.[71] Yet by the end of the month, Johnson was writing to Wilson to warn him of 'the dangers of an unravelling in NATO which could easily get out of hand. With your urgent need to save foreign exchange in Germany, Erhard's budgetary and political difficulties (not to speak of his problems with his brass), my problems with our German offset and with the Congress on troops in Europe – all against the background of the General's antics – there is danger of serious damage to the security arrangements we have worked so hard to construct during the last 20 years'. While the president admitted that there seemed little prospect of the Soviets developing 'itchy fingers', there was no point in the allies letting their guard down.[72]

With the Vietnam War continuing to escalate, the issues surrounding US troop commitments in Europe became more acute. The US needed to renegotiate the amount of payments the Germans would make to them in order for them to maintain troops in Germany. Moreover, the potential political repercussions were pressing and the US worried about the effect troop withdrawals would have on the confidence of Germany and other allies in NATO.[73] By August 1966, the US faced a dilemma in terms of its own obligations to the FRG and the need to dissuade the British from making more cuts. In September, Johnson wrote to Wilson to implore him not to make any precipitous decisions that could help de Gaulle by undermining the solidarity of the alliance. At a time when the nuclear sharing issue was still not fully resolved, Johnson wanted to avoid any action that made the West Germans feel 'they were not full partners in the team'.[74] In turn the Germans were becoming acutely aware of the American dilemma and sought assurances that substantial US force cuts were not about to be made.[75] With the British and Americans united in their concerns about the foreign exchange costs of their troops in Germany, totalling some 51,000 and 262,000, respectively, action needed to be taken.[76] The Americans now saw that discussions with the British and Germans were necessary in order to forestall the need for more substantial cuts and pressed Erhard to accept tripartite talks.[77] Just prior to the collapse of his coalition, Erhard had agreed and in October, John J. McCloy was appointed to head the trilateral commission and conduct a brief review of NATO policy.[78]

From the president's perspective, the Europeans, particularly Britain, France and Germany did not understand the gravity of perpetuating US public support for NATO.[79] As he acknowledged to Wilson in November, the new Congress was likely to be less easy to persuade than its predecessor had been.[80] Johnson was, however, becoming so concerned with the British economic plight and troop withdrawals that he was willing to advocate further purchases of British vessels beyond those he had already committed to as part of the F-111 deal.[81] Johnson's prescience was confirmed as the legislature exerted its influence to try and force drastic troop reductions in Europe. Mike Mansfield, Democratic Senate majority leader from Montana, introduced a resolution proposing cuts that had the backing of forty-three other senators.[82] Even the president had some sympathy with this, commenting that despite American assistance 'all the Europeans say they are neglected'.[83]

A report for the president in November stated that the British balance of payments situation was similar to the American problem but 'much more urgent'. If the British did not receive assurances on this situation, British troops on the Rhine would be reduced accordingly, raising the spectre of further cuts to NATO when the French had made theirs so recently. American agreement to help with this situation by buying British defence equipment was only a short term measure and more direct help might soon be needed.[84] Equally, the US worried that any reduction in their own commitment 'will probably trigger Allied force cuts', which would in turn embolden the USSR because of its increasingly superior conventional capability.[85] A particular fear was that neutralist elements within Germany calling for a reduced US presence in Germany as the Soviet threat receded were already having the effect of changing Bonn's priorities.[86]

Although Dean Rusk acknowledged that many NATO members now regarded the chances of an attack by the Soviets to be remote, he cautioned that 'the political situation could alter quickly, whereas military plans and dispositions took years to evolve; it would be tragic if the Alliance repeated the mistake of too rapid demobilisation which had been made after Second World War. The alliance should not do anything to suggest that it is lowering its guard'. Rusk attempted to assure the allies that the US was not reducing its own commitment to Europe.[87] A paper prepared for the president at the time of the NATO ministerial meeting at the end of 1966 described the political atmosphere as one of 'transition and ferment' as the 'Traditional' European leaders were unable to provide reassurances to small allies about their commitments. Although France presented the greatest challenge here, the paper noted 'a weak, self-centred UK and a Germany governed by an untested coalition excacerbated this'.[88]

Washington remained unsure of the nature of the new German coalition and its chancellor, and was concerned that with de Gaulle's power at its peak, Bonn would increasingly look to Paris rather than Washington.[89] As the trilateral discussions began to meet on a formal basis in January 1967, McCloy was pessimistic about the prospects for NATO. In February he wrote to the president to outline the threats as he saw them, both internal and external. The French challenge was yet to be resolved and British withdrawals were causing strain, and despite a general lessening of tensions with the Warsaw Pact, growing Soviet military strength was a cause for concern, he said. In the face of these challenges, the US needed to show leadership and not precipitate withdrawals.[90] Splits were also emerging between the Pentagon and State Department. With the British making their own cuts to the BAOR, McNamara wanted to pressure both the Germans for a good deal on the US's own economic question and the British not to make further cuts by suggesting that the US might make further drastic cuts of two divisions. In contrast Rusk and others favoured a one division cut and wanted the president to make it clear that there would not be further US reductions unless there was a drastic change in the status of Soviet forces.[91]

The formation of the 'grand coalition' in Germany meant that the trilateral talks could begin in earnest from January 1967.[92] As they got underway, relations between Bonn and Washington remained tense over some of the negative public statements about the US made by the new West German chancellor, Kurt Kiesinger, and particularly progress on an NPT. Working through McCloy, the president carefully pressed the Germans to show their hand about the numbers of British and American withdrawals they would be willing to accept. What is striking here is the ability of the president to press the Germans to accept the need to support a $40 million British shortfall, thus demonstrating the importance to the US of the British maintaining their position.[93] Johnson called on the chancellor to do this in order to maintain alliance solidarity and coerced McNamara into making a further $20 million of defence purchases.[94] Then, in his first visit to Europe as president, Johnson met with Kiesinger to discuss the American need to make cuts. Resorting to direct personal diplomacy he was able to gain the chancellor's sympathy for his own domestic plight with the American Congress. By reducing the number of American troops and aircraft to be rotated out of Germany, the president gained Kiesinger's agreement.[95] The trilateral negotiations were therefore successfully concluded and the three parties signed the new agreement on 28 April. The Germans agreed to make purchases of British defence goods to the value of 250 million deutsche marks, with the US also agreeing to make additional purchases if satisfactory arrangements could be reached. The US agreed to work out financial arrangements in order to deal with the negative effects of rotation of some 35,000 of its troops from Germany.[96]

The Harmel exercise

In contrast to the more pessimistic reports of a collapsing NATO, there was a sense of achievement during the first months of 1967. Moves towards political reform of the alliance in particular were a course of satisfaction in Washington.[97] The exigencies of the balance of payments problems and resultant tripartite talks were also seen to have presented opportunities. A report from the State Department described 'an atmosphere of change and risk in European politics – even of a climax – which gives us an unusual opportunity for Atlantic initiatives' at the beginning of the year. He mentioned the trilateral talks as well as the NPG, a Middle Eastern working party and the 'Belgian Resolution'.[98]

Within NATO, the US and UK largely found agreement on the issue of reform and a move towards détente. In dealing with the final throes of the nuclear sharing issue and de Gaulle's attack, NSAM 345 had called for an examination of how the alliance could work towards greater cohesion, a task delegated by Dean Acheson.[99] Then as the end of 1966 neared, Belgian foreign minister Pierre Harmel, alongside members of the US administration, agreed to undertake a major NATO study examining ways to encourage alliance cohesion and stability. By December, Harmel made his formal proposal to the NAC.[100] Although a long and cumbersome process, with several countries refusing to send a participating rapporteur, work continued through 1967. Crucially, the French were included in discussions and, as expected, raised numerous objections, specifically on the proposal of greater political responsibility for alliance members.

The British took a similar line to the US in discussions, both objecting to the French tactics and, along with the Belgians, refusing to allow a France that had now significantly reassessed its relationship with the alliance to compromise NATO conduct. The UK delegation wished to produce a substantial report combining work from the four sub-groups established as part of the project examining both political and military institutional changes. This set the British, the Americans and Belgians at odds with West Germany, whose representatives were eager to produce a series of reports that the French would accept. The Germans were worried that the exercise would alienate the French further from the rest of the alliance and therefore suggested producing separate reports that confined their initiatives to military matters. Ultimately, the report was produced but with concessions to the French position.[101]

The Harmel Study encouraged alliance collaboration and initiative at a time of strain. Both the British and American Harmel rapporteurs saw the need to increase east–west dialogue, co-ordinate NATO efforts and ensure that other members recognized political and security requirements. As US rapporteur, Foy D. Kohler, told his British opposite number:

> It seems to me that a principal task before the alliance is to find better means of consulting about the security issues that confront us. While our principal objective remains the security of the North Atlantic area, this now involves, to a greater extent, questions of political tactics and actions as well as military issues. There is a greater risk of disagreement amongst us because there are more choices to be made and greater room for manoeuvre. In this environment, it seems to me that maintenance of the NATO organization as a locus for consultation is more important than it has ever been. I know of no better way to improve consultation than to use them more intensively. The existing institutions of NATO at least provide the point of departure.

Kohler urged caution, however, over the military requirements of the alliance and foresaw dangers in moves towards détente, if it was combined with reduced military capability.[102]

The Harmel exercise caused some rifts within the alliance because of the French attitude. Washington noted that Germany had been careful in its attitude towards the whole exercise to avoid any objections from France,[103] and the British remained fearful that it might affect their second application to the EEC.[104] But the Americans also recognized that the British were impatient to press ahead in trying to reorient NATO to cope with the political challenges of a relaxation in east–west tensions.[105]

But by the time of the meeting in Luxembourg in June 1967, and despite the effect of the ongoing crisis in the Middle East on the atmosphere of the proceedings, a US position paper noted that NATO had recently 'been enjoying a period of intense and constructive activity'. Ironically, it was challenge and uncertainty that had in effect united members and driven reform. In part, this had been made possible by the French withdrawal from the military structure, making it less of an 'inhibiting factor' for other nations. Other factors that might have had a negative effect included attacks from the Soviets and other Warsaw Pact countries in response to the Kiesinger government's attitude towards Eastern Europe and the general lack of uncertainty about France's intentions in 1969. The US expressed satisfaction with the course of the Harmel exercise.[106] In October, the Harmel rapporteurs held a series of meetings at Ditchley Park in Oxfordshire reaching a general consensus on the need for maintaining the alliance and for it to make a concerned effort on détente.[107] Moreover, progress on the NPG testified to a renewed atmosphere of progress and cohesion, although 'it would be a serious mistake to confuse current progress with full recovery of what has been a seriously shaken alliance'. Continuing tensions over the course of the NPT and American preoccupation with the situation in Vietnam were clear causes for concern.[108]

Although there were signs of strain between Washington and London both within the alliance and outside by 1967, there was still an understanding between the two allies that showed the centrality of their relationship in NATO. While the US was not willing to support the British without reservation, as Presidential aide Francis Bator pointed out, their should be no limits on their willingness to listen. Bator perceptively highlighted the difficulty Wilson now had in trying to back the US and remain in the Far East, while also supporting the US position on Vietnam, avoiding a balance of payments crisis and/or devaluation. Wilson also had to think about getting re-elected.[109]

In preparation for the year-end NATO ministerial meeting in 1967 Cleveland wrote to McNamara. He emphasized how much had been achieved in the past year, particularly in the Harmel exercise, in adding to the cohesion of the fourteen members against the 'deadweight opposition' of France. Although he warned against complacency and allowing the alliance to let its collective guard down in the face of continued and new Soviet threats, he concluded that '1967 has been a year of impressive progress'.[110]

8

PUTTING NATO FIRST?

By 1967 the need for British reappraisal of its east of Suez role had become much more urgent. Economic difficulties and the end of the Indonesia 'confrontation' against the Malaysian federation in late 1966 led to a major reassessment of British global commitments that resulted in a much stronger focus on the NATO area. By the start of 1968, Britain could no longer maintain the pretence of global status. The Labour government's announcement of its intention to withdraw from east of Suez positions and then to accelerate these withdrawals was the culmination of a long, slow process. Both Tory and Labour governments had tried to soften the impact of withdrawals on allies by demonstrating continued commitment to other areas of defence. This inevitably brought them into conflict with the Americans.

Yet the Anglo-American networks enhanced by years of collaboration could not be dismissed with the end of the British east of Suez presence and there were significant areas of co-operation and understanding. NATO's nuclear posture and re-definition of alliance strategy beyond the massive retaliation led to the adoption of flexible response (MC 14/3) in 1967.[1] Agreement on the NPT in 1968 was a significant achievement in the final months of the Johnson administration. Moreover, many in Washington understood the British dilemma and supported a reorientation of its foreign policy towards the North Atlantic. This was particularly important at a time when they were reapplying for membership of the EEC, a move that heartened many in the US.[2]

NATO force cuts

By 1967, the DOD was searching for ways for its forces in Europe to be further reduced, primarily because their huge defence commitment in Vietnam meant that the North Atlantic seemed a far lesser priority. Within NATO the main focus was placed on land forces: in January the Pentagon produced findings on US naval force posture in NATO, suggesting that there was too much allied concentration on naval forces at the expense of those on land. This report recognized that it would be difficult for a shift in emphasis from sea to land to occur, however. First, a strong naval tradition existed among many of the nations of Europe that could not easily be countered. Second, any savings that European nations could make on naval forces would not necessarily be put into other military land-based projects, as the US government desired.[3]

DOD opinion was informed by its own naval strength, particularly in the Mediterranean. The Polaris base as Rota in Spain had given it an additional element in its maritime approach, particularly in operating Polaris submarines. In December 1966, the Pentagon had announced that it would establish another major naval base at Oeiras, Portugal some 12 miles from Lisbon. The base was placed under the authority of an American and the new area was named the Ibero-Atlantic zone. In February 1967, it came into existence further increasing naval flexibility in the Mediterranean once again.[4]

As a direct result of the war in Vietnam the administration in Washington therefore faced huge pressure over its military policy in Europe. On one hand, the US military was increasing concerned about re-deployments from Europe to Southeast Asia and its effect on NATO. The JCS concluded that the continued withdrawals would 'impair the security of the western world'. Furthermore, such moves threatened to lead to European withdrawals, greater alliance dependence on nuclear arsenals at a time when the conventional aspects of the alliance were coming to dominate strategic thinking and increased scepticism of the US commitment to Europe. They were also representative of declining American influence in the region.[5]

Conversely, others in Washington were less supportive of NATO. By 1966, Mansfield's call to withdraw American troops from Europe was being supported by others and congressmen were openly objecting to the US helping the British when they refused to support US policy in Vietnam. Strains on the US economy caused by the commitment were raising more questions about giving military assistance to NATO partners, especially the UK. Congressman Thomas M. Pelly, a Republican from Washington, stated before Congress that he objected to the 'holier than thou' position Harold Wilson was taking over Vietnam. Referring to the British prime minister's refusal to sell weapons to the Americans if the US openly admitted that they would be used in Vietnam, Pelly argued that the UK was not being consistent.[6]

Pelly's was not a lone voice on the hill. In October 1966 John Byrnes, a Republican Senator for Wisconsin, had gone before Congress to garner support against an arrangement he claimed was 'against the national interest and inimical to the national security'.[7] Byrnes' objection was to the offset agreement over F-111 on non-combatant naval vessels. As his support grew in Congress, he introduced an amendment to existing legislation that no naval vessels used by the US Navy could be produced in foreign shipyards for the fiscal year 1968. Although it did not mention any country by name, it was clear to which country the legislation referred. The British were incensed, although the White House was quick to assure them that an order for 16 minesweepers (nine of which were slated for 1967) would be safe if the British bids were lower than those from the US were and that they could therefore defeat the amendment. Furthermore, if it seemed the Byrnes amendment might be enacted into law, the administration 'would be prepared to look into the matter to see what else could be done'.[8]

With Democrats in a minority, the assurances from the White House were impossible to enforce. On 12 September 1967, the Byrnes Amendment passed in the house by 233 votes to 144. Although it was solely for the fiscal year 1968, it sent a clear message to Whitehall that nothing could be taken as read in the area of military sales. It sent shock waves through the British military establishment, as the increasingly fragile economy now rested on US technology to provide the Royal Navy and RAF with aircraft. There were comments that action such as this threatened seriously to undermine US–UK relations.[9]

The Byrnes Amendment caused consternation in the UK. Following its passage, Healey made a public statement on Independent Television News in Britain that he would consider scrapping the F-111 deal if the amendment ended the offset agreement. He admitted, however, that it would mean 'we would have to abandon those elements of our defence and foreign policy which depend on that type of strike and reconnaissance aircraft'.[10] And in a letter to McNamara, Healey informed him that opinion was running high in Britain over the action. 'We are having considerable difficulty', he said, 'in avoiding damage to Anglo-US relations'.[11]

Yet it was significant that the actions of Byrnes and his colleagues were confined to the hill and did not represent the views of the administration.[12] The Pentagon had to contend with further congressional action against the UK as other amendments were in the pipeline, including one that would have prevented the entire F-111 deal from taking place. McNamara and Healey quickly stepped in to try and soften the blow, with McNamara cautious but conciliatory. The DOD was examining ways that the bid could still be made on a free and fair basis, he said, reassuring his counterpart that even the US press had noted that this action was not in the best interests of the two countries.[13] McNamara attempted to stem the tide of congressional action by confirming the order of minesweepers that remained unaffected, while preventing further moves by Congress to compromise the F-111 agreement. The additional amendment was immediately removed from the congressional timetable. A State Department intelligence report noted that the whole affair had 'tarnished the US image in Britain', although executive and DOD action had had a positive effect and 'put the issue back in its proper perspective'.[14]

The British viewed such executive action with some satisfaction. It was clear that the Johnson administration saw the merits of allowing the offset deal to proceed both in terms of their financial advantage in the F-111 sale and in the strategic opportunities it afforded the British east of Suez. Sir Patrick Dean noted, 'Tactically our wisest move would be to concentrate on the administration rather than on criticizing the Congress.' Furthermore, he suggested that public criticism of American action should be kept to a minimum so that further deals would not be jeopardized.[15] British ministers therefore sought to assure the press that the F-111 arrangement still stood firm. On his way to the US to view both Phantom

F-4 and F-111 aircraft, the minister of state in the Department of Technology, John Stonehouse, told assembled journalists that the F-111 aircraft made sound economic sense and met the RAF's operational requirements, so the British government would be going ahead with the purchase.[16]

In fact, the F-111 deal looked increasingly precarious and the MOD was already searching for ways to save it. Healey had been fighting a rearguard action to prevent cancellation almost since the deal was struck. Certain members of the cabinet, including the prime minister himself, had always been less than keen to sanction the deal and maintained pressure on the MOD.[17] The previous March, Healey had informed McNamara that, although he was struggling for their purchase, the distinct possibility of cancellation now existed.[18] Two months later as another defence review approached, Healey told McNamara that the UK would pull out of Singapore and Malaysia by 1974 or 1975. McNamara expressed his annoyance at this news saying that the US would be seen as 'picking up the pieces'. Once again he advocated an alternative strategy that would involve making savings in Europe. To this end, he suggested that European conventional or strategic nuclear forces could be cut. But Healey stood firm. Despite any reservations Healey might have had, he told the secretary of defense that he saw no tenure for the UK beyond the mid-1970s. 'Herewith Bob McNamara wrestles valiantly, but not to great effect, with Healey', Walt Rostow commented gloomily to the president.[19]

With economic crisis in the UK ongoing, the dates for announced cuts were routinely brought forward. In October 1967, Wilson even had to write to Johnson to reassure him that 'there was not a word of truth' in rumours that the British would withdraw all their troops from Europe if de Gaulle vetoed the British application to the EEC again.[20] By the time of the British devaluation of sterling in November 1967, the planned paying off of HMS *Victorious* was advanced from 1969 to take almost immediate effect.[21] The devaluation placed strain on the dollar and threatened the entire Bretton Woods system of international finance.[22] Following devaluation, McNamara asked Healey what the US could do to help reduce the impact. In response Healey asked for help with 'defence problems that have arisen' as a result, in other words an increase in US procurement of British goods because of the rise in cost of F-111 and Phantom aircraft.[23] A further setback was de Gaulle's announcement at the end of November that he would reject the British application to the EEC, along with a broadside on American policy that further distanced the French president from his NATO allies.[24] By the end of the year, as further cuts were announced, even Britain's strongest supporters in the United States were becoming uneasy. With the strains over Southeast Asia to the fore in the press, cuts in the UK's worldwide force commitments could do little but threaten relations with the US government.[25]

And yet the main focus of British defence cuts continued to be in the east of Suez area meaning that NATO was least affected by the cuts of 1967. A majority of British ministers now favoured playing a more significant role in NATO, a point reinforced by the decision to reapply for EEC membership.[26] As Wilson had prepared for his meeting with the president in June, the official position of the Johnson Administration was still that NATO was in a stronger position than at any time in the recent times and the relationship with the UK was sound. While progress on non-proliferation with the Soviets was still tortuous, 'fundamentally, the United States and the United Kingdom continue to find common ground as strong supporters of the alliance'.[27]

Specifically, the alliance had made gains in the revision of its strategy. France's new position within the organization had actually facilitated progress by reducing its influence and during the ministerial meeting at the close of 1967, the strategy of massive retaliation, which the French had insisted upon, was replaced with that of flexible response, a graduated programme of escalation if the western alliance was ever attacked. This resolved some fundamental issues in US–European relations, perhaps most importantly the question of the American 'nuclear guarantee' to Western Europe, but it was deliberately vague in nature and came at time when conventional forces were being reduced.[28] Reassessment of British and US commitments in Germany alongside this alteration in alliance strategic posture both recognized that previous troop targets envisaging a dogged fight over German soil in the case of a Soviet attack were unrealistic. And the deployment of ICBMs and Polaris submarines meant that aircraft could now be freed up for interception, reconnaissance and ground support instead of being held back for nuclear use.[29]

The final retreat

By January 1968, the British economic situation was so acute that something had to give. In a lengthy and torturous series of cabinet meetings, British ministers ultimately decided that Britain would not sustain its role in the middle and far east beyond March of 1971 and declared that there would be a simultaneous withdrawal from these two areas.[30] Healey's fight for F-111 also came up against even stronger cabinet resolve to cancel the purchase.[31] The prime minister led those in favour of cancellation. When talking to the Americans, however, Healey expressed some optimism that he could still save the order. Healey was now out of step with many of his colleagues and he told the US Embassy that in December matters had gone even further and he had been on the point of resigning over 'lunatic' cabinet judgements on defence cuts that would have jeopardized the British position in Europe as well as the rest of the world.[32]

The final defence cuts by the British caused great distress in Washington, coming at the end of many years spent persuading them to retain a global position. In January, Foreign Secretary George Brown ended his round-the-world trip in Washington, telling an appalled Rusk that the cabinet had decided to withdraw from east of Suez by the early part of the following decade.[33] Rusk expressed his 'deep dismay' at this decision.[34] Despite a last ditch attempt from the president to force a re-consideration on the latter issue, the course was set.[35]

The decision on F-111 disturbed Washington even more. On 12 January, Healey lost the struggle to save the aircraft. Brown had already told Rusk that cancellation of F-111 was almost a certainty, but confirmation was yet another blow for Washington. When the president read news reports from London that termination of the contract would follow, it moved him to write to Wilson reiterating the need for global commitments and urging that F-111 might be the way to achieve it. It was not enough for Johnson that the UK had re-invented itself as a regional power. 'If you decide to forego the acquisition of the F-111, everyone here will regard this as a total disengagement from any commitment whatsoever to the security of areas outside Europe and, indeed, to a considerable extent in Europe as well', the president said.[36]

Wilson replied that he and his colleagues had considered the president's messages and expressed his gratitude that he had set out his views 'with such restraint and understanding'. He stressed that the president was mistaken, however, in thinking that the decisions meant a retreat from the world, instead, their 'determination, once and for all, to hew out a new role for Britain in the world at once commensurate with her real resources yet worthy of her past'. If Britain asserted its total economic strength Wilson insisted that it could be a force for peace and stability in the world. Wilson and colleagues had conceded to American pressure in only one area, a delay of nine months in withdrawing from their commitments in the Middle East. Elsewhere, including the F-111 cancellation, they stood firm with Wilson telling the president he was wrong to say that it represented a disengagement from global and European commitments. Wilson concluded:

> Believe me, Lyndon, the decisions we are having to take now have been the most difficult and the heaviest of any that I, and I think all my colleagues, can remember in our public life. We are not taking them in a narrow or partisan spirit. We are taking them because we are convinced that, in the longer term, only thus can Britain find the new place on the world stage that, I firmly believe the British people ardently desire. And when I say 'the world stage' I mean just that.[37]

On 16 January, Harold Wilson announced in a Statement to the Commons that he hoped the further round of defence cuts would save the government some £716 million. F-111 would not be purchased for the RAF, saving some £400 million alone. He also announced that Britain's carrier force was to be run down by 1971. The Phantom deal would still go through, although at a reduced number with 25 of these aircraft going to the RAF, and another 25 to the Royal Navy. Healey immediately called in to the American Embassy to give details of the cuts, informing Bruce that cancelling Polaris had also been considered although if it had been agreed he would have resigned. Healey reported to the American Embassy that no one in the cabinet would accept the cancellation of Polaris.[38] Finally, he told US Ambassador David Bruce to convey his gratitude to all those in Washington who had supported his position during such troubled times, concluding that it was time to go 'back to the drawing boards'.[39]

US reaction to the east of Suez decision was tempered by a degree of understanding. 'While I regret this unhappy action as you do', Paul Nitze, now the deputy secretary of defense, wrote to Healey, 'I can understand the extra-ordinary political pressures that have been imposed upon you. You have fought a good fight.'[40] A similar feeling of disappointment prevailed in NATO, although some hope remained that other navies of NATO, notably, Italy, Greece and Turkey, would be able to compensate with their own forces.[41] Manlio Brosio pressured the British to maintain at least some naval units in the Mediterranean and then enhancing their contribution to the North Atlantic area. In this way the alliance could make the most of the east of Suez decision.[42]

Such moves could do little to cushion the blow for the president, who had endured previous cut backs, devaluation of sterling and now faced international and domestic opposition to his Vietnam policies. Johnson was advised that there would be no great new military strength in Europe because, in fact, the forces would be predominantly naval, not land or air based as the Pentagon would have preferred.[43] The blow was particularly crushing when it was accompanied by the phasing out of the V-bomber force and cancellation of F-111s. Worse was to come for the president, however. Immediately following the British announcements and cancellations the North Korean seizure of the USS *Pueblo* followed by the North Vietnamese attacks on South Vietnamese towns and military installations in the so-called Tet offensive brought the Johnson administration to its lowest ebb and led directly to Johnson's decision not to run for re-election.[44]

Yet despite ill portents, and perhaps because the president was now so pre-occupied with events in Southeast Asia, Wilson's final visit to the Johnson White House (and Johnson's last with a major European leader) in February, although low key, could be described as cordial and perhaps even successful.[45] Once again American views were tempered by understanding. Walt Rostow told the president that 'Wilson is in trouble at home. His visit here is designed to boost his prestige in Britain.' While his parliamentary majority still looked fine, his inability to deal with the economic problems in Britain had lost him the confidence of his party and country: 'There are even signs he has lost some confidence in himself', Rostow commented.[46] A State Department Research Memorandum concurred with this assessment: 'Prime Minister Wilson comes to Washington... at a time when he knows the UK has never cut a less impressive figure in Washington's eyes.'[47]

Moreover, two significant developments also occurred concurrently with the British announcement. The first was the successful completion of the Anglo-American Polaris project. Despite calls to abandon the deterrent, Labour maintained a belief that it was a fundamental element of British defence. In December 1967, the Defence Review Working Party had recommended the retention of the nuclear capability in Britain because cancellation would damage relations with Europe and within NATO, even though the chances of a nuclear war remained low. In addition, it concluded, 'Abandonment would also lose the United Kingdom the privileged access (albeit declining) which we now enjoy to

American military and technological knowledge in the nuclear field.'[48] On 15 February, the first British Polaris submarine, HMS *Resolution*, successfully launched its first Polaris missile complete with dummy warhead.[49]

The second development was the establishment of the NATO Standing Naval Force Atlantic (SNFL). This force of nationally manned ships grew out of the successful 'Match Maker' exercise held in 1963 and repeated in following years.[50] In June 1967, the meeting of defence ministers tentatively agreed to put SNFL into action and it had been given the green light by outgoing SACLANT. By November, Cleveland was urging his superiors to press forward with the plan 'which can provide tangible further evidence of the alliance's political and military vitality, against the background of other advances emerging from the ministerial meeting'.[51] By the time NATO ministers met in December, preparation was complete. Rusk reported that although ministers expressed concern at the growing security problems in the Mediterranean, the naval force was a pleasing development and ministers were particularly gratified at the widespread support the force had garnered.[52]

In January 1968, Walt Rostow wrote to the president of 'Good News' for NATO. The previous month all NATO countries, with the exception of France, had agreed to create the SNFL. All participating countries contributed equally, regardless of their size. On 13 January 1968, the force had come into being at Portland, England. According to Rostow this was a 'historical moment' and while its military capability was not great, 'the political significance of this decision by NATO is clear'. The force was, in his words, a 'dynamic symbol of the unity of the alliance'.[53] The UK had been of particular importance in the formation of this force. Rostow reported that:

> The British, while initially reluctant to accept the concept, are now wholeheartedly behind it. I understand that they see it [as] a way to participate at modest national cost in a force that can be very meaningful to NATO from a politico-military viewpoint.[54]

The first SNFL Commodore was a British captain and by April 1968 he reported that SNFL could be considered as a success at every level.[55]

Reassessing the NATO role

In the period of reassessment in Washington that followed the British east of Suez announcement the administration came to recognize that there were positives to be taken from the situation, as the British claimed that the withdrawal from east of Suez would allow them to 'take more leadership on NATO defensive matters'.[56] In May, Healey outlined to the NATO Defence Planning Committee what this commitment would entail.[57] The UK still had a substantial air and sea capability, which could now be dedicated to NATO. With the Phantom F-4s, Jaguars, Lightenings and other tactical aircraft available, UK forces would be updated.

The naval element was also impressive in its own right.[58] The DOD predicted that even with the mothballing of carriers, the UK would have the largest European navy and probably the only fleet to have missile firing Polaris and hunter-killer submarines. And with Royal Navy knowledge and the promise of continued conventionally armed nuclear submarines into the 1970s, it seemed that the reduction in UK naval capacity might be negligible.[59]

There was also no shortage of willingness in the UK to help allay US and NATO fears by bolstering commitment in areas such as the Mediterranean, although at least some of these allocations had to be temporary as the withdrawal from other areas proceeded. Forces could be allocated for specific NATO exercises, for example, but the Admiralty cautioned against the quick creation of a standing naval force in the Mediterranean. It recognized that, as all its major naval vessels were to be assigned to NATO, making new commitments in the Mediterranean would increase shortfalls in the Far East as withdrawal took place.[60] Healey also suggested that the renewed British focus on the North Atlantic could presage European defence cooperation.[61]

Furthermore, the change in the structure of British defence also resurrected the issue of a Polaris assignment east of Suez, an option the British had continued to explore.[62] During his trip to Washington in June 1967 Wilson had told the president and McNamara that the British government was still considering the merits of this, but McNamara said he would 'not endorse this proposal if it was regarded as a substitute for maintenance of conventional forces East of Suez'.[63] In the UK, however, the most pressing issue aside from American acquiescence was whether sufficient support facilities could be built to allow a deployment outside of the NATO area.[64] With the major change in British defence policy, however, the capital costs of undertaking such a programme increased dramatically and therefore became much harder to justify in the short term at least. Healey therefore recommended that they should not make provision for deploying east of Suez in the long term, although this option could be restored at five years' notice.[65]

By this time the British had to contend with new developments relating to Polaris. First, its successor Poseidon was being introduced as the British Polaris deterrent neared completion. The Americans developed Poseidon, which increased the payload and accuracy of submarine launched missiles, primarily to counter the Soviet anti-ballistic missile (ABM) capability. They had kept the British informed about this development, although it remained unclear as to whether the US was bound to offer it under the terms of the Nassau pact.[66] In the end, the British made no request for Poseidon in 1967.[67] The Labour government was not, it seemed, willing to be seen completely to rely on the US in the field of weapons development. During a television interview in May 1967, the *New York Times* reported Wilson as saying that Britain did not want to become 'subservient' to America. If the British chose not to buy Poseidon, the newspaper opined, 'It would be, in effect, a deliberate move to break one chain of dependence on American weapons.'[68] The decision against adopting Poseidon was also informed by renewed moves to enter the EEC.[69] The Ministerial Committee on Nuclear

Policy concluded in December 1967 that although Healey was in talks with McNamara to see how Polaris could be improved by the 'hardening' of warheads, there was no point in trying to keep up with the USA or USSR.[70]

Second, the British were becoming concerned about the US announcement that it was accelerating its ABM programme.[71] In public, the British aired concerns about the new arms race this might create and the undermining of the NPT. Yet Bruce suggested that the British were primarily annoyed because of the lack of consultation the Americans had afforded them on this issue, both bilaterally and within the forum of the NPG. But they also believed that the decision was 'just plain wrong' and that Washington had succumbed to domestic pressure. It also cast some doubt onto the efficacy of the British nuclear force, and would encourage the Europeans to look for similar measures and perhaps even 'an AMB [*sic*] "MLF" '.[72] The issue also generated some heated discussion in the NAC.[73] Washington was keen to avoid a spat over this and when the president met George Brown at the end of September, he wanted to apologize about the lack of consultation and assure him that the NPT was not threatened.[74]

The difficult withdrawal decision was compounded by a change in political personnel at the Pentagon during early 1968. In January, it was announced that Robert McNamara would leave his office at the DOD to become head of the World Bank. McNamara's decision to quit was made in large part over the strain he was placed under by the lack of progress in Vietnam, specifically over the North Vietnamese Tet offensive in late January. Washington lawyer and LBJ associate Clark Clifford succeeded him. Clifford's arrival in the Pentagon was significant for the MOD. The connection that Healey had maintained with McNamara was severed and Clifford was far less well disposed to the British, although in the longer term this afforded Healey a more prominent role in NATO and the NPG.[75] But in the short run, Clifford was sceptical of Britain's importance to the US.

In preparation for an NSC meeting in June, the State Department undertook an examination of future UK policy. State now framed all its assertions in light of the UK's role as a regional power. It expressed some optimism about this, claiming 'withdrawals from the Far East and the Persian Gulf have enabled HMG to make an immediate contribution to strengthening NATO's forces in Europe and the Mediterranean'. Specifically, this meant a mobile task force of 20,000 men, a European amphibious force, two frigates in the Mediterranean, a squadron of reconnaissance aircraft in Malta until 1970 and, from 1969, the possibility of a commando carrier with troops for NATO exercises in the Mediterranean. Moreover, State reported, the UK was also exploring a European defence force within NATO and closer co-operation with the EEC and others in defence production and procurement, as well as meetings in NATO on such topics as force levels and strategy. All this was intimately linked to renewed British overtures to join the EEC. While the State Department had been encouraging the UK in European co-operation, unity, strength and burden sharing in NATO, it warned that such initiatives must not be construed as purely Anglo-American. The alliance was regional and must be recognized as such.[76]

In a meeting to discuss the British situation, Rusk presented the State Department line in this manner, describing bilateral relations with the British as 'good', claiming, 'They can take their "sense of special relationship" into Europe by continuing close consultation with us.' The new secretary of defense did not agree with this rosy assessment, highlighting instead the fundamentally different approaches the US and UK now followed. Clifford's main concern was Vietnam and he clearly felt that this British attempt to portray a new regional role for themselves was unhelpful, describing it as 'fluff – not substance'.[77] He was dismissive of British claims that this new look NATO-centric policy would result in great benefits to the alliance, suggesting it was not certain whether they could even maintain their present levels of NATO forces. Newly earmarked forces for NATO were, he claimed, merely bringing them up to levels previously maintained at best. In other areas of the world, notably Asia and the Mediterranean, Clifford noted that British withdrawals were causing the US 'real problems'. This brought a sharp rejoinder from David Bruce, who claimed that Britain seemed to be looking forward to a stronger NATO now they were preparing to get out of the east of Suez area.[78]

Bruce was perhaps being disingenuous. A few days earlier he had told Rusk that the waning Soviet threat in Europe and British withdrawal decision gave no direction to UK foreign policy. Bruce's thoughts, expressed only within his own department, considered the political symbolism of the east of Suez decision, both in light of previous British adherence to an east of Suez strategy and US pressure to maintain it. 'Even the decision to "go European" is more a *faute de mieux* policy than a gripping national objective and, in any event, is largely overshadowed by preoccupation with [the] domestic economy and political concerns', he claimed. The prospects for the renewed emphasis on the European theatre were, in the embassy's opinion, 'not bright' because of the decreasing emphasis on Europe over the previous few years, but NATO might still be 'a modest beneficiary' of the east of Suez withdrawal.[79]

Simultaneously, the JCS continued to argue that threats of further cuts by the UK, other nations and the US could only be implemented if the Soviet Union made further cuts.[80] This seemed unlikely. Despite renewed efforts by the British for mutual force reductions in June,[81] the Soviet Navy had built up considerable power in the Mediterranean.[82] This comprised both surface and submarines elements and by 1965 the Soviets were reported to possess 40 cruise missile submarines, of which between 16 and 18 were nuclear powered.[83] NATO authorities were determined that the Soviet military threat in the Mediterranean and North Atlantic would not go unheeded. SACEUR recommended that the UK should increase its naval presence in the Mediterranean.[84] Following the Middle East crisis of 1967, the Soviets were further consolidating their strategic maritime position in the Mediterranean.[85] In July 1967, Harlan Cleveland reported that the Soviet Navy had 46 warships operating in the area. This included modern guided-missile cruisers and approximately ten submarines. In the first six months of 1967, Cleveland estimated, Soviet naval operations in the Mediterranean were some 400 per cent greater than they had been in 1963.[86] During an NSC meeting in mid-June, the Under Secretary of State, Nicholas Katzenbach, claimed the Soviet presence to be 'primarily political and secondarily military'; although Clark Clifford stressed that it must still be monitored.[87]

The Americans made great efforts in the final six months of 1968 to press allies for a greater contribution in the Mediterranean in order to counter the increased Soviet presence there and to indicate alliance solidarity.[88] There was certainly some satisfaction with the results of pressure to improve NATO commitments more broadly.[89] But NATO authorities were still disappointed that the Europeans were not more forthcoming; Cleveland opined that although the British had 'made considerable public hay' of their strengthened contribution, 'we are inclined to see much of this as more apparent than real'.[90]

US displeasure at the demise of the British carrier force was evident in the planning of these operations. Key elements of flexibility looked likely to be lost as cuts took hold and renewed emphasis on the Mediterranean only heightened concerns. The symbolism of British retrenchment was also important. The US noted that the Soviets were calling at Persian Gulf ports 'within weeks' of the British announcement of their withdrawal from the east of Suez area. They were also shadowing the US Sixth Fleet in the Mediterranean.[91]

In response to these kinds of activities, Cleveland was keen to promote the concept of an international task force in the Mediterranean. This would act something like the SNFL in the Atlantic.[92] This would include at least the US, UK and Italy and perhaps even be extended to non-NATO areas. Unfortunately SNFL still appeared as a bold move and another task force appearing so soon was felt to be a step too far too quickly. When Cleveland proposed the idea, the SACEUR told him that the existing Commander, Allied Forces Southern Europe and Commander, Submarines Allied Naval Forces Mediterranean commands were more than capable of coping with the threat.[93] In the light of the new NATO dominated strategy in the UK, however, Healey acknowledged that any potential standing naval force in the Mediterranean would have to contain some UK elements. He therefore offered two extra naval units for SACEUR's contingency planning, while reserving the right to use them in other areas.[94]

The NATO ministers meeting at Reykjavik in June 1968 examined the possibility of increasing surveillance of the Soviet fleet.[95] Excluding France, all members agreed that this area needed attention (the French flatly refused to acknowledge the Soviet threat at all in the Mediterranean). Members concurred on a Harmel follow up exercise and the need to extend consultation. The proposal of a standing naval force in the area in addition to that in the Atlantic was also discussed, although enthusiasm was still muted because of the provocative nature of such action to Arab nations, as well as to the Soviets.[96] Perhaps because of the increased Soviet naval presence, the diminished role of France and the progress made towards convening Strategic Arms Limitation Talks with the Soviets, Katzenbach reported that the June 1968 meeting in Reykjavik was 'less divisive and more productive than usual'.[97] State official John Leddy reiterated this point, claiming that NATO was changing in a much more positive way than most had predicted and mutual force reduction talks with the Soviets would augment this.[98]

This atmosphere had undoubtedly been helped by the success of the NPT, which had been signed in early June. Slow progress had been made since the breakthrough in late 1966, but Johnson had used the occasion of his withdrawal from the presidential race on 31 March 1968 to press for a renewed assertion of American and Soviet efforts on this. The results of this were very positive and rapid progress was then made. The primary hurdle for the US was, as ever, West Germany. Broadly, Washington had to assure Bonn that the NPT would not contravene German interests while simultaneously recognizing Soviet concerns about West Germany.[99] Specifically, Washington assured Bonn that the NPT would not cut across the work of the NPG and that they would consult with them over the selective release of nuclear weapons on German territory in order to bring them on board.[100] Johnson's announcement on 4 June that the treaty had been agreed was a major achievement in the twilight of his presidency, although it was overshadowed by the assassination of Robert F. Kennedy.[101] Yet even after the NPT had been agreed, Washington and London had to reassure the Germans that the NPT did not affect the integrity of NATO and the NPT was not designed to outlast it.[102]

In the months following Reykjavik, the calming situation in Europe itself was shattered by the Soviet invasion of Czechoslovakia on 21 August, drastically changing the mood within the alliance.[103] As the State Department surmised: 'it has cast into question such matters as the future of détente, the defensive capability of Western Europe, and the future of Communism and independent states of Eastern Europe'. It seemed clear that immediate action would have to be taken at ministerial level or higher, either as in a normal six-monthly meeting or within an extended NPG. The proposal to expand surveillance of Soviet vessels in the Mediterranean was re-examined with a view to speeding it up.[104] Johnson told Wilson in the aftermath of the invasion that although the full implications could not yet be fully known, 'the crisis has served as a stark reminder that the security of Europe and, indeed, world peace depend on the North Atlantic Alliance'.[105]

It was clear to the US delegation that any plans for mutual force reductions would now have to be postponed indefinitely.[106] The Americans therefore sought reassurances that the allies would attempt to augment or at least not reduce their present NATO commitments.[107] This brought American attitudes towards NATO into the spotlight and John Leddy suggested to Rusk that if Washington wanted to 'prod the allies to take meaningful action' in relation to the crisis 'it will be necessary for us to indicate what your own contribution to strengthening NATO might be'.[108] The invasion also threw into question German attitudes towards the NPT.[109] Christian Democrat representative Kurt Birrenbach told the president in September that it signalled that the Soviets were unpredictable, leading Johnson to reiterate that the Europeans needed to renew their commitments to NATO in order to strengthen it.[110] Several member states in NATO also saw the Czech crisis as an opportunity to reassert the main tenets of the alliance and state categorically that it would continue after 1969.[111]

The British response was to reiterate its newfound commitment to NATO.[112] They were now retaining small units in the Mediterranean and placing 20,000 extra troops returning from east of Suez there, as well as increasing the navy's NATO commitment by assigning two assault and two commando ships. At an informal level, the UK reiterated its offer of an increase in its NATO naval contribution.[113] Furthermore, there was military support at the highest level for deployment of suitable ships to the Mediterranean.[114] Following the Czech crisis, military planners in the UK sought contingency measures for dealing with the Soviet threat in Southern Europe and pressure from the US to improve political and military co-operation. From a UK perspective contingency measures for dealing with the Soviet threat in Southern Europe could be achieved at the expense of planned but decreasing force levels east of Suez.[115] This raised objections from SACLANT that such a military policy was made at the expense of Royal Navy deployments to the North Atlantic.[116]

Healey in particular wanted to show how important the British could be as the leading US ally in Europe by pushing towards a new European defensive grouping in NATO.[117] The Americans encouraged this, although the continual problem of German reactions pervaded their response and they did not want to become too closely involved because they wanted it to be seen as arising from 'genuine European initiatives'.[118] Washington was also cautious for fear of upsetting their own and German relations with France, which continued to object to such initiatives.[119] With the Johnson administration in its final days, one of the primary purposes of this new European grouping was to establish a common position for negotiating with the new administration.[120] Yet the Johnson administration officially supported the move, seeing it as a constructive way for the Europeans, and British in particular, to take the lead in NATO affairs.[121]

Yet the US remained cautious about these post-Czech crisis developments.[122] The White House was under further pressure from a newfound domestic isolationism, a mood LBJ noted had not been helped by the British withdrawals.[123] It reiterated that British redeployments would actually mean little in light of the announced retrenchment.[124] And according to the JCS, the British attitude remained uncertain because of force reductions.[125] Moreover, Washington was aware that with British priorities still in the Far East until 1971, any new troops or vessels newly earmarked for NATO could be re-deployed outside the NATO area in a time of emergency.[126] A State Department research memorandum noted 'it appears unlikely that they themselves will offer more than this, particularly in view of their economic difficulties'.[127] Meeting with Foreign Office officials, David Bruce concluded that the British had 'pretty much "scraped bottom of the barrel" regarding specific UK force augmentation to NATO'.[128] But some in the US saw that in the short term at least the Czech crisis offered opportunities to improve the defence posture of the alliance.[129]

The end of the Johnson administration

By 1968, the respective focus of British and American defence policies increasingly diverged. While congressional pressure for American troop withdrawals was 'quiescent', it had not gone away and lack of European assistance in Vietnam was a source of frustration to many.[130] Troop withdrawals that had begun in the early 1960s accelerated as the war in Vietnam expanded. By 1968 the US had reduced its forces in Europe from 417,000 in 1961 by some 51,000 plus approximately 36,000 dependents.[131] At a ministerial meeting with colleagues in NATO in November, Clifford acknowledged that Europe was simply not the primary focus of American policy at that time and pointed out that maintenance of most US commitments in NATO while also having 650,000 troops in Southeast Asia was a 'minor miracle'.[132]

In a summary of bilateral relations with the countries of Western Europe at the end of the Johnson administration, the State Department concluded that the east of Suez withdrawal had been the one major disagreement the United States had had with its ally Great Britain.[133] While the American Embassy in London saw a degree of anti-NATO feeling on the left wing of the Labour Party, it concluded that this was not influential enough to make a difference to the course the government would take.

Instead, in stark contrast to the almost wholly negative assessment he had given to Rusk in June, Bruce and his colleagues saw an opportunity to strengthen NATO in light of recent events. Bruce even suggested that a European defence force based around the UK's Polaris capability might one day be a possibility. He concluded that the 'special relationship' was still important to Britain because its influence in the world was increasingly dependent on the degree to which it could influence the United States, but Bruce also recognized the value of bilateral relations for the US:

> For the United States too this relationship is advantageous: of all our allies, Britain is still the most powerful and most important, still a considerable factor on the world stage, and the support it gives us in our foreign and security policy objectives is of a value which it is hard to overstate.[134]

As the end of the Johnson administration approached and the president sought an arms control summit with the Soviets,[135] it still pushed the British to make greater commitments to NATO in light of the Czech crisis, specifically deploying another brigade in Germany, committing forces returning from the east of Suez area to NATO and extending the service of the *Ark Royal*, committing it to NATO indefinitely. Although Healey could not agree to this, he once again tried to play up other new British defence efforts in the alliance.[136]

With its decision to withdraw from a global commitment, the UK government had recognized the limits of its ability. To the State Department, it seemed that the

UK itself now had less use for a 'special relationship' with the US that it had protected for so long and that had appeared to offer so many benefits within the alliance. As Dean Rusk opined, the new era of defence in the Atlantic could offer invigorated opportunities for its two leading contributors, although they were working on fewer issues in comparison to the early part of the decade.[137]

Yet the continued preferential treatment of the UK in the nuclear field continued. At the time of the Byrnes Amendment, the Johnson administration had approached the dilemma of whether to supply enriched uranium for British submarines with great caution, knowing that congressional opposition existed. The British had requested 400 kilograms of enriched Uranium-235 for the period 1971–1972, with another 200–300 in the years to follow. On 25 October 1967, the Atomic Energy Commission had presented testimony to the Joint Committee of Atomic Energy regarding the UK's request. The commission required the president's approval and he promised that he would consult with the committee before agreeing to the plan. Prominent Democratic Rhode Island senator and chairman of the joint committee, John O. Pastore, then wrote to the president in November when he became aware of the possibility that the UK might benefit in this way, stating that it would not be in the interests of the US to supply them. For one, Pastore argued, the UK would be shown favourable treatment above Italy and the Netherlands, both of which had also asked for help in nuclear propulsion for submarines. In addition, providing the UK would free up its nuclear industry to make nuclear fuel for commercial purposes to compete with the US on the international nuclear power market. Third, he argued continued British trade with North Vietnam, Communist China and Cuba should not be encouraged by practising double standards.[138]

The administration rejected this objection. Katzenbach told the president that the State view on this was that it would represent a 'slap in the face' for Harold Wilson if the US government now refused to honour this commitment. Johnson's reply to Pastore stated, 'Their [the UK's] support for our Vietnam policies has been a great source of strength to us all. In the light of this steadfast friendship, we should think long and hard before taking steps that could only injure this close relationship'.[139] Johnson also vigorously sold the proposition to Congress telling them that supplying the fuel would 'substantially enhance the ability of the United Kingdom to contribute to our mutual defense, particularly in the North Atlantic area'. The irony was almost certainly not lost on Congress coming as it did only months after the Labour government's decision to withdraw from their worldwide role to concentrate on NATO commitments.[140]

In January the following year, representatives of the Defense Department and Atomic Energy Commission wrote to the president recommending the continuation of the *Agreement for Co-operation on the Uses of Atomic Energy for Mutual Defense Purposes* for one more year. It had expired on 31 December 1968. They concluded: 'The transfer of materials . . . will not adversely affect our defense programs and will add to the United Kingdom's defense capability without unnecessary duplication of effort and facilities.' In effect, this recognized the nuclear relationship once more; as did the State Department, which recommended compliance, and the president, who stated in his reply that the transfer of material and parts would 'promote and ... not constitute an unreasonable risk to the common defense and security'. On 18 January 1969, in one of his final acts as president, Johnson signed the memorandum.[141]

CONCLUSION

Shortly after Lyndon Johnson left office and was succeeded by Richard Nixon in early 1969, Michael Stewart addressed the left-wing, London-based Fabian Society in a seminar on the state of Anglo-American relations. Stewart acknowledged the difficulties that presently existed between the two countries, but also tried to explain exactly why the relationship was so important. He outlined the vitality of democratic institutions, the relationship with Europe more broadly and within NATO, and the fact that both worked at the highest level in the United Nations. In particular he noted that since France had opted out of the NATO integrated military structure, only Britain had such a 'unique connection' with the United States.[1]

As Stewart recognized, the years since Harold Wilson had become prime minister had been fraught with difficulties. Escalation of the war in Vietnam and then the British global withdrawal were just the two most prominent examples of division, but there were others. The east of Suez decision had undone many years of work by the US government to ensure that it was not the sole world policemen. British efforts to convince Washington that NATO was a beneficiary of the cuts therefore received a mixed reception and some American policy-makers claimed the British were really maintaining rather than increasing their contribution. Moreover, with progress on arms control limitations talks, temporarily undone by the invasion of Czechoslovakia in August 1968, and the development of détente policies, some allies questioned the need for strengthening NATO. However upsetting the British renouncing their east of Suez defence commitments, American policy-makers maintained a degree of understanding, especially as they were experiencing their own series of crises with the war in Vietnam, balance of payments problems and massive domestic unrest. The British decision could also be seen as timely in the context of broader alliance reform and the need to check the burgeoning Soviet naval threat in the Mediterranean and the invasion of Czechoslovakia.[2]

Relations between London and Washington therefore need to be understood in the context of renegotiation rather than decline during this period. First, this is because the British consistently attempted to pursue a policy of 'interdependence' from the end of the 1950s whereby increased reliance on the US, especially in the field of nuclear technology, was intended to be complemented by American agreement to become more closely involved in British defence concerns. This policy met with limited success even during the Macmillan years. Most obviously this can be seen in the Kennedy administration's decision to cancel the Skybolt missile.[3] Yet the Skybolt cancellation must be set in its context: it was a short-term misunderstanding between the two powers and fits into the pattern of negotiation of the British role. Moreover, the policy of interdependence was pursued with equal if not greater vigour by the Wilson government for the very reason that the basic aims of British foreign policy, pursuit of global defensive commitments, remained the same.

Second, dire British economic problems meant that both the Conservatives and especially Labour had to recognize the difficulties of maintaining this global role. As Saki Dockrill suggests, the idea that the British decision to withdraw from east of Suez was a 'breathless one' made between January 1966 and 1968 is not convincing.[4] The British had in fact been renegotiating their role since at least the beginning of the decade, if not well before. Ultimately it seems that the Wilson government came to recognize that the British role had to be reassessed and British diplomatic influence would increasingly come through connections within the Commonwealth and NATO in place of military hard military power.[5] Moreover, for all its apparent disgust with the Labour decisions regarding east of Suez and the focus on NATO, the Conservative government of Edward Heath that took power in 1970 found it impossible to reverse the decision, especially when it was committed to Britain entering the EEC.[6]

Neustadt's ideas about 'crises' in Anglo-American relations can therefore be applied only within a limited context in order to aid an understanding of this period. Understandably, the Skybolt episode broadly fits his model; 'disappointed expectations' were easy to find in London during November and December 1962, although some of the British 'paranoid reactions' can be questioned. The short term nature of the Skybolt debacle meant that resolution of the crisis was underway almost as soon as the British realized that the Americans had decided to cancel the missile. Thorneycroft and McNamara met with relatively clear, albeit limited, briefs and agreed on many points while the president had also set others to work on resolving the crisis. The British were therefore never in serious danger of being abandoned and many in London knew that.

It is more challenging to explain longer term difficulties using Neustadt's model. The MLF negotiations do not fit as well, for example. There were relatively few 'muddled perceptions' over MLF as both broadly understood the other's position. Despite the divergence in policy aims there was no crisis, even in December 1964, because both sides strove to understand each other. Moreover, 'stifled communications' were generally not an issue as both sides understood the others' respective position. There was also relatively little disappointment afterwards even as the British became aware of the broad commitments they had made at Nassau and the full implications these had.

Instead, the series of incidents in this book suggests that the notion of 'instrumental interdependence' most usefully explains US–UK relations during this period because the relationship was broadly one of mutual co-operation where this was necessary. 'Sentiment' or 'empathetic interdependence' as advanced by Rosencrance and Dawson was far less important. While it may have had a place in Kennedy's decision to provide Macmillan with Polaris as a replacement for Skybolt, Kennedy based his decision primarily on the perceived costs of not providing the British with what they desired. Just as Eisenhower had viewed the decision to amend the McMahon act in 1958 as a necessity in light of the Sputnik launch, so his successor believed that failure to provide the British with Polaris would damage relations between the two countries at a time of renewed tension over Berlin and Cuba and perhaps force the British to look towards nuclear co-operation with the French. Moreover, provision of Polaris at a relatively cheap price gave them the opportunity to invest further in their conventional roles in NATO and east of Suez, thus helping the Americans to maintain their commitments.

Despite the relative weakening of their power, in key areas, especially NATO, the British remained very influential. Although the Polaris project involved a high degree of reliance on the goodwill of Washington, the project was a huge success, completed on time and within budget. The British were also successful in gaining an association between Polaris and NATO on their terms. Kennedy's agreement to provide the British with an affordable, reliable and prestigious nuclear weapons system for use in the NATO area was designed to allow the British to play out its worldwide conventional role. By exacting a vague conventional commitment from them at Nassau, Kennedy reiterated his administration's concerns about NATO but the infamous 'escape clause' in the Nassau agreement was intended to give the British peace of mind by allowing them to use the weapon anywhere they had major concerns. In the first months after the Nassau agreement they managed to place the multinational element of the agreement high on the NATO agenda while maintaining a relatively loose association between the deterrent and the alliance.

Acquisition of Polaris also gave the British greater diplomatic bargaining power that they were able to exploit over the following years and they were pivotal in shaping Kennedy and Johnson's actions on MLF. With German support, if not assured then at least likely, and the French absent from the debates, Britain would be the power around which others gathered. Yet with a Polaris force secured and their promise of its assignment to NATO, the British had no need for another commitment. This resulted in a bluffing game from both sides of the Atlantic, with the US saying that although Britain was an integral member of the alliance and therefore the proposed MLF, it would proceed without the UK if necessary, and the UK saying it might not bother to join now as it had Polaris. Yet the British knew that failure to participate in such a major project would leave them open to accusations of undermining the force and failure to create the political cohesion necessary in NATO in the long term. They found it impossible to renege after having made such a public commitment at Nassau.

The NATO nuclear sharing issue undoubtedly caused tension in US–UK relations, but, outside of the State Department, many in Washington understood the British attitude of resistance including both Kennedy and Johnson. Kennedy was never a strong MLF enthusiast and his primary aim was to maintain some interest in the force and to explore all options with a view to an acceptable solution in the long term. His untimely death raises the prospect of exactly what he would have done had he had to make decisions on the MLF in a potential second term. Yet it seems clear that with British opposition and German divisions Kennedy may well have had to make the same kind of decision. Indeed, Johnson's eventual compromise was based on his reading of Kennedy's attitude towards the force.

The solution that evolved after December 1964 very much suited the British and facilitated progress in NATO. The MLF was therefore a crucial issue: it was a hugely ambitious programme that ultimately was deemed to be too complex to complete, but it was illustrative of broader debates within the alliance. Anglo-American policy during this period remained primarily concerned with a solution to the 'German (nuclear) problem', as the MLF showed, and in order to do this the US needed Britain as a strong ally in NATO. The MLF policy was also intended to deal with Gaullist elements that might wreck the NATO project. Certainly the MLF was divisive at the time but again the US came to a better understanding of other allies' positions within the alliance that allowed progress to be made. The eventual compromise produced a more realistic assessment of alliance nuclear and military affairs through the creation of the NPG, the Harmel exercise, the adoption of flexible response and even the symbolism of SNFL.

But in other areas, as the British withdrew from their global role, the Anglo-American relationship undoubtedly became less important. In light of the changes in their global defensive posture in 1968, the State Department's Director of Intelligence was stark in his summary of US relations with the UK in the previous few years. The characteristics of the relationship had changed significantly since Churchill's time, he concluded. The relationship was now far less one of interdependence than one of dependence and clientage. Yet with its place as the third largest nuclear power, its intention to carry a small but high quality air and naval force into the 1970s and its continued strategic positions in the Rhine, Cyprus and Malta it could still be highly useful to the US:

> Its interests will still converge with ours more than with those of any other ally. It will continue to be the world's No. 3 nuclear power. It will still have unparalleled experience, expertise, and entree and will therefore be able to carry out undertakings of benefit to the US in diplomacy, intelligence, and technology. For all its loss of power, it will reckon that it still has a strong claim to the position of the United States' favored partner. It will hope the US agrees.[7]

The networks and links with the US built up in the previous years still existed – they would not be broken as a result of the east of Suez withdrawal. Within its context, the east of Suez decision represented British recognition of its new role as a regional rather than global power in a regional alliance, with a nuclear capability and looking towards a place in the European Community.

Finally, this study supports the notion that the Johnson administration's foreign policies were broadly successful in dealing with NATO and European allies. In Walt Rostow's words, Johnson left NATO 'in extremely good shape for your successor, given de Gaulle, Vietnam, balance of payments problems, etc'.[8] Undoubtedly Johnson's war in Vietnam had many negative political and military consequences for this alliance, yet considerable progress was made in the final years of the Johnson presidency. Johnson's decisions on the nuclear affairs of the alliance had been particularly astute. After initial hesitancy he recognized that alliance attitudes did not permit a quick solution to the nuclear sharing issue and formulated a policy that very much suited the circumstances despite huge continued pressure from the State Department. In this instance Johnson was able to use his advisory process well and formulate workable policies.

In other areas, with the exception of the tripartite talks and the NPT, Johnson took a far less direct interest as the war in Vietnam became more pressing. Yet at working level the US moved forward with a series of reforms that made the alliance more progressive and viable and allowed the president to develop his détente policies despite the war in Vietnam and Soviet invasion of Czechoslovakia. The ability of Robert McNamara and others to advance alliance reform through the NPG demonstrated American leadership and a realistic assessment of alliance structures at a time when the very existence of the alliance was under threat. Indeed, the Johnson administration's handling of de Gaulle's challenge to NATO and the question of British troops in the FRG showed a realism and deftness of touch that is not in keeping with the prevailing view of Johnson and his attitude towards foreign affairs. As Thomas Schwartz concludes, 'The Vietnam War should not be allowed to block a more dispassionate assessment of Johnson's foreign and domestic policies.'[9]

Examining the Kennedy–Johnson years together provides a picture of US–UK relations that was complex and shifting. There were more areas of contention between Washington and London by the end of the decade than there had been at the start and with the announcement of rapid withdrawal from global commitments they were working on far fewer areas of mutual concern. But there were also many continued areas of agreement, particularly in NATO. Thus, the US–UK relationship during the second half of the 1960s cannot be dismissed as unimportant and while the strains must be acknowledged, so must the achievements.

NOTES

INTRODUCTION

1 *Foreign Relations of the United States*, 1964–1968, vol. XII, *Western Europe*, Memorandum of Conversation, 11 January 1968, pp. 603–8; R. Crossman, *The Diaries of a Cabinet Minister, vol. 2*, London: Hamish Hamilton, 1976, p. 646.

2 D. Dimbleby and D. Reynolds, *An Ocean Apart: The Relationship Between Britain and America in the Twentieth Century*, London: BBC/Hodder & Stoughton, 1988, pp. 221–44; A. Horne, 'The Macmillan Years and Afterwards', in W.M.R. Louis and H. Bull (eds) *The 'Special Relationship': Anglo-American Relations Since 1945*, Oxford: Clarendon, 1986, p. 101.

3 See, for example, C.J. Bartlett, *'The Special Relationship': A Political History of Anglo-American Relations Since 1945*, London: Longman, 1992, pp. 88–101; J. Dumbrell, *A Special Relationship: Anglo-American Relations in the Cold War and After*, Basingstoke: Macmillan, 2001, pp. 49–58; D. Nunnerley, *President Kennedy and Britain*, London: The Bodley Head, 1972; R. Ovendale, *Anglo-American Relations in the Twentieth Century*, Basingstoke: Macmillan, 1998, pp. 120–31; D.C. Watt, *Succeeding John Bull: America in Britain's Place, 1900–1975*, Cambridge: Cambridge University Press, 1984, pp. 138–43.

4 Watt, *Succeeding John Bull*, p. 146.

5 S.A. Ellis, 'Lyndon Johnson, Harold Wilson and the Vietnam War: A *Not* So Special Relationship?' in J. Hollowell (ed.) *Twentieth Century Anglo-American Relations*, Basingstoke: Palgrave, 2001, pp. 180–204.

6 S.A. Ellis, *Britain, America and the Vietnam War*, Westport and London: Praeger, 2004; J. Colman, *A 'Special Relationship'? Harold Wilson, Lyndon B. Johnson and Anglo-American Relations 'at the Summit', 1964–68*, Manchester: Manchester University Press, 2004; J. Dumbrell, 'The Johnson Administration and the Labour Government: Vietnam, the Pound and East of Suez', *Journal of American Studies*, vol. 30, no. 2, 1996, pp. 211–31; A.P. Dobson, 'The Years of Transition: Anglo-American Relations, 1961–1967', *Review of International Studies*, vol. 16, 1990, pp. 239–58. See also Bartlett, *The 'Special Relationship'*, p. 101–9.

7 Dobson, 'The Years of Transition', pp. 239–58. Colman, *A 'Special Relationship'?* pp. 168–71.

8 S. Dockrill, *Britain's Retreat from East of Suez: The Choice Between Europe and the World?* Basingstoke: Palgrave, 2002.

9 N.J. Ashton, 'Harold Macmillan and the "Golden Days" of Anglo-American Relations Revisited, 1957–63', *Diplomatic History*, vol. 29, no. 4, 2005, pp. 691–723; N.J. Ashton, *Kennedy, Macmillan and the Cold War: The Irony of Interdependence*, Basingstoke and New York: Palgrave-Macmillan, 2002, pp. 16–17; W.S. Lucas, 'The Cost of Myth: Macmillan and the Illusion of the "Special Relationship"', in R. Aldous

and S. Lee (eds) *Harold Macmillan: Aspects of a Political Life*, Basingstoke: Macmillan, 1999, pp. 16–31.

10 R.E. Neustadt, *Alliance Politics*, New York: Columbia University Press, 1970, p. 56.

11 L. Richardson, *When Allies Differ: Anglo-American Relations During the Suez and Falklands Crises*, New York: St Martin's Press, 1995, p. 5.

12 D. Reynolds, 'A "Special Relationship?" America, Britain and the International Order Since the Second World War', *International Affairs*, vol. 62, no. 1, 1985/1986, pp. 1–20; W. Scott Lucas 'Neustadt Revisited', in A. Gorst, L. Johnman and W.S. Lucas (eds) *Post-War Britain: Themes and Perspectives*, London: Pinter, 1989.

13 R.O. Keohane, *After Hegemony: Cooperation and Discord in the World Political Economy*, Princeton: Princeton University Press, 1984, pp. 122–3.

14 R. Dawson and R. Rosencrance, 'Theory and Reality in the Anglo-American Alliance', *World Politics*, vol. 19, no. 1, 1966, pp. 21–51.

15 Dumbrell, *A Special Relationship*, pp. 1–15.

16 J. Baylis, 'The Anglo-American Relationship and Alliance Theory', *International Relations*, vol. 8, 1985, pp. 368–79.

17 M. Trachtenberg, *A Constructed Peace: The Making of a European Settlement, 1945–1963*, Princeton: Princeton University Press, 1999.

18 Lyndon B. Johnson Library, Oral History, Harlan Cleveland I, p. 13.

19 T.A. Schwartz, *Lyndon Johnson and Europe: In the Shadow of Vietnam*, Cambridge and London: Harvard University Press, 2003; W.I. Cohen and N.B. Tucker, *Lyndon Johnson Confronts the World: American Foreign Policy, 1963–1968*, Cambridge: Cambridge University Press, 1994; H.W. Brands, *The Wages of Globalism: Lyndon Johnson and the Limits of American Power*, Oxford and New York: Oxford University Press, 1995; J. Dumbrell, *President Lyndon Johnson and Soviet Communism*, Manchester and New York: Manchester University Press, 2004.

20 Schwartz, *Lyndon Johnson and Europe*, pp. 1–8.

1 ANGLO-AMERICAN DEFENCE RELATIONS IN NATO

1 See, for example, C.J. Bartlett, *'The Special Relationship': A Political History of Anglo-American Relations Since 1945*, London: Longman, 1992, pp. 34–43; J. Baylis, *The Diplomacy of Pragmatism: Britain and the Formation of NATO, 1942–49*, Basingstoke: Macmillan, 1993; S. Greenwood, *Britain and the Cold War, 1945–91*, Basingstoke: Macmillan, 2000.

2 R. Ovendale, *Anglo-American Relations*, Basingstoke: Macmillan, 1998, pp. 58–79.

3 D. Reynolds, 'A "Special Relationship?" America, Britain and the International Order Since the Second World War', *International Affairs*, vol. 62, no. 1, 1985/1986, p. 10.

4 J. Baylis, 'Exchanging Nuclear Secrets: Laying the Foundations of the Anglo-American Nuclear Relationship', *Diplomatic History*, vol. 25, no. 1, 2001, pp. 33–62.

5 J. Simpson, *The Independent Nuclear State: The United States, Britain and the Military Atom*, London and Basingstoke: Macmillan, 1983, pp. 76–89.

6 D. Campbell, *The Unsinkable Aircraft Carrier: American Military Power in Britain*, London: Paladin, 1986, pp. 27–31.

7 S. Twigge and A. Macmillan, 'Britain, the United States, and the Development of NATO Strategy, 1950–1964', *Journal of Strategic Studies*, vol. 19, no. 2, 1996, pp. 260–81.

8 A.J. Pierre, *Nuclear Politics: The British Experience with an Independent Strategic Force, 1939–1970*, London: Oxford University Press, 1972, p. 144; J. Baylis, *Anglo-American Defence Relations, 1939–1981*, London and Basingstoke: Macmillan, 1981, pp. 62–3.

9 D.C. Watt, 'Demythologizing the Eisenhower Era', in W.M. Roger Louis and H. Bull (eds) *The Special Relationship: Anglo-American Relations Since 1945*, Oxford: Oxford University Press, 1986, pp. 72–4.

10 S. Dockrill, *Eisenhower's New-Look, 1953–61*, Basingstoke and London: Macmillan, 1996, pp. 1–5.

11 Dockrill, *Eisenhower's New-Look National Security Policy*, pp. 72–9.

12 Dockrill, *Eisenhower's New-Look*, pp. 79–85; Baylis, *Ambiguity and Deterrence: British Nuclear Strategy, 1945–1964*, Oxford: Clarendon, 1995, pp. 130–1.

13 Baylis, *Ambiguity and Deterrence*, pp. 131–2.

14 Baylis, *Ambiguity and Deterrence*, pp. 133–51.

15 Dockrill, *Eisenhower's New-Look*, pp. 85–8.

16 J.L. Gaddis, *Strategies of Containment: A Critical Appraisal of Postwar American National Security Policy*, Oxford and New York: Oxford University Press, 1982, pp. 147–50.

17 Gaddis, *Strategies of Containment*, pp. 150–1; Jan S. Breemer, *US Naval Developments*, London: Frederick Warne, 1983, p. 21. Dulles soon toned this down for domestic and allied consumption. See J.F. Dulles, 'Policy for Security and Peace', *Foreign Affairs*, vol. 32, no. 3, 1954, pp. 353–64.

18 Gaddis, *Strategies of Containment*, p. 150.

19 Dulles, 'Policy for Security and Peace', pp. 355–7.

20 Gaddis, *Strategies of Containment*, pp. 152–3.

21 I. Clark and N.J. Wheeler, *The British Origins of Nuclear Strategy, 1945–55*, Oxford: Oxford University Press, 1989, pp. 179–80; Baylis, *Ambiguity and Deterrence*, pp. 158–60.

22 Dockrill, *Eisenhower's New-Look*, p. 89.

23 Dockrill, *Eisenhower's New-Look*, pp. 92–8.

24 Diary entry of Evelyn Shuckburgh, 14 December 1953, quoted in Dockrill, *Eisenhower's New-Look*, p. 87.

25 Twigge and Macmillan, 'Development of NATO Strategy, 1950–1964', p. 263.

26 F.S. Northedge, *Descent from Power: British Foreign Policy, 1945–1973*, London: George Allen & Unwin, pp. 290–1.

27 Command Paper (CMND) 124, Defence: Outline of Future Policy, 1957.

28 See W.S. Lucas, *Divided we Stand: Britain, the US and the Suez Crisis*, London: Hodder & Stoughton, 1991.

29 E.J. Grove, 'British Naval Policy', in A. Gorst, L. Johnman and W.S. Lucas (eds) *Post-War Britain, 1945–1964: Themes and Perspectives*, London: Pinter, 1989, pp. 160–1.

30 CMND 9075, Statement on Defence, 1954.

31 E.J. Grove, *Vanguard to Trident: British Naval Policy since World War II*, London: The Bodley Head, 1987, pp. 199–200.

32 Public Record Office (hereafter referred to as PRO), CAB 21/4444, Brook to Eden, 16 July 1956.

33 P. Darby, *British Defence Policy East of Suez, 1947–1968*, London: Royal Institute of International Affairs/Oxford University Press, 1973, p. 99; Grove, 'British Naval Policy', in Gorst, Johnman and Lucas, *Post-War Britain*, pp. 163–4.

34 M. Chalmers, *Paying for Defence: Military Spending and British Decline*, London: Pluto Press, 1985, p. 71; Darby, *British Defence Policy East of Suez*, pp. 111–12; Grove, 'British Naval Policy', in Gorst, Johnman and Lucas, *Post-War Britain*, p. 164.

35 Baylis, *Anglo-American Defence Relations*, p. 57; D. Murray, *Kennedy, Macmillan and Nuclear Weapons*, Basingstoke: Macmillan, 2000, pp. 17–18; G.W. Rees, 'Brothers in Arms', in Gorst, Johnman and Lucas (eds) *Post-War Britain*, p. 206.

36 For conflicting views of the success of Macmillan's policy see E.B. Geelhoed and A.O. Edwards, *Eisenhower, Macmillan and Allied Unity, 1957–1961*, Basingstoke

and New York: Palgrave, 2003; Watt, 'Demythologizing the Eisenhower Era', in Louis and Bull (eds) *The Special Relationship*, pp. 74–8.

37 S.J. Ball, 'Macmillan and British Defence Policy', in R. Aldous and S. Lee (eds) *Harold Macmillan and Britain's World Role*, Basingstoke and London: Macmillan, 1996, pp. 74–81.

38 I. Clark, *Nuclear Diplomacy and the Special Relationship: Britain's Deterrent and America, 1957–1962*, Oxford: Clarendon Press, 1994, pp. 27–8.

39 See R. Dietl, ' "Sole Master of the Western Nuclear Strength"? The United States, Western Europe and the Elusiveness of a European Defence Identity, 1959–1964', in W. Loth (ed.) *Europe, Cold War and Coexistence*, London and Portland: Frank Cass, 2004, pp. 132–72.

40 Naval Historical Center, Operational Archives Branch (hereafter referred to as NHC, OAB), Papers of Harvey M. Sapolsky , series I, box 6, Special Projects Office File (History), 1953–1963, Note on meeting between Charles Wilson and Duncan Sandys, undated (1954).

41 H.M. Sapolsky, *The Polaris System Development: Bureaucratic and Pragmatic Success in Government*, Cambridge: Harvard University Press, 1972, Chapter 2; Peter Nailor, *The Nassau Connection: The Organisation and Management of the British Polaris Project*, London: Her Majesty's Stationary Office, 1988, pp. 2–3.

42 Murray, *Kennedy, Macmillan and Nuclear Weapons*, p. 19.

43 See N.J. Ashton, 'Harold Macmillan and the "Golden Days" of Anglo-American Relations Revisited, 1957–1963', *Diplomatic History*, vol. 29, no.4, 2005, pp. 699–700.

44 *Public Papers of the Presidents of the United States: Dwight D. Eisenhower*, 1957, President Eisenhower and Harold Macmillan, Declaration of Common Purpose, 25 October 1957, pp. 768–73.

45 PRO, DEFE 13/126, Note of talk between Admiral Sir Michael Denny and Mountbatten, 2 September 1959; Ashton, 'Harold Macmillan and the "Golden Days" '.

46 CMND 537, Atomic Energy Agreement, 3 July 1958.

47 Baylis, *Anglo-American Defence Relations*, p. 65.

48 Murray, *Kennedy, Macmillan and Nuclear Weapons*, p. 17; Baylis, *Anglo-American Defence Relations*, p. 60.

49 NHC, OAB, Series of Interviews on the Subject of Polaris, interview with Admiral William F. Raborn, p. 20.

50 PRO, ADM 205/179, Burke to Mountbatten, 29 November 1957.

51 PRO, ADM 205/172, Mountbatten of Burma Newsletter, 9 February 1958, p. 4.

52 See R. Moore, *The Royal Navy and Nuclear Weapons*, London and Portland: Frank Cass, 2001, pp. 163–6. This view has been the subject of some historiographical debate. For the most recent account see K. Young, 'The Royal Navy's Polaris Lobby, 1955–62', *Journal of Strategic Studies*, vol. 25, no. 3, 2002, pp. 56–86.

53 PRO, ADM 1/27375, Selkirk to Hailsham, 1 January 1958; Murray, *Kennedy, Macmillan and Nuclear Weapons*, pp. 39–40.

54 PRO, ADM 167/153, Board Memo B1273, 22 June 1959; PRO, DEFE, 4/123, COS (59), 1 December 1959; Moore, *The Royal Navy and Nuclear Weapons*, 156–9.

55 PRO, ADM 205/179, DCNS to Mountbatten, 3 March 1958.

56 PRO, ADM 205/179, Report of Working Party and Proposed Future Action, undated (March 1958).

57 PRO, ADM 1/27275, DCNS to Mountbatten, 30 June 1958.

58 See Twigge and Macmillan, 'Development of NATO Nuclear Strategy, 1950–1964', pp. 262–6.

59 See PRO, ADM 205/179, DCNS to Controller, 19 February 1958; PRO, ADM 205/179, DCNS to Admiralty Board, 3 March 1958; PRO, ADM 205/172, Minutes of First Sea Lord's Weekly Meeting, 26 March 1958.

60 PRO, ADM 205/172, Minutes of First Sea Lord's Weekly Meeting, 17 September 1958; Mountbatten of Burma Newsletter, 29 September 1958, p. 12.

61 PRO, ADM 205/179, DCNS to Mountbatten, 6 March 1958.

62 PRO, ADM 205/179, DCNS to Mountbatten, 6 March 1958.

63 PRO, ADM 205/179, DCNS to Mountbatten, 1 May 1958.

64 PRO, ADM 205/179, Memorandum for the Board, 3 March 1958.

65 PRO, ADM 205/179, Report of Working Party and Proposed Future Action, undated (March 1958).

66 PRO, ADM 205/179, Goodwin to Brockman, 15 April 1958; *New York Times*, 12 April 1958.

67 PRO, ADM 205/179, Burke to Mountbatten, 14 April 1958.

68 PRO, ADM 205/179, Mountbatten to Burke, 8 May 1958; PRO, ADM 205/179, Burke to Mountbatten, 16 May 1958.

69 PRO, ADM 205/179, Brundrett to Mountbatten, 27 May 1958; PRO, ADM 205/179, Mountbatten to Burke, 9 June 1958; PRO, ADM 205/179, Message to Admiralty, British Joint Services Mission (BJSM), Washington, undated (July 1958).

70 PRO, ADM 1/27389, Burke to Mountbatten, 6 February 1959.

71 PRO, ADM 1/27389, Burke to Mountbatten, 28 February 1959.

72 PRO, ADM 205/179, Admiralty, BJSM to Admiralty, 3 October 1958; PRO, ADM 205/179, Admiralty, BJSM to Admiralty, 27 September 1958.

73 PRO, ADM 1/27839, Meeting of Defence Committee, 8 April 1960; PRO, DEFE 7/1328, British Controlled Contribution to the Nuclear Deterrent, MOD Paper, 31 December 1959; PRO, DEFE 7/1328, Brief for Minister of Defence, 19 February 1960.

74 PRO, ADM 1/27389, Selkirk to Mountbatten, 1 June 1959.

75 T.J. Botti, *The Long Wait: The Forging of the Anglo-American Nuclear Alliance, 1945–1958*, Westport: Greenwood Press, 1987, pp. 229–34.

76 Clark, *Nuclear Diplomacy and the Special Relationship*, pp. 159–61.

77 Botti, *The Long Wait*, p. 241.

78 See Clark, *Nuclear Diplomacy and the Special Relationship*, pp. 176–89.

79 See PRO, ADM 1/27389, Memorandum of Understanding on Skybolt, 6 June 1960.

80 Clark, *Nuclear Diplomacy and the Special Relationship*, pp. 251–4; Murray, *Kennedy, Macmillan and Nuclear Weapons*, pp. 40–1.

81 PRO, ADM 1/27389, Burke to Lambe, 27 March 1960.

82 PRO, ADM 1/27389, Couchman to Burke, 26 April 1960.

83 PRO, ADM 1/27839, Polaris submarines for the UK: Timing of Alternative Programmes, Admiralty report for the MOD, undated (April 1960); PRO, ADM 1/27839, Director of Tactical and Weapons Policy to Mountbatten, 29 April 1960; PRO, ADM 1/27839, Director of Tactical and Weapons, Policy note on Skybolt, 27 April 1960.

84 C. Grayling and C. Langdon, *Just Another Star? Anglo-American Relations since 1945*, London: Harrap, 1988, p. 45.

85 PRO, ADM1/27839, Couchman to Thisleton Smith, 26 April 1960.

86 Clark, *Nuclear Diplomacy and the Special Relationship*, p. 260; Murray, *Kennedy, Macmillan and Nuclear Weapons*, p. 46.

87 Clark, *Nuclear Diplomacy and the Special Relationship*, pp. 264–74; Murray, *Kennedy, Macmillan and Nuclear Weapons*, pp. 41–3.

88 J.D. Steinbruner, *The Cybernetic Theory of Decision: New Dimension of Political Analysis*, Princeton: Princeton University Press, 1974, p. 176.

89 Steinbruner, *The Cybernetic Theory of Decision*, p. 185.

90 C. Newton, 'Polaris Major Factor in Proposed 1000-Missile Force for NATO', *Missiles and Rockets* (July 1960), pp. 12–13; C.A. Pagedas, *Anglo-American Strategic Relations and the French Problem, 1960–1963: A Troubled Partnership*, London and

Portland: Frank Cass, 2000, p. 67; Steinbruner, *The Cybernetic Theory of Decision*, p. 188.

91 Pagedas, *Anglo-American Strategic Relations and the French Problem*, pp. 74–5.

92 PRO, DEFE 11/311, Foreign Office to British Embassy, Washington, 24 February 1960, p. 2.

93 See PRO, PREM 11/3714, Macmillan to Eisenhower, 26 October 1960.

94 Clark, *Nuclear Diplomacy and the Special Relationship*, pp. 274–7.

95 PRO, PREM 11/3713, Note of a meeting at 10 Downing Street, 15 June 1960.

96 PRO, PREM 11/3713, Bligh to Macmillan, 2 June 1960; PREM 11/3713, Caccia to Foreign Office, 2 June 1960.

97 Clark, *Nuclear Diplomacy and the Special Relationship*, pp. 280–1; Nailor, *The Nassau Connection*, p. 2.

98 PRO, PREM 11/3713, de Zulueta to Macmillan, 4 July 1960.

99 PRO, PREM 11/3713, de Zulueta to Macmillan, 4 July 1960; PRO, PREM 11/3713, Eisenhower to Macmillan, 30 June 1960; PRO, PREM 11/3713, Bishop to Macmillan, 22 June 1960.

100 PRO, PREM 11/3713, de Zulueta to Macmillan, 4 July 1960.

101 Clark, *Nuclear Diplomacy and the Special Relationship*, pp. 292–5.

102 Clark, *Nuclear Diplomacy and the Special Relationship*, pp. 31–3; W. Park, *Defending the West: A History of NATO*, Brighton: Wheatsheaf, 1986, p. 27; Baylis, *Anglo-American Defence Relations*, pp. 43–9.

103 Pagedas, *Anglo-American Strategic Relations and the French Problem*, pp. 12–13.

104 Pagedas, *Anglo-American Strategic Relations and the French Problem*, pp. 22–43.

105 Pagedas, *Anglo-American Strategic Relations and the French Problem*, pp. 56–87.

106 H.W. Gatzke, *Germany and the United States: A 'Special Relationship'?* Cambridge and London: Harvard University Press, 1980, p. 182; Pagedas, *Anglo-American Strategic Relations and the French Problem*, pp. 24–5.

107 Pagedas, *Anglo-American Strategic Relations and the French Problem*, pp. 114–15.

108 United States Declassified Documents Series (hereafter referred to as USDD), 424A/366, Memorandum of Conversation: NATO MRBM Force, 3 October 1960.

109 USDD, 424A/366, Memorandum of Conversation: NATO MRBM Force, 3 October 1960, pp. 2–3; USDD, 58B/177, 1/1/79, Memorandum for the National Security Council, NATO MRBM Force, 22 December 1960; Pagedas, *Anglo-American Strategic Relations and the French Problem*, pp. 83–5; Steinbruner, *The Cybernetic Theory of Decision*, pp. 188–90.

2 SKYBOLT, POLARIS AND NASSAU

1 F.J. Gavin, 'The Myth of Flexible Response: United States Strategy in Europe During the 1960s', *International History Review*, vol. 23, no. 4, pp. 847–75.

2 John F. Kennedy Library (hereafter referred to as JFK), National Security Files (hereafter referred to as NSF), Regional Security Files (hereafter referred to as RSF), NATO, General, Rostow, 1/61-11/61 [Folder 2 of 4], Herter's Explanatory note, 16 December 1960; United States Declassified Documents Series (hereafter referred to as USDD), 44/673, 1/1/84, NATO and MRBM Proposal, undated (late 1960).

3 See R. Aldous, ' "A Family Affair": Macmillan and the Art of Personal Diplomacy', in R. Aldous and S. Lee (eds) *Harold Macmillan and Britain's World Role*, London and Basingstoke: Macmillan, 1996, pp. 9–36.

4 See N.J. Ashton, 'Harold Macmillan and the "Golden Days" of Anglo-American Relations', *Diplomatic History*, vol. 29, no. 4, 2005, especially pp. 714–23.

5 *Public Papers of the Presidents of the United States: John F. Kennedy*, 1962, Joint Statement between President Kennedy and Harold Macmillan, 21 December 1962, pp. 908–10.

6 For example, D. Murray, *Kennedy, Macmillan and Nuclear Weapons*, Basingstoke: Macmillan, 2000; I. Clark, *Nuclear Diplomacy and the Special Relationship: Britain's Deterrent and America, 1957–1962*, Oxford: Clarendon, 1994; A.J. Pierre, *Nuclear Politics: The British Experience with an Independent Strategic Force, 1939–1970*, London: Oxford University Press, 1972; R.E. Neustadt, *Alliance Politics*, New York: Columbia University Press, 1970; R.E. Neustadt, *Report for JFK: The Skybolt Crisis in Perspective*, Ithaca and London: Cornell University Press, 1999. See also, H. Brandon 'Skybolt: The Full Inside Story of How a Missile Nearly Split the West', *The Sunday Times*, 8 December 1963.

7 Neustadt, *Report to JFK*, pp. 94–5.

8 M. Trachtenberg, *A Constructed Peace: The Making of a European Settlement, 1945–1963*, Princeton: Princeton University Press, 1999, p. 362.

9 J. Baylis, *Anglo-American Defence Relations, 1939–1981*, London and Basingstoke: Macmillan, 1981, pp. 70–1; Clark, *Nuclear Diplomacy and the Special Relationship*, 370–1; C.A. Pagedas, *Anglo-American Strategic Relations and the French Problem, 1960–1963: A Troubled Partnership*, London and Portland: Frank Cass, 2000, pp. 198–9.

10 David Bruce described the Skybolt episode as 'The single most exaggerated thing since my stay in England...I was astonished at the outcry'. JFK, Papers of David Nunnerley (hereafter referred to as Nunnerley Papers), Transcripts, Ball – Douglas-Home, David Bruce interview.

11 See N.J. Ashton, *Kennedy, Macmillan and the Cold War: The Irony of Interdependence*, Basingstoke and New York: Palgrave-Macmillan, 2002, pp. 16–17.

12 Pagedas, *Anglo-American Strategic Relations and the French Problem*, p. 135; Foreign Relations of the United States (hereafter referred to as FRUS), 1961–1963, vol. XIII, *Western Europe and Canada*, Policy Directive: NATO and the Atlantic Nations, 20 April 1961, pp. 285–91.

13 FRUS, 1961–1963, vol. XIII, Policy Directive: NATO and the Atlantic Nations, 20 April 1961, p. 289.

14 Public Record Office (hereafter referred to as PRO), PREM 11/3715, Caccia to Foreign Office, 17 March 1961; PRO, CAB 21/4978, Summary of Washington Telegram, no. 695, Anglo-American discussion on NATO Strategy and Nuclear Weapons, 29 March 1961; Ramsbotham to Mottershead, 7 March 1961.

15 *Public Papers of the Presidents of the United States: John F. Kennedy*, 1961, Address before the Canadian Parliament, 17 May 1961, pp. 382–7; *New York Times*, 18 May 1961.

16 T.C. Sorenson, *Kennedy*, New York: Harper & Row, 1965, p. 567. This caused some suspicion within NATO. The Germans in particular were concerned and requested immediate clarification, especially as to whether Kennedy's proposal would require further amendments to the McMahon Act and whether the US really believed France would participate in such a project. See JFK, NSF, RSF, box 222, NATO General, Cables, 1/61-2/62 [1 of 4], Finletter to Rusk, 18 May 1961.

17 See United States National Archives (hereafter referred to as USNA), Record Group (hereafter referred to as RG)59, Deputy Assistant Secretary for Politico-Military Affairs, Subject Files, 1961–1968, Lot 65D134, NN3-059-93-20, (hereafter referred to as Politico-Military Affairs), Polaris, McNamara to Rusk, 5 December 1961.

18 Pagedas, *Anglo-American Strategic Relations and the French Problem*, pp. 135–6, J.D. Steinbruner, *The Cybernetic Theory of Decision: New Dimension of Political Analysis*, Princeton: Princeton University Press, 1974, p. 225.

19 JFK, NSF, RSF, box 216A, Multilateral Force, General, 1/61-6/62, Kohler and McGhee to Rusk, 27 October 1961; FRUS, 1961–1963, vol. XIII, Rusk to McNamara, 29 October 1961, pp. 333–5. See also USDD, 266/3179, 11/1/97, Rusk to McNamara, 20 September 1962; USDD, 266/3178, 11/1/97, Political Implications of MRBM Land Basing, State Department Memorandum, 19 September 1962.

20 See D.L. Dileo, 'George Ball and the Europeanists in the State Department, 1961–1963', in D. Brinkley and R.T. Griffiths (eds) *John F. Kennedy and Europe*, Baton Rouge: Louisiana State University Press, 1999, pp. 263–80.

21 See JFK, NSF, RSF, box 216A, Multilateral Force, General, 1/61-6/62, Position Paper: MRBM's, 4 December 1961.

22 USNA, RG 59, Politico-Military Affairs, Macmillan Visit (1962), Position Paper: Assistance for Military Nuclear Programs, 16 December 1962, p. 2.

23 USNA, RG 59, Politico-Military Affairs, Macmillan Visit (1962), Position Paper: Assistance for Military Nuclear Programs, 16 December 1962, p. 4.

24 USNA, RG 59, Politico-Military Affairs, Macmillan Visit (1962), Position Paper: Defense Policies, 18 December 1961, pp. 1–8.

25 USNA, RG 59, Bureau of European Affairs, NATO and Atlantic Political Affairs (EUR/RPM), Records Relating to NATO Affairs, 1959–1966, Lot 67D516 (hereafter referred to as EUR/RPM), Defense Affairs NATO, Def 12 Nuclear Force – European Opinion, Collins to Kohler, 24 January 1962.

26 FRUS, 1961–1963, vol. XIII, Memorandum for the President, undated (July 1962), pp. 432–3.

27 R.S. Jordan, *Generals in International Politics: NATO's Supreme Allied Commander, Europe*, Lexington: University of Kentucky Press, 1987, pp. 89–91.

28 See Ashton, *Kennedy, Macmillan and the Cold War*, p. 137.

29 A recent study argues that de Gaulle used this (Anglo-American) fear in order to try and extract aid for his own nuclear programme. See E.R. Mahan, *Kennedy, De Gaulle and Western Europe*, Basingstoke: Palgrave, 2002, pp. 71–3.

30 FRUS, 1961–1963, vol. XIII, Memorandum of Meeting, 15 March 1962, pp. 366–8.

31 Steinbruner, *The Cybernetic Theory of Decision*, pp. 226–8; Pagedas, *Anglo-American Strategic Relations and the French Problem*, pp. 139–41; FRUS, 1961–1963, vol. XIII, Minutes of Meeting, 16 April 1962, p. 380; FRUS, 1961–1963, vol. XIII, NSAM 147, 18 April 1962, Subject: NATO Nuclear Program, pp. 384–7; USDD, 153/2744, 9/1/89, Washington to US Mission to NATO, 17 April 1962.

32 FRUS, 1961–1963, vol. VII, *Arms Control and Disarmament*, William Y. Smith to General Maxwell D. Taylor, 10 August 1962, pp. 548–9; National Intelligence Estimate, NIE 11-2-63, 2 July 1963, pp. 762.

33 FRUS, 1961–1963, vol. XIII, NSAM 147, 18 April 1962, pp. 386–7.

34 USNA, RG 330, Secretary of Defense Files, 334, NATO Ministerial Mtng, December 1962, Memorandum of Conversation, 2 May 1962.

35 USNA, RG 330, Secretary of Defense Files, 334, NATO Ministerial Mtng, December 1962, Memorandum of Conversation, 3 May 1962.

36 PRO, DEFE 11/223, British Embassy Washington to the Foreign Office, 8 June 1962; Foreign Office to British Embassy, Washington, 14 June 1962.

37 JFK, NSF, RSF, box 216A, Multilateral Force, General, 1/61-6/62, Kennedy to Finletter, 15 June 1962.

38 PRO, PREM 11/3715, Watkinson to Macmillan, 18 June 1962.

39 PRO, PREM 11/3715, Shuckburgh to Foreign Office, 18 June 1962; Home to Macmillan, 21 June 1962.

40 PRO, PREM 11/3715, Home to Macmillan, 21 June 1962.

41 See USDD, 88B/206, Missiles Panel to President's Scientific Advisory Committee, 12 July 1960.

42 Clark, *Nuclear Diplomacy and the Special Relationship*, p. 341–6; Murray, *Kennedy, Macmillan and Nuclear Weapons*, p. 47; Neustadt, *Alliance Politics*, p. 36; PRO, FO 371/159649, Information Department, BDS Washington to Foreign Office, 6 January 1961.

43 Clark, *Nuclear Diplomacy and the Special Relationship*, p. 346; PRO, FO 371/159649, Foreign Office to BDS, Washington, 13 January 1961; Neustadt, *Alliance Politics*, p. 36.

44 PRO, DEFE 13/409, Note for the Record, 3 November 1961; PRO, DEFE 13/409, Zuckerman to Watkinson, 30 November 1961; PRO, DEFE 13/409, Minute of meeting between McNamara and Watkinson, 11 December 1961; A.C. Enthoven and K.W. Smith, *How Much is Enough? Shaping the Defense Program*, New York: Harper & Row, 1971, pp. 253–4. McNamara may have been referring to an American position paper prepared at the same time that recognized the UK was counting on Skybolt. See USNA, RG 59, Politico-Military Affairs, Macmillan Visit 1962, Bermuda Meeting with PM Macmillan, 21–22 December 1961, Position Paper, undated (December 1961).

45 PRO, DEFE 13/409, Minute of meeting between McNamara and Watkinson, 11 December 1961.

46 Naval Historical Center, Operational Archives Branch, Papers of Harvey M. Sapolsky, series I, box 6, Special Projects Office File (History) 1953–1963, McNamara to Connally, 28 January 1961; McNamara to Kennedy, 28 January 1961.

47 PRO, DEFE 13/126, British Embassy, Washington to Foreign Office, 30 March 1961.

48 M. Simeon, 'Watching Brief, 1958–60', in J.E. Moore (ed.) *The Impact of Polaris: The Origins of Britain's Seaborne Nuclear Deterrent*, Huddersfield: Richard Netherwood, 1999, p. 37.

49 D. Nunnerley, *President Kennedy and Britain*, London: The Bodley Head, 1972, pp. 133–5.

50 Trachtenberg, *A Constructed Peace*, pp. 315–17. McNamara's speeches followed an approach to confrontation with the Soviets approved by the president in October the previous year. See S. Twigge and A. Macmillan, 'Britain, the United States and the Development of Nuclear Strategy, 1950–64', *Journal of Strategic Studies*, vol. 19, no. 2, 1996, pp. 274–5.

51 L.S. Kaplan, *The Long Entanglement: NATO's First Fifty Years*, Westport: Praeger, 1999, pp. 101–10; Steinbruner, *The Cybernetic Theory of Decision*, pp. 220–1.

52 JFK, NSF, box 398, McGeorge Bundy Correspondence, Chronological File, 5/6/61-5/15/61, Kennedy to Macmillan, 8 May 1961.

53 J.W. Young, *Britain and European Unity, 1945–1999*, Basingstoke and London: Palgrave, 2000, p. 68.

54 Young, *Britain and European Unity*, pp. 69–70.

55 Pagedas, *Anglo-American Strategic Relations and the French Problem*, pp. 151–4.

56 USNA, RG 59, Deputy Assistant Secretary for Politio-Military Affairs, Subject Files of the Special Asst for Atomic Energy and Aerospace, 1950–1966, Nuclear Sharing – France 1962/61 Assistance to, Gavin to Ball, 17 March 1962. See also E.R. Mahan, *Kennedy, De Gaulle and Western Europe*, pp. 75–7.

57 Pagedas, *Anglo-American Strategic Relations and the French Problem*, pp. 189–93.

58 JFK, NSF, box 171, United Kingdom, Macmillan Correspondence, 1/20/61-9/7/61, Kennedy to Macmillan, 6 May 1961.

59 Pagedas, *Anglo-American Strategic Relations and the French Problem*, pp. 193–7.

60 FRUS, 1961–1963, vol. XIII, Bundy to Kennedy, 24 April 1962, pp. 1068–9.

61 See, for example, USNA, RG 59, Politico-Military Affairs, Macmillan Visit (1962), NATO STRATEGY Paper, 21 April 1962, pp. 4–5; FRUS, 1961–1963, vol. XIII, Kohler to Rusk, 24 May 1962, pp. 1073–6; Rusk to McNamara, 8 September 1962, pp. 1078–80.

62 FRUS, 1961–1963, vol. XIII, Kohler to Rusk, 24 May 1962, pp. 1073–76.

63 Pagedas, *Anglo-American Strategic Relations and the French Problem*, pp. 209–10.

64 Pagedas, *Anglo-American Strategic Relations and the French Problem*, pp. 202–6; House of Commons Debates, 1961–1962, 24 May 1962, vol. 660, col. 667–8.

65 USNA, RG 59, Politico-Military Affairs, Macmillan Visit 1962, NATO STRATEGY Paper, 21 April 1962. The paper also claimed that a reason to oppose such action was that it might then encourage the West German government to seek similar treatment from the British.

66 USNA, RG 59, Deputy Assistant Secretary for Politico-Military Affairs, Subject Files of the Special Asst for Atomic Energy and Aerospace, 1950–1966, Nuclear Sharing – France 1963 and Prior, Battle to Bundy, 9 May 1962. The president continued to probe the problems, however. See JFK, Papers of Richard E. Neustadt (hereafter referred to as Neustadt Papers), box 20, Government Consulting, 1959–66, NATO Nuclear Weapons/AID, 1962, 1 of 2, McNamara to Kennedy, 16 June 1962.

67 JFK, NSF, RSF, box 222, NATO, General, 3/1/62-6/14/62 [4 of 4], Rusk to American Embassy, Paris, 8 June 1962; PRO, PREM 11/3715, Dixon to Foreign Office, 12 June 1962; Macmillan's handwritten note on Ormsby Gore to Foreign Office, 15 June 1962.

68 PRO, PREM 11/3715, Macmillan to Home, 24 June 1962.

69 FRUS, 1961–1963, vol. XIII, American Embassy, London to Department of State, 26 June 1962, p. 423–5.

70 Pagedas, *Anglo-American Strategic Relations and the French Problem*, pp. 229–30.

71 USNA, RG 330, United Kingdom 333, September – December 1962, Memorandum of Conversation, 13 September 1962; Pagedas, *Anglo-American Strategic Relations and the French Problem*, pp. 232–3.

72 USDD, 266/3180, 11/1/97, Discussion with Lord Home on Nuclear/MRBM Issues, State Department to Bundy, 28 September 1962.

73 USNA, RG 59, Lot Files, Bureau of European Affairs Deputy Assistant Secretary Subject Files, J. Robert Schaetzel, 1961–1966, Lot 66D439, MLF, Tyler to Rusk, 25 October 1962; Pagedas, *Anglo-American Strategic Relations and the French Problem*, pp. 234–5.

74 PRO, DEFE 13/409, Zuckerman to Watkinson, 8 August 1962; PRO, DEFE 13/409, BDS Washington to MOD, 14 August 1962; JFK, Neustadt Papers, box 19, Government Consulting, 1959–66, Skybolt/Atlantic Affairs, 8/62-11/62, Skybolt-Nassau, Miscellaneous, Classified – Folder 1, Wilson to Brown, 14 August 1962.

75 JFK, Neustadt Papers, box 19, Government Consulting, 1959–66, Skybolt/Atlantic Affairs, 8/62-11/62, Skybolt-Nassau, Miscellaneous, Classified – Folder 1, Jones to Rusk, 31 August 1962; Ashton, *Kennedy, Macmillan and the Cold War*, pp. 165–6.

76 Neustadt, *Alliance Politics*, p. 40.

77 Murray, *Kennedy, Macmillan and Nuclear Weapons*, p. 51.

78 Enthoven and Smith, *How Much is Enough?* p. 261.

79 PRO, DEFE 13/409, DRS, Washington to MOD, 31 October 1962.

80 JFK, Neustadt Papers, Skybolt/Atlantic Affairs, 8/62-11/62, Skybolt-Nassau, Miscellaneous, Classified – Folder 2, Tyler to Rusk, 8 November 1962; Neustadt, *Report to JFK*, pp. 33–4.

81 FRUS, 1961–1963, vol. XIII, Department of State Memorandum, Implications for the United Kingdom of Decision to Abandon Skybolt, 31 October 1962, pp. 1083–5.

82 JFK, Neustadt Papers, Skybolt/Atlantic Affairs, 8/62-11/62, Skybolt-Nassau, Miscellaneous, Classified – Folder 2, Thorneycroft to McNamara, 5 November 1962.

83 JFK, Neustadt Papers, Skybolt/Atlantic Affairs, 8/62-11/62, Skybolt-Nassau, Miscellaneous, Classified – Folder 2, McNamara to Thorneycroft, 7 November 1962, Nitze to McNamara, 7 November 1962.

84 PRO, DEFE 13/409, Memorandum for Minister of Defence, 7 November 1962.

85 PRO, DEFE 13/409, BDS Washington to MOD, 7 November 1962.

86 PRO, PREM 11/3716, RAFS Washington to Air Ministry, 13 November 1962.

87 FRUS, 1961–1963, vol. XIII, Note of Conversations Relating to Skybolt by McNamara, 9 November 1962, pp. 1085–6; JFK, Neustadt Papers, Skybolt/Atlantic Affairs, 8/62-11/62, Skybolt-Nassau, Miscellaneous, Classified – Folder 2,

McNamara to Bruce, 12 November 1962; Murray, *Kennedy, Macmillan and Nuclear Weapons*, pp. 53–4.

88 PRO, DEFE 13/409, Hockaday to Thorneycroft, 9 November 1962; PRO, DEFE 13/409, Note for the Record 'Skybolt', 14 November 1962.

89 Clark, *Nuclear Diplomacy and the Special Relationship*, pp. 354–6.

90 PRO, PREM 11/3716, Thorneycroft to Macmillan, 7 December 1962. For his previous thoughts on the matter see PRO, PREM 11/3716, Godfrey to de Zulueta, 15 November 1962.

91 See PRO DEFE 11/222, Chiefs of Staff Committee Papers on Nuclear Defence and Europe, 6 December 1962.

92 Ashton, *Kennedy, Macmillan and the Cold War*, p. 170.

93 PRO, PREM 11/3716, Macmillan to Thorneycroft, 7 December 1962.

94 Ashton, *Kennedy, Macmillan and the Cold War*, pp. 168–9. Only the Joint Chiefs of Staff recommended continuing with Skybolt. See JFK, NSF, RSF, box 227, NATO, Weapons, Cables, Skybolt, 3/63 [1 of 2], Joint Chiefs of Staff to McNamara, 20 November 1962; JFK, Nunnerley Papers, Transcripts, John-Norstad, Lemnitzer interview, 11 February 1970.

95 JFK, NSF, RSF, box 227, NATO, Weapons, Cables, Skybolt, 3/63 [1 of 2], Bruce to Rusk, 21 November 1962.

96 JFK, Neustadt Papers, box 19, Government Consulting, 1959–66, Skybolt/Atlantic Affairs, 8/62-11/62, Skybolt-Nassau, Miscellaneous, Classified – Folder 3, Kitchen to Rusk, 30 November 1962.

97 Murray, *Kennedy, Macmillan and Nuclear Weapons*, pp. 54–5.

98 PRO, CAB 21/5967, Foreign Office to British Embassy, Washington, 6 December 1962; PRO, CAB 21/5967, Gore to Foreign Office, 7 December 1962.

99 PRO, CAB 21/5967, Note for the record, 29 November 1962.

100 USNA, RG 59, Conference Files, Lot 65D533 (hereafter referred to as Conference Files), CF2208, Schedule for Nassau Meeting, undated; PRO, CAB 21/5967, Gore to Foreign Office, 4 December 1962.

101 USNA, RG 59, Conference Files, CF2209, Bruce to Rusk, 3 December 1962; JFK, Neustadt Papers, box 19, Government Consulting, 1959–66, Skybolt/Atlantic Affairs, 8/62-11/62, Skybolt-Nassau, Miscellaneous, Classified – Folder 2, Kitchen to Rusk, undated (7 or 9 November 1962); USNA, RG 59, Central Decimal File, 1960–1963, 741.5/1-2562, American Embassy, London to Rusk, 14 December 1962.

102 PRO, CAB 21/5697, Foreign Office to British Embassy, Washington, 6 December 1962; Ormsby Gore to Foreign Office, 7 December 1962.

103 PRO, PREM 11/3716, Note for the Record, 9 December 1962.

104 PRO, PREM 11/3716, de Zulueta to Ormsby Gore, 11 December 1962.

105 Clark, *Nuclear Diplomacy and the Special Relationship*, p. 358; Murray, *Kennedy, Macmillan and Nuclear Weapons*, pp. 64–6; D. Kiker, 'The Education of Robert McNamara', *The Atlantic*, vol. 219, no. 3, 1967, pp. 49–55.

106 Neustadt, *Report to JFK*, p. 69.

107 PRO, PREM 11/3716, Record of talks between McNamara and Thorneycroft, 11 December 1962; JFK, NSF, RSF, box 227, NATO, Weapons, Cables, Skybolt, 3/63 [1 of 2], Bruce to Rusk, Personal for President from McNamara, 11 December 1962.

108 Neustadt, *Alliance Politics*, p. 47; Murray, *Kennedy, Macmillan and Nuclear Weapons*, pp. 55–6. See also Clark, *Nuclear Diplomacy and the Special Relationship*, pp. 358–9; Neustadt, *Report to JFK*, pp. 69–76.

109 JFK, NSF, RSF, box 227, NATO, Weapons, Cables, Skybolt, 3/63 [1 of 2], Bruce to Rusk, Personal for President from McNamara, 11 December 1962.

110 JFK, Neustadt Papers, box 19, Government Consulting, 1959–66, Skybolt/Atlantic Affairs, 8/62-11/62, Skybolt-Nassau, Classified – Folder 3, Last Conversation with

the President before NATO Meeting of December 1962, 10 December 1962 (13 December 1962).

111 JFK, Nunnerley Papers, Transcripts, Thorneycroft-Wright, Thorneycroft interview, 18 June 1969, p. 18; Murray, *Kennedy, Macmillan and Nuclear Weapons*, p. 79; Ashton, *Kennedy, Macmillan and the Cold War*, pp. 172–3.

112 Ashton, *Kennedy, Macmillan and the Cold War*, pp. 171–2.

113 See Clark, *Nuclear Diplomacy and the Special Relationship*, p. 358. The Pentagon had already conducted a study on alternatives to Skybolt in November. See Neustadt, *Report to JFK*, pp. 40–1.

114 USNA, RG 59, Conference Files, CF2212, Kennedy–Macmillan Nassau Meeting, 19–20 December 1962 [1 of 2], Wiesner to President, 14 December 1962.

115 USNA, RG 59, Conference Files, CF2212, Kennedy–Macmillan Nassau Meeting [1 of 2], Gilpatric to Bundy, 15 December 1962.

116 See, for example, JFK, NSF, RSF, box 224, NATO, Second Defence Policy conference, 11/30/62, Rusk to McNamara, 24 November 1962. This letter was written by Henry Owen. See Neustadt, *Report to JFK*, p. 47.

117 USNA, RG 59, Conference Files, CF2212, Kennedy–Macmillan Nassau Meeting [1 of 2], Memorandum, Subject: Nuclear Aspects of Macmillan Visit, 15 December 1962, p. 4.

118 USNA, RG 59, Conference Files, CF2212, Kennedy–Macmillan Nassau Meeting [1 of 2], Memorandum, Subject: Nuclear Aspects of Macmillan Visit, 15 December 1962, p. 7.

119 USNA, RG 59, Conference Files, CF2212, Kennedy–Macmillan Nassau Meeting [1 of 2], Memorandum, Subject: Nuclear Aspects of Macmillan Visit, 15 December 1962 (No drafting information is included), p. 9.

120 FRUS, 1961–1963, vol. XIII, Memorandum of Conversation, 16 December 1962, pp. 1088–91. See also Ashton, *Kennedy, Macmillan and the Cold War*, pp. 173–4.

121 Neustadt, *Alliance Politics*, pp. 50–1; Murray, *Kennedy, Macmillan and Nuclear Weapons*, pp. 82–3. Ashton suggests that Kennedy offered the 50–50 deal primarily in order to consolidate his negotiating position for three reasons. First, because he did not want to be seen to be reneging on a deal his predecessor had made. Second, in case the Nassau talks broke down he could show that he had made an offer and third because he wanted to 'smooth over' the divisions within his own administration. See Ashton, *Kennedy, Macmillan and the Cold War*, p. 175. This is convincing: Kennedy had said at his meeting with McNamara and Rusk on 10 December 'that he was not eager to join in a large share of further development costs for a weapon to be supplied only to the British'. JFK, Neustadt Papers, box 19, Government Consulting, 1959–66, Skybolt/Atlantic Affairs, 8/62-11/62, Skybolt-Nassau, Miscellaneous, Classified – Folder 3, Last Conversation with the President before NATO Meeting of December 1962, 10 December 1962 (13 December 1962).

122 See JFK, NSF, RSF, box 227, NATO, Weapons, Cables, Skybolt, 3/63 [1 of 2], Owen to Ball, 16 December 1962; JFK, Neustadt Papers, box 19, Government Consulting, 1959–66, Skybolt/Atlantic Affairs, 8/62-11/62, Skybolt-Nassau, Miscellaneous, Classified – Folder 4, Tyler to Ball, 18 December 1962.

123 USNA, RG 59, EUR/RPM, Nassau United Kingdom Negotiations, Tyler and Rostow to Rusk, 17 December 1962.

124 USNA, RG 59, Conference Files, CF2212, Rostow to Kennedy, 17 December 1962.

125 Murray, *Kennedy, Macmillan and Nuclear Weapons*, pp. 79–80.

126 PRO, DEFE 13/619, Scott to Thorneycroft, 18 December 1962.

127 Baylis, *Ambiguity and Deterrence: British Nuclear Strategy, 1945–1964*, Oxford: Clarendon, 1995, pp. 319–26; Clark, *Nuclear Diplomacy and the Special Relationship*, pp. 409–18; Murray, *Kennedy, Macmillan and Nuclear Weapons*,

pp. 84–93; Pierre, *Nuclear Politics*, pp. 231–43; Ashton, *Kennedy, Macmillan and Nuclear Weapons*, pp. 174–85.

128 See Nunnerley Papers, Transcripts, Ball – Douglas-Home, David Bruce interview, 5 December 1968; First Lord Harlech interview, p. 29.

129 Neustadt, *Report to JFK*, pp. 88–90; Murray, *Kennedy, Macmillan and Nuclear Weapons*, pp. 82–4.

130 PRO, CAB 21/5967, Record of Meeting held at Bali-Hai, the Bahamas, 9.50 am, Wednesday 19 December 1962, p. 3; FRUS, 1961–1963, vol. XIII, Memorandum of Conversation, Nassau, 9.45 am, 19 December 1962, pp. 1091–7. See also PRO, PREM 11/4230, Visit of the Prime Minister to Chateau de Rambouillet, 15–16 December 1962, Record of Conversation, 15 December 1962; Harold Macmillan, *At the End of the Day*, Basingstoke: Macmillan, 1973, p. 348.

131 FRUS, 1961–1963, vol. XIII, Memorandum of Conversation, Nassau, 4.30 pm, 19 December 1962, p. 1103.

132 FRUS, 1961–1963, vol. XIII, Memorandum of Conversation, Nassau, 4.30 pm, 19 December 1962, pp. 1102–5.

133 FRUS, 1961–1963, vol. XIII, Memorandum of Conversation, Nassau, 9.45 am, 19 December 1962, p. 1096.

134 FRUS, 1961–1963, vol. XIII, Rusk to Nassau, 20 December 1962, p. 1108.

135 See also Clark, *Nuclear Diplomacy and the Special Relationship*, pp. 417–18.

136 PRO, CAB 21/5967, Macmillan to First Secretary of State, Codel 24, 20 December 1962.

137 PRO, DEFE 13/619, Thorneycroft to Macmillan, 19 December 1962, pp. 2–4.

138 Ashton, *Kennedy, Macmillan and the Cold War*, p. 182.

139 PRO, DEFE 13/619, Telephone advanced summary from Chief Whip, Codel 62, Annex U, 21 December 1962.

140 PRO, DEFE 13/619, Telephone advanced summary, Annex T, 21 December 1962.

141 PRO, DEFE 13/619, Scott and Zuckerman to Thorneycroft, 21 December 1962.

142 Nunnerley, *President Kennedy and Britain*, p. 149.

143 USNA, RG 59, Conference Files, CF2212, Nassau Meeting, 19–20 December 1962, Memorandum of Conversation between Ball and Rostow, 20 December 1962. His later recollections of the Nassau conference contradict this optimistic assessment. See G.W. Ball, *The Discipline of Power: Essentials of a Modern World Structure*, Boston and Toronto: Little, Brown and Co., 1968, pp. 102–7; G.W. Ball, *The Past Has Another Pattern: Memoirs*, New York and London: W.W. Norton, 1982, p. 107.

144 USNA, RG 59, Conference Files, CF2212, Macmillan Nassau Meeting [2 of 2], Rostow to Rusk, 20 December 1962.

145 JFK, NSF, RSF, box 219, Multilateral Force, Subjects, De Gaulle Correspondence, Kennedy to de Gaulle, 21 December 1962.

146 JFK, NSF, RSF, box 228, NATO, Weapons, Nassau Agreement, 11/21/62-3/25/63 [1 of 3], Rusk to American Embassy, Bonn, 21 December 1962.

147 USNA, RG 59, Politico-Military Affairs, Steering Comm Post Nassau, Salinger to Manning, 22 December 1962, Ball–McNamara Press Conference, 21 December, pp. 7–8.

148 USNA, RG 59, Politico-Military Affairs, Steering Comm Post Nassau, Salinger to Manning, 22 December 1962, Ball–McNamara Press Conference, 21 December, pp. 18–19.

149 USNA, RG 59, Conference Files, CF2212, Macmillan Nassau Meeting [2 of 2], Ball to Rusk, 21 December 1962.

150 USNA, RG 59, Bureau of European Affairs, Office of Atlantic Political and Military Affairs, Records Relating to NATO, 1957–1964, NATO 1962 8–2 Council (Pol Consultation), Rostow to Tyler, 21 December 1962; Rostow to Tyler, 26 December 1962.

3 THE POLARIS PROJECT AND NATO

1 John F. Kennedy Library (hereafter referred to as JFK), National Security Files (hereafter referred to as NSF), Regional Security Files (hereafter referred to as RSF), NATO, General, Cables, 6/15/62-3/31/63 [5 of 5], Rusk to Finletter, 27 December 1962.

2 United States National Archive (hereafter referred to as USNA), Record Group (hereafter referred to as RG), 59, Deputy Assistant for Politico-Military Affairs, Subject Files, 1961–1968, Lot 65D134, NN3-059-93-20 (hereafter referred to as Politico-Military Affairs), Folder 5, Rostow Strategy Paper, Post Nassau Strategy, 27 December 1962.

3 JFK, NSF, RSF, box 228, NATO, Weapons, Cables, Nassau Agreement, 3/29/60-1/31/63, Allied Reactions to Nassau Agreement, 8 January 1963, p. 6.

4 M. Middeke, 'Anglo-American Nuclear Weapons Cooperation After the Nassau Conference: The British Policy of Interdependence', *Journal of Cold War Studies,* vol. 2, no. 2, 2000, p. 95.

5 *Public Papers of the Presidents of the United States: John F. Kennedy*, 1962, Joint Statement between President Kennedy and Harold Macmillan, 21 December 1962, pp. 908–10.

6 I.J. Galantin, *Submarine Admiral: From Battlewagons to Ballistic Missiles*, Urbana and Chicago: University of Illinois Press, 1995, pp. 289–90.

7 A. Priest, 'In American Hands: Britain, the United States and the Polaris Nuclear Project, 1962–1968', *Contemporary British History*, vol. 19, no. 3, 2005, pp. 353–76.

8 USNA, RG 59, Politico-Military Affairs, Steering Comm Post Nassau, Steering Group on Implementing the Nassau Decisions, Minutes of First Meeting, 27 December 1962.

9 Public Record Office (hereafter referred to as PRO), FO 371/173449, Mottershead to Grieg, 30 January 1963.

10 M. Middeke, 'Britain's Global Military Role, Conventional Defence and Anglo-American Interdependence After Nassau', *Journal of Strategic Studies*, vol. 24, no. 1, 2001, pp. 143–64.

11 See E.R. Mahan, *Kennedy, De Gaulle and Western Europe*, Basingstoke and London: Palgrave-Macmillan, 2003, pp. 55–8.

12 PRO, DEFE 11/222, Note of a Meeting between Thorneycroft and Stikker, 29 January 1963.

13 USNA, RG 218, NND 941071, Folder 337, S/Def Staff Mtgs, Secretary of Defense Staff Meeting, 7 January 1963, p. 9.

14 PRO, ADM 1/29269, Carrington to Thorneycroft, 31 December 1962.

15 See USNA, RG 59, Politico-Military Affairs, I Technical and Financial Agreement with UK, Burdett to Kitchen, undated (11 January 1963).

16 PRO, FO 371/173515, MOD to BDS, Washington, 7 January 1963; PRO, ADM 1/29269, Foreign Office to British Embassy, Washington, 7 January 1963; PRO, ADM 1/29269, Home to Macmillan, 8 January 1963; *The Times*, 18 January 1963.

17 PRO, ADM 1/29269, MOD to BDS, Washington, 7 January 1963.

18 USNA, RG 59, Central Decimal File (hereafter referred to as CDF), 741.5/1-2562, American Embassy, London to USIA, 3 January 1963; USNA RG 59, Conference Files, Lot 66D110, CF2217, Steering Group on Implementing Nassau [2 of 2], American Embassy, Paris to Secretary of State, 3 January 1963.

19 JFK, NSF, RSF, box 229, NATO, Weapons, Cables, Secretary Ball in Paris and Bonn, Finletter to Rusk, 12 January 1963.

20 USNA, RG 218, NND 941071, Folder 337, S/Def Staff Mtgs, Secretary of Defense Staff Meeting, 7 January 1963, p. 6.

21 USNA, RG 218, NND 941071, Folder 337, S/Def Staff Mtgs, Secretary of Defense Staff Meeting, 7 January 1963, p. 6; JFK, Papers of George W. Ball, box 6, NATO, 1/31/61-10/28/63, McNamara and Ball telephone conversation, 8 January 1963.

22 PRO, ADM 1/28987, Record of Meeting between Polaris Fact Finding Team and US Navy Special Projects Office, 9 January 1963; USNA, RG 218, NND 941071, Folder 337, S/Def Staff Mtgs, Secretary of Defense Staff Meeting, 7 January 1963, p. 7.

23 PRO, ADM 1/28987, Report of Fact Finding Mission to Washington, 15 January 1963.

24 PRO, ADM 1/28987, Notes of meeting between Polaris fact-finding team and US Navy Special Projects Office, 9 January 1963.

25 PRO, ADM 1 /29269, Carrington to Thorneycroft, 31 December 1962.

26 PRO, ADM 1/29269, Admiralty to Chief of the British Naval Staff, 18 January 1963.

27 See PRO, FO 371/173515, Zuckerman to Thorneycroft, 10 January 1963.

28 USNA, RG 59, CDF, 741.5/1-2562, Kitchen to American Embassy, London, 13 January 1963; USNA, RG 59, Bureau of European Affairs, NATO and Atlantic Political Affairs (EUR/RPM), Records Relating to NATO Affairs, 1959–1966, Lot 67D516 (hereafter referred to as EUR/RPM), NATO United Kingdom Negotiations, Steering Group on Implementing the Nassau Decisions, Minutes of Third Meeting, 10 January 1963, p. 3.

29 PRO, DEFE 13/619, Thorneycroft to Macmillan, 2 January 1963.

30 USNA, RG 59, CDF, 741.5/1-2562, British Embassy, London to Rusk, 2 January 1963.

31 PRO, AIR 20/10057, Macmillan to Thorneycroft, 26 December 1962; PRO, ADM 1/27890, Amery to Thorneycroft, 15 January 1963.

32 PRO, DEFE 7/1752, NASSAU Agreement, note of meeting held on 17 January 1963 (24 January 1963). See also JFK, Papers of George W. Ball, box 6, NATO, Multilateral Force (MLF), 1/31/61-10/28/63, Telephone conversation between Ball and McNamara, 8 January 1963, 12.30 pm.

33 PRO, ADM 1/28987, Report of Fact Finding Mission to Washington, 15 January 1963. See also PRO, DEFE 7/1752, NASSAU Agreement, note of meeting held on 17 January 1963 (24 January 1963).

34 USNA, RG 218, NND 941071, Folder 337, S/Def Staff Mtgs, Secretary of Defense Staff Meeting, 7 January 1963, p. 5.

35 PRO, FO 371/173515, McNamara to Thorneycroft, 13 January 1963.

36 PRO, PREM 13/228, Thorneycroft to Macmillan, undated; PRO, PREM 11/5088, Telephone conversation between Macmillan and Kennedy, 19 January 1963; DEFE 7/1752, Thorneycroft to Macmillan, 22 January 1963.

37 USNA, RG 59, EUR/RPM, NATO United Kingdom Negotiations, Steering Group on Implementing the Nassau Decisions, Minutes of Third Meeting, 10 January 1963, p. 1.

38 USNA, RG 218, NND 941071, Folder 337, S/Def Staff Mtgs, Secretary of Defense Staff Meeting, 28 January 1963, pp. 3–4; P. Nailor, *The Nassau Connection: The Organisation and Management of the British Polaris Project*, London: Her Majesty's Stationary Office, 1988, p. 18.

39 USNA, RG 218, NND 941071, Folder 337, S/Def Staff Mtgs, Secretary of Defense Staff Meeting, 7 January 1963, pp. 4–7.

40 USNA, RG 59, Politico-Military Affairs, Mr Ball's Presentation to NAC, Speech given by Under Secretary of State, George W. Ball, at a meeting of the North Atlantic Council, 11 January 1963; USNA, RG 59, Politico-Military Affairs, Mr Ball's Presentation to NAC, Finletter to Secretary of State, 11 January 1963; USNA, RG 59, Politico-Military Affairs, Multilateral Force, Text of Remarks made by Sir Evelyn Shuckburgh in the North Atlantic council, 11 January 1963; JFK, NSF, McGeorge Bundy Correspondence, Memos to the President, 1/1/63-1/20/63, Bundy to Kennedy, 12 January 1963.

41 USNA, RG 59, Politico-Military Affairs, Multilateral Force 2, Steering Group in Implementing the Nassau Decisions, Assignment of Forces to NATO, Submitted by Sub-Group II, 25 January 1963.

42 USNA, RG 59, Deputy Assistant Secretary for Politico-Military Affairs, Subject Files of the Special Asst for Atomic Energy and Aerospace, 1950–1966, Notes by John McNaughton of meeting with president on Nassau Implementation, 12 January 1963.

43 USNA, RG 59, EUR/RPM, Nassau United Kingdom Negotiations, Tyler and Rostow to Rusk, 17 December 1962; Foreign Relations of the United States (hereafter referred to as FRUS), 1961–1963, vol. XIII, *Western Europe and Canada*, Points Memorandum for the Record, 12 January 1963, p. 475; Kitchen to Rusk, 4 January 1963, p. 1124.

44 Although de Gaulle told them he would be 'prudent' when he came to discuss Polaris at his upcoming press conference. PRO, FO 146/4620, Summary record of discussion with General De Gaulle, 2 January 1963; C.A. Pagedas, *Anglo-American Strategic Relations and the French Problem, 1960–1963: A Troubled Partnership*, London and Portland, Frank Cass, 2000, p. 258.

45 FRUS, 1961–1963, vol. XIII, Record of Meeting, 28 December 1963, p. 1116; Bohlen to State Department, 4 January 1963, pp. 745–8.

46 R. Davis, 'Why Did the General Do It? De Gaulle, Polaris and the French Veto of Britain's Application to Join the Common Market', *European History Quarterly*, vol. 28, no. 3, 1998, p. 387.

47 Pagedas, *Anglo-American Strategic Relations and the French Problem*, pp. 258–62. Richard Davis suggests that the American offer of Polaris on 'similar' terms to the British 'did more harm than good to relations between Paris and their British and American counterparts'. Davis, 'Why Did the General Do It?' p. 387.

48 JFK, NSF, RSF, box 214, Europe, Subjects, PR Group, Unnumbered Series, 1963 [1 of 2], De Gaulle's Press Conference, Elysee Palace, 14 January 1963; JFK, NSF, RSF, box 212, Europe, General, 9/62-1/24, 63 [1 of 2], Bohlen to Secretary of State, 15 January 1963.

49 JFK, NSF, RSF, 9/62-1/24 63 [2 of 2], Dowling to Rusk, 28 January 1963. In fact, even the French record shows that Macmillan had at the very least implied he wanted submarine launched missiles, a point de Gaulle later conceded. See G. Warner, 'Why the General Said No', *International Affairs*, vol. 78, no. 4, 2002, p. 879.

50 JFK, NSF, RSF, 9/62-1/24 63 [1 of 2], Bohlen to Rusk, 19 January 1963.

51 JFK, NSF, RSF, 9/62-1/24 63 [1 of 2], Bohlen to Rusk, 16 January 1963.

52 G. Warner, 'Why the General Said No', pp. 880–1. Although Richard Davis agrees that the Nassau agreement did not have a direct impact, he plays up the importance of defence issues in de Gaulle's veto and suggests that it changed the tone of the press conference. Davis, 'Why did the General Do It?', pp. 387–90.

53 JFK, NSF, RSF, 9/62-1/24 63 [1 of 2], Bohlen to Rusk, 19 January 1963.

54 FRUS, 1961–1963, vol. XIII, Rusk to Bohlen, 19 January 1963, pp. 748–9.

55 FRUS, 1961–1963, vol. XIII, Rusk to US Embassy, Bonn, 21 December 1962, pp. 467–8; US Embassy, Bonn to Rusk, 3 January 1963, p. 468, fn.

56 USNA, RG 59, Politico-Military Affairs, Mr Ball's Presentation to NAC, Bohlen to Secretary of State, 11 January 1963.

57 PRO, CAB 21/5967, Macmillan to Kennedy, 24 December 1962.

58 PRO, PREM 11/5088, Telephone conversation between Macmillan and Kennedy, 19 January 1963, p. 1.

59 Pagedas, *Anglo-American Strategic Relations and the French Problem*, p. 265; Middeke, 'Anglo-American Nuclear Weapons Cooperation', p. 74.

60 See, for example, *The Times*, 22 December 1962; *Guardian*, 22 December 1962.

61 PRO, PREM 11/5088, Telephone conversation between Macmillan and Kennedy, 19 January 1963, p. 2.

62 JFK, NSF, box 173, United Kingdom, Macmillan Correspondence 6/20/62-4/15/63, Macmillan to Kennedy, T.24/63, 15 January 1963.

63 JFK, NSF, RSF, 9/62-1/24 63 [1 of 2], Bruce to Rusk, 24 January 1963.

64 JFK, President's Office Files, box 127A, United Kingdom, Security, 1/63-4/63, McGeorge Bundy to Kennedy, 6 February 1963; JFK, NSF, RSF, box 218, Multilateral Force, Cables, 3/1/63-3/10/63, MacArthur to Rusk, 7 March 1963.

65 JFK, NSF, RSF, box 228, NATO, Weapons, Nassau Agreement, Cables, 11/21/62–3/25/63 [3 of 3], Rusk to London and Paris, 18 February 1963; Rusk to American Embassies, London and Paris, 20 February 1963; Rusk to American Embassies, London and Paris, 22 February 1963; JFK, Papers of Richard E. Neustadt, box 21, Government Consulting, 1959–66 – Skybolt/Atlantic Affairs – NATO/MLF, 1963 [3 of 3], Tyler to Finletter, 25 February 1963.

66 JFK, Papers of Richard E. Neustadt, box 21, Government Consulting, 1959–66, Skybolt/Atlantic Affairs – NATO/MLF, 1963 [2 of 3], Rusk to Kennedy, 6 March 1963.

67 USNA, RG 59, Central Files, Pol US–UK, Memorandum of Conversation, Subject: Post-Nassau Arrangements, 11 February 1963; FRUS 1961–1963, vol. XIII, Bundy to Rusk and McNamara, 11 March 1963, p. 524; Memorandum for the Record, 14 March 1963, p. 526.

68 JFK, NSF, RSF, box 218, Multilateral Force, Cables, 3/11/63-3/15/63, Kennedy to Macmillan, 14 March 1963.

69 JFK, NSF, RSF, box 218, Multilateral Force, Cables, 3/16/63-3/31/63, Ball to Rusk, 16 March 1963.

70 JFK, NSF, RSF, Multilateral Force, Subjects, Macmillan Correspondence, Macmillan to Kennedy, 16 March 1963.

71 PRO, DEFE 11/222, Chiefs of Staff Committee, Papers on nuclear defence and Europe, 6 December 1962; PRO, DEFE 7/2346, Note from Chief of Defence Staff, prime minister's proposed statement on assignment of V-bombers and Polaris, 29 January 1963; PRO, DEFE 11/223, Chiefs of Staff Committee Joint Planning Staff Meeting, 26 April 1963; Chiefs of Staff Committee Meeting, 30 April 1963; Note on adoption of 26 April report recommendations by MOD, 21 June 1963.

72 PRO, PREM 11/4589, Ormsby-Gore to Foreign Office, 31 March 1963. Kennedy told Macmillan in May that he would 'be glad to turn some of our zealous admirals loose on Admiral Mountbatten'; PRO, CAB 21/4978, Kennedy to Macmillan, 10 May 1963.

73 Command Paper (CMND) 1995, Polaris Sales Agreement, 6 April 1963.

74 PRO, FO 371/173516, Rose to Wilkinson, 14 February 1963; PRO, FO 371/173517, Thorneycroft to Home, 20 February 1963.

75 PRO, ADM 1/28970, Report on Polaris Manning and Training Mission to the United States, visit P.E. 1260/5, 8–20 April 1963.

76 FO 371/173517, Home to Ormsby Gore, 16 March 1963; Ormsby Gore to Home, 16 March 1963.

77 JFK, NSF, RSF, NATO, Weapons, Cables, Jupiter/Polaris, 3/1/63-9/3/63, Rusk to Ormsby Gore, 6 April 1963; Brubeck to Bundy, 24/4/63; Rusk to Various American Embassies, 24 April 1963; PRO, FO 371/173520, Rose to Hood, 22 April 1963; PRO, FO 371/173520, Rose to Arthur, 23 May 1963.

78 Lyndon B. Johnson Library, Oral History, David K. Bruce, p. 9.

79 PRO, ADM 1/28839, Notes on Meetings in Washington, undated (January 1963).

80 Nailor, *The Nassau Connection*, pp. 69–72; Priest, 'In American Hands', pp. 357–60.

81 JFK, NSF, RSF, box 218, Multilateral Force, Subjects, Macmillan Correspondence, Kennedy to Macmillan, 10 May 1963.

82 JFK, NSF, RSF, box 218, Multilateral Force, General, 5/15/63-5/21/63, McNaughton to McNamara, 16 May 1963.

83 PRO, FO 371/173521, Hood Minute, Polaris Presentation, 4 November 1963.

84 JFK, Oral History, Caspar John, pp. 12–13.

85 JFK, Oral History, Lord Harlech, pp. 56–7.

4 THE MLF AFTER NASSAU

1 *Public Papers of the Presidents of the United States: John F. Kennedy*, 1962, Joint Statement between President Kennedy and Harold Macmillan, 21 December 1962, pp. 908–10.

2 United States National Archive (hereafter referred to as USNA), RG 59, Deputy Assistant Secretary for Politico-Military Affairs, Subject Files, 1961–1968, Lot 65D134, NN3-059-93-20 (hereafter referred to as Politico-Military Affairs), Multilateral Force 2, Nassau Multilateral Polaris Force, 5 January 1963.

3 USNA, RG 330, 334, NATO, November–December 1962, D.C. Strother to Joint Chiefs of Staff, 13 December 1962; J. Baylis, *Anglo-American Defence Relations, 1939–1981*, London and Basingstoke: Macmillan, 1981, pp. 78–9; A.J. Pierre, *Nuclear Politics: The British Experience with an Independent Strategic Force, 1939–1970*, London: Oxford University Press, 1972, p. 246.

4 John F. Kennedy Library (hereafter referred to as JFK), National Security Files (hereafter referred to as NSF), Regional Security Files (hereafter referred to as RSF), box 228, NATO, Weapons, Cables, Nassau Agreement, 3/29/60-1/31/63, Hughes to Rusk, Allied Reactions to the Nassau Agreement, 8 January 1963, pp. 4–5. See also Record of Meeting between Stikker and Home, Public Record Office (hereafter referred to as PRO), DEFE 11/222, at which Stikker reported that Adenauer had originally been 'suspicious of Anglo-American motives at Nassau'.

5 R. Morgan, 'Kennedy and Adenauer', in D. Brinkley and R.T. Griffiths (eds) *John F. Kennedy and Europe*, Baton Rouge: Louisiana State University Press, 1999, pp. 16–31.

6 H.W. Gatzke, *Germany and the United States: A 'Special Relationship'?* Cambridge and London: Harvard University Press, 1980, p. 192. Gatzke states that the Cuban missile crisis had encouraged them to 'settle their differences'. See also J.L. Richardson, *Germany and the Atlantic Alliance: The Interaction of Strategy and Politics*, Cambridge: Harvard University Press, 1966, p. 63.

7 Foreign Relations of the United States (hereafter referred to as FRUS), 1961–1963, vol. XIII, *Western Europe and Canada*, US Embassy, Bonn to Rusk, 14 January 1963, p. 478; JFK, NSF, RSF, box 219, Multilateral Force, Adenauer Correspondence, Adenauer to Kennedy, 17 January 1963.

8 See, for example, JFK, NSF, RSF, box 212A, Tuthill to Rusk, 2 February 1963; J.D. Steinbruner, *The Cybernetic Theory of Decision: New Dimensions of Political Analysis*, Princeton: Princeton University Press, 1974, p. 251. Richardson, *Germany and the Atlantic Alliance*, pp. 83–4.

9 T.C. Sorenson, *Kennedy*, New York: Harper & Row, 1965, p. 569.

10 For assessments of Kennedy's attitude towards MLF by those who worked with him see JFK, Papers of David Nunnerley (hereafter referred to as Nunnerley Papers), Transcripts, Ball – Douglas-Home, McGeorge Bundy interview, 30 January 1970, p. 4; Lord Harlech interview, 13 May 1969, p. 10. JFK, Oral History, Lord Harlech, pp. 58–9; Walt Whitman Rostow, 11 April 1964, p. 103. Dean Rusk suggested that the MLF may have succeeded if the British had been more positive. JFK, Nunnerley Papers, Notes, MacDonald – Zuckert, Rusk interview, supplementary, p. 3.

11 FRUS, 1961–1963, vol. XIII, Department of State to Certain Missions, 20 December 1962, p. 466.

12 USNA, RG 59, Politico-Military Affairs, Mr Ball's Presentation to NAC, Finletter to Rusk, 12 January 1963.

13 Richardson, *Germany and the Atlantic Alliance*, p. 205.

14 H.A. Kissinger, *The Troubled Partnership: A Re-appraisal of the Atlantic Alliance*, New York: McGraw-Hill, 1965, p. 141.

15 JFK, NSF, McGeorge Bundy Correspondence, box 405, Memos to the President, 1/1/63-1/20/63, Bundy to Kennedy, 12 January 1963.

16 PRO, DEFE 7/2313, Working Group on Implementation of the Nassau Nuclear Agreement, Annex, 'NATO Nuclear Force', 16 January 1963; Working group Meeting, 21 January 1963.

17 PRO, ADM 1/29269, Thorneycroft to Macmillan, 7 January 1963.

18 JFK, NSF, RSF, box 22, NATO, Weapons, Nassau Agreement, Cables, 11/21/63-3/25/63 [3 of 3], Finletter to Rusk, 17 January 1963.

19 USNA, RG 59, Politico-Military Affairs, Multilateral Force 2, Steering Group on Implementing Nassau Decisions, Integrated Seaborne Force, Submitted by Sub-Group IV, 25 January 1963.

20 JFK, President's Office Files (hereafter referred to as POF), Special Correspondence, box 28, Bruce, David K.E., 2/4-5/63, Kennedy to Bruce, 5 February 1963.

21 L.S. Kaplan, 'The MLF Debate', in Brinkley and Griffiths (eds) *John F. Kennedy and Europe*, pp. 54–5.

22 USNA, RG 59, Records of Deputy Assistant Secretary for Politico-Military Affairs, Subject Files, 1961–1963, box 2, Memoranda [5 of 5], Memorandum of Conversation, 26 January 1963.

23 USNA, RG 59, Bureau of European Affairs, NATO and Atlantic Political Affairs (EUR/RPM), Records Relating to NATO Affairs, 1959–1966, Lot 67D516, Nassau United Kingdom Negotiations, Steering Group on Implementing the Nassau Decisions, Memorandum no. 15, 6 February 1963; FRUS, 1961–1963, vol. XIII, Summary Record of NSC Executive Committee Meeting no. 41, 12 February 1963, pp. 494–5.

24 JFK, NSF, RSF, box 219, NATO, Weapons, Nassau, Sub-Group IV Multilateral Force Planning, Lloyd to Nassau Steering Group, 14 February 1963; Kennedy to Merchant, undated (February 1963).

25 FRUS, 1961–1963, vol. XIII, Summary Record of NSC Executive Committee Meeting no. 41, 12 February 1963, p. 498.

26 FRUS, 1961–1963, vol. XIII, Memorandum of Conversation, 18 February 1963, p. 502.

27 JFK, Papers of George W. Ball (hereafter referred to as Ball Papers), box 6, Multilateral Force (MLF), 1/27/63-10/25/63, Telephone conversation between Kennedy and Ball, 25 February 1963, 11.40 am.

28 NSF, McGeorge Bundy Correspondence, box 405, Memos to the President, 3/63/4/63, Bundy to Kennedy, 6 March 1963.

29 JFK, NSF, RSF, box 217, Multilateral Force, General, Merchant, 3/9/63-3/28/63, Finletter to Rusk, 28 February 1963; Memorandum, Status of Nassau NATO Follow-up Activities, 5 March 1963.

30 JFK, NSF, RSF, box 219, Multilateral Force, Cables, 3/1/63-3/10/63, Morris to Rusk, 6 March 1963.

31 JFK, NSF, box 171, United Kingdom, 1/1/63-11/22/63, Bruce to Kennedy and Rusk, 5 March 1963.

32 PRO, FO 371/173301, Buchan to Home, 5 March 1963.

33 PRO, PREM 11/4587, Macmillan to Kennedy, 8 March 1963.

34 Steinbruner, *The Cybernetic Theory of Decision*, p. 274.

35 JFK, NSF, RSF, box 219, Multilateral Force, Cables, 3/11/63-3/15/63, Bruce to Rusk, 12 March 1963; Bruce to Rusk, 13 March 1963.

36 PRO, PREM 11/4587, Conversations between Livingston Merchant and the prime minister, 12 March 1963, 10.15 am.

37 JFK, NSF, RSF, box 219, Multilateral Force, Cables, 3/11/63-3/15/63, Bruce to Rusk, 12 March 1963.

38 JFK, NSF, RSF, box 219, Multilateral Force, Cables, 3/11/63-3/15/63, Bruce to Rusk, 13 March 1963.

39 PRO, PREM 11/4587, Conversations between Livingston Merchant and the Foreign Secretary, 13 March 1963, 11 am.

40 FRUS 1961–1963, vol. XIII, Bundy to Rusk and McNamara, 11 March 1963, p. 524; Memorandum for the Record, 14 March 1963, p. 526.

41 JFK, NSF, RSF, box 219, Multilateral Force, Cables, 3/11/63-3/15/63, Kennedy to Macmillan, 14 March 1963.

42 FRUS, 1961–1963, vol. XIII, Department of State to US Embassy, London, 14 March 1963, pp. 527–8.

43 See, for example, JFK, Papers of Richard E. Neustadt, box 20, Government Consulting, 1959–66, Skybolt/Atlantic Affairs – NATO/MLF, 1963 [1 of 3], Rostow to Rusk, 30 March 1963.

44 PRO, CAB 21/4978, Trend to Macmillan, 25 March 1963.

45 FRUS, 1961–1963, vol. XIII, Merchant to Rusk, 20 March 1963, pp. 532–3.

46 United States Declassified Documents Series (hereafter referred to as USDD), 146/1736, 5/1/95, Memorandum for the President, Subject: The British Political Situation, 25 March 1963; A.M. Schlesinger, *A Thousand Days: John F. Kennedy in the White House*, London: Deutsch, 1965, p. 753.

47 JFK, Papers of Arthur M. Schlesinger, White House Files, box WH-41, Multilateral Forces, 1963, Schlesinger to Bundy, 27 March 1963.

48 FRUS, 1961–1963, vol. XIII, Adenauer to Kennedy, 2 May 1963; JFK, NSF, RSF, box 219, Multilateral Force, Adenauer Correspondence, Kennedy to Adenauer, 4 May 1963.

49 FRUS, 1961–1963, vol. XIII, Memorandum for the Record, 3 May 1963, p. 568.

50 JFK, NSF, RSF, box 217A, Multilateral Force, General, 5/1/63-5/7/63, Ball to Bruce, 5 May 1963.

51 JFK, NSF, RSF, box 217A, Multilateral Force, General, 4/11/63-4/23/63, Bruce to Rusk, 9 May 1963; See also Bruce to Rusk, 6 May 1963; Bruce to Rusk, 10 May 1963.

52 Although Bundy told de Zulueta 'he does not mean in any way to put this topic ahead of the test ban matter' JFK, POF, box 127A, United Kingdom, Security, 5/63–6/63, Bundy to de Zulueta, 10 May 1963; PRO, CAB 21/4978, Kennedy to Macmillan, 10 May 1963.

53 JFK, POF, box 127A, United Kingdom, Security, 5/63-6/63, Bundy to Kennedy, 15 May 1963; JFK, Papers of Richard E. Neustadt, box 20, Government Consulting, Skybolt/Atlantic Affairs – MLF/Europe General, 1963 [1 of 2], Bundy to Bruce, 15 May 1963.

54 PRO, CAB 130/191, Minutes of Third Cabinet Meeting on NATO Nuclear Force, 17 May 1963.

55 PRO, CAB 130/191, Minutes of Fourth Cabinet Meeting on NATO Nuclear Force, 19 May 1963.

56 PRO, CAB C (63) 95, Separate memoranda by the Foreign Secretary and Secretary of Defence, 28 May 1963.

57 JFK, NSF, RSF, box 218, Multilateral Force, General, 5/15/63-5/21/63, Rusk to State, 21 May 1963.

58 JFK, NSF, RSF, box 218, Multilateral Force, General, 5/22/63-5/31/63, Bundy to Rusk, 22 May 1963. See also Bruce to Rusk, 4 June 1963.

59 PRO, ADM 1/29109, Mountbatten to Thorneycroft, 24 May 1963.

60 PRO, PREM 11/4589, Macmillan to Thorneycroft, undated (June 1963).

61 PRO, ADM 1/29109, Record of Meeting between Admiral Ricketts and Thorneycroft, 4 June 1963.

62 PRO, PREM 11/4589, Thorneycroft to Macmillan, 7 June 1963; Memorandum by Lord Hailsham, Mixed Manned Force of Surface Ships, 5 June 1963.

63 JFK, White House Central Files, box 984, TR 56/CO 305, undated note.

64 With the MLF such a prominent feature of American policy, the Soviets refused to consider negotiations for a non-dissemination treaty with the British and Americans. K. Oliver, *Kennedy, Macmillan and the Nuclear Test Ban Debate, 1961–1963*, Basingstoke: Macmillan, 1998, p. 191.

65 USDD, 305B/280, 7/1/79, President's European Trip: June 1963, Scope Paper on Britain, 18 June 1963, p. 9.

66 M. Middeke, 'Anglo-American Nuclear Weapons Cooperation After the Nassau Conference: The British Policy of Interdependence', *Journal of Cold War Studies*, vol. 2, no. 2, 2000, pp. 82–4.

67 J.P.G. Freeman, *Britain's Nuclear Arms Control Policy in the Context of Anglo-American Relations, 1957–68*, New York: St Martin's Press, 1986, p. 172.

68 Freeman, *Britain's Nuclear Arms Control Policy*, p. 290, n.

69 See JFK, NSF, RSF, box 218, Multilateral Force, General, 6/20/63-6/30/63, Bundy to President, 'The MLF and Adenauer', 20 June 1963; Gatzke, *Germany and the United States*, p. 209.

70 In mid June, Stikker expressed his concern about the lack of new initiative on the MLF, claiming the whole venture might now fail. He suggested to the State Department that this failure would have a significant effect on US 'prestige' and offered to take on the burden of promoting MLF in Europe himself. USNA, RG 59, Bureau of Europe Affairs, Office of Atlantic Political and Military Affairs, Records Relating to NATO, 1957–1964, Political Affairs and Related Visits (SYG Stikker Visits 63), Getz to Tyler, 18 June 1963.

71 FRUS, 1961–1963, vol. XIII, Bundy to Kennedy, 15 June 1963, pp. 592–5; JFK, NSF, RSF, box 218, Multilateral Force, General, 6/18/63-6/19/63, Klein to Bundy, 18 June 1963. Yet Kennedy made a major speech promoting MLF as a force for European unity in Frankfurt. *Public Papers of the Presidents of the United States: John F. Kennedy*, 1963, Address in the Assembly Hall at the Paulskirche in Frankfurt, pp. 516–21.

72 FRUS, 1961–1963, vol. VII, *Arms Control and Disarmament*, Memorandum of Conversation, 29 June 1963, p. 754. See also FRUS, 1961–1963, vol. VII, Memorandum for the Record, Washington, 10 July 1963, p. 790; FRUS, 1961–1963, vol. XIII, Memorandum of Conversation, 30 June 1963, p. 600; Bundy to Rusk, 11 July 1963, pp. 603–4. Macmillan told Kennedy of his 'true feelings of gratitude to you for the great success of our meeting at Birch Grove House'. JFK, POF, box 127, Countries, United Kingdom, General, 7/63-11/63, Macmillan to Kennedy, 4 July 1963.

73 JFK, NSF, RSF, box 218, Multilateral Force, General, 7/1/63-7/20/63, Bundy to Rusk, 11 July 1963.

74 PRO, PREM 11/3714, Ramsbotham to Hood, 22 December 1960.

75 FRUS, 1961–1963, vol. XIII, NSAM 253, 13 July 1963 p. 604.

76 JFK, NSF, RSF, box 218, Multilateral Force, General, 7/1/63-7/20/63, Klein to Bundy, 19 July 1963.

77 Oliver, *Kennedy, Macmillan and the Test Ban*, pp. 204–5.

78 JFK, POF, Special Correspondence, box 31, Ormsby Gore, David (Lord Harlech), 6/26/62-5/9/63, Ormsby Gore to Kennedy, 2 August 1963.

79 JFK, NSF, RSF, box 218, Multilateral Force, General, 8/11/63-8/31/63 and Undated, Notes on Conversations re the MLF with Mr McGeorge Bundy, 30 August 1963.

80 PRO, FO 371/173461, Mixed-manning Demonstration, Aide-Memoire 11 September 1963, pp. 2–3.

81 PRO, CAB 129/114, C (63) 151, The Multilateral Force, memorandum by Home, 12 September 1963.

82 JFK, NSF, RSF, box 218, Multilateral Force, General, 9/1/63-9/26/63, Jones to Rusk, 13 September 1963; Tyler to Rusk, 24 September 1963; JFK, Ball Papers, box 6, Multilateral Force (MLF), 1/27/63-10/25/63, Telephone Conversation between Rusk and Ball, 25 September 1963, 1.25 pm.

83 FRUS, 1961–1963, vol. XIII, Memorandum of Conversation, 4 October 1963, pp. 613–14; PRO, FO 371/173461, British Embassy, Washington to Foreign Office, 4 October 1963; JFK, Oral History, William R. Tyler.

84 JFK, Ball Papers, box 6, Multilateral Force (MLF), 1/27/63-10/25/63, Telephone conversation between Ball and Chayes, 9 October 1963, 10.30 am.

85 PRO, CAB 21/6044, New York to Foreign Office, Multilateral NATO Nuclear Force: Statement of Her Majesty's Government's position, 27 September 1963.

86 *Economist*, 5 October 1963, p. 21.

87 PRO, FO 371/173461, Record of first meeting of MLF Steering Group, 11 October 1963; Shuckburgh to Foreign Office, 11 October 1963.

88 PRO, FO 371/173461, 2739/16/10/63, Draft directive to the UK representative on the Multilateral Force Steering Group, Annex A, Appendix A, NATO Multilateral Force: Statement of HMG's Position, 16 October 1963; *New York Times*, 4 October 1963.

89 PRO, FO 371/173463, Minute by the Foreign Secretary, 11 December 1963.

90 PRO, FO 371/173461, 2739/16/10/63, MLF Steering Group, Paris. Item 2: Mixed-manning Demonstration. Draft Brief by Foreign Office, 9 October 1963; Draft Directive to the United Kingdom Representative on the Multilateral Force Steering Group, Annex A, 9 October 1963.

91 PRO, ADM1/29109, Memorandum by Mottershead, undated (October 1963).

92 PRO, FO 371/173461, Proposed Amendments to Foreign Office Draft Briefs: MLF Steering Group, Paris by Mottershead, 10 October 1963, Item 2, Paragraph 2; note by Fielding.

93 JFK, NSF, box 171, United Kingdom 1/1/63-11/22/63, Lampson to Department of State, 'Current British Foreign Office Thinking about France', 15 October 1963.

94 USDD, 128E/849, 1/1/76, American Embassy, London to Department of State, 15 October 1963.

95 PRO, FO 371/173462, Thomson to Barnes, 25 October 1963, item 4.

96 PRO, FO 371/173461, Barnes to Shuckburgh, 9 October 1963, item 4.

97 PRO, FO 371/173462, Terms of Reference for the Multilateral Force Working Group, 17 October 1963.

98 PRO, FO 371/173464, Multilateral Force Working Group (Sixth Meeting), 25 October 1963, Annex A to UK delegation.

99 PRO, FO 371/173465, MLF – Invitation to Participate in Mixed-Manned Experiment, 4 December 1963, Annex NATO Multilateral Force – US Proposal for Demonstration, refs. (a) COS.363/63, (b) Military Sub-Group's Report of Findings of Mixed Manned Demonstration, 25 October, 1963; PRO, ADM 1/29109, First Sea Lord to Mountbatten, 18 November 1963.

100 PRO, DEFE 25/32, Joint Foreign Office and MOD Memorandum, undated (December 1963); Wright to Hockaday, 8 November 1963.

101 USNA, RG 59, Central File 1963 DEF (MLF) 9/1/63, Ball to Bundy, 16 October 1963; Bundy to Pastore, 17 October 1963.

102 JFK, NSF, RSF, box 218, Multilateral Force, General, 11/15/63-11/30/63, Merchant to Ball, 21 November 1963; Briefing on MLF, 20 November 1963.

103 JFK, Oral History, Thomas K. Finletter, pp. 8–9.

104 JFK, Nunnerley Papers, transcripts, Ball – Douglas-Home, McGeorge Bundy interview, 30 January 1970.

105 JFK, Oral History, William R. Tyler.

5 WASHINGTON AND THE LABOUR PARTY

1 J. Dumbrell, *A Special Relationship: Anglo-American Relations in the Cold War and After*, Basingstoke: Macmillan, 2001, pp. 60–6; N.J. Ashton, *Kennedy, Macmillan and the Cold War: The Irony of Interdependence*, Basingstoke: Palgrave-Macmillan, 2002, p. 220.

2 C. Ponting, *Breach of Promise: Labour in Power, 1964–1970*, London: Hamish Hamilton, 1989, pp. 7–11; D. Keohane, *Labour Party Defence Policy Since 1945*, London: Leicester University Press, 1993, pp. 22–3.

3 Keohane, *Labour Party Defence*, p. 2.

4 Keohane, *Labour Party Defence*, pp. 8–9.

5 Keohane, *Labour Party Defence*, pp. 14–18.

6 R.G. Hughes, ' "We Are Not Seeking Strength for its own Sake": The British Labour Party, West Germany and the Cold War, 1951–1964', *Cold War History*, vol. 3, no. 1, October 2002, pp. 67–94.

7 P. Jones, *America and the British Labour Party: The 'Special Relationship' at Work*, London and New York: I.B. Tauris, 1997, p. 107.

8 Jones, *America and the British Labour Party*, pp. 106–12.

9 For an explanation of how the 1960 vote was passed, see Jones, *America and the British Labour Party*, pp. 113–16.

10 Jones, *America and the British Labour Party*, p. 116.

11 A. Thorpe, *A History of the British Labour Party*, Basingstoke and London: Macmillan, 1997, pp. 151–2.

12 John F. Kennedy Library (hereafter referred to as JFK), National Security Files (hereafter referred to as NSF), Regional Security Files (hereafter referred to as RSF), box 228, NATO, Weapons, Nassau Agreement, 11/21/62-3/25/63 [1 of 3], Jones to Rusk, 21 December 1962.

13 JFK, NSF, RSF, box 228, NATO, Weapons, Nassau Agreement, 3/29/60-1/31/63, Research Memorandum: Allied Reactions to the Nassau Agreement, 8 January 1963, p. 7.

14 See House of Commons Debates, 1962–1963, 30–31 January 1963, vol. 670, col. 955–1074 and col. 1139–260.

15 Thorpe, *A History of the British Labour Party*, p. 153.

16 JFK, NSF, Country Files, box 171, United Kingdom, 1/1/63-11/22/63, Hughes to Rusk, Possible Successors to UK Labor Leader Gaitskell, 17 January 1963.

17 House of Commons Debates, 1962–1963, 30–31 January 1963, vol. 670, col. 1240–9; JFK, NSF, Country Files, box 175, United Kingdom, Wilson Talks, 1/63-4/63, Hilsman to Rusk, 8 March 1963.

18 JFK, President's Office Files (hereafter referred to as POF), Countries, box 127A, United Kingdom, Security, 1/63-4/63, Irving to Department of State, James Harold Wilson, 'Next British Prime Minister', 21 February 1963, p. 2.

19 JFK, POF, Countries, box 127A, United Kingdom, Security, 1/63-4/63, Irving to Department of State, 21 February 1963, p. 3.

20 JFK, POF, Countries, box 127A, United Kingdom, Security, 1/63-4/63, Irving to Department of State, 21 February 1963, p. 5.

21 JFK, NSF, RSF, box 213A, Europe, General, 2/21/63-3/31/63 [1 of 3], Jones to Rusk, 27 February 1963.

22 JFK, NSF, RSF, box 213A, Europe, General, 2/21/63-3/31/63 [3 of 3], Fuller to Rostow, 22 March 1963.

23 United States National Archive (hereafter referred to as USNA), Record Group (hereafter referred to as RG 59), Central File, Pol US–UK, Jones to Department of State, 16 March 1963.

24 USNA, RG 59, Central File, Pol US–UK, Jones to Department of State, 16 March 1963. In reply, the Deputy Chief of Mission 'doubted that the Labor Party could, as a practical matter, wholly give up nuclear weapons, even if it wanted to do this. The UK was a nuclear power and it was stuck with this power.'

25 JFK, POF, Countries, box 127A, United Kingdom, Security, 1/63-4/63, Irving to Department of State, 27 March 1963.

26 JFK, POF, Countries, box 127A, United Kingdom, Security, 1/63-4/63, Bruce to Rusk, 27 March 1963.

27 JFK, NSF, Country Files, box 170, United Kingdom, 1/21/63-12/31/62, Schlesinger to Kennedy, 25 March 1963.

28 JFK, POF, Countries, box 127A, United Kingdom, Security, 1/63-4/63, Brubeck to Bundy, 30 March 1963; Note of a Meeting between Wilson and Rostow, 30 March 1963.

29 JFK, POF, Countries, box 127A, United Kingdom, Security, 1/61-4/63, Schlesinger to Kennedy, 1 April 1963.

30 JFK, NSF, Country Files, box 175, United Kingdom, Wilson Talks, 1/63-4/63, Memorandum of Conversation between Dean Rusk and Harold Wilson, 1 April 1964.

31 Churchill Archive Centre (hereafter referred to as CA), Papers of Patrick Gordon Walker, GNWR 1/15, Notes of talk with Merchant, 12 March 1963.

32 JFK, NSF, Country Files, box 170, United Kingdom, 1/21/63-12/31/62, Irving to Rusk, 28 March 1963.

33 JFK, NSF, Country Files, box 170, United Kingdom, 1/21/63-12/31/62, Memorandum of Conversation, 29 May 1963. Splits within the German government also seemed to have hardened Gordon Walker's opinion. In April he had met Schroeder and Helmut Schmidt and while Schroeder told him that the MLF would strengthen NATO, Schmidt told that it had 'no military sense'. CA, Papers of Patrick Gordon Walker, GNWR 1/15, Notes of talk with Schroeder, 6 April 1963; Note on Talk with Schmidt, 5 April 1963.

34 JFK, NSF, Country Files, box 170, United Kingdom, 1/21/63-12/31/62, Memorandum of Conversation between Patrick Gordon Walker and the President, 29 May 1963; CA, Papers of Patrick Gordon Walker, GNWR 1/15, Notes of talk with the president, 29 May 1963; Notes of talk with McNamara, 31 May 1963; Note of talks with Dean Rusk, 31 May 1963.

35 JFK, NSF, RSF, box 218, Multilateral Force, General, 5/22/63-5/31/63, Memorandum of Conversation between Merchant and Gordon Walker, 29 May 1963.

36 In July, Bruce reported Wilson claiming Kennedy had said that the MLF was tantamount to arming the FRG with nuclear weapons and thus it would prevent any non-proliferation treaty as well as ending any east–west understanding and be as decisive as Hitler marching into the Rhineland. JFK, NSF, Country Files, box 171, United Kingdom, 1/1/63-11/22/63, Bruce to Rusk, 4 July 1963.

37 United States Declassified Documents Series (hereafter referred to as USDD), 305B/280, 7/1/79, President's European Trip: June 1963, Scope Paper on Britain, 18 June 1963, p. 9.

38 JFK, NSF, McGeorge Bundy Correspondence, Memos to the President, 9/63-11/63, Bundy to Kennedy, 24 October 1963.

39 JFK, NSF, Country Files, box 171, United Kingdom, 1/1/63-11/22/63, Schlesinger to Bundy, 29 October 1963.

40 JFK, NSF, RSF, box 218A, Multilateral Force, General, 11/1/63-11/14/63, Bruce to Rusk, 14 November 1963.

41 Lyndon B. Johnson Library (hereafter referred to as LBJ), NSF, Country Files, United Kingdom, box 213, Rostow to Tyler, 17 February 1964.

42 USDD, 133/1632, 5/1/93 NATO and the Atlantic Nations, 24 January 1964 (Revision of NSC Memorandum of 20 April 1961).

43 LBJ, NSF, Country File, United Kingdom, box 213, Press conference in Washington by Harold Wilson, 3 March 1964.

44 USDD, 118/1456, 8/1/96, Memorandum of Conversation, Department of State, Subject: Tour d'horizon with Harold Wilson, Leader of the British Labour Party, 2 March 1964, pp. 2–3; LBJ, NSF Country File, United Kingdom, box 213, Memorandum of Conversation between Wilson and McNamara, 5 March 1964.

45 P.C.G. Walker, 'The Labour Party's Defence and Foreign Policy', *Foreign Affairs*, vol. 42, no. 3, April 1964, pp. 393–4; A.J. Pierre, *Nuclear Politics: The British Experience with an Independent Strategic Force, 1939–1970*, London: Oxford University Press, 1972, p. 266.

46 Walker, 'The Labour Party's Defence and Foreign Policy', pp. 392–3.

47 The Labour Party, *Let's go with Labour for the New Britain: The Labour Party's Manifesto for the 1964 General Election*, London: Transport House, 1964, p. 23.

48 Ponting, *Breach of Promise*, p. 8; Pierre, *Nuclear Politics*, p. 264.

49 L. Beaton, 'Britain's Bomb' in *Economist*, 12 September 1964.

50 Thorpe, *A History of the British Labour Party*, p. 154–5.

51 LBJ, NSF Country File, United Kingdom, box 213, Rusk to Johnson, 24 October 1964, 16a-1, p. 2.

52 Public Record Office (hereafter referred to as PRO), DEFE 13/510, Note of meeting between Lord Harlech and Denis Healey, 21 October 1964.

53 LBJ, Papers of George Ball, Britain II [12/2/63-11/23/64], 28, Telephone conversation between George Ball and McGeorge Bundy, 20 October 1964, pp. 1–2.

54 USNA, RG 59, Lot Files, Records of Under Secretary of State George W. Ball, 1961–1966, Lot 74D272, MLF#1, Memorandum for Henry Owen, 24 October 1964.

55 PRO, DEFE 13/350, CNS to Healey, 19 October 1964; CPE to Healey, 19 October 1964; D. Healey, *The Time of my Life*, London: Penguin, 1989, p. 302.

56 PRO, DEFE 13/350, DUS (P&B) to Healey, 21 October 1964; Record of Meeting with Denis Healey at Polaris Management Centre, 23 October 1964.

57 PRO, DEFE 13/350, CNS to Healey, 17 November 1964.

58 H. Wilson, *The Labour Government, 1964–1970: A Personal Record*, London: Penguin, 1971, pp. 68–9.

59 Healey, *The Time of my Life*, p. 302.

60 Wilson, *The Labour Government*, pp. 68–9.

61 Pierre, *Nuclear Politics*, p. 287; Healey, *The Time of my Life*, p. 302.

62 See Foreign Relations of the United States (hereafter referred to as FRUS), 1961–1963, vol. XIII, *Western Europe and Canada*, Memorandum of Conversation, 19 December 1962, p. 1101; Pierre, *Nuclear Politics*, pp. 285–7; Healey, *The Time of my Life*, p. 250.

63 Pierre, *Nuclear Politics*, pp. 288–9.

64 PRO, PREM 13/222, Healey to Wilson, 21 December 1964.

65 PRO, PREM 13/222, Healey to Wilson, 21 December 1964 and Wilson's handwritten note.

66 FRUS, 1964–1968, vol. XIII, Bundy to Johnson, 8 November 1964, p. 104.

67 USNA, RG 59, Lot Files, Records of Under Secretary of State George W. Ball, 1961–1966, Lot 74D272, MLF#3, Staff Message Branch, Department of the Air Force to Department of State, 26 November 1964.

68 FRUS, 1964–1968, vol. XIII, Ball to Rusk, 2 December 1964, p. 132.

69 Wilson, *The Labour Government*, p. 85; House of Commons Debates, 1964–1965, 16 December 1964, vol. 704, col. 427–41.

70 CA, Papers of Patrick Gordon Walker, GNWR 3/4, Thoughts on Foreign Policy, August 1964.

71 C. Wrigley, 'Now you see it, now you don't: Harold Wilson and Labour's Foreign Policy, 1964–70', in R. Coopey, S. Fielding and N. Tiratsoo (eds) *The Wilson Governments, 1964–1970*, London and New York: Pinter, 1993, p. 123.

72 Jones, *America and the British Labour Party*, p. 118.

6 THE END OF THE MLF AND NUCLEAR SHARING

1 Paul Hammond says that the evidence as to whether Johnson was aware of Kennedy's reservations remains 'inconclusive'. P.Y. Hammond, *LBJ and the Presidential Management of Foreign Relations*, Austin: University of Texas Press, 1992, p. 110.

2 Lyndon B. Johnson Library (hereafter referred to as LBJ), Papers of George W. Ball (hereafter referred to as Ball Papers), MLF [12/2/63–12/64], Record of Conversation, 2 December 1963; Andrew J. Pierre, *Nuclear Politics: The British Experience with an Independence Strategic Force, 1939–1970*, London: Oxford University Press, 1972, p. 251.

3 *New York Times*, 29 November 1963; J.D. Steinbruner, *The Cybernetic Theory of Decision: New Dimensions of Political Analysis*, Princeton: Princeton University Press, 1974, p. 285.

4 Hammond, *LBJ and the Presidential Management of Foreign Relations*, p. 116.

5 A. Priest, 'In Common Cause: The NATO Multilateral Force and Mixed-Manning Demonstration on USS *Claude V. Ricketts*, 1964–1965', *Journal of Military History*, vol. 69, no. 3, 2005, p. 780.

6 United States National Archive (hereafter referred to as USNA), Record Group (hereafter referred to as RG 59), Subject Files, Office of Special Assistant to the Secretary of State for MLF Negotiations, 1963–1966 (hereafter referred to as Office of S/MF), Coordination MLF – Navy, Admiral David L. MacDonald to Paul Nitze, 7 October 1964; USNA, RG 200, Proposals for Nuclear Sharing, November 1964–1965, McNamara to Johnson, 5 December 1964.

7 B. Castle, *The Castle Diaries, 1964–1970*, London: Weidenfeld and Nicolson, 1984, p. 4; J.W. Young, 'Killing the MLF? The Wilson Government and Nuclear Sharing in Europe, 1964–66', *Diplomacy and Statecraft*, vol. 14, no. 2, 2003, pp. 295–324.

8 S. Schrafstetter and S. Twigge, *Avoiding Armageddon: Europe, the United States, and the Struggle for Nuclear Nonproliferation, 1945–1970*, Westport: Praeger, 2004, pp. 145–8; S. Schrafstetter and S. Twigge, 'Trick or Truth? The British ANF Proposal, West Germany and US Nonproliferation Policy, 1964–1968', *Diplomacy and Statecraft*, vol. 11, no. 2, 2000, p. 162. See also J.W. Young, *The Labour Governments, 1964–70, vol. 2: International Policy*, Manchester and New York: Manchester University Press, 2003, p. 117.

9 Foreign Relations of the United States (hereafter referred to as FRUS), vol. XIII, 1961–1963, W*estern Europe and Canada*, Memorandum of Conversation, Washington, 26 November 1963, pp. 1136–8.

10 FRUS, vol. XIII, 1961–1963, Johnson to Home, 24 December 1963, pp. 1136–9; FRUS, 1964–1968, vol. XII, *Western Europe*, 1964–1968, Johnson to Home, 28 February 1964.

11 FRUS, 1961–1963, vol. XIII, NATO Ministerial Meeting, Paris 16–18 December 1963, Scope Paper Prepared in the Department of State, 6 December 1963, p. 635.

12 LBJ, National Security File (hereafter referred to as NSF), International Meetings and Travel File, boxes 33 and 34, NATO Ministerial Meeting, 16–18 December 1963, Draft paper, 30 November 1963.

13 LBJ, NSF, International Meetings and Travel File, boxes 33 and 34, 5, NATO Ministerial Meeting, the Hague, 12–14 May 1964, Strategy Paper, undated.

14 FRUS, 1961–1963, vol. XIII, NATO Ministerial Meeting, Paris 16–18 December 1963, Scope Paper Prepared in the Department of State, 6 December 1963, p. 639.

15 LBJ, NSF, International Meetings and Travel File, boxes 33 and 34, NATO Ministerial Meeting, 16–18 December 1963, Draft Paper, 30 November 1963, 6; Draft remarks by Secretary McNamara, undated.

16 USNA, RG 59, Conference Files, Lot 66D110, CF 2345, Rusk to State Department, 17 December 1963.

17 Public Record Office (hereafter referred to as PRO), FO 371/173464, Shuckburgh to Foreign Office, 6 December 1963.

18 FRUS, 1964–1968, vol. XII, Memorandum of Conversation, 13 February 1964, pp. 17–20; USNA, RG 218, NND 471071, 471.6, Atomic and Nuclear Weapons (June 1963–March 1964), Telegram to Finletter, 19 January 1964; USNA RG 218, CM-1964-1294-64-1344-64, Taylor to Director, Joint Staff, 14 April 1964.

19 PRO, CAB 129/114, C (63) 151, Memorandum by Home, 12 September 1963, pp. 228–9.

20 PRO, CAB 129/114, C (63) 151, Memorandum by Home, 12 September 1963, p. 222.

21 *The Times*, 11 January 1964; FRUS, 1964–1968, vol. XIII, *Western Europe Region*, Rusk to Johnson, 16 January 1964, p. 7.

22 House of Commons Debates, 1963–1964, 11 December 1963, vol. 686, col. 374–5.

23 PRO, CAB 129/116, C (64), Multilateral Force: Experiment in Mixed-manning, Note by the Secretary of the Cabinet, 9 January 1964.

24 PRO, FO 371/179022, Thomson to Barnes, 24 January 1964; PRO, PREM 11/4739, Note by the Prime Minister, 29 January 1964.

25 LBJ, NSF, Country File – UK, box 212, Prime Minister Home Visit Briefing Book, 12–13 February 1964 [1 of 2], 2a.

26 J. Baylis, *Anglo-American Defence Relations, 1939–1981*, London and Basingstoke: Macmillan, 1981, p. 79.

27 FRUS, 1964–1968, vol. XIII, Memorandum of Conversation, 26 April 1964, pp. 41–3.

28 USNA, RG 59, Office of S/MF, MLF – UK, Bureau of intelligence and Research Paper, Department of State, 29 April 1964.

29 USNA, RG 59, Bureau of European Affairs, NATO and Atlantic Politico-Military Affairs, Records Relating to Political Affairs, 1957–1966, EUR/RPM, POL 7, Visits/Meetings (May 1964), Record of Meeting with Mr McNaughton in preparation for NATO Ministerial Meeting, 4 May 1964, p. 6.

30 LBJ, Oral History, Thomas K. Finletter, pp. 13–14.

31 LBJ, NSF, Subject File, box 25, MLF – Ricketts, box 25, Rusk to Johnson, 8 April 1964.

32 LBJ, NSF, Subject File, MLF – Ricketts, box 25, Rusk to Johnson, 8 April 1964.

33 FRUS, 1964–1968, vol. XIII, Memorandum of Discussion, 10 April 1964, pp. 35–6.

34 Hammond, *LBJ and the Presidential Management of Foreign Relations*, p. 117.

35 LBJ, NSF, Agency File, box 35, NATO – General, vol. 1 12/63–7/64 [1 of 3], Klein to Bundy, 7 April 1964.

36 LBJ, Oral History, Thomas K. Finletter, pp. 14–16.

37 LBJ, Oral History, Thomas K. Finletter, pp. 14–16; FRUS, 1964–1968, vol. XIII, Memorandum of Discussion, 10 April 1964, pp. 36–7.

38 LBJ, NSF, Subject File, box 25, MLF – Ricketts, The MLF: What and Why? Note attached to correspondence from Rusk to Johnson, 8 April 1964, pp. 4–5; FRUS, 1964–1968, vol. XIII, p. 36, n 2. Labour's Richard Crossman reinforced this optimistic attitude the following month when he told Arthur Schlesinger that MLF would offer Wilson a way out of the nuclear dilemma and he would have to join if the Americans persisted. USNA, RG 59, Office of S/MF, MLF US–UK, Schlesinger to Finletter, 22 May 1964.

39 PRO, PREM 11/4740, Shuckburgh to Foreign Office, 21 April 1964; Home to Butler, 21 April 1964; PRO, PREM 11/4740, Harlech to Foreign Office, 28 April 1964.

40 PRO, FO 371/179064, Dixon to Foreign Office, 25 April 1964; Foreign Office submission, 'France and NATO', 8 May 1964.

41 USNA, RG 59, NATO, 1957–1966, EUR/RPM, box 7, POL 7, Visits/Meetings (May 1964), Record of Meeting with Mr McNaughton in preparation for NATO Ministerial Meeting, 4 May 1964, p. 6.

42 PRO, PREM 11/4740, Roberts to Foreign Office, 11 June 1964.

43 *Public Papers of the Presidents of the United States: Lyndon B. Johnson*, 1963–1964, vol. II, Joint Communiqué issued by President Johnson and Chancellor Erhard, 12 June 1964, pp. 771–3; NSF, Files of McGeorge Bundy, box 2, Chron File, April 1964 [3 of 3], Bundy to Johnson, 12 January 1965.

44 FRUS, 1964–1968, vol. XIII, Telegram From the Department of State to the Mission to the North Atlantic Treaty Organisation and European Regional Organisation, Washington, 3 July 1964, p. 59.

45 A. Kopkind (ed.) 'A Document of the Sixties: Memorandum on the British Labour Party and the MLF', by R.E. Neustadt, 6 July 1964, *New York Review of Books*, vol. XI, no. 10, 5 December 1968, pp. 37–46.

46 Kopkind (ed.) 'A Document of the Sixties', p. 46.

47 PRO, ADM 1/29109, Thorneycroft to Home, 8 May 1964.

48 PRO, PREM 11/4740, Thorneycroft to Home, 30 June 1964; Butler to Home, 30 June 1964.

49 In a hand-written note, Home's private secretary said that this latest correspondence from Thorneycroft supplemented the 'barrage of minutes' he had produced recently on MLF. PRO, PREM 11/4740, Thorneycroft to Home, 23 July 1964.

50 LBJ, NSF, Subject File MLF – Ricketts, box 25, Memorandum for General Clifton, 29 April 1964.

51 LBJ, NSF, NS-Defense, Ex-ND 16, Ships-Submarines, Clifton to Johnson, 9 July 1964.

52 USNA, RG 59, Office of S/MF, Mixed Manning Demonstration, Remarks of Secretary Nitze at Name Changing Ceremony of USS Claude V. Ricketts (DDG-5), Norfolk, VA, 28 July 1964; Naval Historical Center, Ships History Branch, Office of Assistant Secretary of Defense (Public Affairs), News Release, 13 October 1964, USS Claude Ricketts (DDG-5) to visit Washington Navy Yard; LBJ, NSF, Committee File, Committee on Nuclear Proliferation, boxes 6–7, Mixed-Manned Demonstration ship visits Washington, Remarks of Dean Rusk on 20 October 1964, Department of State Bulletin, 51: 661–2, 9 November 1964.

53 USNA, RG 59, Deputy Assistant Secretary for Politico-Military Affairs, Subject Files of the Special Asst for Atomic Energy and Aerospace, 1950–1966, Nuclear Sharing – MLF 1962–1964, Hughes to Rusk, Stiffer Soviet Position on MLF Expressed in July 11 Notes, 13 July 1964; PRO, PREM 11/4740, Trevelyan to Foreign Office, 29 July 1964; Foreign Office to UK NATO Delegation, 30 July 1964.

54 C. McArdle Kelleher, *Germany and the Politics of Nuclear Weapons*, New York and London: Columbia University Press, 1975, pp. 246–59; FRUS, 1964–1968, vol. XIII, Erhard to Johnson, 30 September 1964, pp. 78–9; *The Times*, 8 October 1964.

55 P. Geyelin, *Lyndon B. Johnson and the World*, New York: Praeger, 1966, p. 169.

56 *New York Times*, 4 August 1964; LBJ, NSF, Ex-ND, National Security – Defense, box 1, George McGovern, Lee Metcalf, Eugene McCarthy, Philip A. Hart, Maurine Neuberger, Gaylord Nelson and Gale McGhee to Johnson, 7 September 1964.

57 FRUS, 1964–1968, vol. XIII, Bundy to Johnson, 8 November 1964, p. 106.

58 'And I must say, and I shall probably edit this, this was not a glorious episode in American foreign policy', Finletter concluded. LBJ, Oral History, Thomas K. Finletter, pp. 16–18.

59 LBJ, NSF, Special Head of State Correspondence, box 17, Germany, 11/22/63-2/4/65, Erhard to Johnson, 30 September 1964; Hammond, *LBJ and the Presidential Management of Foreign Relations*, pp. 121–3.

60 FRUS, 1964–1968, vol. XIII, Memorandum of Conversation, 6 October 1964, p. 81

61 *Sunday Telegraph*, 11 October 1964; FRUS, 1964–1968, vol. XII, Bruce to State Department, 16 October 1964, pp. 464–7.

62 USNA, RG 59, Lot Files, Records of Under Secretary of State George W. Ball, 1961–1966, Lot 74D272 (hereafter referred to as Ball Records), MLF#1, Ball to Rusk, 9 November 1964.

63 USNA, RG 59, Deputy Assistant Secretary for Politico-Military Affairs, Subject Files of the Special Asst for Atomic Energy and Aerospace, 1950–1966, Nuclear Sharing – MLF 1962–1964, Memorandum of Conversation, 19 October 1964.

64 USNA, RG 59, Office of S/MF, Subject Files, MLF UK, Spiers to Rusk, 20 October 1964.

65 LBJ, NSF, Committee File, Committee on Nuclear Proliferation, boxes 6–7, NSAM 318, 14 November 1964.

66 PRO, PREM 13/25, Note on meeting with Shuckburgh, 26 October 1964; Harlech to Foreign Office, 27 October 1964.

67 PRO, PREM 13/25, MOD Note of Conversation with Roswell Gilpatric, 24 October 1964. The task force met for the first time on 7 December as the Committee on Nuclear Proliferation. See FRUS, 1964–1968, vol. XI, *Arms Control and Disarmament*, NSAM 320, 25 November 1964, p. 126; LBJ, NSF, Committee File, Committee on Nuclear Proliferation, boxes 6–7, Bundy Memorandum, 7 December 1964.

68 FRUS, 1964–1968, vol. XIII, Department of State to the American Embassy, Bonn, 29 October 1964, pp. 93–5.

69 PRO, PREM 13/25, Record of Discussion at the State Department, 26 October 1964.

70 LBJ, Ball Papers, MLF I, Record of conversation between Dean Rusk and George Ball, 27 October 1964. FRUS, 1964–1968, vol. XIII, Department of State to American Embassy, Bonn, 29 October 1964, pp. 93–5.

71 PRO, PREM 13/25, Record of a lunchtime discussion at the State Department, 27 October 1964.

72 LBJ, Ball Papers, MLF I, Conversation between William Tyler and George Ball, 28 October 1964; FRUS, 1964–1968, vol. XIII, Memorandum of Conversation, 31 October 1964, p. 97.

73 PRO, PREM 13/25, Shuckburgh to Foreign Office, 10 November 1964.

74 Although it should be noted that David Bruce later claimed the ANF 'was never seriously considered here'. LBJ, Oral History, David K. Bruce, p. 5.

75 Bundy also sketched out the various views of Johnson's main advisers on MLF and the dangers of allowing low level personnel to dominate the MLF process by imposing their own views of Atlantic co-operation onto America's allies. FRUS, 1964–1968, vol. XIII, Bundy to Johnson, 8 November 1964, p. 102.

76 PRO, PREM 13/27, Outline of Proposal for ANF, undated (November 1964), p. 40.

77 PRO, PREM 13/26, Harlech to Foreign Office, 19 November 1964.

78 PRO, DEFE 13/350, Hockaday to Chief of Naval Staff, 12 November 1964.

79 PRO, CAB 130/211, Defence Study Group, Proposal for ANF, 17 November 1964.

80 PRO, PREM 13/26, Trend to Wilson, 19 November 1964.

81 FRUS, 1964–1968, vol. XIII, American Embassy, Bonn to State Department, 4 November 1964, pp. 100–3.

82 *The Times*, 13 November 1964; *Economist*, 14 November 1964, pp. 671–2; PRO, PREM 13/25, Harlech to Foreign Office, 14 November 1964.

83 RG 59, Ball Records, MLF#2, Ball to Rusk, 17 November 1964; PRO, PREM 13/25, Harlech to Foreign Office, 14 November 1964.

84 PRO, PREM 13/25, Note of meeting between Harold Wilson and Patrick Gordon Walker, 29 October 1964.

85 PRO, PREM 13/25, Zuckerman to Healey, 9 November 1964, p. 3.

86 PRO, PREM 13/26, Trend to Wilson, 19 November 1964.

87 S. Dockrill, 'Britain's Power and Influence: Dealing with Three Roles and the Wilson Government's Defence Debate at Chequers in November 1964', *Diplomacy and Statecraft*, vol. 11, no. 1, March 2000, pp. 230–1.

88 PRO, PREM 13/26, Trend to Wilson, 19 November 1964.

89 Schrafstetter and Twigge, 'Trick or Truth?', pp. 168–9.

90 Schrafstetter and Twigge, 'Trick or Truth?', p. 170.

91 LBJ, NSF, International Meetings and Travel File, box 34, 48, NATO Parliamentarians Conference, Statement Delivered by Lord Kennet, 19 November 1964.

92 H. Wilson, *The Labour Government, 1964–1970: A Personal Record*, London: Penguin, 1971, pp. 70–3.

93 House of Commons Debates, 1964–1965, 23 November 1964, vol. 702, col. 943–6.

94 LBJ, Ball Papers, Britain II [12/2/63-11/23/64], 43, Record of Conversation, 23 November 1964; PRO, PREM 13/27, Record of Meeting, 27 November 1964.

95 FRUS, 1964–1968, vol. XIII, Bundy to Ball, 25 November 1964, p. 121.

96 Hammond, *LBJ and the Presidential Management of Foreign Relations*, pp. 124–5.

97 *Public Papers of the Presidents of the United States: Lyndon B. Johnson*, 1963–1964, vol. II, Remarks at 175th Anniversary Convocation of Georgetown University, 3 December 1964, pp. 1632–5.

98 PRO, PREM 13/27, Gordon Walker to Wilson, 30 November 1964.

99 PRO, PREM 13/27, Record of meeting between George Ball, David Bruce, Harold Wilson, Patrick Gordon Walker and Oliver Wright, 27 November 1964.

100 PRO, PREM 13/27, Gordon Walker to Wilson, 30 November 1964.

101 PRO, PREM 13/27, Harlech to Gordon Walker, 3 December 1964.

102 PRO, PREM 13/27, [US] Memorandum of Conversation, 19 November 1964, attached to Gordon Walker to Wilson, 30 November 1964.

103 PRO, PREM 13/27, Caradon to Foreign Office, 29 November 1964; S. Dockrill, 'Forging the Anglo-American Global Defence Partnership: Harold Wilson, Lyndon Johnson and the Washington Summit, December 1964', *Journal of Strategic Studies*, vol. 23, no. 4, 2000, p. 115.

104 PRO, PREM 13/27, Harlech to Foreign Office, 27 November 1964.

105 LBJ, NSF, International Meetings and Travel File, box 34, 32d, Memorandum of Conversation, undated (early December 1964).

106 United States Declassified Documents Series (hereafter referred to as USDD), 431A/391, 10/1/78, Ball to Johnson, 5 December 1964.

107 Hammond, *LBJ and the Presidential Management of Foreign Relations*, p. 129.

108 USDD, 137/1701, 5/1/96, Memorandum of Conversation, and the MLF, 5 December 1964, pp. 6–9.

109 USDD, 137/1701, 5/1/96, Memorandum of Conversation, 5 December 1964, pp. 6–9.

110 LBJ, NSF, Files of McGeorge Bundy, box 5, Chron File, December 1–10, 1964 [2 of 2], Bundy to Johnson, 4 December 1964.

111 USDD, 137/1701, 5/1/96, Memorandum of Conversation, 5 December 1964, p. 9.

112 LBJ, NSF, Files of McGeorge Bundy, box 5, Chron File, December 1–10, 1964 [2 of 2], 'Suggested Answers to Wilson's Likely Arguments Against Englishmen on Surface Ships', 5 December 1964; Bundy to Johnson, 5 December 1964.

113 LBJ, NSF, Files of McGeorge Bundy, box 5, Chron File, December 1–10, 1964 [2 of 2], Bundy to President, 5 December 1964.

114 USDD, 138/1702, 5/1/96, Memorandum of Conversation, 6 December 1964, pp. 1–5; FRUS, vol. XIII, 1964–1968, Diary Entry by David Bruce, 6 December 1964, pp. 133–4.

115 USDD, 138/1702, 5/1/96, Memorandum of Conversation, 6 December 1964, p. 4.

116 USDD, 137/1701, 5/1/96, Memorandum of Conversation, 5 December 1964, p. 8.
117 Dockrill, 'Forging the Anglo-American Global Defence Partnership', p. 117.
118 FRUS, vol. XIII, 1964–1968, Bundy to Johnson, 6 December 1964, p. 137.
119 LBJ, NSF, Files of McGeorge Bundy, box 5, Chron File, December 1–10, 1964 [2 of 2], Bundy to President, 'Last Minute Papers for Wilson Visit', 6 December 1964.
120 USDD, 138/1701, 5/1/96, Memorandum of Conversation, 5 December 1964, p. 9; USDD, 138/1702, 5/1/96, Memorandum of Conversation, 6 December 1964, p. 4.
121 FRUS vol. XIII, 1964–1968, Memorandum for the Record by Bundy, 7 December 1964, pp. 137–9. Johnson had described the meeting to Bundy over the telephone at 1.30 pm.
122 Wilson, *The Labour Government*, p. 81.
123 FRUS, 1964–1968, vol. XIII, Memorandum of Conversation, 8 December 1964, pp. 146–52; FRUS, 1964–1968, vol. XIII, US Comments on UK Proposal of a Project for an Atlantic Nuclear Force, 8 December 1964, pp. 153–6; Geyelin, *Lyndon B. Johnson and the World*, pp. 173–4.
124 Dockrill, 'Forging the Anglo-American Defence Partnership', pp. 118–19.
125 USNA, RG 59, Central File, Subject Numeric File, 1964–1966, Pol UK–US, Memorandum of Conversation, 7 December 1964.
126 *Public Papers of the Presidents of the United States: Lyndon B. Johnson*, 1963–1964, vol. II, President Johnson and Harold Wilson, Joint Statement, 7 December 1964, 797, pp. 1649–50.
127 FRUS, 1964–1968, vol. XIII, Bundy to Johnson, 10 December 1964, pp. 158–60.
128 FRUS, 1964–1968, vol. XIII, Bundy to Bruce, 9 December 1964, pp. 156–8.
129 See LBJ, NSF, Files of McGeorge Bundy, box 5, Chron File, December 1–10, 1964 [2 of 2], Possible Political Advantages to the US in the ANF as against the MLF, 8 December 1964.
130 FRUS, 1964–1968, vol. XIII, NSAM 322, 17 December 1964, pp. 165–7.
131 Hammond, *LBJ and the Presidential Management of Foreign Relations*, p. 133.
132 LBJ, NSF, Ex-ND National Security – Defense, box 1, file 4, Dutton to Bundy, 9 December 1964.
133 *New York Times*, 22 December 1964; PRO, DEFE 11/366, Dixon to Foreign Office, 22 December 1964.
134 LBJ, Oral History, Dean Rusk, vol. IV, p. 11.
135 PRO, PREM 13/27, Record of a meeting between Harold Wilson and Gerhard Schroeder at 10 Downing Street, 11 December 1964.
136 LBJ, White House Central File, Countries, CO 305, United Kingdom, box 77, file 1, Folder 5, Donald M. Wilson (Deputy Director, United States Information Agency) to Johnson, 27 January 1965.
137 PRO, PREM 13/222, Healey to Wilson, 21 December 1964.
138 PRO, DEFE 13/350, See CNS to Healey, 17 November 1964; Draft statement by MOD (RN), undated (January 1965).
139 PRO, FO 371/184536, Z/12/8/G, Note by Arthurs, 21 January 1965.
140 PRO, FO 371/184536, Z/12/11, Arthurs to Barnes, 2 February 1965; Z/12/15, Shuckburgh to Foreign Office, 13 February 1965; Z/12/3/G, Foreign Office to Washington, 4 February 1965.
141 PRO, PREM 13/222, Foreign Office to UK Delegation to NATO, 11 February 1965.
142 LBJ, NSF, Name File, box 7, Neustadt Memos, Neustadt to Bundy, 8 January 1965.
143 LBJ, NSF, Committee File, Committee on Nuclear Proliferation, boxes 6–7, McCloy to Gilpatric, 8 January 1965, pp. 4–7.
144 LBJ, NSF, Files of McGeorge Bundy, box 5, Chron File, December 1–10, 1964 [2 of 2], Bundy to Johnson, 12 January 1965.
145 LBJ, NSF, Files of Spurgeon Keeny, box 1, Gilpatric Panel, A Report to the President by the Committee on Nuclear Proliferation, 21 January 1965, p. 8; LBJ, NSF, Files of

Spurgeon Keeny, box 7, Gilpatric Panel, Minutes of First Meeting, 13 and 14 December 1964, Issue Paper, p. 21.

146 FRUS, 1964–1968, vol. XIII, Rusk to Schroeder, 13 January 1965, p. 173. See also LBJ, NSF, Files of McGeorge Bundy, box 6, Chron File, 1–14 January 1965 [2 of 2], Bundy to Rostow, 10 January 1965.

147 USNA, RG 59, Ball Records, MLF#5, Bundy to Ball, 31 January 1965.

148 USNA, RG 59, Office of S/MF, Poseidon and MLF, Colbert to Owen, 21 January 1965.

149 PRO, DEFE 25/33, Scott to Barnes, 15 February 1965.

150 FRUS, 1964–1968, vol. XIII, Bundy to Rusk, 4 March 1965, pp. 187–8.

151 FRUS, 1964–1968, vol. XIII, Tyler to Rusk, 8 March 1965, pp. 188–9; C. Ponting, *Breach of Promise: Labour in Power, 1964–1970*, London: Hamish Hamilton, 1989, p. 29.

152 LBJ, NSF, Head of State Correspondence, box 9, United Kingdom, vol. 1 [2 of 2], PM Wilson Correspondence, March 4, 1964–August 30 1965, Wilson to Johnson, 11 March 1965. Johnson's bland reply was that there should be 'a very careful review of this whole problem'. LBJ, NSF, Head of State Correspondence, box 9, United Kingdom, vol. 1 [1 of 2], PM Wilson Correspondence, March 4, 1964–August 30 1965, Johnson to Wilson, 24 March 1965.

153 PRO, PREM 13/225, Note by Wilson, 26 March 1965.

154 PRO, PREM 13/452, Record of meeting between Denis Healey and the Secretary General of NATO, 13 May 1965.

155 Mountbatten, 'Britain's Armed Forces', *NATO Letter*, May 1965, pp. 22–5.

156 FRUS, 1964–1968, vol. XIII, Rusk to Department of State, 14 May 1965, p. 209.

157 LBJ, NSF, National Intelligence Estimates, Number 23–65, Prospects for West German Foreign Policy, 22 April 1965, p. 7.

158 Priest, 'In Common Cause', pp. 775–80.

159 PRO, DEFE 25/32, Westlake to MOD, 25 June 1965.

160 LBJ, NSF, Subject File MLF – Ricketts, box 25, American Embassy, Brussels to Rusk, 28 January 1965, Rusk to American Embassy, Rome, 28 January 1965; American Embassy, London to Ball, 29 January 1965; Klein to Bundy, 29 January 1965.

161 PRO, DEFE 25/32, McDonnell to Jones, 6 January 1965.

162 PRO, PREM 13/226, Wilson's hand-written note on minute from Tom Bridges to J.O. Wright, 18 January 1965.

163 USNA, RG 59, Office of S/MF, Sub-Group and Paris Working Group Files, 1963–1965, Miscellaneous: Ricketts, Kaiser to Rusk, 2 April 1965.

164 PRO, PREM 13/226, Harold Wilson's hand-written note on minute from Bridges to Wright, 1 June 1965.

165 *The Times*, 4 June 1965.

166 USDD, 355D/129, 10/1/78, Remarks by McNamara at NATO Defense Ministers Meeting, Paris, 31 May 1965; J.E. Stromseth, *The Origins of Flexible Response*, Basingstoke: Macmillan, 1988, p. 80. A. Priest, 'From "Hardware" to "Software": The End of the MLF-ANF Debate and the Rise of the NATO Nuclear Planning Group', in A. Wenger, C. Nuenlist and A. Locher (eds) *Transforming NATO in the Cold War: Challenges beyond Deterrence* (forthcoming, Routledge, 2006).

167 PRO, DEFE 25/92, Shuckburgh to Foreign Office, 1 June 1965; Dean to Foreign Office, 4 June 1965.

168 PRO, PREM 13/666, Note of a meeting at between Healey and McNamara, 2 June 1965.

169 PRO, FO 371/184417, NATO Intermediate Review: 1965, UK Submission, 22 June 1965, p. 3.

170 LBJ, NSF, Name File, box 5, NATO – Select Committee on Defense Ministers 6/65-5/67, Klein to Bundy, 15 June 1965.

171 PRO, DEFE 25/92, Shuckburgh to Foreign Office, 8 July 1965.

172 PRO, DEFE 25/59, Dean to Foreign Office, 7 October 1965.

173 LBJ, NSF, Agency File, NATO – Atlantic Nuclear Problem, September 21, 1965 (Briefing Book), Ball Paper; LBJ, NSF, Agency File, NATO – George W. Ball Analysis of a Collective Nuclear System, Ball to Rusk, McNamara and Bundy, The Case for a Strong American Lead to Establish a Collective Nuclear System That Would Help Save the Western World From Repeating An Old Mistake, 27 October 1965, and Tab A: 'The Dangers of a Psychotic Germany'; USNA, RG 59, Ball Records, The Nuclear Problem, The Case for a Fresh Start on Atlantic Nuclear Defence (with no mixed manned forces or plans for such forces), by Bundy, 18 October 1965; Comments on the Proposal to substitute bilateral 'consultation' with Germany for a collective nuclear system, by Ball.

174 USNA, RG 59, Ball Records, Spiers to Leddy, 18 October 1965.

175 USNA, RG 59, Office of S/MF, Sub-Group and Paris Working Group, Miscellaneous USS Ricketts, Schaetzel to Baker, 2 December 1965.

176 PRO, DEFE 49/11, Kelly to CBNS, Washington, 27 July 1965; PRO, DEFE 13/490, Healey to Shuckburgh, 8 December 1965.

177 USNA, RG 200, Proposals for Nuclear Sharing, November 1964–1965, Memorandum of Conversation, 20 October 1965.

178 PRO, PREM 13/681, Wright to Wilson, 22 November 1965.

179 PRO, DEFE 13/490, Healey to Shuckburgh, 8 December 1965. The State Department still wanted to at hold open the concept of mixed-manning on any future NATO force. See USNA, RG 59, Deputy Assistant Secretary for Politico-Military Affairs, Office of Operations, Subject Files, 1962–1966, Def-Defense Affairs, 6/65-12/65, United Kingdom, Rusk to Johnson, 13 December 1965.

180 PRO, PREM 13/681, Record of Conversation between McNamara and Wilson, 10 Downing Street, 26 November 1965; *The Sunday Times*, 21 November 1965.

181 PRO, PREM 13/453, Speech by Denis Healey to NATO Nuclear Special Committee, 27 November 1965.

182 FRUS, 1964–1968, vol. XII, Visit of Prime Minister Wilson, 15–19 December 1965, Memorandum Prepared by Read, undated, pp. 510–12; PRO, PREM 13/805, Extract of Meeting at the White House, 16 December 1965; FRUS, 1964–1968, vol. XIII, Note of Meeting by Bundy, 16 December 1965, pp. 284–5.

183 LBJ, NSF, Files of McGeorge Bundy, box 13, Chron File, 11–19 December 1965 [1 of 2], Bundy to Johnson, 16 December 1965.

184 LBJ, NSF, Agency File, box 39, Papers on a Pressing Problem Confronting the North Atlantic Alliance, Memo by Finletter, 7 December 1965.

185 FRUS, 1964–1968, vol. XIII, Memorandum of Conversation, Subject: Nuclear Sharing, 20 December 1965, pp. 292–5.

186 PRO, PREM 13/805, Roberts to Foreign Office, 3 December 1965; Roberts to Foreign Office, 7 December 1965; Erhard to Wilson, 22 December 1965; Shuckburgh to Foreign Office, 17 December 1965.

187 LBJ, NSF, Head of State Correspondence File, box 9, United Kingdom, vol. 2 [2 of 2], PM Wilson Correspondence, August 30, 1965–February 27, 1966, Wilson to Johnson, 5 January 1966.

188 LBJ, NSF, Head of State Correspondence File, box 9, United Kingdom, vol. 2 [2 of 2], PM Wilson Correspondence, August 30, 1965–February 27, 1966, Bundy to Johnson, 6 January 1966.

189 FRUS, 1964–1968, vol. XIII, Bundy to Rusk, 17 January 1966, pp. 300–1.

190 PRO, DEFE 13/673, Dean to Foreign Office, 15 February 1966.

191 PRO, PREM 13/805, Wright to Maclehose, 4 March 1966; Draft Reply to President Johnson, undated (late February 1966); FRUS, 1964–1968, vol. XIII, Wilson to Johnson, 26 February 1966, p. 318.

192 The Labour Party, *Time for Decision: Manifesto of the Labour Party, General Election, 1966*, London: Transport House, 1966, p. 21.

193 USNA, RG 59, Ball Records, Briefing Book: France and NATO, Book 3, Wilson to Johnson, 29 March 1966, p. 2.
194 FRUS, 1964–1968, vol. XIII, Rusk to Johnson, 11 April 1966, pp. 363–5. In contrast, Walt Whitman Rostow told the president that 'at the moment the Germans do not have the political and psychological base to foreclose a hardware option once and for all without a major concession from Moscow in the direction of German unity'. LBJ, NSF, Files of Walt W. Rostow, box 15, Non-Vietnam: April–July 1966, Rostow to Johnson, 17 April 1966.
195 LBJ, NSF, Files of Robert W. Komer, box 1, NATO, Komer to President, 16 March 1966.
196 FRUS, 1964–1968, vol. XIII, NSAM 345, Rostow to Rusk and McNamara, 22 April 1966, pp. 374–5; Rusk and McNamara to Johnson, 28 May 1966, pp. 402–3.
197 PRO, DEFE 13/673, Dean to Gore Booth, 12 May 1966.
198 FRUS, 1964–1968, vol. XIII, Johnson to Wilson, 21 May 1966, pp. 396–8. Wilson reported that he and Erhard did not even discuss the issue of nuclear sharing. LBJ, NSF, Head of State Correspondence, box 9, United Kingdom, vol. 4, PM Wilson Correspondence, March 23, 1966–June 3, 1966, Wilson to Johnson, 26 May 1966.
199 PRO, DEFE 13/673, Record of Meeting between Denis Healey and Paul Nitze, 16 May 1966.
200 FRUS, 1964–1968, vol. XIII, Note of Meeting with the President, 23 June 1966, pp. 418–19.
201 FRUS, 1964–1968, vol. XIII, McGhee to State Department, 2 July 1966, pp. 427–30.
202 PRO, CAB 133/347, Background note, Prime Minister's Visit to Washington, undated (July 1966).
203 LBJ, NSF, Files of Walt W. Rostow, box 11, Non-Proliferation, Rostow to Rusk, 3 September 1966; Bator to President, 7 September 1966.
204 Kelleher, Germany and the Politics of Nuclear Weapons, p. 263; Schrafstetter and Twigge, 'Trick or Truth?' p. 177.
205 PRO, PREM 13/808, Record of conversation between Wilson and Eugene Rostow, 21 November 1966; PRO, DEFE 25/99, Roberts to Foreign Office, 7 December 1966.
206 Hammond, LBJ and the Presidential Management of Foreign Relations, p. 163.
207 Hammond, LBJ and the Presidential Management of Foreign Relations, p. 148.
208 LBJ, NSF, International Meetings and Travel File, NATO Ministerial Meeting, Paris, December 1966 [1 of 3], Position Paper, 8 December 1966.
209 LBJ, NSF, Agency File, box 36, NATO – General, vol. 4, 5/66-3/67 [2 of 2], Hughes to Rusk, 22 September 1966.
210 USNA, RG 59 Central File, Subject Numeric File, 1964–1966, NATO 3, FR (PA), Department of State Circular, Press Conference by John M. Leddy, 12 December 1966.
211 LBJ, NSC Meetings, vol. 4, box 2, Summary Notes of 566th NSC Meeting, 13 December 1966; LBJ, NSF, Files of Walt Whitman Rostow, box 1, Meetings with the President, April–December 1966, Note of Meeting with the President, 17 December 1966, p. 5.

7 ALLIES UNDER STRAIN

1 Lyndon B. Johnson Library (hereafter referred to as LBJ), Oral History, Harlan Cleveland, pp. 41–2.
2 G.C. Herring, America's Longest War: The United States and Vietnam, 1950–1975, New York: McGraw-Hill, 2002, p. 182.
3 LBJ, Oral History, Admiral Thomas H. Moorer, vol. II, p. 17; Naval Historical Center, Operational Archives Branch, Post Command File, CNO Series, Annual Reports (Statements Before Congress, 1955 [Final] – 1971), Statement of Admiral

David L. McDonald, 1 February 1967 for FY 1968, p. 9; Statement of Admiral Thomas H. Moorer, May 1968 for FY 1969, pp. 14–15.

4 T.A. Schwartz, *Lyndon Johnson and Europe: In the Shadow of Vietnam*, Cambridge and London: Harvard University Press, 2003, pp. 99–100.

5 L.B. Johnson, *The Vantage Point: Perspectives of the Presidency, 1963–1969*, New York: Holt, Rhinehart and Winston, 1971, p. 305.

6 J.W. Young, *The Labour Governments, 1964–70, vol. 2: International Policy*, Manchester and New York: Manchester University Press, 2003, pp. 121.

7 H. Wilson, *The Labour Government, 1964–1970: A Personal Record*, London: Penguin, 1971, p. 23.

8 D.B. Kunz, 'Cold War Dollar Diplomacy: The Other Side of Containment', in D.B. Kunz (ed.) *The Diplomacy of the Crucial Decade: American Foreign Relations During the 1960s*, New York: Columbia University Press, 1994, pp. 94–6; R. Roy, 'No Secrets Between "Special Friends": America's Involvement in British Economic Policy, October 1964–April 1965', *History*, vol. 89, no. 295, 2004, pp. 399–423.

9 Public Record Office (hereafter referred to as PRO), DEFE 13/673, Dean to Stewart, 30 September 1965.

10 J. Fielding, 'Coping with Decline: US Policy Toward the British Defense Reviews of 1966', *Diplomatic History*, vol. 23, no. 4, 1999, pp. 634–5.

11 J. Dumbrell, *A Special Relationship: Anglo-American Relations in the Cold War and After*, Basingstoke: Macmillan, 2001, pp. 150–4; D. Dimbleby and D. Reynolds, *An Ocean Apart: The Relationship between Britain and America in the Twentieth Century*, London: BBC/Hodder & Stoughton, 1988, pp. 250–3.

12 J. Dumbrell and S.A. Ellis, 'British Involvement in Vietnam Peace Initiatives, 1966–1967: Marigolds, Sunflowers, and "Kosygin Week"', *Diplomatic History*, vol. 27, no. 1, 2003, pp. 113–49; Y. Mizumoto, 'Harold Wilson's Efforts at a Negotiated Settlement of the Vietnam War, 1965–67', *Electronic Journal of International History*, 2005, pp. 1–43.

13 For a broader dicsussion of developments, see Schwartz, *Lyndon Johnson and Europe*, pp. 140–86.

14 D. Healey, *The Time of my Life*, London: Penguin, 1989, pp. 306–7.

15 PRO, DEFE 25/97, Healey to McNamara, 21 February 1966.

16 LBJ, Oral History, Dean Rusk, vol. IV, p. 18.

17 Dimbleby and Reynolds, *An Ocean Apart*, p. 253.

18 PRO, DEFE 13/436, Healey Memorandum, 5 March 1965; M. Chalmers, *Paying for Defence: Military Spending and British Decline*, London: Pluto Press, 1985, p. 82.

19 M. Middeke, 'Britain's Global Military Role, Conventional Defence and Anglo-American Interdependence After Nassau', *Journal of Strategic Studies*, vol. 24, no. 1, 2001, p. 157.

20 PRO, DEFE 13/436, The Case for CVA.01, MOD Paper, 18 November 1964; PRO, FO 371/184417, NATO Intermediate Review: 1965, UK Submission, Part II (b) (Naval), 22 June 1965; P. Darby, *British Defence Policy East of Suez*, London: Royal Institute of International Affairs/Oxford University Press, 1973, p. 271.

21 PRO, FO 371/184417, Barnes to Shuckburgh, 18 June 1965; PRO, FO 371/184418, Foreign Office telegram, 17 August 1965.

22 PRO, PREM 13/212, Trend to Wilson, 17 February 1965.

23 Healey, *The Time of my Life*, p. 302.

24 United States National Archive (hereafter referred to as USNA), RG 59, Lot Files, Records of Under Secretary of State George W. Ball, 1961–1966, Lot 74D272 (hereafter referred to as Ball Records), NATO, Memorandum of Conversation, 30 May 1965, p. 4.

25 USNA, RG 59, Ball Records, NATO, Memorandum of Conversation, 30 May 1965, p. 5.

26 Foreign Relations of the United States (hereafter referred to as FRUS), 1964–1968, vol. XII, *Western Europe*, Memorandum of Conversation, 30 June 1965, pp. 493–4.

27 FRUS, 1964–1968, vol. XII, Bator to Bundy, 29 July 1965, pp. 501–2.

28 Fielding, 'Coping with Decline', p. 634.

29 USNA, RG 59, Deputy Asst for Politico-Military Affairs, Office of Operations, Subject Files, 1962–1966, Visit of Prime Minister Wilson, 15–19 December, 1965, Memorandum of Conversation, 11 October 1965.

30 LBJ, National Security Files (hereafter referred to as NSF), Files of McGeorge Bundy, box 13, Chron File, Dec 11–19, 1965 [1 of 2], Memorandum for the Record, 17 December 1965.

31 PRO, CAB 164/713, Deployment of Polaris, undated note (January 1966).

32 FRUS, 1964–1968, vol. XII, Rostow to Johnson, 20 January 1966, pp. 512–14.

33 FRUS, 1964–1968, vol. XIII, *Western Europe Region*, Memorandum of Conversation, 27 January 1966, pp. 303–6.

34 FRUS, 1964–1968, vol. XII, Memorandum of Conversation, 22 January 1966, pp. 514–15; FRUS, 1964–1968, vol. XII, Memorandum of Conversation, 27 January 1966, pp. 526–7.

35 FRUS, 1964–1968, vol. XII, Memorandum of Conversation, 27 January 1966, p. 524.

36 F.S. Northedge, *Descent from Power: British Foreign Policy, 1945–1973*, London: George Allen & Unwin, 1974, pp. 297–8; K. Speed, *Sea Change: The Battle for the Falklands and the Future of Britain's Navy*, Bath: Ashgrove Press, 1982, pp. 9–11.

37 FRUS, 1964–1968, vol. XII, Memorandum of Conversation, 27 January 1966, p. 522.

38 PRO, DEFE 13/436, Healey to Permanent Under-Secretary, 10 November 1964; The Case for CVA 01, 18 November 1964; Chalmers, *Paying for Defence*, p. 84.

39 PRO, CAB 130/211, Paper on the Atlantic Nuclear Force by the Defence Study Group, 17 November 1964, p. 39.

40 PRO, DEFE 13/673, Note by Henry Kuss on US/UK co-operation on offset procurement, 8 December 1965.

41 FRUS, 1964–1968, vol. XII, Memorandum of Conversation, 27 January 1966, p. 523.

42 FRUS, 1964–1968, vol. XIII, Memorandum of Conversation, 27 January 1966, pp. 305–6.

43 LBJ, NSF, box 215, 3F, UK Defense Review 1966, Joint State-Defense Scope Paper, 27 January 1966; LBJ, NSF, box 215, 2L, UK Defense Review 1966, Position Paper: UK Position in Malta, 27 January 1966.

44 FRUS, 1964–1968, vol. XII, Bator to President, 16 February 1966, p. 529.

45 United States Declassified Documents Series (hereafter referred to as USDD), 238/2936, 9/1/94, Johnson to Wilson, 25 February 1966.

46 USDD 94/1322, 4/1/85, Johnson to Wilson, 25 February 1966; PRO, DEFE 13/673, Johnson to Wilson, 3 March 1966.

47 USNA, RG 200, ASW – Draft Memos, McNamara to Johnson, 9 October 1964; USNA, RG 59, DOS Top Secret Foreign Policy Files, 1964–1966, NATO, p. 8, Department of State to Various Embassies, 23 December 1964.

48 USDD, 46/0525, Bowman to Rostow, 14 May 1966.

49 PRO, FO 371/179139, Foreign Office to British Embassy, Bonn, 19 March 1966.

50 LBJ, NSF, Agency File, box 35, NATO – General, vol. 3, 12/64-5/66 [2 of 2], Special Report: Developments in NATO, CIA, Office of Current Intelligence, 4 February 1966, p. 1.

51 LBJ, NSF, Agency File, box 35, NATO – General, vol. 3, 12/64-5/66 [2 of 2], Special Report: Developments in NATO, CIA, Office of Current Intelligence, 4 February 1966, pp. 5–6.

52 FRUS, vol. XIII, Circular telegram from the Department of State to Posts in NATO Capitals, 4 May 1964, pp. 48–50.

53 USDD, 1/31/86, Memorandum of Conversation between Wheeler and McCloy, undated; USDD, 11/1/92, NATO and France, Department of State Policy Planning Council Paper, 6 May 1964.
54 FRUS, 1964–1968, vol. XIII, Department of State to Certain Europeans Posts, 10 February 1966, pp. 312–14.
55 FRUS, 1964–1968, vol. XIII, Ball to Johnson, 2 March 1966, pp. 318–19.
56 FRUS, 1964–1968, vol. XIII, Rusk to the Posts in NATO Capitals, 2 March 1966, pp. 319–21.
57 FRUS, 1964–1968, vol. XIII, Bohlen to Rusk, 7 March 1966.
58 FRUS, 1964–1968, vol. XIII, de Gaulle to Johnson, 7 March 1966, pp. 325–6.
59 FRUS, 1964–1968, vol. XIII, Bator to Johnson, 8 March 1966, p. 330.
60 FRUS, 1964–1968, vol. XIII, Komer to Johnson, 16 March 1966, pp. 335–8.
61 FRUS, 1964–1968, vol. XIII, Memorandum of Conversation, 17 March 1964, p. 342.
62 USNA, RG 59, Ball Records, Briefing Book: France and NATO, Book 3, Wilson to Johnson, 29 March 1966.
63 USDD, 293B/311, 10/1/78, American Embassy, London to Department of State, 23 May 1966; USDD, 81/0891, 3/1/95, American Embassy, London to Department of State, 25 May 1966.
64 J. Dumbrell, 'The Johnson Administration and the British Labour Government: Vietnam, the Pound and East of Suez', *Journal of American Studies*, vol. 30, no. 2, 1996, p. 221.
65 Kunz, 'Cold War Dollar Diplomacy', in Kunz (ed.) *Diplomacy of the Crucial Decade*, p. 100.
66 K. Boyle, 'The Price of Peace: Vietnam, the Pound and the Crisis of American Empire', *Diplomatic History*, vol. 27, no. 1, 2003, p. 44.
67 LBJ, NSF, Files of Walt W. Rostow, box 12, Wilson Visit, Bator to Johnson, 21 July 1966.
68 USDD, 208A/599, 10/1/78, Ball to Johnson, 22 July 1966.
69 USDD, 86/1096, 3/1/90, Rostow to President, 13 June 1966.
70 J. Colman, *A 'Special Relationship'? Harold Wilson, Lyndon B. Johnson and Anglo-American Relations 'at the summit', 1964–68*, Manchester and New York: Manchester University Press, 2004, pp. 115–17.
71 PRO, DEFE 13/673, Dean to MacLehose, 6 August 1966.
72 FRUS, 1964–1968, vol. XIII, Johnson to Wilson, undated.
73 F.J. Gavin, 'The Myth of Flexible Response: United States Strategy in Europe during the 1960s', *International History Review*, vol. 23, no. 4, 2001, pp. 867–71.
74 FRUS, 1964–1968, vol. XIII, Johnson to Wilson, undated, pp. 460–1.
75 FRUS, 1964–1968, vol. XIII, Schroeder to Rusk, 8 August 1966, pp. 442–3.
76 Young, *The Labour Governments*, p. 124.
77 LBJ, NSF, Agency File, box 36, NATO – General vol. 4, 5/66–3/67 [2 of 2], Bator to Johnson, 23 August 1966; FRUS, 1964–1968, vol. XIII, Johnson to Erhard, 7 September 1966; Ball to American Embassy, Bonn, 8 September 1966, pp. 464–6.
78 *Public Papers of the Presidents of the United States: Lyndon B. Johnson*, 1966, vol. II, Washington: p. 506; FRUS, 1964–1968, vol. XIII, McCloy to Johnson, 21 November 1966, pp. 495–7. Thomas Alan Schwartz suggests that McCloy's appointment was intended to reassure the Federal Republic that the Americans were not abandoning their NATO commitments and it had the effect of upsetting the British. Schwartz, *Lyndon Johnson and Europe*, pp. 143–6.
79 LBJ, NSF, National Security Council Meetings, box 2, vol. 4, tab 48, Summary Notes of 566th NSC Meeting, 13 December 1966.

80 FRUS, 1964–1968, vol. XIII, Johnson to Wilson, 15 November 1966, pp. 491–2.
81 PRO, PREM 13/808, Johnson to Wilson, 15 November 1966; Wilson to Johnson, 17 November 1966; Johnson to Wilson, 19 November 1966; Record of Conversation, 21 November 1966.
82 LBJ, Administrative History of the Department of State, vol. 1, Chapters 1–3, box 1, 2: The Troop Problem and Burden Sharing, p. 16.
83 LBJ, NSF, National Security Council Meetings, box 2, vol. 4, tab 51, Summary Notes of 569th NSC Meeting, 3 May 1967.
84 LBJ, NSF, Agency File, box 39, NATO, Report to the President, US Forces for the NATO Central Region, November 1966, pp. 7–10, 'The British Situation'.
85 LBJ, NSF, Agency File, box 39, NATO, Report to the President, US Forces for the NATO Central Region, November 1966, 'Conclusions and Recommendations'.
86 LBJ, NSF, NIE, Folder 23, West Germany, Number 23–67, Bonn's Policies under the Kiesinger government, 30 March 1967, p. 5.
87 PRO, FO 371, UK Delegation to NATO to Foreign Office, 15 December 1966.
88 LBJ, NSF, International Meeting and Travel File, box 35, NATO Ministerial Meeting, Paris, December 1966 [1 of 3], Scope Paper, 7 December 1966.
89 Schwartz, *Lyndon Johnson and Europe*, pp. 147–9.
90 LBJ, NSF, Agency File, box 35, NATO – General, vol. 3 12/64-5/66 [2 of 2], McCloy to Rostow, 17 February 1966; USDD, 88/1025, 3/1/86, McCloy to Johnson, 23 February 1967.
91 LBJ, NSF, Files of Walt W. Rostow, [Non-Vietnam, January–Febrauary 1967], Bator to Johnson, 25 February 1967.
92 Young, *The Labour Governments*, p. 125; Schwartz, *Lyndon Johnson and Europe*, p. 151.
93 As Johnson said, he would not see NATO 'go down' over $40 million. USDD, 70/1092, 3/1/87, Record of Meeting, 9 March 1967.
94 Schwartz, *Lyndon Johnson and Europe*, pp. 153–7.
95 Schwartz, *Lyndon Johnson and Europe*, pp. 159–64.
96 FRUS, 1964–1968, vol. XIII, Final Report on Trilateral Talks, undated (April 1967), pp. 562–70.
97 LBJ, NSF, International Meeting and Travel File, box 35, NATO Ministerial Meeting, Paris, December 1966 [1 of 3], Position Paper, 6 December 1966.
98 USNA, RG 59, Central Foreign Policy Files (hereafter referred to as CFPF), 1967–1969, Political and Defense, DEF 4 NATO 1-1-67, Eugene Rostow to Rusk, 9 January 1967.
99 FRUS, 1964–1968, vol. XIII, Memorandum by the Acheson Group, undated, pp. 406–9.
100 H. Haftendorn, *NATO and the Nuclear Revolution: A Crisis of Credibility, 1966–1967*, Oxford: Clarendon Press, 1996, pp. 320–6.
101 Haftendorn, *NATO and the Nuclear Revolution*, pp. 355–62.
102 FRUS, 1964–1968, vol. XIII, Kohler to Watson, 13 July 1967, pp. 591–5.
103 See also USNA, RG 59, CFPF, 1967–1969, Political and Defense, DEF 4 NATO, State to US Mission to NATO, 4 November 1967.
104 NSF, Agency File, box 35, NATO, General, vol. 5, 3/67-12/67 [1 of 2], CIS Intelligence Memorandum, The Harmel Study – NATO Looks to its Future, 7 December 1967, p. 5.
105 USNA, RG 59, CFPF, 1967–1969, Political and Defense, DEF 4 NATO, US Mission to NATO to Rusk, 1 November 1967.
106 LBJ, NSF, International Meetings and Travel File, box 35, NATO Ministerial Meeting, Luxembourg, June 13–14, 1967 [1 of 2], Position Paper: The Study on the Future of

the Alliance, 5 June 1967. See also FRUS, 1964–1968, vol. XIII, Cleveland to Rusk, 17 June 1967, pp. 585–90.

107 USNA, RG 59, CFPF, 1967–1969, Political and Defense, DEF 4 NATO, 9/1/67, Bowie to Rusk, 16 October 1967.

108 LBJ, NSF, International Meetings and Travel File, box 35, NATO Ministerial Meeting, Luxembourg, June 13–14, 1967 [1 of 2], Position Paper: Issues Paper, 5 June 1967.

109 USDD, 131/2305, 9/1/91, Bator to Johnson, 2 June 1967.

110 USNA, RG 59, CFPF, 1967–1969, Political and Defense, DEF 1 NATO 9-9-67, Cleveland to McNamara, 5 December 1967.

8 PUTTING NATO FIRST?

1 J.E. Stromseth, *The Origins of Flexible Response: NATO's Debate over Strategy in the 1960s*, New York: St Martin's Press, 1988, pp. 175–6.

2 Foreign Relations of the United States (hereafter referred to as FRUS), 1964–1968, vol. XIII, *Western Europe Region*, Memorandum of Conversation, 18 April 1967, pp. 559–60; Rusk to Certain posts in Europe, 2 May 1967, p. 570, Memorandum of Conversation, 2 June 1967, pp. 579–80; Max Guderzo, 'Johnson and European Integration: A Missed Chance for Transatlantic Power', *Cold War History*, vol. 4, no. 2, 2004, pp. 89–114.

3 United States Declassified Documents Series (hereafter referred to as USDD), 122/1484, 5/1/93, Rusk to McNamara, 13 January 1967.

4 Congressional Record – Senate, vol. 113, part 13, 90th Congress, 1st Session, 21–28 June 1967, 16640, Speech by Supreme Allied Commander Atlantic, Thomas H. Moorer (USN), on the Occasion of the Change of Command Ceremonies, Norfolk, VA, 17 June 1967.

5 USDD, 202/2571, 9/1/86, Department of State Paper, Military Redeployments from Europe, 2 February 1967.

6 Congressional Record – Senate, vol. 112, part 12, 89th Congress, 2nd Session, 1966, p. 15780.

7 Congressional Record – House, vol. 111, Part 21, 89th Congress, 1st Session, 22 October 1965, pp. 28499–504.

8 Public Record Office (hereafter referred to as PRO), DEFE 13/510, Report on the Byrnes Amendment, 15 June 1967; Lyndon B. Johnson Library (hereafter referred to as LBJ), National Security Files (hereafter referred to as NSF), Country File, United Kingdom, box 211, Benjamin Read to Walt Whitman Rostow, 1 July 1967; Draft reply to Ridley British Embassy, Washington on Byrnes Amendment, undated.

9 PRO, DEFE 13/510, Talking points used by foreign secretary in talks with Eugene Rostow, 14 September 1967.

10 PRO, DEFE 13/530, Transcript of Interview with Denis Healey by Reginald Bosanquet, 14 September 1967 for ITN *News At Ten* Programme.

11 PRO, DEFE 13/530, Healey to McNamara, 14 September 1967.

12 PRO, PREM 13/1891, Dean to Foreign Office, 15 September 1967; British Embassy, Washington to Foreign Office, 23 September 1967.

13 FRUS, 1964–1968, vol. XII, *Western Europe*, Rusk to US Embassy, London, 14 September 1967, p. 581; DEFE PRO, 13/530, McNamara to Healey, 16 September 1967.

14 United States National Archive (hereafter referred to as USNA), RG 59, Central Foreign Policy Files (hereafter CFPF), 1967–1969, POL 1 UK–US 1/1/67, Department of State Intelligence Note, 20 September 1967.

15 PRO, DEFE 13/530, Dean to Foreign Office, 23 September 1967.

16 *Evening News*, 4 October 1967.

17 D. Healey, *The Time of my Life*, London: Penguin, 1989, p. 273.
18 USDD, 181/2064, 7/1/95, Meeting between Healey and McNamara, 4 March 1967.
19 LBJ, NSF, box 211, vol. XI, 13a, Rostow's comment on correspondence from Bruce to Rusk, 10 May 1967.
20 LBJ, NSF, Head of State Correspondence File, box 10, Wilson to Johnson, 30 October 1966.
21 D. Wettern, *The Decline of British Seapower*, London: Jane's, 1982, p. 299.
22 D.B. Kunz, 'Cold War Dollar Diplomacy: The Other Side of Containment', in D.B. Kunz (ed.) *The Diplomacy of the Crucial Decade: American Foreign Relations During the 1960s*, New York: Columbia University Press, 1994, pp. 105–7; Kunz, ' "Somewhat Mixed up Together": Anglo-American Defence and Financial Policy During the 1960s', *Journal of Imperial and Commonwealth History*, vol. 27, no. 2, 1999, pp. 223–8; J. Dumbrell, 'The Johnson Administration and the British Labour Government: Vietnam, the Pound and East of Suez', *Journal of American Studies*, vol. 30, no. 2, pp. 224–7.
23 PRO, DEFE 13/510, Healey to McNamara, 27 November 1967.
24 T.A. Schwartz, *Lyndon Johnson and Europe: In the Shadow of Vietnam*, Cambridge and London: Harvard University Press, 2003, pp. 194–5.
25 A.P. Dobson, 'The Years of Transition: Anglo-American Relations, 1961–1967', *Review of International Studies*, vol. 16, 1990, p. 256.
26 S. Dockrill, *Britain's Retreat from East of Suez: The Choice Between Europe and the World?* Basingstoke: Palgrave, 2002, pp. 196–7.
27 LBJ, NSF, box 216, 34, Visit of Prime Minister Harold Wilson [1 of 2], Background Paper: NATO Problems, 2 June 1967.
28 C. Bluth, 'Reconciling the Irreconcilable: Alliance Politics and the Paradox of Extended Deterrence', *Cold War History*, vol. 1, no. 2, 2001, pp. 97–8.
29 *Economist*, 16 December 1967, pp. 1136–7.
30 Dockrill, *Britain's Retreat*, pp. 202–3.
31 R. Crossman, *The Diaries of a Cabinet Minister, vol. 2*, London: Hamish Hamilton, 1976, pp. 634–5.
32 FRUS, 1964–1968, vol. XII, Bruce to Department of State, 9 January 1968, pp. 599–602. Embassy staff suggested Healey had not resigned because 'he is relatively young, politically ambitious, and has no place else to go'. USNA, RG 59, CFPF, 1967–1969, POL 15-1 UK 1/1/68, American Embassy, London to Rusk, 24 January 1968.
33 Crossman, *The Diaries of a Cabinet Minister, vol. 2*, p. 646; LBJ, NSF, Head of State Correspondence File, box 10, Rostow to Johnson, 11 January 1968.
34 USDD, 81/0895, 3/1/95, Katzenbach to Johnson, 11 January 1968.
35 FRUS, 1964–1968, vol. XII, Johnson to Wilson, 11 January 1968, pp. 608–9.
36 FRUS, 1964–1968, vol. XII, Johnson to Wilson, 15 January 1968, pp. 609–11.
37 LBJ, NSF, Files of Walt W. Rostow, box 16, Non-Vietnam: January–February 1968, Wilson to Johnson, 15 January 1968.
38 USDD, 19/0206, 1/1/96, Bruce to Rusk, 16 January 1968; Although Barbara Castle claims in her diaries that she supported cancellation. Barbara Castle, *The Castle Diaries, 1964–1970*, London: Weidenfeld & Nicholson, 1984, p. 356.
39 USDD, 19/0206, 1/1/96, Bruce to Rusk, 16 January 1968; Healey, *The Time of My Life*, p. 273.
40 LBJ, NSF, Country File, United Kingdom, box 212, vol. XII, Nitze to Healey, 17 January 1968.
41 Naval Historical Center (hereafter referred to as NHC), Operational Archive Branch (hereafter referred to as OAB), Oral History, Admiral Thomas Moorer, vol. I, interview 10, p. 464; vol. I, interview 9, p. 412.

42 FRUS, 1964–1968, vol. XIII, Department of State to US mission to NATO, 22 February 1968, pp. 671–2.

43 LBJ, NSF, Country File, United Kingdom, box 216, Visits of Prime Minister Wilson Briefing Book, Background Paper: New British Defence Posture, 2 February 1968.

44 See G.C. Herring, *America's Longest War: The United States and Vietnam, 1950–1975*, New York: McGraw-Hill, 2002, pp. 229–36.

45 Schwartz, *Lyndon Johnson and Europe*, pp. 198–9; J. Colman, *A 'Special Relationship'? Harold Wilson, Lyndon B. Johnson and Anglo-American Relations 'at the Summit', 1964–68*, Manchester: Manchester University Press, 2004, pp. 159–62.

46 LBJ, NSF, Files of Edward R. Fried, box 2, CHRON, DEC. 1967-FEB. 1968, Rostow to Johnson, 7 February 1968.

47 USNA, RG 59, CFPF, Political and Defense, 1967–1969, POL 7 UK, Thomas L. Hughes to Rusk, 7 February 1968, p. i.

48 PRO, CAB 134/3120, Report by the Defence Review Working Party, British Nuclear Policy, 1 December 1967.

49 M. Henry, 'A CO's Story', in J.E. Moore, *The Impact of Polaris: The Origins of Britain's Seaborne Nuclear Deterrent*, Huddersfield: Richard Netherwood, 1999, pp. 246–7; NHC, OAB, Papers of Harvey M. Sapolsky, series I, box 5, Miscellaneous 1956–1968 (Folder 2), Harvey M. Sapolsky's notes.

50 Congressional Record – Senate, vol. 113, part 13, 90th Congress, 1st Session, 21–28 June 1967, pp. 16639–41.

51 USNA, RG 59, CFPF, 1967–1969, DEF 1 NATO 9/9/67, Cleveland to Rusk, 28 November 1967.

52 FRUS, 1964–1968, vol. XIII, Rusk to Department of State, 14 December 1967, p. 651.

53 USDD, 298/3535, 1/11/93, Rostow to Johnson, 12 January 1968.

54 USDD, 298/3535, 1/11/93, Rostow to Johnson, 12 January 1968; Congressional Record – Senate, vol. 113, part 27, 90th Congress, 1st Session, 13–15 December 1967, p. 36738; FRUS, 1964–1968, vol. XIII, Department of State to US mission to NATO, 22 February 1968, p. 671.

55 Congressional Record – Senate, vol. 114, part 8, 90th Congress, 2nd Session, 22 April 1968, p. 10140.

56 LBJ, NSF, Agency File, box 37, NATO Messages, vol. 2, 9/67-9/68 [1 of 2], Cleveland to Rusk, 8 May 1968.

57 USNA, RG 59, CFPF, 1967–1969, DEF 1 NATO 5/1/68, Cleveland to Rusk, 11 May 1968; USNA, RG 59, CFPF, 1967–1969, Political and Defense, DEF 6 NATO, 5/1/68, Cleveland to Rusk, 13 May 1968; Clifford to American Embassy, London, 14 May 1968.

58 In contrast to this view, Michael Stewart noted in his diary following discussions with Healey that the increased contributions were 'very modest'. Churchill College Archive, Papers of Michael Stewart, STWT 8/1/5, journal entry, 1 May 1968.

59 USDD, 267/3226, 11/1/95, Visit of Prime Minister Wilson. Background Paper: New British Defense Posture, undated; *Economist*, 15 June 1968, pp. 22–3.

60 PRO, DEFE 13/627, The increased Significance of the Flanks of NATO, Paper drafted by the Defence Secretariat, Annex A to COS 1110/15/2/68, February 1968; Note for secretary of state's speech to NATO Defence Planning Committee on 10 May 1968, undated.

61 FRUS, 1964–1968, vol. XIII, Rusk to Cleveland, 9 May 1968, p. 695.

62 See for example, PRO, CAB 134/3120, Ministerial Committee on Nuclear Policy, 1966, note by Chairman on Polaris, 14 December 1966; PRO, CAB 164/713, Paper by Working Party for Consideration of Nuclear Policy Committee, The Deployment of Polaris Submarines, 10 November 1966, p. 11; Healey to Wilson, 2 January 1967.

63 PRO, FCO 16/241, Extract from record of conversation between the prime minister and President Johnson, 2 June 1967.

64 PRO, CAB 164/713, Healey to Wilson, 2 January 1967; Healey to Wilson, 3 August 1967.

65 PRO, CAB 164/713, Healey to Wilson, 5 June 1968.

66 See DEFE 13/350, Healey to Wilson, 22 January 1965.

67 USNA, RG 59, Central; Foreign Policy Files, Political and Defense, 1967–1969, POL 15 UK–US, Bendall to Kitchen, 3 April 1967; USNA, RG 59, CFPF, Political and Defense 1967–1969, POL 15 UK, US Embassy, London to Rusk, 17 April 1967. With the likelihood of the British adopting Poseidon increasingly remote, they began seriously to reconsider co-operation with the French in the nuclear field. PRO, FCO 46/153, Note on Discussion between Denis Healey and Pierre Messmer, 19 January 1967; Chalfont to Healey, 23 January 1967; Bendell to Sykes, 15 May 1967.

68 *New York Times*, 10 May 1967.

69 C. Grayling and C. Langdon, *Just Another Star? Anglo-American Relations since 1945*, London: Harrap, 1988, p. 56.

70 PRO, CAB 134/3120, Ministerial Committee on Nuclear Policy, minutes, 5 December 1967.

71 Schwartz, *Lyndon Johnson and Europe*, p. 207; LBJ, NSF, Files of Spurgeon Keeny, box 1, ABMI 1966–67, Healey to McNamara, 15 September 1967; Research Memorandum, 18 December 1967.

72 LBJ, NSF, Files of Spurgeon Keeny, box 1, ABMI 1966–67, Bruce to Rusk, 22 September 1967. See also Kohler to US Embassy, Moscow, 22 February 1967.

73 LBJ, NSF, Files of Spurgeon Keeny, box 1, ABMI 1966–67, Cleveland to Rusk, 14 September 1967.

74 LBJ, NSF, Files of Edward R. Fried, box 2, CHRON September 1, 1967–November 30, 1967 [2 of 2], Rostow to Johnson, 26 September 1967.

75 C.J. Bartlett, *The 'Special Relationship: A Political History of Anglo-American Relations since 1945*, Harlow: Longman, 1992, p. 122; B. Reed and G.L. Williams, *Denis Healey and the Policies of Power*, London: Sidwick & Jackson, 1971, pp. 254–63.

76 FRUS, 1964–1968, vol. XII, Paper Prepared in the Department of State, undated (June 1968), pp. 620–621; USDD, 133/1622, 5/1/93, Record of NSC Meeting, 5 June 1968; W. Schütze, 'European Defence Co-operation and NATO', in The Atlantic Institute, *The Atlantic Papers*, New York: University Press of Cambridge, 1970, p. 30; Bartlett, *The 'Special Relationship'*, p. 123.

77 LBJ, NSF, Files of Edward R. Fried, box 2, CHRON, May 2–July 31, 1968, NSC Meeting on the UK, 5 June 1968 (7 June 1968), pp. 1–2.

78 USDD, 82/1212, 4/1/85, Summary Notes of 587th NSC Meeting [Extract], 5 June 1968.

79 LBJ, NSF, Country File, United Kingdom, box 212, 178, Bruce to Rusk, 1 June 1968.

80 USNA, RG 218, 0015, 092.2, NATO, Donaldson to Wheeler (Extract from JCS 1924/202-2 [7 June 1967]), 12 April 1968.

81 USNA, RG 59, CFPF, 1967–1969, Political and Defense, DEF 6, NATO, 6/1/67, Memorandum of Conversation, 11 June 1968.

82 Congressional Record – Senate, vol. 113, part 13, 90th Congress, 1st Session, 21–28 June 1967, pp. 16639–40, Speech by Supreme Allied Commander Atlantic, Thomas H. Moorer (USN), on the Occasion of the Change of Command Ceremonies, Norfolk, VA, 17 June 1967.

83 USDD, 245/2609, 9/1/91, Rusk to Department of State, Third Session, NATO Ministerial Meeting, 15 December 1965; B. Ranft and G. Till, *The Sea in Soviet Strategy*, Basingstoke: Macmillan, 1983, p. 92.

84 PRO, DEFE 13/720, SACEUR Force Proposals, 1969–1973, undated.

85 J.J. Herzog, 'Perspectives on Soviet Naval Development', in P.J. Murphy (ed.) *Naval Power in Soviet Policy*, Washington DC: United States Government Printing Office for the United States Air Force, 1978, p. 40.

86 Congressional Record – Senate, vol. 114, part 1, 90th Congress, Second Session, Extension of Remarks, p. 1111; NHC, OAB, Post 1946 Command File, CNO Series, Annual Reports (Statements before Congress), 1955 (Final) – 1971, Statement of Thomas H. Moorer, May 1968 for FY 1969, p. 13.

87 LBJ, NSF, Files of Edward R. Fried, box 2, CHRON, May 2–July 31, 1968, Summary Note of NSC Meeting, 19 June 1968.

88 LBJ, NSF, Agency file, box 40, NATO Ministerial Meeting, Brussels, 14–16 November 1968, Position Paper: Actions Taken on Mediterranean Security, 6 November 1968.

89 LBJ, NSF, Files of Walt W. Rostow, box 2, Meetings with the President, July–December 1968 [1], Issues for the NATO Ministerial Meeting, Brussels, 14–16 November 1968.

90 USNA, RG 59, CFPF, 1967–1969, Political and Defense, DEF 6 NATO 9/1/68, Cleveland to Rusk, 18 September 1968.

91 NHC, OAB, Post 1946 Command File, Sec Nav Series, Statements before Congress, Statement of John H. Chafee, Secretary of the Navy, before Defense Sub-Committee of Committee on Appropriations, 14 July 1969.

92 USDD, 298/3535, 1/11/93, Rostow to Johnson, 12 January 1968; Congressional Record – Senate, vol. 113, part 27, 90th Congress, 1st Session, 13–15 December 1967, 36738; FRUS, 1964–1968, vol. XIII, Department of State to US mission to NATO, 22 February 1968, p. 671.

93 USNA, RG 218, 0015, 092.2, Memorandum of Conversation, 10 October 1967.

94 PRO, DEFE 13/627, Draft Statement by Denis Healey to NATO Defence Planning Committee, 10 May 1968, COS 27/68, Annex A; PRO, DEFE 13/628, Note on DPC Meeting, 10 May 1968.

95 FRUS, 1964–1968, vol. XIII, Paper prepared in the Department of State, The Reykjavik Ministerial Meeting of NATO, undated (June 1968), p. 713.

96 FRUS, 1964–1968, vol. XIII, Intelligence Note, no. 512, 28 June 1968, pp. 723–4; see also PRO, DEFE 13/627, Mulley to Healey, 9 February 1968; *Economist*, 13 July 1968, p. 28.

97 LBJ, Cabinet Papers, box 14, Minutes of Cabinet Meeting, 26 June 1968, p. 1; LBJ, Oral History, Dean Rusk, vol. IV, pp. 19–20.

98 USDD, 26/0391, 1/1/88, Minutes of NSC Meeting, 19 June 1968; FRUS, 1964–1968, vol. XIII, Memorandum of conversation, 23 June 1968, pp. 719–20; Intelligence note no. 512, pp. 722–5.

99 Schwartz, *Lyndon Johnson and Europe*, p. 208.

100 FRUS, 1964–1968, vol. XIII, Rusk and Clifford to Johnson, 16 March 1968, p. 679; A. Wenger, 'Crisis and Opportunity: NATO's Transformation and Multilateralization of Détente, 1966–1968', *Journal of Cold War Studies*, vol. 6, no. 2, 2004, pp. 71–2.

101 Schwartz, *Lyndon Johnson and Europe*, p. 210.

102 LBJ, NSF, Files of Edward R. Fried, box 2, CHRON, September 1, 1967–November 30, 1967 [2 of 2], Rostow to Johnson, 14 June 1968.

103 Washington and Moscow were also about to announce the start of the Strategic Arms Limitation Talks (SALT). LBJ, Oral History Dean Rusk, vol. IV, pp. 19–20; J.G. McGinn, 'The Politics of Collective Inaction: NATO's Response to the Prague Spring', *Journal of Cold War Studies*, vol. 1, no. 3, 1999, pp. 111–38.

104 FRUS, 1964–1968, vol. XIII, Paper Prepared in the Department of State, The United States, Europe, and the Czechoslovakia Crisis, undated (late August/early September 1968), pp. 744–9.

105 LBJ, NSF, Agency File, NATO General, vol. 6, 2/68-9/68, Johnson to Wilson (draft), undated.

106 USNA, RG 59, CFPF, DEF 6 NATO, 7/1/68, US Mission to NATO to Rusk, 26 August 1968.

107 FRUS, 1964–1968, vol. XIII, Cleveland to Rusk, 26 August 1968, p. 739; USNA, RG 59, CFPF, 1967–1969, DEF 4 NATO, 8/1/68, Leddy to Rusk, 29 August 1968; LBJ, NSF, Agency File, box 37, NATO General, vol. 6, 2/68-9/68, DOS Research Memorandum, The NATO Response to the Czechoslovak Crisis, 27 September 1968, pp. 1–2.

108 LBJ, NSF, Agency File, box 35, NATO – General, vol. 6, 2/68-9/68, Rostow to Johnson, 13 September 1968; Leddy to Rusk, 13 September 1968.

109 FRUS, 1964–1968, vol. XIII, Paper prepared in Department of State: The United States, Europe, and the Czechoslovakia Crisis, undated, p. 748.

110 FRUS, 1964–1968, vol. XIII, Memorandum for the Record, 13 September 1968, pp. 756–9.

111 USNA, RG 59, CFPF, 1967–1969, DEF 4 NATO 10/1/68, Cleveland to Rusk, 4 October 1968.

112 USNA, RG 59, CFPF, 1967–1969, DEF 4 NATO, 9/15/68, Memorandum of Conversation, 23 September 1968; USNA, RG 59, CFPF, 1967–1969, DEF 1 NATO 9/1/68, Bruce to Rusk, 26 September 1968.

113 USDD, 74/0732, 3/1/93, Research Memorandum, undated (October 1968); LBJ, NSF, Country File, United Kingdom, box 212, 127, Rostow to Johnson, 10 October 1968.

114 PRO, DEFE 13/627, CDS to Healey, 8 October 1968.

115 PRO, DEFE 11/629, Relative Naval and Maritime Priorities – NATO and east of Suez, Chiefs of Staff Committee Paper, September 1968; Minutes of COS 50th Meeting, 1 October 1968.

116 PRO, DEFE 11/630, Acting Chief of Defence Staff to Healey, undated.

117 For a summary see USNA, RG 59, CFPF, 1967–1969, DEF 4 NATO 10/1/68, Hughes to Rusk, 'British Proposals for a New Intra-NATO Defense Grouping, 12 November 1968.

118 USNA, RG 59, CFPF, 1967–1969, DEF 4 NATO 5/1/68, McGhee to Rusk, 9 May 1968.

119 LBJ, NSF, Agency File, box 40, NATO Ministerial Meeting, Brussels, 14–16 November 1968, Position Paper: Future European Defense Arrangements, 4 November 1968.

120 USNA, RG 59, CFPF, 1967–1969, DEF 12 NATO 10/1/68, Lodge to Rusk, 25 November 1968.

121 USNA, RG 59, CFPF, 1967–1969, Political and Defense, DEF 12 NATO, 10/1/68, Cleveland to Rusk, 5 October 1968. USNA, RG 59, CFPF, 1967–1969, Political and Defense, DEF 12 NATO 1/1/69, Cleveland to Rusk, 13 January 1969.

122 FRUS, 1964–1968, vol. XIII, Intelligence Memorandum, no. 2049/68, The Response of NATO Countries to the Invasion of Czechoslovakia, 4 November 1968, pp. 778–80.

123 USDD, 37/0485, 1/1/96, Rostow to Johnson, 10 October 1968; USDD, 37/0486, 1/1/96, Memorandum of Conversation, undated.

124 USDD, 74/0732, 3/1/93, Research Memorandum, undated (October 1968); LBJ, NSF, Country File, United Kingdom, box 212, 127, Rostow to Johnson, 10 October 1968.

125 FRUS, 1964–1968, vol. XIII, Summary Notes of 590th Meeting of the National Security Council, 4 September 1968, p. 753.

126 *Economist*, 18 May 1968, p. 37.

127 LBJ, NSF, Agency File, box 37, NATO General, vol. 6, 2/68-9/68, DOS Research Memorandum, The NATO Response to the Czechoslovak Crisis, 27 September 1968, pp. 8–9.

128 USNA, RG 59, CFPF, 1967–1969, Political and Defense, DEF 1 NATO, 9/1/68, Bruce to Rusk, 11 September 1968.

129 LBJ, NSF, Files of Walt W. Rostow, Meetings with the President, July–December 1968 [1], Scope Paper: Effects of the Czech Crisis, undated.

130 USDD, 114/1735, 5/1/87, Record of President's Meeting with Congressional Leadership, 27 February 1968; FRUS, 1964–1968, vol. XIII, Rostow to Johnson, 22 March 1968, pp. 683–4.

131 FRUS, 1964–1968, vol. XIII, Talking Paper prepared in Department of Defense, undated, p. 729.

132 USNA, RG 59, CFPF, 1967–1969, Political and Defense, DEF 1 11/1/68, Cleveland to Rusk, 14 November 1968.

133 LBJ, Administrative History of the Department of State, vol. 1, chapters 1–3, box 1, Section D: Bilateral Relations with Western Europe, 1: Great Britain.

134 USNA, RG 59 CFPF, 1967–1969, Political and Defense, POL 2 UK, 'Britain – a Review and Outlook', Paper Prepared by American Embassy, London, 21 November 1968.

135 Schwartz, *Lyndon Johnson and Europe*, pp. 220–2.

136 LBJ, NSF, Agency File, box 39, NATO Strategy and Forces, Ministerial Meeting, Brussels, 14–16 November, 1968 Tab D, p. 9.

137 LBJ, NSF, National Security Council Meetings, box 2, vol. 5, tab 69, Current Issues Affecting US/UK Relations, Summary notes of 587th NSC Meeting, 5 June 1968.

138 LBJ, NSF, Country File, United Kingdom, Memos, vol. XII, box 211, Pastore to Johnson, 20 November 1967. See also additional correspondence in LBJ, White House Central Files, CO, box 78, File 1.

139 LBJ, NSF, Country File, United Kingdom, Memos, vol. XII, box 211, Draft reply to Senator Pastore, 12 December 1967.

140 LBJ, White House Central Files, CO 305, United Kingdom, box 77, file 1, President Johnson to Congress on Amendment to Agreement on United Kingdom and United States Co-operation on the uses of Atomic Energy for Mutual Defense purposes of 3 July 1958 (signed 27 September 1968), 11 October 1968.

141 FRUS, 1964–1968, vol. XII, Katzenbach to Johnson, 22 November 1968, pp. 632–5; Nitze and Seabourg to Johnson, 15 January 1969; LBJ, NSF, Country File, United Kingdom, Cables and Memos, vol. XIV, box 212, Johnson to McNamara and Seaborg, 18 January 1969.

CONCLUSION

1 Churchill Archive Centre, Papers of Michael Stewart, PTWT 12/3/6, Lectures Given to the Fabian Society, 22 February 1969.

2 S. Dockrill, *Britain's Retreat from East of Suez: The Choice Between Europe and the World?* Basingstoke: Palgrave, 2002, p. 219.

3 N.J. Ashton, *Kennedy, Macmillan and the Cold War: The Irony of Interdependence*, Basingstoke and New York: Palgrave-Macmillan, 2002, pp. 223–4.

4 Dockrill, *Britain's Retreat*, p. 209.

5 Dockrill, *Britain's Retreat*, pp. 215–16.

6 Dockrill, *Britain's Retreat*, p. 225.

7 United States National Archive, Record Group 59, Central Foreign Policy Files, Political and Defense, 1967–1969, POL 7 UK, Thomas L. Hughes to Rusk, 7 February 1968, p. 15.

8 Lyndon B. Johnson Library, National Security Files, Agency File, box 39, NATO Filed by LBJ Library, Rostow to President, 17 November 1968.

9 T.A. Schwartz, *Lyndon Johnson and Europe: In the Shadow of Vietnam*, Cambridge and London: Harvard University Press, 2003, p. 225.

BIBLIOGRAPHY

Primary sources

United Kingdom

Public Record Office, Kew, London

ADM 1	Admiralty and Secretariat Papers
ADM 205	First Sea Lord Papers
ADM 328	Admiralty and Ministry of Defence: Contracts and Purchase Department
CAB 21	Cabinet Office Registered Papers
CAB 48	Cabinet Office Papers
CAB 128	Cabinet Minutes and Memoranda
CAB 129	Cabinet Memoranda
CAB 130	Cabinet: Miscellaneous Committees: Minutes and Papers
CAB 133	Commonwealth and International Conferences Minutes and Papers
CAB 134	Miscellaneous Committees – Minutes and Papers
CAB 148	Cabinet Office: Defence and Overseas Policy Committees and Sub-Committees: Minutes and Papers
CO 926	Colonial Office: Mediterranean and Atlantic Department
DEFE 7	Ministry of Defence Registered Files, General
DEFE 10	Major Defence Committee Working Parties Papers
DEFE 11	Chiefs of Staff Committees Registered Files
DEFE 13	Private Office MOD Registered Files
DEFE 24	Ministry of Defence: Defence Secretariat Branches
DEFE 25	Chief of Defence Staff Registered Files
DEFE 49	Ministry of Defence: Navy Department: Personnel
FCO 46	Foreign and Commonwealth Office: Defence Department
FO 371	Foreign Office Files, General Correspondence
PREM 11	Prime Minister's Office: Correspondence and Papers
PREM 13	Prime Minister's Office: Correspondence and Papers

Churchill Archive Centre, Cambridge

Sir Frank Kenyon Roberts Papers
Sir Frederick Brundrett Papers

(Baron) (John) Selwyn Brooke Lloyd Papers
(Baron) Patrick Chrestien Gordon-Walker Papers
(Baron) (Robert) Michael Maitland Stewart Papers

Published sources

Command Papers (CMND)
House of Commons Debates

United States

John F. Kennedy Library, Boston, MA

National Security Files (NSF)
Oral Histories
Personal Papers
President's Office Files (POF)
White House Central File (WHCF)

Lyndon Baines Johnson Presidential Library, Austin, TX

Administrative History
Cabinet Papers
National Security File (NSF)
Office of the White House Aides Files
Oral Histories
Personal Papers
White House Central Files (WHCF)

National Archives, College Park, MD

RG 59   General Records of Department of State
RG 200   Records of Robert S. McNamara
RG 218   Records of Joint Chiefs of Staff
RG 330   Secretary of Defense Files

Naval Historical Center, Washington, DC

Ships History Branch
Department of Defence records

Operational Archives Branch
Oral Histories
Polaris Study Files of Harvey M. Sapolsky, 1953–1969
Post 1946 Command File
Series of Interviews on the Subject of Polaris

Published sources

1961–1963, vol. VII, *Arms Control and Disarmament*
1961–1963, vol. XIII, *West Europe and Canada*
1964–1968, vol. XI, *Arms Control and Disarmament*
1964–1968, vol. XII, *Western Europe*
1964–1968, vol. XIII, *Western Europe Region*
Congressional Record – House and Senate, 1962–1968
Dwight D. Eisenhower, 1953–1961
Foreign Relations of the United States, Washington: United States Government Printing Office, 1994–2001
John F. Kennedy, 1961–1963
Lyndon B. Johnson, 1963–1969
The Public Papers of the Presidents of the United States, Washington: United States Government Printing Office, 1954–1970
US Declassified Documents Series, Washington DC: 1976–1998

Newspapers

United Kingdom

Economist
Evening News
Guardian
Sunday Telegraph
The Sunday Times
The Times

United States

New York Times

Secondary sources

Books

Aldous, R. and Lee, S. (eds), *Harold Macmillan and Britain's World Role*, Basingstoke: Macmillan, 1996.
—— *Harold Macmillan: Aspects of a Political Life*, Basingstoke: Macmillan, 1999.
Asthon, N.J., *Kennedy, Macmillan and the Cold War: The Irony of Interdependence*, Basingstoke and New York: Palgrave-Macmillan, 2002.
Atlantic Institute, *The Atlantic Papers*, New York: University Press of Cambridge, 1970.
Baer, G.W., *One Hundred Years of Seapower: The US Navy, 1890–1990*, Stanford: Stanford University Press, 1994.
Ball, G.W., *The Discipline of Power: Essentials of a Modern World Structure*, Boston, MA and Toronto: Little, Brown & Co, 1968.
—— *The Past Has Another Pattern: Memoirs*, New York and London: W.W. Norton, 1982.

Bange, O., *The EEC Crisis of 1963: Kennedy, Macmillan, De Gaulle and Adenauer in Conflict*, Basingstoke: Macmillan, 1999.

Bartlett, C.J., *'The Special Relationship': A Political History of Anglo-American Relations since 1945*, Harlow: Longman, 1992.

Baylis, J., *Anglo-American Defence Relations, 1939–1981*, London and Basingstoke: Macmillan, 1981.

—— *The Diplomacy of Pragmatism: Britain and the Formation of NATO, 1942–49*, Basingstoke and London: Macmillan, 1993.

—— *Ambiguity and Deterrence: British Nuclear Strategy, 1945–1964*, Oxford: Clarendon, 1995.

Beer, F.A. and Baylis, J., *Britain, NATO and Nuclear Weapons: Alternative Defence Verses Alliance Reform*, London: Macmillan, 1989.

Botti, T.J., *The Long Wait: The Forging of the Anglo-American Nuclear Alliance, 1945–1958*, Westport, CT: Greenwood Press, 1987.

Brands, H.W., *The Wages of Globalism: Lyndon Johnson and the Limits of American Power*, New York and Oxford: Oxford University Press, 1995.

Breemer, J.S., *US Naval Developments*, London: Frederick Warne, 1983.

Brinkley, D. and Griffiths, R.T., *John F. Kennedy and Europe*, Baton Rouge: Louisiana State University Press, 1999.

Buchan, A., *NATO in the 1960s*, London: Chatto & Windus, 1963.

Buffet, C. and Heuser, B., *Haunted by History: Myths in International Relations*, Oxford: Berghahn, 1998.

Burk, K. and Stokes, M. (eds), *The United States and the European Alliance Since 1945*, Oxford and New York: Berg, 1999.

Busch, P., *All the Way with JFK? Britain, the US and the Vietnam War*, Oxford: Oxford University Press, 2003.

Calleo, D., *The Atlantic Fantasy: The US, NATO and Europe*, Baltimore, MD and London: Johns Hopkins Press, 1970.

Campbell, D., *The Unsinkable Aircraft Carrier: American Military Power in Britain*, London: Palladin, 1985.

Castle, B., *The Castle Diaries, 1964–1970*, London: Weidenfeld & Nicolson, 1984.

Chalmers, M., *Paying for Defence: Military Spending and British Decline*, London: Pluto Press, 1985.

Clark, I., *Nuclear Diplomacy and the Special Relationship: Britain's Deterrent and America, 1957–1962*, Oxford: Clarendon Press, 1994.

Clark, I. and Wheeler, N.J., *The British Origins of Nuclear Strategy, 1945–1955*, Oxford: Clarendon, 1989.

Clarke, M. and Hague, R. (eds), *European Defence Co-operation: America, Britain and NATO*, Manchester: Manchester University Press in Association with the Fulbright Commission, 1990.

Cohen, W.I. and Tucker, N.B. (eds), *Lyndon Johnson Confronts the World: American Foreign Policy, 1963–1968*, Cambridge: Cambridge University Press, 1994.

Colman, J., *A 'Special Relationship'? Harold Wilson, Lyndon B. Johnson and Anglo-American Relations 'at the Summit', 1964–68*, Manchester: Manchester University Press, 2004.

Coopey, R., Fielding, S. and Tiratsoo, N. (eds), *The Wilson Governments, 1964–1970*, London and New York: Pinter, 1995.

Costigliola, F., *France and the United States: The Cold Alliance Since World War II*, New York: Twayne, 1992.

Crossman, R., *The Diaries of a Cabinet Minister, vol. 1*, London: Hamish Hamilton, 1975.

—— *The Diaries of a Cabinet Minister, vol. 2*, London: Hamish Hamilton, 1976.

Daalder, I.H., *The Nature and Practice of Flexible Response: NATO Strategy and Theater Nuclear Forces Since 1967*, New York: Columbia University Press, 1991.

Darby, P., *British Defence Policy East of Suez, 1947–1968*, London: Royal Institute of International Affairs/Oxford University Press, 1973.

Dimbleby, D. and Reynolds, D., *An Ocean Apart: The Relationship between Britain and America in the Twentieth Century*, London: BBC/Hodder & Stoughton, 1988.

Dockrill, S., *Eisenhower's New-Look National Security Policy, 1953–61*, Basingstoke and London: Macmillan, 1996.

—— *Britain's Retreat from East of Suez: The Choice Between Europe and the World?* Basingstoke and New York: Palgrave-Macmillan, 2002.

Dumbrell, J., *A Special Relationship: Anglo-American Relations in the Cold War and After*, Basingstoke: Macmillan, 2001.

—— *President Lyndon Johnson and Soviet Communism*, Manchester: Manchester University Press, 2004.

Dunn, D.H. (ed.), *Diplomacy at the Highest Level: The Evolution of International Summitry*, Basingstoke: Macmillan, 1996.

Ellis, S.A., *Britain, America and the Vietnam War*, Westport, CT and London: Praeger, 2004.

Enthoven, A.C. and Wayne Smith, K. *How Much is Enough? Shaping the Defense Program, 1961–1969*, New York: Harper & Row, 1971.

Fox, W.T.R. and Fox, A.B., *NATO and the Range of American Choice*, New York: Columbia University Press, 1967.

Freeman, J.P.G., *Britain's Nuclear Arms Control Policy in the Context of Anglo-American Relations, 1957–68*, New York: St Martin's Press, 1986.

Gaddis, J.L., *Strategies of Containment: A Critical Appraisal of Postwar American National Security Policy*, Oxford: Oxford University Press, 1982.

Galantin, I.J., *Submarine Admiral: From Battlewagons to Ballistic Missiles*, Urbana and Chicago, IL: University of Illinois Press, 1995.

Gatzke, H.W., *Germany and the United States: A 'Special Relationship'?* Cambridge, MA and London: Harvard University Press, 1980.

Geelhoed, E.B. and Edmonds, A.O., *Eisenhower, Macmillan and Allied Unity, 1957–1961*, Basingstoke: Palgrave-Macmillan, 2003.

Geyelin, P., *Lyndon B. Johnson and the World*, New York: Praeger, 1966.

Gorst, A., Johnman, L. and Lucas, W.S., *Post-War Britain: Themes and Perspectives*, London: Pinter, 1989.

Grayling, C. and Langdon, C., *Just Another Star? Anglo-American Relations since 1945*, London: Harrap, 1988.

Greenwood, S., *Britain and the Cold War, 1945–91*, London and Basingstoke: Macmillan, 2000.

Grove, E.J., *Vanguard to Trident: British Naval Policy since World War II*, London: The Bodley Head, 1987.

Haftendorn, H., *NATO and the Nuclear Revolution: A Crisis of Credibility, 1966–1967*, Oxford: Clarendon Press, 1996.

Hammond, P.Y., *LBJ and the Presidential Management of Foreign Relations*, Austin, TX: University of Texas Press, 1992.

Healey, D., *The Time of My Life*, London: Penguin, 1990.

Herring, G.C., *America's Longest War: The United States and Vietnam, 1950–1975*, New York: McGraw-Hill, 2002.

Hollowell, J. (ed.), *Twentieth Century Anglo-American Relations*, Basingstoke: Palgrave, 2001.

Horne, A., *Macmillan, 1857–1986*, London: Macmillan, 1989.

Johnson, L.B., *The Vantage Point: Perspectives of the Presidency, 1963–1969*, New York: Holt, Rinehart & Winston, 1971.

Jones, P., *America and the British Labour Party: The Special Relationship at Work*, London and New York: I.B. Taurus, 1997.

Jordan, R.S., *Generals in International Politics: NATO's Supreme Allied Commander, Europe*, Lexington: University of Kentucky Press, 1987.

Kaiser, K. and Roper, J. (eds), *British-German Defence Co-operation: Partners within the Alliance*, London: Jane's, 1988.

Kaplan, L.S., *The United States and NATO: The Formative Years*, Lexington, KY: University Press of Kentucky, 1984.

—— *The Long Entanglement: NATO's First Fifty Years*, Westport, CT: Praeger, 1999.

Keohane, D., *Labour Party Defence Policy since 1945*, London and Leicester: Leicester University Press, 1993.

Keohane, R.O., *After Hegemony: Cooperation and Discord in the World Political Economy*, Princeton, NJ: Princeton University Press, 1984.

Kissinger, H.A., *The Troubled Partnership: A Re-appraisal of the Atlantic Alliance*, New York: McGraw-Hill, 1965.

Kunz, D.B. (ed.), *Diplomacy of the Crucial Decade: American Foreign Policy During the 1960s*, New York: Columbia University Press, 1994.

Labour Party, *Let's go with Labour for the New Britain: The Labour Party's Manifesto for the 1964 General Election*, London: Transport House, 1964.

—— *Time for Decision: Manifesto of the Labour Party, General Election 1966*, London: Transport House, 1966.

Loth, W. (ed.), *Europe, Cold War and Coexistence*, London and Portland: Frank Cass, 2004.

Louis, W.M.R. and Bull, H., *The 'Special Relationship': Anglo-American Relations Since 1945*, Oxford: Clarendon Press, 1986.

Lucas, W.S., *Divided We Stand: Britain, the US and the Suez Crisis*, London: Hodder & Stoughton, 1996.

McArdle Kelleher, C., *Germany and the Politics of Nuclear Weapons*, New York and London: Columbia University Press, 1975.

McDonald, I.S. (ed.), *Anglo-American Relations Since the Second World War*, New York: St Martin's Press, 1974.

Macmillan, H., *At the End of the Day*, Basingstoke: Macmillan, 1973.

McNamara, R.S., *The Essence of Security: Reflections in Office*, London: Hodder & Stoughton, 1968.

Mahan, E.R., *Kennedy, De Gaulle and Western Europe*, Basingstoke: Palgrave, 2002.

Moore, J.E., *The Impact of Polaris: The Origins of Britain's Seaborne Nuclear Deterrent*, Huddersfield: Richard Netherwood, 1999.

Moore, R., *The Royal Navy and Nuclear Weapons*, London: Frank Cass, 2001.

Morgan, R., *The United States and West Germany, 1945–1973: A Study in Alliance Politics*, London: Oxford University Press for the Institute of International Affairs, 1974.

Murphy, P.J. (ed.), *Naval Power in Soviet Policy*, Washington, DC: United States Government Printing Office for the United States Air Force, 1978.

Murray, D., *Kennedy, Macmillan and Nuclear Weapons*, Basingstoke: Macmillan, 2000.

Nailor, P., *The Nassau Connection: The Organisation and Management of the British Polaris Project*, London: Her Majesty's Stationary Office, 1988.

Neustadt, R.E., *Alliance Politics*, New York: Columbia University Press, 1970.

—— *Report to JFK: The Skybolt Crisis in Perspective*, Ithaca, NY and London: Cornell University Press, 1999.

Newhouse, J., *De Gaulle and the Anglo-Saxons*, London: Andre Deutsch, 1970.

Northedge, F.S., *Descent from Power: British Foreign Policy, 1945–1973*, London: George Allen & Unwin, 1974.

Nunnerley, D., *President Kennedy and Britain*, London: The Bodley Head, 1972.

Oliver, K., *Kennedy, Macmillan, and the Nuclear Test-Ban Debate, 1961–63*, Basingstoke: Macmillan, 1998.

Ovendale, R., *Anglo-American Relations in the Twentieth Century*, Basingstoke: Macmillan, 1998.

Pagedas, C.A., *Anglo-American Strategic Relations and the French Problem, 1960–1963: A Troubled Partnership*, London and Portland: Frank Cass, 2000.

Park, W., *Defending the West: A History of NATO*, Brighton: Wheatsheaf, 1986.

Paxton, R.O. and Wahl, N. (eds), *De Gaulle and the United States: A Centennial Reappraisal*, Oxford and Providence: Berg, 1994.

Pierre, A.J., *Nuclear Politics: The British Experience with an Independent Strategic Force, 1939–1970*, London: Oxford University Press, 1972.

Pimlott, B., *Harold Wilson*, London: Harper Collins, 1993.

Ponting, C., *Breach of Promise: Labour in Power, 1964–1970*, London: Hamish Hamilton, 1989.

Ranft, B. and Till, G., *The Sea in Soviet Strategy*, Basingstoke: Macmillan, 1983.

Reed, B. and Williams, G., *Denis Healey and the Policies of Power*, London: Sidwick & Jackson, 1971.

Richardson, J.L., *Germany and the Atlantic Alliance: The Interaction of Strategy and Politics*, Cambridge, MA: Harvard University Press, 1966.

Richardson, L., *When Allies Differ: Anglo-American Relations During the Suez and Falklands Crises*, New York: St Martin's Press, 1996.

Richey, G., *Britain's Strategic Role in NATO*, Basingstoke: Macmillan, 1986.

Rostow, W.W., *The Diffusion of Power: An Essay in Recent History*, New York: Macmillan, 1972.

Saplosky, H.M., *The Polaris System Development: Bureaucratic and Pragmatic Success in Government*, Cambridge, MA: Harvard University Press, 1972.

Schlesinger, A.M., *A Thousand Days: John F. Kennedy in the White House*, London: Deutsch, 1965.

Schoenbaum, T.J., *Waging Peace and War: Dean Rusk in the Truman, Kennedy & Johnson Years*, New York: Simon & Schuster, 1988.

Schrafstetter, S. and Twigge, S., *Avoiding Armageddon: Europe, the United States and Struggle for Nuclear Nonproliferation, 1945–1970*, Westport, CT and London: Praeger, 2004.

Schwartz, T.A., *Lyndon Johnson and Europe*, Cambridge, MA and London: Harvard University Press, 2003.

Shapley, D., *Promise and Power: The Life and Times of Robert McNamara*, Boston, MA: Little Brown, 1993.

Simpson, J., *The Independent Nuclear State: The United States, Britain and the Military Atom*, London and Basingstoke: Macmillan, 1983.

Sorenson, T.C., *Kennedy*, New York: Harper & Row, 1965.

Speed, K., *Sea Change: The Battle for the Falklands and the Future of Britain's Navy*, Bath: Ashgrove Press, 1982.

Spinardi, G., *From Polaris to Trident: The Development of US Fleet Ballistic Missile Technology*, Cambridge: Cambridge University Press, 1994.

Steinbruner, J.D., *The Cybernetic Theory of Decision: New Dimensions of Political Analysis*, Princeton, NJ: Princeton University Press, 1974.

Stromseth, J.E., *The Origins of Flexible Response*, Basingstoke: Macmillan, 1988.

Thorpe, A., *A History of the British Labour Party*, Basingstoke and London: Macmillan, 1997.

Trachtenberg, M., *A Constructed Peace: The Making of a European Settlement, 1945–1963*, Princeton, NJ: Princeton University Press, 1999.

Twigge, S. and Scott, L., *Planning Armageddon: Britain, the United States and the Command and Control of Western Nuclear Forces, 1945–1964*, Amsterdam: Harwood, 2000.

Watt, D.C., *Succeeding John Bull: America in Britain's Place, 1900–1975*, Cambridge: Cambridge University Press, 1984.

Wenger, A., Nuenlist, C. and Locher, A. (eds) *Transforming NATO in the Cold War: Challenges Beyond Deterrence* (forthcoming, Routledge, 2006).

Wettern, D., *The Decline of British Seapower*, London: Jane's, 1982.

Wilson, H., *The Labour Government 1964–1970: A Personal Record*, London: Penguin, 1971.

Young, J.W., *Britain and European Unity, 1945–1999*, Basingstoke: Macmillan, 2000.

—— *The Labour Governments, 1964–70, vol. 2: International Policy*, Manchester and New York: Manchester University Press, 2003.

Zeiler, T.W., *Dean Rusk: Defending the American Mission Abroad*, Wilmington: Scholarly Resources, 2000.

Articles

Allen, H.C., 'The Anglo-American Relationship in the Sixties', *International Affairs*, vol. 39, 1963, pp. 37–48.

Ashton, N.J., 'Harold Macmillan and the "Golden Days" of Anglo-American Relations', *Diplomatic History*, vol. 29, no. 4, 2005, pp. 691–723.

Baylis, J., 'The Anglo-American Relationship and Alliance Theory', *International Relations*, vol. 8, 1985, pp. 368–79.

—— 'Exchanging Nuclear Secrets: Laying the Foundations of the Anglo-American Nuclear Relationship', *Diplomatic History*, vol. 25, no. 1, 2001, pp. 33–61.

Bluth, C., 'Reconciling the Irreconcilable: Alliance Politics and the Paradox of Extended Deterrence in the 1960s', *Cold War History*, vol. 1, no. 2, 2001, pp. 73–102.

Boulton, J., 'NATO and the MLF', *Journal of Contemporary History*, vol. 7, no. s 3/4, 1973, pp. 275–94.

Boyle, K., 'The Price of Peace: Vietnam, the Pound, and the Crisis of American Empire', *Diplomatic History*, vol. 27, no. 1, 2003, pp. 37–72.

Brown, N., 'Britain's Strategic Weapons: I. Manned Bombers', *The World Today*, vol. 20, 1964, pp. 293–8.

—— 'Britain's Strategic Weapons: II. The *Polaris* A3', *The World Today*, vol. 20, 1964, pp. 358–64.

Brzezinski, Z., 'Moscow and the MLF: Hostility and Ambivalence', *Foreign Affairs*, vol. 43, 1964/1965, pp. 126–34.

Buchan, A., 'The Multilateral Force: A Study in Alliance Politics', *International Affairs*, vol. 40, no. 4, 1964, pp. 619–37.

—— 'The Multilateral Force: An Historical Perspective', *Adelphi Papers*, no. 13, London, Institute for Strategic Studies, 1964.

Catterall, P. (ed.), 'Witness Seminar: The East of Suez Decision', *Contemporary Record* (now *Contemporary British History*), vol. 7, no. 3, 1993, pp. 612–53.

Church, F., 'US Policy and the "New Europe"', *Foreign Affairs*, vol. 45, no. 1, October 1966, pp. 49–57.

Cleveland, H., 'NATO After the Invasion', *Foreign Affairs*, vol. 47, no. 2, 1969, pp. 251–65.

Davis, R., ' "Why Did the General Do It?" De Gaulle, Polaris and the French Veto of Britain's Application to Join the Common Market', *European History Quarterly*, vol. 28, no. 3, 1998, pp. 373–97.

Dawson, R. and Rosencrance, R., 'Theory and Reality in the Anglo-American Alliance', *World Politics*, vol. 19, no. 1, 1966, pp. 21–51.

Dobson, A.P., 'Labour or Conservative: Does it Matter in Anglo-American Relations?' *Journal of Contemporary History*, vol. 25, 1990, pp. 387–407.

—— 'The Years of Transition: Anglo-American Relations, 1961–1967', *Review of International Studies*, vol. 16, 1990, pp. 239–57.

Dockrill, S., 'Forging the Anglo-American Global Defence Partnership: Harold Wilson, Lyndon Johnson and the Washington Summit, December 1964', *Journal of Strategic Studies*, vol. 23, no. 4, 2000, pp. 107–29.

—— 'Britain's Power and Influence: Dealing with Three Roles and the Wilson Government's Defence Debate at Chequers in November 1964', *Diplomacy & Statecraft*, vol. 11, no. 1, 2000, pp. 211–40.

Dulles, J.F., 'Policy for Security and Peace', *Foreign Affairs*, vol. 32, no. 3, 1954, pp. 353–64.

Dumbrell, J., 'The Johnson Administration and the British Labour Government: Vietnam, the Pound and East of Suez', *Journal of American Studies*, vol. 30, no. 2, 1996, pp. 211–31.

Dumbrell, J. and Ellis, S.A., 'British Involvement in Vietnam Peace Initiatives, 1966–1967: Marigolds, Sunflowers, and "Kosygin Week"', *Diplomatic History*, vol. 27, no. 1, 2003, pp. 113–49.

Fielding, J., 'Coping with Decline: US Policy Toward the British Defense Reviews of 1966', *Diplomatic History*, vol. 23, no. 4, 1999, pp. 633–56.

Gavin, F.J., 'The Myth of Flexible Response: United States Strategy in Europe during the 1960s', *International History Review*, vol. 23, no. 4, 2001, pp. 847–75.

Gordon Walker, P.C., 'Labour's Foreign and Defence Policy', *Foreign Affairs*, vol. 42, no. 3, 1964, pp. 391–8.

Guderzo, M., 'Johnson and European Integration: A Missed Chance for Transatlantic Power', *Cold War History*, vol. 4, no. 2, 2004, pp. 89–114.

Healey, D., 'A Conventional Alternative to Nuclear Retaliation: Turning Point for NATO', *New Republic*, vol. 21, no. 24, 1961, p. 7.

Hughes, R.G., ' "We Are Not Seeking Strength for its own Sake": The British Labour Party, West Germany and the Cold War, 1951–1964', *Cold War History*, vol. 3, no. 1, 2002, pp. 67–94.

Jones, M., 'Anglo-American Relations after Suez, the Rise and Decline of the Working Group Experiment, and the French Challenge to NATO, 1957–59', *Diplomacy and Statecraft*, vol. 14, no. 1, 2003, pp. 49–79.

Karber, P.A. and Combs, J.A., 'The United States, NATO and the Soviet Threat to Western Europe: Military Threats and Policy Options, 1945–1963', *Diplomatic History*, vol. 22, no. 3, 1998, pp. 399–429.

Kiker, D., 'The Education of Robert McNamara', *The Atlantic*, vol. 219, no. 3, 1967, pp. 49–55.

Kissinger, H., 'NATO's Nuclear Dilemma', *Reporter*, vol. 28, 1963, pp. 22–37.

—— 'Coalition Diplomacy in a Nuclear Age', *Foreign Affairs* vol. 42, 1964, pp. 525–45.

Kohl, W.L., 'Nuclear Sharing in NATO and the Multilateral Force', *Political Science Quarterly*, vol. 80, 1965, pp. 88–109.

Kopkind, A. (ed.), 'Memorandum on the British Labour Party and the MLF' by R.E. Neustadt, *New York Review of Books*, vol. 11, no.10, 1968, pp. 37–46.

Kunz, D.B., 'Lyndon Johnson's Dollar Diplomacy', *History Today*, vol. 42, no. 4, 1992, pp. 45–51.

—— ' "Somewhat Mixed up Together": Anglo-American Defence and Financial Policy during the 1960s', *Journal of Imperial and Commonwealth History*, vol. 27, no. 2, 1999, pp. 213–32.

McGinn, J.G., 'The Politics of Collective Inaction: NATO's Response to the Prague Spring', *Journal of Cold War Studies*, vol. 1, no. 3, 1999, pp. 111–38.

Melissen, J., 'Pre-Summit Diplomacy: Britain, the United States and the Nassau Conference, December 1962', *Diplomacy and Statecraft*, vol. 7, no. 3, 1996, pp. 652–87.

Middeke, M., 'Anglo-American Nuclear Weapons Co-operation After the Nassau Conference: The British Policy of Interdependence', *Journal of Cold War Studies*, vol. 2, no. 2, 2000, pp. 69–96.

—— 'Britain's Global Military Role, Conventional Defence and Anglo-American Interdependence after Nassau', *Journal of Strategic Studies*, vol. 24, no. 1, 2001, pp. 143–64.

Mizumoto, Y., 'Harold Wilson's Efforts at a Negotiated Settlement of the Vietnam War, 1965–67', *Electronic Journal of International History*, 2005, 1–43.

Mountbatten, 'Britain's Armed Forces', *NATO Letter*, 1965, pp. 22–5.

Mulley, F.W., 'NATO's Nuclear Problems: Control or Consultation', *Orbis*, vol. 8, no.1, 1964, pp. 21–35.

Newton, C., 'Polaris Major Factor in Proposed 1000-Missile Force for NATO', *Missiles and Rockets*, 1960, pp. 12–13.

Nuti, L., ' "Me Too, Please": Italy and the Politics of Nuclear Weapons, 1945–1975' *Diplomacy and Statecraft*, vol. 4, no. 1, 1993, pp. 114–48.

Priest, A., ' "In Common Cause": The Multilateral Force and Mixed-Manning Demonstration on USS Claude V. Ricketts, 1964–1965', *Journal of Military History*, vol. 69, no. 3, 2005, pp. 759–89.

—— 'In American Hands: Britain, the United States and the Polaris Nuclear Project, 1962–1968', *Contemporary British History*, vol. 19, no. 3, 2005, pp. 353–376.

Reynolds, D., 'A "Special Relationship"? America, Britain and the International Order Since the Second World War', *International Affairs*, vol. 62, no. 1, 1985/1986, pp. 1–20.

—— 'Re-thinking Anglo-American Relations', *International Affairs*, vol. 65, no. 1, 1988/1989, pp. 89–111.

Roy, R., 'No Secrets Between "Special Friends": America's Involvement in British Economic Policy, October 1964–April 1965', *History*, vol. 89, no. 295, 2004, pp. 399–423.

Schrafstetter, S. and Twigge, S., 'Trick or Truth? The British ANF Proposal, West Germany and US Nonproliferation Policy, 1964–1968', *Diplomacy & Statecraft*, vol. 11, no. 2, 2000, pp. 161–84.

Twigge, S. and Macmillan, A., 'Britain, the United States, and the Development of NATO Strategy, 1950–1964', *Journal of Strategic Studies*, vol. 19, no. 2, 1996, pp. 260–81.

Twigge, S. and Scott, L. 'Learning to Love the Bomb: The Command and Control of British Nuclear Forces, 1953–1964', *Journal of Strategic Studies*, vol. 22, no. 1, 1999, pp. 29–53.

Verrier, A., 'Defense and Politics After Nassau', *Political Quarterly*, vol. 34, 1963, pp. 269–78.

Warner, G., 'The Nassau Agreement and NATO', *The World Today*, vol. 19, 1963, pp. 61–69.

—— 'The Anglo-American Special Relationship', *Diplomatic History*, vol. 13, no. 4, 1989, pp. 479–500.

—— 'Why the General said No: *Documents diplomatiques français*', *International Affairs*, vol. 78, no. 4, 2002, pp. 869–82.

Wenger, A., 'Crisis and Opportunity: NATO's Transformation and the Multilateralization of Détente, 1966–1968', *Journal of Cold War Studies*, vol. 6, no. 2, 2004, pp. 22–74.

Williams, R.G., 'Skybolt and American Foreign Policy', *Military Affairs*, vol. 30, no. 3, 1966, pp. 153–160.

Windsor, P., 'Recent Developments in NATO', *The World Today*, vol. 22, 1966, p. 227.

—— 'NATO and European Détente', *The World Today*, vol. 23, 1967, pp. 361–69.

Young, J.W., 'Killing the MLF? The Wilson Government and Nuclear Sharing in Europe, 1964–66', *Diplomacy and Statecraft*, vol. 14, no. 2, 2003, pp. 295–324.

Young, K., 'The Royal Navy's Polaris Lobby, 1955–62', *Journal of Strategic Studies*, vol. 25, no. 3, 2002, pp. 56–86.

—— 'The Skybolt Crisis of 1962: Muddle or Mischief?', *Journal of Strategic Studies*, vol. 27, no. 4, 2004, pp. 614–35.

INDEX

For Product Safety Concerns and Information please contact our EU
representative GPSR@taylorandfrancis.com
Taylor & Francis Verlag GmbH, Kaufingerstraße 24, 80331 München, Germany

www.ingramcontent.com/pod-product-compliance
Lightning Source LLC
Chambersburg PA
CBHW050428280326
41932CB00013BA/2027

9 780415 649490